Henry Theophilus Finck

Romantic Love and Personal Beauty

Their Development, Casual Relations, Historic and National Peculiarities

Henry Theophilus Finck

Romantic Love and Personal Beauty
Their Development, Casual Relations, Historic and National Peculiarities

ISBN/EAN: 9783744769839

Printed in Europe, USA, Canada, Australia, Japan

Cover: Foto ©ninafisch / pixelio.de

More available books at **www.hansebooks.com**

ROMANTIC LOVE

AND

PERSONAL BEAUTY

THEIR

DEVELOPMENT, CAUSAL RELATIONS
HISTORIC AND NATIONAL PECULIARITIES

BY

HENRY T. FINCK

IN TWO VOLUMES
VOL. II

London
MACMILLAN AND CO.
AND NEW YORK
1887

All rights reserved

CONTENTS

	PAGE
NATIONALITY AND LOVE	1
French Love	1
Italian Love	14
Spanish Love	19
German Love	25
English Love	37
American Love	47
SCHOPENHAUER'S THEORY OF LOVE	59
Love is an Illusion	60
Individuals Sacrificed to the Species	60
Sources of Love	62
(1) Physical Beauty	62
(2) Psychic Traits	63
(3) Complementary Qualities	64
FOUR SOURCES OF BEAUTY	74
I. Health	74
Greek Beauty	77
Mediæval Ugliness	80
Modern Hygiene	82
II. Crossing	85
III. Romantic Love	92
IV. Mental Refinement	95
EVOLUTION OF TASTE	101
Savage Notions of Beauty	101
Non-Æsthetic "Ornamentation"	103
Personal Beauty as a Fine Art	103

	PAGE
Negative Tests of Beauty	106
(a) Animals	106
(b) Savages	110
(c) Degraded Classes	111
(d) Age and Decrepitude	112
(e) Disease	112
POSITIVE TESTS OF BEAUTY	118
(a) Symmetry	118
(b) Gradation	120
(c) Curvature	123
Masculine and Feminine Beauty	125
(d) Delicacy	127
(e) Smoothness	129
(f) Lustre and Colour	130
(g) Expression, Variety, Individuality	134
THE FEET	140
Size	140
Fashionable Ugliness	141
Tests of Beauty	145
A Graceful Gait	149
Evolution of the Great Toe	152
National Peculiarities	156
Beautifying Hygiene	157
Dancing and Grace	160
Dancing and Courtship	161
Evolution of Dance Music	166
The Dance of Love	169
Ballet-Dancing	170
THE LOWER LIMBS	171
Muscular Development	171
Beautifying Exercise	174
Fashionable Ugliness	178
The Crinoline Craze	179
THE WAIST	183
The Beauty-Curve	183
The Wasp-Waist Mania	184
Hygienic Disadvantages	186

	PAGE
Æsthetic Disadvantages	188
Corpulence and Leanness	190
The Fashion Fetish Analysed	195
Individualism *versus* Fashion	201
Masculine Fashions	204
CHEST AND BOSOM	208
Feminine Beauty	208
Masculine Beauty	213
Magic Effect of Deep Breathing	214
A Moral Question	217
NECK AND SHOULDER	219
ARM AND HAND	221
Evolution and Sexual Differences	221
Calisthenics and Massage	224
The Second Face	226
Finger Nails	228
Manicure Secrets	230
JAW, CHIN, AND MOUTH	232
Hands *versus* Jaws	232
Dimples in the Chin	238
Refined Lips	240
Cosmetic Hints	252
THE CHEEKS	255
High Cheek Bones	255
Colour and Blushes	259
THE EARS	266
A Useless Ornament	266
Cosmetics and Fashion	270
Physiognomic Vagaries	272
Noise and Civilisation	273
A Musical Voice	276
THE NOSE	277
Size and Shape	277
Evolution of the Nose	279
Greek and Hebrew Noses	283
Fashion and Cosmetic Surgery	287
Nose-Breathing and Health	291

	PAGE
Cosmetic Value of Odours	292
THE FOREHEAD	296
Beauty and Brain	296
Fashionable Deformity	299
Wrinkles	301
THE COMPLEXION	304
White *versus* Black	304
Cosmetic Hints	315
Freckles and Sunshine	319
THE EYES	323
Colour	324
Lustre	331
Form	335
Expression	339
(*a*) Lustre	341
(*b*) Colour of Iris	345
(*c*) Movements of the Iris	347
(*d*) ,, ,, Eyeball	348
(*e*) ,, ,, Eyelids	352
(*f*) ,, ,, Eyebrows	356
Cosmetic Hints	357
THE HAIR	358
Cause of Man's Nudity	358
Beards and Moustaches	362
Baldness and Depilatories	367
Æsthetic Value of Hair	371
BRUNETTE AND BLONDE	375
Blonde *versus* Brunette	375
Brunette *versus* Blonde	377
Why Cupid Favours Brunettes	380
NATIONALITY AND BEAUTY	389
FRENCH BEAUTY	390
ITALIAN BEAUTY	399
SPANISH BEAUTY	405
GERMAN AND AUSTRIAN BEAUTY	416
ENGLISH BEAUTY	427
AMERICAN BEAUTY	438

NATIONALITY AND LOVE

ROMANTIC Love — commonly considered immutable — not only displays countless individual variations in regard to duration and degrees of intensity, but has a sort of "local colour" in each country; or, to keep up our old metaphor, a varying clang-tint, depending on the greater or less prominence of certain "overtones."

To describe all these varieties of Love would require a separate volume. And since all the most interesting forms of the romantic passion are to be met with in France, Italy, Spain, Germany, England, and America, it will suffice to briefly characterise Love in those countries.

FRENCH LOVE

As literary luck would have it, the subject of French Love follows naturally upon the subject of the last chapter, the *Remedia Amoris*.

The French are too clever a nation to leave to individual effort the difficult task of curing the mind of such an obstinate thing as Love. All the papas and mammas in the land have put their heads together and devised two methods of *killing Love wholesale*, compared with which all the remedies named in the last chapter are mere fly-bites.

These two methods are Chaperonage and Parental Choice, as opposed to Courtship and Individual Sexual Selection.

Paradoxical as it may seem, there is in the midst of modern Europe a nation which, in the treatment of women, Love, and marriage, stands on the same low level of evolution as the ancient, mediæval, and Oriental nations.

This is not a theory, but a fact patent to all, and attested by the best English, German, and French authors.

One of the deepest of French thinkers, whose eyes were opened by travel and comparison, De Stendhal, in 1842, says in his book *De l'Amour:* " Pour comprendre cette passion, que depuis trente ans la peur du ridicule cache avec tant de soin parmi nous, il faut en parler comme d'une maladie "—" To understand this passion, which during the last thirty years has been concealed among us with so much solicitude, from fear of ridicule, it is necessary to speak of it as a malady."

But Stendhal greatly understates the case. It was not only within thirty years from the time when he wrote, and by means of ridicule, that the French had tried hard to kill Love. They have never really emancipated themselves from mediæval barbarism. Pure Romantic Love between two young unmarried persons has never yet flourished in France—because it has never been allowed to grow. To-day, as in the days of the Troubadours, the only form of Love celebrated in French plays and romances is the form which implies conjugal infidelity.

"Marriage, as treated in the old French epics," says Ploss, "is rarely based on love;" the woman marries for protection, the man for her wealth or social affiliations. In the eighteenth century girls were compelled from their earliest years to live only for appearance sake: "The most harmless natural enjoyment, every childish ebullition, is interdicted as improper. Her mother denies her the expression of tender emotion as too bourgeois, too common. The little one grows up in a dreary, heartless vacuum; her deeper feelings remain undeveloped. . . . Real love would be too ordinary a motive of marriage, and therefore extremely ridiculous. It is not offered her, accordingly, nor does she feel any."

Heine wrote from Paris in 1837 that "girls never fall in love in this country." "With us in Germany, as also in England and other nations of Germanic origin, young girls are allowed the utmost possible liberty, whereas married women become subjected to the strict and anxious supervision of their husbands.

"Here in France, as already stated, the reverse is the case: young girls remain in the seclusion of a convent until they either marry or are introduced to the world under the strict eye of a relative. In the world, *i.e.* in the French salon, they always remain silent and little noticed, for it is neither good form here nor wise to make love to an unmarried girl.

"There lies the difference. We Germans, as well as our Germanic neighbours, bestow our love always on unmarried girls, and these only are celebrated by our poets; among the French, on the other hand, married women only are the object of love, in life as well as in literature."

The difficulty of becoming acquainted with a young lady, Mr. Hamerton tells us, is greatest "in what may be called the 'respectable' classes in country-towns and their vicinities. In Parisian society young ladies go out into *le monde*, and may be seen and even spoken to at evening-parties."

"And even spoken to" is good, is very good. What a privilege for the young men! The iron bars which formerly separated them from the young ladies have actually been removed, and they are allowed to speak to them—in presence of a heart-chilling, conversation-killing dragon. No wonder Parisian society is so corrupt!

Mr. Hamerton has given in *Round My House* the most realistic and fascinating account of French courtship and marriage-customs ever written. He is a great admirer of the French, always ready to excuse their foibles, and his testimony is, therefore, doubly valuable as that of an absolutely impartial witness. He had an opportunity for many years of studying French provincial life with an artist's trained faculties ; and here are a few sentences culled from his descriptions :—

"It is not merely difficult, in our neighbourhood, for a young man in the respectable classes to get acquainted with a young lady, but *every conceivable arrangement is devised to make it absolutely impossible.* Balls and evening-parties are hardly ever given, and when they are given great care is taken to keep young men out of them, and young marriageable girls either dance with each other or with mere children."

Whereas in England "a young girl may go where she likes, without much risk to her good name," a French girl "may not cross a street alone, nor open a book which has not been examined, nor have an opinion about anything." "The French ideal of a well-brought-up young lady is that she should not know anything whatever about love and marriage, that she should be both innocent and ignorant, and both in the supreme degree—both to a degree which no English person can imagine."

"The young men are not to blame; they would be ready enough, perhaps, to fall in love if they had the chance, like any Englishman or German, but the respectable parents of the young lady take care that they shall *not* have the chance of falling in love."

The only opportunity a young man has of seeing a girl is at a distance, at church or in a religious procession. Here he may see her face; her character he can only ascertain through gossip, a lady friend, or the parish priest. It is much more respectable, however, to show no such curiosity, for its absence implies the absence of such a ridiculous thing as Love. "*There is nothing which good society in France disapproves of so much as the passion of Love*, or anything resembling it." "When Cœlebs asks for the hand of a girl he has seen for a minute, he may just possibly be in love with her, which is a degrading supposition; but if he has never seen her, you cannot even suspect him of a sentiment so unbecoming."

There is but one way for the young man to gain admission to a house where there is a marriageable young lady: "He must first, through a third party, ask to marry the young lady, and, if her *parents* consent, he will then be admitted to see her and speak to her, but not otherwise. *The respectable order of affairs is that the offer and acceptance should precede and not follow courtship.*"

Would it be possible to conceive a more diabolically ingenious social machinery for massacring Romantic Love *en gros?*

"Marriages in France are generally arranged by the exercise of reason and prudence, rather than by either passion or affection." Mr. Hamerton gives an amusing account of how he was asked to be matrimonial ambassador by a young man who had never seen the girl he wanted to marry. Mr. Hamerton obliged the young man, but was told by the mother that if the young man would wait two years he might have a fair chance, provided a *richer* or *nobler* suitor did not turn up in the meantime.

Money and Rank *versus* Love. French mammas have at least one virtue. They are not hypocrites.

The Countess von Bothmer, who lived in France a quarter of a century, says in her *French Home Life:* "Where we so ordinarily listen to what we understand by love—to the temptations of the young heart in all their forms (however transitory), to our individual impressions and our own opinions—the French consult fitness of relative situation, reciprocities of fortune and position, and harmonies of family intercourse."

To annihilate the last resource of Love—elopement—the *Code Napoléon* forbids all marriages without either the consent of the father and mother, or proof that they are both dead. "It is very troublesome to get married in France; the operation is surrounded by difficulties and formalities which would make an Englishman stamp with rage."

Social life, of course, suffers as much from this idiotic system as Romantic Love. French hospitality "does not extend beyond the family circle," we are informed by M. Max O'Rell, who also gives this amusing instance of the imbecility or mental slavery (he does not use these words) produced by the French system of education and chaperonage:—

"I remember I was one day sitting in the Champs Elysées with two English ladies. Beside us was a young French girl with her father and mother. The person on the right of papa rose and went away, and we heard the young innocent say to her mother: 'Mamma, may I go and sit by papa?' It was a baby of about eighteen or twenty. Those English ladies laugh over the affair to this day."

Boys suffer as well as girls. As the author of an article on "Parisian Psychology" remarks: "There are no mothers in France; it is a nation of 'mammas,' who, in the most unlimited sense of the word, spoil their boys, weaken them in body and soul, dwarf their thought, dry their hearts, and lower them to below even their own level, hoping thereby to rule over them through life, as they too often do. Frenchwomen having been at best but half-wives, regard their children as a sort of compensation for what they have themselves not had; and after the mischievous fashion of weak 'mammas,' prolong babyhood till far into mature life."

The French, in fact, are a nation of babies. Their puerile conceit, which prevents them from learning to read any language but their own, and thus finding out what other nations think of them, is responsible in part for the mediæval barbarism of their matrimonial arrangements. The Parisian is the most provincial animal in the world. In any other metropolis—be it London, New York, Vienna, or Berlin—people understand and relish whatever is good in literature, art, and life, be it English, American, French, German, or Italian. But the Parisian understands only what is narrowly and exclusively French. And this is the dictionary definition of Provincialism.

The consequences of this mediævalism and provincialism in modern France are thus eloquently summed up by a writer in the *Westminster Review* (1877):—

"Such education as girls receive is not only not a preparation for the wedded state, it is a positive disqualification for it. They are not taught to read, they are not taught to reason; they are *launched into life without a single intellectual interest.* The whole effort of their early training goes to fill their mind with puerilities and superstitions. As regards God, they are instructed to believe in relics and old bones; as regards man, they are instructed to believe in dress, in mannerisms, and coquetry. Their love of appreciation, after being enormously developed, is bottled up and tied down until a husband is found to draw the cork. What else, then, can we look for but an explosion of frivolity? Can we expect that such a provision of coquettishness will be reserved for the husband's exclusive use? He will be tired of it in three months—unless it is tired of him before; and then the pent-up waters will forsake their narrow bed and overflow the country far and wide."

No wonder Napoléon remarked that "Love does more harm than good." And right he was, most emphatically, for the only kind of Love *possible* in France does infinite harm. It poisons life and literature alike.

We can now understand the fierceness of Dumas's attacks on *mariages de convenance:* "The manifest deterioration of the race touches him; it does not touch us. Nor do we at all realise the next to impossibility of a man ever marrying for love in France. There are those who have tried to do it, but they can never get on in life; they are reputed of 'bad example'" (*St. James's Gazette*).

And now we come upon a paradox which has puzzled a great many thinkers. The Countess von Bothmer, while deploring the absence of Love in French courtship, endeavours to show that domestic happiness and conjugal affection are, nevertheless, not rare in France. French husbands "are ordinarily with their wives, accompany them wherever they can, and share their friendships and distractions." Mr. Hamerton likewise bears witness that French girls "become excellent wives, faithful, orderly, dutiful, contented, and economical. They all either love their husbands, *or conduct themselves as if they did so.*" He says the notion fostered by novels "that Frenchmen are always occupied in making love to their neighbours' wives" is nonsense; that there is no more adultery than elsewhere. "There exists in foreign countries, and especially in England, a belief that Frenchwomen are very generally adulteresses.

The origin of the belief is this,—the manner in which marriages are generally managed in France leaves no room for interesting love-stories. Novelists and dramatists *must* find love-stories somewhere, and so they have to seek for them in illicit intrigues."

This is all very ingenious, but the argument is not conclusive. Even granted for a moment that Mr. Hamerton is right in his defence of French conjugal life, is it not a more than sufficient condemnation of the French system of "courtship" that one-half of the nation are prevented from reading its literature because it is so foul and filthy—because Love has been made synonymous with adultery?

But Mr. Hamerton's assertion loses its probability when viewed in the light of the following considerations. He himself admits that the French are anxious to read about Love, that the novelists and dramatists *must* find stories of Love somewhere—mind you, not of conjugal but of Romantic Love—and the Paris *Figaro* not long ago denounced the French novelists of the period for devoting their stories to Love almost exclusively, whereas Balzac, Dumas, Thackeray, and Scott, at least introduced various other matters of interest. Now French novels have the largest editions of any books published; and if so vast an interest is displayed by the French in reading about Love, is it likely that their interest is purely literary? Certainly not. They will seek it in real life. And in real life it can only be found in one sphere, which elsewhere is protected against such invasions, by the young being allowed to meet one another. "It is to be feared that they who marry where they do not love, will love where they do not marry." In *this* respect human nature is the same the world over. The testimony of scores of unprejudiced authors on this head cannot be ignored.

This, however, is only one of the evils following from the French suppression of pre-matrimonial Love. The parents may or may not suffer through conjugal jealousy and infidelity, one thing is certain, —that the children suffer from it, in body and mind. It is leading to the depopulation of France. It was M. Jules Rochard who called attention to the fact that "France, which two centuries ago included one-third of the total population of Europe, now contains but one-tenth;" although the death-rate is smaller in France than in most European countries, and although there has been a gradual increase of wealth throughout the country.

That the suppression of Romantic Love and of all opportunities for courtship is the principal cause of the decline of France, is apparent from the fact that the countries in which population increases most rapidly—as America and Great Britain—are those in which Romantic Love is the chief motive to marriage.

Romantic Love goes by complementary qualities, the defects of the parents neutralising one another in the offspring; so that the children who are the issue of a love-match are commonly more beautiful than their parents. In France there is no selection whatever, except with reference to money and rank. Not even Health is considered, the *sine qua non* of Love as well as Beauty. Hence the absence of Love in France has led to the almost absolute absence of beauty. And it would be nothing short of a miracle if the offspring of a young maiden, still in her teens, and an old broken-down sinner, chosen by her parents for his wealth or social position, were any different from the puny, hairy men and coarse-featured, vulgar women that make up the bulk of the French nation.

In Paris one does occasionally see a fine figure and a rather pretty face, but they almost always belong to the lower classes. As the lower classes allow the young considerable freedom, it would seem as if beauty in this class ought to be as common an article as in England or the United States. But the incapacity of the young women for feeling and reciprocating Love neutralises these opportunities. For of what use is it for a man to feel Love if the woman invariably bases her choice on money? This matter is most clearly brought out by Mr. Hamerton :—

"Amongst the lower classes, the peasantry and workmen . . . girls have as much freedom as they have in England. The great institution of the *parlement* gives them ample opportunities for becoming acquainted with their lovers; indeed the acquaintance, in many cases, goes further than is altogether desirable. A peasant girl requires no parental help in looking after her own interests. She admits a lover to the happy state of *parlement*, which means that he has a right to talk with her when they meet, and to call upon her, dance with her, etc. The lover is always eager to fix the wedding-day, the girl is not so eager. She keeps him on indefinitely until a richer one appears, on which No. 1 has the mortification of seeing himself excluded from *parlement*, whilst another takes his place. In this way a clever girl will go on for several years, amusing herself by torturing amorous swains, until at length a sufficiently big fish nibbles at the bait, when she hooks him at once, and takes good care that *he* shall not escape. Nothing can be more pathetically ludicrous than the condition of a young peasant who is really in love, especially if he is able to write, for then he pours forth his feelings in innumerable letters full of tenderness and complaint. On her part the girl does not answer the letters, and has not the slightest pity for the unhappy victim of her charms. After seeing a good deal of such love-affairs I have come to the conclusion that in humble life young men do really very often feel

>" 'The hope, the fear, the jealous care,
> The exalted portion of the pain
> And power of love.'

And they 'wear the chain' too. Young women, on the other hand, seem only to amuse themselves with all this simple-hearted devotion—

>" 'And mammon wins his way where seraphs might despair.' "

Schopenhauer pointed out that the French lack the *Gefühl für das Innige* — the tenderness and emotional depth which characterise the Germans and Italians. It is this that accounts for the inability of the French to appreciate Love, and for the fact that even vice is coarser in France than elsewhere, as remarked by Mr. Lecky, who, in his *History of European Morals*, contrasts "the coarse, cynical, ostentatious sensuality, which forms the most repulsive feature of the French character," with "the dreamy, languid, and æsthetical sensuality of the Spaniard or Italian." And it remained for the French to attempt to deify vice as in that over-rated and repulsive story of *Manon Lescaut*.

Mme. de Staël, who suffered so much from the provincialism (*alias* patriotism) of her countrymen, saw clearly the immorality of the French system of marrying girls without consulting their choice. Brandes relates the following anecdote of her: "One day, speaking of the unnaturalness of marriages arranged by the parents, as distinguished from those in which the young girls choose for themselves, she exclaimed, 'I would *compel* my daughter to marry the man of her choice!'"

An attempt is being made at present in Paris to introduce the Anglo-American feminine spirit into society. The word *flirter* has been adopted, and the thing itself experimented with. But the French girl does not know how to draw the line between coquetry and flirtation. She needs a better education before she can flirt properly. This education the Government is trying to give her at present; but it meets with stubborn resistance from the priests, and from the old notion that intellectual culture is fatal to feminine charms and the capacity for affection. If this book should accomplish nothing else than prove that without intellect there can be no deep Love, it will not have been written in vain.

ITALIAN LOVE

In Italy, in the sixteenth century, women were kept in as strict seclusion as to-day in France; and with the same results,—conjugal infidelity and a great lack of Personal Beauty, as noted by Montaigne, who remarks at the same time that it was regarded as something quite extraordinary if a young lady was seen in public.

Byron wrote in 1817 that "Jealousy is not the order of the day in Venice;" and that the Italians "marry for their parents, and love for themselves."

In Crowe and Cavalcaselle's *Life and Times of Titian* we read that "Though chroniclers have left us to guess what the state of society may have been in Venice at the close of the fifteenth century, they give us reason to believe that it was deeply influenced by Oriental habit. The separation of men from women in churches, the long seclusion of unmarried females in convents or in the privacy of palaces, were but the precursors to marriages in which husbands were first allowed to see their wives as they came in state to dance round the wedding supper-table."

But even at this early period when women were still treated as babies unable to take care of themselves, we find at least one trace of the Gallantry which is so essential an element in modern love. It was customary for the men, on festive occasions, to stand behind their wives' chairs at table and serve them.

Extremely ungallant, on the other hand, are some of the Italian proverbs about women of this and other periods. "A woman is like a horse-chestnut—beautiful outside, worthless inside." "Two women and a goose make a market." "Married man—bird in cage." "In buying a horse and taking a wife shut your eyes and commend your soul to heaven."

Her exuberant health makes an Italian woman naturally prone to Love; but though she falls in love most readily, the passion is apt to be fugitive and superficial. She rarely loves with the passionate ardour of a Spanish woman. "What we notice especially in Italian women," says Schweiger-Lerchenfeld, "is the absence of that alternation between those extremes of temperament which are so conspicuous in other Southern women. Energy is almost as unknown to her as the moral power of resignation and sacrifice. Hence it can hardly surprise us that Italian history records so few heroic women or pious female martyrs. Italy has produced neither a Jeanne d'Arc nor an Elizabeth of Thuringia; the crowns were too oppressive to be borne by these beauties, and life too enchanting for them to invite to tragic self-sacrifice."

Probably the most realistic, and certainly the most fascinating, account of Italian love-making ever given is to be found in Mr. Howells's *Venetian Life*. As it is too long to quote, I will attempt to condense it, though at some sacrifice of that literary "bouquet," as an epicure would say, which constitutes the unique charm of Mr. Howells's style:—

"The Venetians have had a practical and strictly businesslike way of arranging marriages from the earliest times. The shrewdest provision has always been made for the dower and for the good of the state; private and public interest being consulted, the small matters of affection have been left to the chances of association.

"Herodotus relates that the Assyrian Veneti sold their daughters at auction to the highest bidder;

and the fair being thus comfortably placed in life, the hard-favoured were given to whomsoever would take them, with such dower as might be considered a reasonable compensation. The auction was discontinued in Christian times, but marriage-contracts still partook of the form of a public and half-mercantile transaction.

"These passionate, headlong Italians look well to the main chance before they leap into matrimony, and you may be sure Todaro knows, in black and white, what the Biondina has to her fortune before he weds her."

"With the nobility and with the richest commoners marriage is still greatly a matter of contract, and is arranged without much reference to the principals, though it is now scarcely probable in any case that they have not seen each other. But with all other classes, except the poorest, who cannot or will not seclude the youth of either sex from each other, and with whom, consequently, romantic contrivance and subterfuge would be superfluous, love is made to-day in Venice as in the *Capa y espada* comedies of the Spaniards, and the business is carried on with all the cumbrous machinery of confidants, *billets-doux*, and stolen interviews."

The "operatic method of courtship" thence resulting commonly assumes this form :—

"They follow that beautiful blonde, who, marching demurely in front of the gray-moustached papa and the fat mamma, after the fashion in Venice, is electrically conscious of pursuit. They follow during the whole evening, and, at a distance, softly follow her home, where the burning Todaro photographs the number of the house upon the sensitised tablets of his soul. This is the first step in love: he has seen his adored one, and she knows that he loves her with an inextinguishable ardour."

The next step consists in his frequenting the *caffè*, where she goes with her parents, and feasting his eyes on her beauty. After some time he may possibly get a chance to speak a few words to her under her balcony; or, what is more likely, he will bribe her servant-maid to bring her a love-letter. Or else he goes to church to admire her at a convenient distance.

"It must be confessed that if the Biondina is not pleased with his looks, his devotion must assume the character of an intolerable bore to her; and that to see him everywhere at her heels—to behold him leaning against the pillar near which she kneels at church, the head of his stick in his mouth, and his attitude carefully taken with a view to captivation—to be always in deadly fear lest she shall meet him in promenade, or turning round at the *caffè* encounter his pleading gaze—that all this must drive the Biondina to a state bordering upon blasphemy and finger-nails. *Ma, come si fa? Ci vuol pazienza?* This is the sole course open to ingenuous youth in Venice, where confessed and unashamed acquaintance between young people is extremely difficult; and so this blind pursuit must go on till the Biondina's inclinations are at last laboriously ascertained." Then follow the inquiries as to her dowry, after which nothing remains but "to demand her in marriage of her father, *and after that to make her acquaintance.*"

Topsy-turvy as this last arrangement may seem to Anglo-American notions, here at least Love has some chance to bring about real Sexual Selection, for a Southerner's passions are momentarily inflamed, and the Italian Cupid needs but a moment to fix his choice. And what distinguishes Italy still more favourably from France is that, whereas the French consider Love ridiculous, and have made the most ingenious contrivances for annihilating it, the Italians worship it, revel in it, and are inclined rather to make too many concessions to it than to ignore it.

The result is patent to all eyes. For every attractive Frenchwoman there are to-day a hundred beautiful Italians. And were Anglo-American methods of courtship introduced in Italy, beauty would again be doubled in amount. It must not be forgotten, however, that Love, as a beautifier of mankind, has in Italy very strong allies in the balmy air and sunshine, tempting to constant outdoor life, which mellows the complexion, brightens the eyes, and fills out the figure to those full yet elegant proportions which instantaneously arouse the romantic passion.

SPANISH LOVE

Spanish veins contain more Oriental blood than those of any other European nation; and to the present day Eastern methods of treating women cast their shadow on Spanish life. But the shadow is so light, and so much mitigated by the rosy hue of romance, that the "local colour" of Love in Spain presents an unusually fascinating spectacle, which countless literary artists have attempted to depict.

During the sixteenth and seventeenth centuries

the Oriental shadow was much darker, and kept the women in extreme subjection and ignorance. "Their life," says Professor Scherr, speaking even of the queens, "passed away in a luxurious tedium which dulled the sentiments to the point of idiocy. They were only crowned slaves. As an instance of their absolute deprivation of liberty may be cited the case of Elizabeth, wife of Philip II., who, when in 1565 she went to Bayonne to meet her mother, had to wait three days before the gates of Burgos before it was possible to ascertain the king's decision whether the queen should pass through the city or around it."

"Women of rank," he continues, "lived in a seclusion bordering on that of a convent, if not surpassing it. For nuns were at least allowed to speak to male visitors behind bars, whereas married women were strictly forbidden to receive the visit of a man, except with the special permission of the husband. And only during the first year of their wedded life were they allowed to frequent public drives in open carriages by the side of their husband; subsequently they were only allowed to go out in closed carriages. Of cosy family life not a trace. . . . Even the table did not unite the husband and wife; the master took his meal alone, while his wife and children sat respectfully on the floor on carpets, with their legs crossed in Oriental fashion.

"The poor women, excluded from every refined social diversion, were confined to manual work, gossip with their duennas, mechanical praying, playing with their rosaries, and—intriguing. For the greater the subjection of women, the more does their cunning grow, the more passionate becomes their desire to avenge themselves on their tyrants. The Spaniards found this out to their cost. The most inexorable spirit of revenge, all the parade of 'Spanish honour,' bordering in its excess on clownishness, could not prevent the Spanish dames from loving and being loved."

In course of time this Oriental despotism, with its fatal consequences to conjugal fidelity—as in France—has been greatly mitigated in Spain. In Pepys's *Diary*, 1667, we read of an informant who told the writer "of their wooing [in Spain] by serenades at the window, and that their friends do always make the match; but yet they have opportunities to meet at masse at church, and there they make love."

In an interesting book on Spain, written almost two and a quarter centuries after Pepys's *Diary*—Mr. Lathrop's *Spanish Vistas*—we still read concerning this ecclesiastic Love-making, in the Seville Cathedral: "Every door was guarded by a squad of the decrepit army, so that entrance there became a horror. These sanctuary beggars serve a double purpose, however. The black-garbed Sevillan ladies, who are perpetually stealing in and out noiselessly under cover of their archly-draped lace veils—losing themselves in the dark, incense-laden interior, or emerging from confession into the daylight glare again—are careful to drop some slight conscience-money into the palms that wait. Occasionally, by pre-arrangement, one of these beggars will convey into the hand that passes him a silver piece, a tightly-folded note from some clandestine lover. It is a convenient underground mail, and I am afraid the venerable church innocently shelters a good many little transactions of this kind."

How greatly the facilities for falling in love and for making love have been increased in modern Spain is vividly brought out in the following citation from Schweiger-Lerchenfeld regarding the scenes to be witnessed every evening on the crowded promenade or Rambla at Barcelona:—

"Are these elegantly-attired ramblers one and all suitors, since they put no limit nor restraint on their whispered flatteries? No, that is simply the custom in Barcelona. The women and girls are beautiful, and though they are well aware of it, they nevertheless allow their charms to be whispered in their ears hundreds of times every evening—a freedom of intercourse which is only possible on Spanish soil. . . . And thus one of these adored beauties walks up and down in the glare of the lamps, and sweet music is wafted to her ears: 'Your beauty dazzles me,' whispers one voice; and another, 'Happiness and anguish your eyes are burning into my soul.' One compliments the chosen one on her hair, another on her figure, a third on her graceful gait. Young adorers feel a thrill running down their whole body if her mantilla only touches them; while mature lovers are contented with nothing less than a pressure of the hand. It is a picture that is possible, conceivable only in Spain."

The same writer quotes some specimens of Spanish Love-songs, one of which may be transferred to this page—

"Échame, niña bonita,
Lágrimas en tu pañuelo,
Y los llevaré a Madrid
Que los engarce un platero."

"Show me, my little charmer, the tear in your handkerchief; to Madrid will I take it and have it set by a jeweller."

What a contrast between this modern complimentary and poetic form of Gallantry and the form prevalent in the good old times when lovers endeavoured to win a maiden's favour by flagellating themselves under her window until the blood ran down their backs; and when, as Scherr adds, "it was regarded as the surest sign of supreme gallantry if some of the blood bespattered the clothes of the beauty to whom this crazy act of devotion was addressed!"

Nevertheless, the Spanish still have much to learn from England and America regarding the proper methods of Courtship; for, according to a writer in *Macmillan's Magazine* (1874), the unmarried maiden of the higher classes, "like her humbler sister, can never have the privilege of seeing her lover in private, and very rarely, indeed, if ever, is he admitted into the *sala* where she is sitting. He may contrive to get a few minutes' chat with her through the barred windows of her *sala;* but when a Spaniard leads his wife from the altar, he knows no more of her character, attainments, and disposition than does the parish priest who married them, and perhaps not so much."

In one respect Spanish lovers have a great advantage over their unfortunate colleagues in France. There marriage is impossible without parental consent, whereas in Spain a law exists concerning which the writer just quoted says:—

"Should a Spanish lad and lassie become attached

to one another, and the parents absolutely forbid the match, and refuse their daughter liberty and permission to marry, the lover has his remedy at law. He has but to make a statement of the facts on paper, and deposit it, signed and attested, with the alcalde or mayor of the township in which the lady's parents dwell. The alcalde then makes an order, giving the young man the right of free entry into the house in question, within a certain number of days, for the purpose of wooing and carrying off his idol. The parents dare not interfere with the office of the alcalde, and the lady is taken to her lover's arms. From that moment he, and he alone, is bound to provide for her: by his own act and deed she has become his property." Should he prove false "the law comes upon him with all its force, and he is bound to maintain her, in every way, as a wife, under pain of punishment."

Thus a Spanish girl is protected against perfidious lovers as well as is an English and American girl through the possibility of suing for breach of promise. If the short stories told in *Don Quixote* may be taken as examples, faithless lovers were very common in Spain at that time; which, doubtless, accounts for the origin of this law. The girls on their part erred by yielding too easily to the promises of the men; though they are partially excused by the great strength of their passions.

In his work on Suicide, Professor Morselli has statistics showing that more women take their life in Spain than in any other country; and he attributes this to the force of their passions, which is greater than in Italy, where the number of female suicides is considerably lower.

Thus Love has a more favourable ground in Spain than either in Italy or in France, notwithstanding certain restrictions. And the result shows itself in this, that all tourists unite in singing the praises of Spanish Beauty. Spain, indeed, unites in itself all the conditions favourable to Beauty: a climate tempting to outdoor life; a considerable amount of intellectual culture and æsthetic refinement; a mixture of nationalities, fusing *ethnic* peculiarities into a harmonious whole; and Love, which fuses *individual* complementary qualities into a harmonious ensemble of beautiful features, graceful figure, amiable disposition, and refined manners.

GERMAN LOVE

When Tacitus penned his famous certificate of good moral character for the Germans of his time, he little suspected how many thousand times it would be quoted by the grateful and proud descendants of those early Teutons, and pinned to the lapels of their coats as a sort of prize medal in the competition for ancestral virtue. The more candid historians, however, admit that the Roman historian somewhat overdrew his picture in order to teach his own profligate countrymen a sort of Sunday school lesson, by the vivid contrast presented by these inhabitants of the northern virgin forests.

There is no question that women were held in considerable honour among these early Germans. Many of them served as priestesses, and adultery was punished with death. Polygamy existed only among the chiefs, and even among them it was not common. Yet the men did not treat the women as their equals. "They had more duties than privileges," says Schweiger-Lerchenfeld. Their husbands were addicted to excessive drinking and gambling when not engaged in war or the chase, leaving the hard domestic and field labour to the women: and all this cannot have tended to refine the women.

"Marriage in the old Germanic times," says Ploss, "was mostly an affair of expediency.... In the choice of a wife beauty was of less moment than property and good social antecedents. Love *before* the betrothal rarely occurs."

Gustav Freytag, in his *Pictures of German Life*, during the fifteenth, sixteenth, and seventeenth centuries, remarks: "Marriage was considered by our ancestors less as a union of two lovers than as an institution replete with duties and rights, not only of married people towards one another, but also towards their relatives, as a bond uniting two corporate bodies.... Therefore in the olden time the choice of husband and wife was always an affair of importance to the relatives on both sides, so that a German wooing from the oldest times, *even until the last century*, had the appearance of a business transaction, which was carried out with great regard to suitability."

And a business transaction it is, unfortunately, to the present day, in the vast majority of cases. A certain amount of dower or property on the bride's part is the first and most essential requisite. Second in importance is the desirability of not descending even a step in the social ladder, though an extra lump of gold commonly suffices to pull down social Pride to a lower level. Health, temper, Personal

Beauty, and mutual suitability—these are the trifles which, other things being equal, come in as a third consideration. And thus is the order of Sexual Selection, as ordained by Love, commonly reversed.

What would an English or American youth of twenty-two say to his father if the latter should undertake to write to all his relatives, asking them to look about for an eligible partner for his son, and capping the climax by starting himself on a trip in search of a bride for his son? Would he accept without a murmur the girl thus found, and would an English or American girl thus allow herself to be given away like a cat in a bag, not knowing whither she was going? I have seen several such cases with my own eyes. One of them was most pathetic. For when the blooming bride, a sweet and refined girl, was introduced to the bridegroom selected for her by her parents—a repulsive-looking brute, twice her age—she conceived a perfect loathing for him, and almost wept out her eyes before the wedding-day. But the man was rich, and that settled the matter.

What aggravated this outrage was the fact that the bride's father also was rich. And herein, in fact, lies the canker of the German system. Money is such a comfortable thing to have that it is useless to preach against it. There are money-marriages enough in England and America. But in these countries it is generally considered sufficient if one party has the money. Not so in Germany. It is not so much the comfort ensured by a certain amount of money that is aimed at as the superior social influence ensured by a large amount of wealth.

Hence the rich marry the rich, regardless of other consequences, and poor Cupid is left shivering in the cold. So that, after all, the silly pride of social position is a greater enemy of Romantic Love than money.

And the consequences of such a matrimonial system? They have been most eloquently set forth by the blind old philosopher, Dr. Dühring:—

"The amalgamation of fortunes, and the resulting enervating luxury of living, are the ruling matrimonial motives; and the want of mutual adaptation of the individuals becomes the cause of the degenerate appearance of the offspring. The loathsome products of such marriages then walk about as ugly embodiments and witnesses of such a degraded system of legalised prostitution (*Kuppelwirthschaft*). They bear the stamp of incongruity on body and mind; for their appearance shows them to be the offspring of disharmonious parents, blindly associated, or even, in many cases, of parents who themselves are already products of this new matrimonial method. This degeneracy necessarily continues from one generation to another, and in this manner maltreated Nature avenges herself by leading to personal decrepitude and the formation of a new sort of idiocy."

"It is true," he adds, "that love is not an infallible sign of mutual suitability; but when it is absent, or even replaced by aversion, it is certain that it is useless to expect a specially harmonious composition of the offspring."

Is this one of the reasons why Personal Beauty is so rare, comparatively, in Germany?

But Individual Preference is not the only element of Love which thus suffers in Germany through false Pride and parental tyranny. Gallantry is another factor which needs mending. German women are sweet and amiable. In fact, they are *too* sweet and good-natured. They have spoiled the men, who in consequence are excessively selfish in their relations to women—the most selfish men in the world, outside of Turkey or China. True, the German officer in a ballroom seems to be the very essence of officious Gallantry. But his motives are too transparently Ovidian: it is not true Anglo-American politeness of the heart that inspires his conduct. He is either after forbidden sweets or parading his uniform and his vanity. Take the same man and watch him at home. His wife has to get him his chair, move it up to the fire, bring him his slippers, put the coffee in his hand, and do errands for him. When he goes out she puts on his overcoat and buttons it up carefully for him as if he were a helpless big baby. This would be all very well—for why should not women be gallant too?—if he would only retaliate. But he never dreams of it. Even if it comes to a task which calls for masculine muscular power—the carrying of bundles, etc.—he makes the wife do it. He is, in fact, matrimonially considered, not only a big baby but also a big brute, the very incarnation of masculine selfishness.

In former centuries it was customary in Germany, as it is now with us, for women to bow first to men. The modern German has reversed this. Woman has no right to bow until her lord and superior has invited her to do so by doffing his hat.

The German girl, says the Countess von Bothmer in *German Home Life*, "is taught that to be womanly she must be helpless, to be feminine she must be feeble, to endear herself she must be dependent, to charm she must cling." "To keep carefully to the sheep-walk, to applaud in concert and condemn in chorus, is the only behaviour that can be tolerated." "They have one bugbear and one object of idolatry, these monotonous ladies,—a fetish which they worship under the name of Mode; a monster between public opinion and Mrs. Grundy. To say a thing is not 'Mode' here, is to condemn it as if by all the laws of Media and Persia. It is not her centre [*sic*], but the system of her social education, that renders the German woman so hopelessly provincial."

Of course it is the men who are responsible for this social education and this feminine ideal of absolute dependence. It suits their selfish pleasure to be worshipped and obeyed by the women without any efforts at gallant retaliation on their part.

A native writer tells us that "a true German philosophises occasionally while he embraces his sweetheart; while kissing even, theories will sprout in his mind."

No wonder, therefore, that one of the German metaphysicians, Fichte, should have made a sophistic attempt to reduce masculine selfishness to a system. He proves to his own satisfaction that it is woman's duty to sacrifice herself in man's behalf; while man, on his part, has no such obligations. His reasoning is too elaborate to quote in full; but is too amusingly naïve to be omitted, so I will translate the summary of it given by Kuno Fischer in his *History of Philosophy* :—

"What woman's natural instincts demand is self-abandonment to a man; she desires this abandonment not for her own sake, but for the man's sake; she gives herself to him, for him. Now abandoning oneself for another is self-sacrifice, and self-sacrifice from an instinctive impulse is LOVE. Therefore love is a kind of instinctive impulse which the sexual instinct in woman necessarily and involuntarily assumes. She feels the necessity of loving. . . . This impulse is peculiar to woman alone; woman alone loves [!!!]; only through woman does love appear among mankind. . . . The woman's life should disappear in the man's without a remnant, and it is this relation that is so beautifully and correctly indicated in the fact that the wife no longer uses her own name, but that of her husband [!]."

The latest (and it is to be hoped the last) of the German metaphysicians, the pessimist Hartmann, goes even a step beyond Fichte in arrogating for man special privileges in Love. If Fichte makes Love synonymous with Self-Sacrifice—feminine, mind you, not masculine—Hartmann tries to prove that man may love as often as he pleases, but woman only once. And what aggravates the offence, he does it in such a poetic manner. "Though it may be doubtful," he says, "whether a man can truly love two women at the same time, it is beyond all doubt that he can love several in succession with all the depth of his heart; and the assertion that there is only one true love is an unwarranted generalisation to all mankind of a maxim which is true of woman alone. . . . Woman can learn but once by experience what love is, and it is painful for the lover not to be the one who teaches her first. True it is that a tree nipped by a spring frost brings forth a second crown of leaves, but so rich and luxuriant as the first it will not be; thus does a maiden-heart produce a second bloom, if the first had to wither before maturity, but its full and complete floral glory is unfolded only where love, aroused for the first time, passes in full vigour through all its phases."

Yet it is not ungallant selfishness alone that prompts German men to bring up their women so that they shall be mere playthings at first and drudges after marriage, never real soul-mates. They have the same old stupid continental fear that culture of the intellect weakens the feelings. This fear is based on slovenly reasoning—on the inference that because a few blue-stockings have at all ages made themselves ridiculous by assuming masculine attributes and parading their lack of tenderness and feminine delicacy, therefore intellectual training must be fatal to feminine charms. As if there were not plenty of masculine blue-stockings, or pedants, without disproving the fact that the men of the greatest intellectual power—men of genius—are also the most emotional and refined of all men; or the fact proved by this whole monograph, that Love and general emotional refinement grow with the general intellectual culture of women.

A typical illustration of German feeling on the subject of female education is to be found in Schweiger-Lerchenfeld's *Frauenleben der Erde*, p. 530. Referring to the attempts now being made in France to give young girls a rational education, he quotes the opinion of a French legislator that a girl thus brought up would not love less deeply than heretofore, while she would love more intelligently ; and then comments as follows : " How far this anticipation may be realised cannot be decided now or in the near future. At any rate we must leave to the French themselves the task of getting along with this classical female generation of the future. Certain it is that their experiment will hardly be imitated, and that the old Romans and Greeks may eventually become more dangerous to masculine supremacy (Autorität) than the pilgrimage stories of Lourdes."

It is time for German woman to rise in revolt against this mediæval masculine selfishness. Not in active revolt, for a warlike woman is an abomination. But in passive revolt. Let them cease to spoil the men, and these bears will become more gallant. Germany is later in almost every phase of literary and social culture than England. It was not an accident that Shakspere came before Heine, the English before the German poet of Love ; for Love is much less advanced in Germany than in England. It has not even passed the stage where a harsh sort of Coyness is still in place. German women want to learn the cunning to be strange. They are too deferential to the men, too easily won. They want to learn to indulge in harmless flirtation, and they want the education which will give them wit enough to flirt cleverly and make the men mellow.

It must be admitted, however, notwithstanding all these strictures, that there is much genuine Romantic Love in Germany, often differing in no wise from Anglo-American Love. At first sight it seems, indeed, as if chaperonage were as strict as in

France; and no doubt many German girls are brought up on the spring-chicken-coyness system which regards every man as a hawk, and a signal for hiding away in a corner. But in general German girls have much more freedom than French girls. They may walk alone in the street in the daytime, go alone to the conservatory to attend a music-lesson. They meet the young men freely at evening-parties, dances, musical entertainments, etc.; and the chaperons are not nearly so obtrusive and offensive as in France. The mothers appear to have taken to heart Jean Paul's saying that "in the mother's presence it is impossible to carry on an edifying conversation with the daughter." So that there is plenty of opportunity for falling in love; and were it not for parental dictation, Love-matches would perhaps be as common as in England. But the girls lack independence of spirit to defy parental tyranny, which it is their *moral duty* to defy where money or rank are pitted against Love. For the health and happiness of the next generation are at stake.

German girls also enjoy an advantage over the French in having a literature which is pure and wholesome; and by reading about Romantic Love they train and deepen their feelings. It is often said that Heine's influence has been chiefly negative. The truth is, *Heine is the greatest emotional educator Germany has ever had.* More young men and girls have wept over his pathetic lyrics than over any other poetry. His *Buch der Lieder* has done more to foster the growth of Romantic Love in Germany than all other collections of verse combined; not only by their own unadorned beauty, but through the soulful music wedded to these poems by Schubert, Schumann, and other magicians of the heart. The fact that the copyright on Heine's works was soon to expire, and the country to be flooded with cheap editions, has long caused Master Cupid to rub his hands in gleeful anticipation of brisk business; and he has just given orders in his arsenal for one hundred thousand new golden arrows.

Heine indeed fathomed the secrets of Love much more deeply than Goethe. Whereas Heine sang of Love in every major and minor key, Goethe appears to have emphasised chiefly its transitoriness. "Love, as Goethe knows it," says Professor Seeley, "is very tender, and has a lyric note as fresh as that of a song-bird. In his *Autobiography* one love-passage succeeds another, but each comes speedily to an end. How far in each case he was to blame is a matter of controversy. But he seems to betray a way of thinking about women such as might be natural to an Oriental sultan. 'I was in that agreeable phase,' he writes, 'when a new passion had begun to spring up in me before the old one had quite disappeared.' About Frederika he blames himself without reserve, and uses strong expressions of contrition; but he forgets the matter strangely soon. In his distress of mind he says he found riding, and especially skating, bring much relief. This reminds us of the famous letter to the Frau von Stein about coffee. He is always ready in a moment to shake off the deepest impressions and receive new ones; and he never looks back. . . . Goethe was a man of the old *régime*. . . . Had he entered into the reforming movement of his age, he might have striven to elevate women. . . . He certainly felt at times that all was not right in the status of women ('woman's fate is pitiable'), and how narrowly confined was their happiness (wie enggebunden ist des Weibes Glück) . . . but he was not a reformer of institutions."

A reformer of institutions, however, has apparently just arisen in Berlin. For we read that at a private female seminary the girls received the following subject for an essay: "There is from the Ideas of Plato, the atoms of Democritus, the Substance of Spinoza, the monads of Leibnitz, and from the subjective mental forms of Kant, the proof to bring, that the philosophy it never neglected has the to-be-calculated results of their hypotheses with their into-perception-falling effects to compare."

Such subjects, so elegantly expressed, are no doubt eminently calculated to bring out the latent possibilities of feminine feeling and culture.

To close this chapter with a sweet, soothing concord—major triad, horns and 'cellos, *smorzando*—it must be admitted that the Germans have one ingredient of Romantic Love which all other nations must envy them. They have one more thrill in the drama of Love, in the ascending scale of familiarities, than we have, namely, the word *Du*, which is something very different from the stilted *Thou*, because still a part of everyday language. The second person singular is used in Germany towards pet animals and children, between students, intimate friends, relatives, and lovers. French "lovers" do not say *tu* to each other till after marriage, and even then they do not use it in public. But the German lover has the privilege, as soon as he is engaged, of exchanging the formal *Sie* for the affectionate *Du ;* and the first *Du* that comes from her lips can hardly be less sweet than the first kiss.

There is a game of cards, popular among young folks in Germany, during which you have to address every one with *Du* whom you otherwise would have to call *Sie*, and *vice versâ ;* cards have to be called spoons, white black, etc. If there is a young man in the company secretly in love with a young lady, you can always "spot" him by the eagerness he shows to speak to her, and the fact that he always gets the *Du* right and everything else wrong ; while she, strange to say, appears to have never heard of such a thing at all as a personal pronoun.

ENGLISH LOVE

Concerning Romantic Love in England and America, there is less to be said under the head of National Peculiarities than in case of the continental nations of Europe, for the simple reason that almost everything said in the pages on Modern Love refers especially to these two countries. Anglo-American Love is Romantic Love, pure and simple, as first depicted by Shakspere, and after him, with more or less accuracy, by a hundred other poets and novelists. There is no lack of colour in this Love —colour warm and glowing—but it is no longer a mere local colour, a national or provincial peculiarity, but Love in its essence, its cosmopolitan aspect ; Love such as will in course of time prevail throughout the world, when the Anglisation of this planet —which is only a question of time—shall have been completed.

England has many a bright jewel in the crown of her achievements in behalf of civilisation, but the brightest of all is this, that she was the first country in the world—ancient, mediæval, or modern—that removed the bars from woman's prison-windows, opened every door to Cupid, and made him thoroughly welcome and comfortable. And grateful Cupid has retaliated by setting up English manners and customs as a model which all other nations are slowly but surely copying. Eighteen million souls in the United States, or almost two persons in every five, are not of English origin; yet of these there are not one million who have not given up their old country methods of courtship as antiquated, and adopted the Anglo-American style. The Germans in America make love not after the German but after the English fashion. So do the French, though somewhat more reluctantly and tardily. In San Francisco and Chicago it is said that but one name in ten is of English origin; yet who ever heard of a San Franciscan or Chicagoan making love in foreign style? During the last hundred years the majority of the immigrants to America have come from non-English countries; yet, though the parents enter the country as adults with all their national traditions stamped on their memories, they invariably allow their sons and daughters to court and be courted in American style. And now that England is gradually extending her influence to every one of the five continents, Romantic Love—to whose sway, quite as much as to their outdoor active life, the English owe the fact that they are to-day the handsomest and most energetic race in the world—is also rapidly extending its sphere, and will finally oust the last vestiges of Oriental despotism, feminine suppression, and mediæval masculine barbarism.

For some centuries woman has been more favoured by law, and especially by national custom, in England than in any other European state. It is true that the Englishman who beats his wife is the most brutal savage on the face of the globe, but he is to be found only among the lowest classes. Nor has wife-selling ever been quite such a universal custom in England as foreigners imagine; although cases are on record as far back as 1302 and as late as 1884. In an article in *All the Year Round* (Dec. 20, 1884) more than twenty cases are enumerated with full details, the price of a wife varying from twenty-five guineas to a pint or half a pint of beer, or a penny and a dinner; and the *Times* of July 22, 1797, remarks sarcastically: "By some mistake or omission, in the report of the Smithfield market, we have not learned the average price of wives for the week. The increasing value of the fair sex is esteemed by several eminent writers the certain criterion of increasing civilisation. Smithfield has, on this ground, strong pretensions to refined improvement, as the price of wives has risen in that market from half a guinea to three guineas and a half."

That these cases occurred only among the lowest classes is self-evident; yet even the lowest classes often resented the brutal transaction by pelting the offenders with stones and mud; whereas, as far as the women were concerned, the offence was mitigated by the fact that in all cases on record they appear to have been only too glad to be sold, so as to get rid of their tyrants.

It cannot be said that English women are all exempt from the hardest manual labour even to-day; but the tendency to relieve them of tasks unsuited to feminine muscular development has existed longer in England than elsewhere. The difference can be best observed with regard to agricultural labour. Any one who travels through Italy, Switzerland, France, or Germany in the autumn, gets the impression that most of the harvesting is done by the women; whereas in England, as shown by statistics, there are twenty-two men to every woman engaged as field-labourers. Yet even at that rate there are still 64,840 women in England engaged in agricultural labour unsuited to their sex.

On the other hand, English women, like American women, are manifesting a great disposition at present to try their hand or brain at almost every employment heretofore considered exclusively masculine. The census enumerates 349 different classes of work, and of these all but about 70 have been invaded by women; including 5 horse-dealers, 14 bicycle makers and dealers, 16 sculptors, 18 fence makers, 19 fossil diggers, etc.; whereas there are as yet no female pilots, dentists, police officers, shepherds, law students, architects, cab-drivers, commercial travellers, barristers, etc. [Full list in *Pall Mall Gazette*, Oct. 3, 1884.]

Inasmuch as there are almost a million more women than men in England, it is not surprising that women should thus seek to extend their sphere of usefulness. We live in an experimental epoch, when it is to be ascertained what is and what is not becoming to woman regarded as a labourer. It is therefore of the utmost importance that there should be some standard by which each employment is to be judged. And this standard, fortunately, is supplied by Romantic Love.

We have seen that the tendency of civilisation has been to differentiate the sexes more and more in appearance, character, and emotional susceptibilities, and that on this differentiation depends the existence and power of Love, because it *individualises* man and woman, and Love is the more intense the more it is individualised.

Hence every employment which tends to make woman masculine in appearance or habits is to be tabooed by her because antagonistic to Love. If she, nevertheless, persists in it, Love will have its revenge by eliminating her through Sexual Selection. No man will marry a masculine woman, or fall in love with her, so that her unnatural temperament will not be transmitted to the next generation and multiplied.

But what is to be accepted as the standard of femininity? The answer is given us by Nature. Throughout the animal world, with a few insignificant exceptions, the sexes are differentiated distinctly; and the female is the more tender and gentle of the two, the more devoted to domestic affection and the care and education of the young, the more amiable, and, above all, less aggressive, bold, and pugnacious than the male. "Any education which women undergo," says the *Spectator*, " should be an education not for the militant life of war against evil, but for the spiritual life inspiring a persuasive or patient charity. . . . Even in a field properly suited to them — the field of charitable institutions, of poor-law work, of educational representation — women no sooner take up the cudgels than they lose their appropriate influence, and are either unsexed or paralysed."

According to Mr. Ruskin, "woman's work is—(1) To please people. (2) To feed them in dainty ways. (3) To clothe them. (4) To keep them orderly. (5) To teach them."

Statistics concerning the employments instinctively sought by the majority of women bear out Mr. Ruskin's table quite well. Woman's first duty is to please people by being beautiful, amiable, and fascinating in conversation and manners. No man would marry a woman unless she pleased him in one way or another; hence matrimony is the most successful female profession, which in England includes 4,437,962 women. But there are other ways in which women seek to please and prosper; hence there are in England 2368 actresses as against 2197 actors, and 11,376 women whose profession is music, as against 14,170 men.

Domestic service, which includes the "feeding in dainty ways" (though too often the "dainty" must be omitted), employs 1,230,406 women in England — about 30,000 fewer than industrial employments, which are somewhat more popular owing to the greater individual liberty they allow the employed. Yet domestic service is a much better preparation for married life than labour in a manufactory; so that, other things being equal, a labouring man looking for a wife would be apt to select one who has learned how to take care of his home. This thought ought to help to render domestic service more popular.

"To clothe them." Dressmaking, staymaking (alas!), and millinery, employ 357,995 women in England.

"To keep them orderly." Bathing and washing service employ 176,670 women; medicine and nursing, almost 50,000; missions, 1660.

"To teach them." This, one of woman's special vocations, eminently suited to her capacity, employs 123,995 females.

If I have failed in correctly interpreting Mr. Ruskin's oracle, I stand subject to correction from that earnest labourer in the task of finding for woman her proper sphere—a work for which he has not yet received the recognition and thanks he deserves.

That marriage, and not miscellaneous employment, is woman's true destiny, is shown by the way in which Cupid influences statistics. Thus there are in England about 29,000 school-mistresses aged 15-20, and 28,500 aged 25-45; but the time from 20-25, the period of courtship and marriage, has only 21,000. In the case of dressmakers this fact is brought out still more strikingly: 15-20—84,000; 20-25—76,000; 25-45—129,000, in round numbers.

Although, therefore, as Emerson remarks, "the circumstances may be easily imagined in which woman may speak, vote, argue cases, legislate, and drive coaches, if only it comes by degrees;" facts show that there is more philosophy of the future in Mrs. Hawthorne's remark that "Home, I think, is the great arena for women, and there, I am sure, she can wield a power which no king or emperor can cope with."

A consideration of all the foregoing facts shows that Love may be safely accepted as a guiding-star in making a proper division of the world's labour between men and women. And the reason why England and America have made so much more progress than other nations in ascertaining woman's true capacity and sphere, is because she has been educated to a point where she can assert her independence, and where she can inspire as well as feel Love—thus making man humble, gallant, gentle, ready to make concessions and remove restrictions. It is in England and America alone that Love plays a more important *rôle* in marriage than money and social position; that the young are generally permitted to consult their own heart instead of parental command; and that the opportunities for courtship are so liberal and numerous that the young are enabled to fall in love with one another not only for dazzling qualities of Personal Beauty, viewed for a moment, but for traits of character, emotional refinement, and a cultured intellect.

These two nations alone have fully taken to heart and heeded Addison's maxim that "Those marriages generally abound most with love and constancy that are *preceded by a long courtship*. The passion should strike root and gather strength before marriage be grafted on it. A long course of hopes and expectations fixes the idea in our minds, and habituates us to a fondness of the person beloved."

There is, however, a difference between English

and American Love which shows that we have learned Addison's lesson even better than his own countrymen. As Mr. Robert Laird Collier remarks in *English Home Life:* "The American custom, among the mass of the people, of leaving young men and young women free to associate together and to keep company with each other for an indefinite length of time, without declaring their intentions, is almost unknown in any country of Europe. It is not long after a young man begins to show the daughter attentions before the father gives intimation that he wishes to know what it means, and either the youth declares his intentions or is notified to 'cut sticks.'" "Courtships in England are short, and engagements are long."

The London *Standard* doubtless exaggerates the difference between English and American girls and their attitude toward men in the course of an article, part of which may, nevertheless, be cited: "American girls offer a bright example to their English sisters of a happy, unclouded youth, and instances seem to be few of their abusing the liberty which is accorded to them. Perhaps their immunity from sentimental troubles arises from the fact that from earliest childhood they have been comrades of the other sex, and are therefore not disposed to turn a man into a demi-god because they only see one at rare intervals under the eagle eye of a mother or aunt. A great revolution in public opinion would be required ere English girls could be emancipated to the extent which prevails on the other side of the Atlantic, and even then it is doubtful whether the system would work well. The daughters of

Albion, with but few exceptions, are single-hearted, earnest, and prone to look upon everything seriously. They often make the mistake of imagining that a man is in love because he is decently civil."

Yet in *German Home Life*, written from an English point of view, we read that "There is no such thing as country life, as we understand it, in Germany; no cosy sociability, smiling snugness, pleasant bounties and hospitalities; and, above all, for the young folk, no freedom, flirtation, boatings, sketchings, high teas, scamperings, and merriments generally." And again: "The sort of frank 'flirtation,' beginning openly in fun and ending in amusement, which is common amongst healthy, high-spirited boys and girls in England, and has no latent element of intrigue or vanity in it, but is born of exuberant animal spirits, youthful frolics, and healthy pastimes shared together, is forbidden to her" (the German girl).

The *Standard* itself apparently contradicts itself in another article on "Flirtation," concerning which it says: "It is usually so innocent that it has become part of the education most of our young women pass through in their training for society. The British matron smiles contentedly when she sees that her daughter, just entered on her teens, exhibits a partiality for long walks and soft-toned confabulations with her cousin Fred or her brother's favourite schoolmate. Three or four such juvenile attachments will do the girl no harm, if they are gently watched over by the parental eye. They serve to evolve the sexually social instincts in a gradual way. Through them the bashful maiden learns the nature of man in the same fashion as she takes lessons on the piano. In a word, she is 'getting her hand in' for the real game of matrimony that is to be played in a few years. Her youthful swains, of course, derive their own instruction from these innocent amours. . . . Chivalrous feeling is developed which it takes a deal of worldly wisdom to smother in after years. . . . When we observe this sentimentality in a boy, we derive great amusement from it, but it should raise the lad in our estimation. He has something in him to which ideals appeal, and his early-developed susceptibility will—to use a beautiful but forgotten word—engentle his nature."

Perhaps the difference between English and American courtship and flirtation is not so great as often painted, and is becoming less every year, owing to the Americanisation of Europe.

AMERICAN LOVE

It is in the United States of America that Plato's ideal—so completely ignored by his countrymen—that young men and women should have ample opportunity to meet and get acquainted with one another before marriage, is most perfectly realised ; as well as Addison's supplementary advice that marriage should be preceded by a long courtship.

As boys and girls in America are commonly educated in the same schools, they are initiated at an early age into the sweets and sorrows of Calf-love Courtship, which has such a refining influence on the boys, and renders the girls more easy and natural in society when they get older ; destroying among other puerilities that spring-chicken Coyness which makes many of their European sisters appear so silly. In the Western country-schools each girl has her "beau"—a boy of fourteen to seventeen—who brings her flowers, apples, or other presents, accompanies her home, and performs various other gallant services; nor has any harm ever been known to result from this juvenile Courtship—except an occasional elopement, in case of a prematurely frivolous couple, whom it was just as well to get rid of in that way as any other.

When they get a little older, the young folks go to picnics without a chaperon, or they enjoy a drive or sleigh-ride, or go a-skating together; and after a party, dance, church fair, or other social gathering, where the elders commonly keep out of the way considerately, each young man accompanies a young lady home. Were you to insinuate to him the advisability of having a chaperon for the young lady, he would inform you pointedly that the young lady needed no protection inasmuch as he was a *gentleman* and not a tramp. It is this high sense of gentlemanly honour that protects women in America—a hundred times better than all the barred windows of the Orient and the dragons of Europe. Thanks to this feeling of modern chivalry, a young lady may travel all alone from New York to Chicago, or even to San Francisco, and, if her manners are modest and refined, she will not once be insulted by word or look, not even in passing through the roughest mining regions.

It is the consciousness of this chivalrous code of honour among the men that gives an American girl the frank and natural gaze which is one of her greatest charms, and that allows her to talk to a man just introduced as if they were old acquaintances. It is a knowledge of this gentlemanly code that makes parents feel perfectly at ease in leaving their daughter alone in the parlour all the evening with a visitor. In a word, American customs prove that if you treat a man as a gentleman he will behave like a gentleman.

Unquestionably there are girls who abuse the liberty allowed them, and encourage the men to encourage them in their freedom. Mr. Henry James has done a most valuable service in holding up the mirror to one of these girls, to serve as a warning to all Daisy Millers and semi-Daisy Millers. There are not a few of the latter kind, and I have myself met three full-fledged specimens of the real "Daisy" in Europe—girls who would not have hesitated to go out rowing on a lake at eleven o'clock in the evening with a man known to them only a few hours, or to go next day with him to visit an old tower, or to say that mamma "always makes a fuss if I introduce a gentleman. But I *do* introduce them—almost always. If I didn't introduce my gentlemen friends to mother, I shouldn't think I was natural." It is this class of American tourists that have, unfortunately, given foreigners a caricatured notion of the American girl's deportment.

Etiquette differs somewhat in various American cities and among the different classes. For instance, a young lady of the "upper circles," who in Chicago is permitted to drive to the theatre in a carriage with a young man, is not allowed the same privilege in New York.

The New York *Sun*, an excellent authority in social matters, gives the whole philosophy of American Courtship and Love in answering a young man's question as to whether, in asking a young lady of the highest circles to accompany him to a place of amusement, it is necessary to invite a chaperon at the same time. He is told that he must,—in those circles :—

"But these people are only a few among the many. What is called society more exclusively in New York comprises, all told, no more than a hundred or two hundred families. Outside of them, of course, there are larger circles, to which they give the law to a greater or less extent, but the whole number of men and women in this great town of a million and a half of inhabitants who pay obedience to that law is not over a few thousand.

"Nine girls out of ten in New York, with the full consent of their parents and as a matter of course, accompany young men to amusements without taking a chaperon along. They feel, and they are, entirely able to look out for themselves, and they would regard the whole fun as spoiled if a third person was on hand to watch over them. A large part of the audience at every theatre is always made up of young men and young women who have come out in pairs, and who have no thought of violating any rule of propriety. Very many of these girls would never be invited to the theatre by their male acquaintances if they were under the dominion of such a usage, for the men want them to themselves, else they would not ask their company, and besides do not feel able to pay for an extra ticket for an obnoxious third person; or, if they have a little more money to spare, they prefer to expend it at an ice-cream saloon after the play.

"Nor can it be said that the morals of these less formal young people are any worse than those of the more exacting society. Probably they are better on the average, and if the laws of Murray Hill prevailed throughout this city, the marriage-rate of New York would be likely to decline, for nothing discourages the passion of the average young man so much as his inability to meet the charmer except in the presence of a third person, who acts as a buffer between him and her. He feels that he has no show, and cannot appear to good advantage under the eyes of a cool critic, whereas if he could walk with the girl alone in the shades of the balmy evening, the courage to declare his affection would come to him.

"Therefore it is that engagements, even in the most fashionable society, are commonly made in the country during the summer, where the young people come together more freely and more constantly than in the town."

The attempt made in certain corners of New York "Society" to introduce the foreign system of chaperonage is one of the most absurd and incongruous efforts at aping foreign fashions (which are on the decline even in Europe) ever witnessed in our midst. In Europe Chaperonage is in so far excusable, as it is a modified survival from barbarous times when men were mostly brutes, being drunk half the time and on military expeditions the other half. To treat American men, who are brought up as gentlemen, and commonly behave as such, as mediæval ruffians, is a gratuitous insult, which they ought to resent by avoiding those houses where Oriental experiments are being tried with the daughters. That would bring the "mammas" to reason very soon.

Yet it would seem as if New York "Society" had already had enough of the Oriental experiment; for the same high authority just quoted asserted last autumn that "A regular stampede in favour of the liberty of the young unmarried female is to be undertaken this winter by a number of 'three-years-in-society' veterans, supported and encouraged by nearly all this season's *débutantes.* The first step is to be the establishment of a right on the part of young girls to form parties for theatre *matinées* and afternoon concerts, untrammelled by the presence of even a matron of their own age, and to which all 'reliable and well-behaved young men are to be eligible.' . . . Rule No. 2 establishes beyond all dispute the often-mooted question whether the presence of a brother and sister in a party of young people going to any place of evening amusement throws a shield of respectability over the others of the party. Society long ago frowned upon this mongrel kind of chaperonage; but upon the principle that no young man would permit indiscretions or improprieties in a party of which his sister made one, the 'veterans' have voted in favour of it. The young man with a sister is therefore to enact the part of dragon on these occasions, and will be largely in demand. Failing a convenient sister, he may get a cousin, perhaps, to take her place."

When it comes to the cousin, the reversion to Americanism, pure and simple, will be complete.

The gentlemanliness and Gallantry of Americans have at all times been acknowledged by observers of all nationalities; and it is indeed hardly too much to say that the average American is disposed to treat the whole female sex with a studied Gallantry, which in most European countries is reserved by men for the one girl with whom they happen to be in love. Even the irate and vituperative Anthony Trollope in his book on North America was obliged to admit that "It must be borne in mind that in that country material wellbeing and education are more extended than with us, and that therefore men there have learned to be chivalrous who with us have hardly progressed so far. The conduct of the men to the women throughout the states is always gracious. . . . But it seems to me that the women have not advanced as far as the men have done. . . . In America the spirit of chivalry has sunk deeper among men than it has among women."

Anthony Trollope is by no means the only writer who has put his finger on the greatest foible of American women. No doubt they have, as a class, been spoiled by excessive masculine Gallantry. They do not, like the women of the Troubadour period, who were similarly spoilt, go quite so far as to send their knights on crusades and among lepers, but they often shroud themselves in an atmosphere of selfishness which is very unfeminine—to choose a complimentary adjective.

In the East, where there is already a large excess of women over men, this evil is less marked than in the West, where women are still in a minority. Thus the Denver *Tribune*, in an article on "The Impoliteness of Women," remarks: "If there is any characteristic of Americans of which they are more proud than any other, it is the courtesy which the men who are natives of this country exhibit towards women, and the respect which the gentler sex receives in public. This is a trait of the American character of which Americans are justly proud, and in which they doubtless excel the people of any other country. But while this is true of the men, it is a matter to be deeply regretted that as much cannot be said of the women of this country." After praising American women for their beauty, vivacity, high moral character, and other charms, the *Tribune* adds that they "seem very generally to be prompted in their conduct in public by a spirit of selfishness which very often finds expression in acts of positive rudeness." They are ungrateful, it continues, to the men who give up their seats in street-cars; they compel men to step into a muddy street, instead of walking one behind the other at a crossing; and at such places as the stamp-window of the post-office they do not wait for their turn, but force the men to stand aside.

Another Western paper, the Chicago *Tribune*, complains that in that city there are 10,000 homes in which the daughters are ignorant of the simplest kind of household duties. It adds "That they do not desire to learn; that, having been brought up to do nothing except appear gracefully in society, their object in life is to marry husbands who can support them in idle luxury; that this state of things has substituted for marriages founded on love and respect a market in which the men have quoted money-values, and where a young man, however great his talents, has no chance of winning a wife from the charmed circle."

So that the pendulum has apparently swung to the other extreme. In mediæval times the women were married for their money by the lazy, selfish men; now the women are lazy and selfish, while the men toil and are married for their money.

Yet there is much exaggeration in this view, which applies to only a small portion of the American people. We are far from the times when Miss Martineau complained of the feeble health of American women, and attributed it to the vacuity of their minds. Their health is still, on the average, inferior to that of English and German damsels, from whom they could also learn useful lessons in domestic matters; but intellectually the American woman has no equal in the world; while her sweetness, grace, and proverbial beauty combine into an ensemble which makes Cupid chuckle whenever he looks at a susceptible young man.

Goldsmith says somewhere that "the English love with violence, and expect violent love in return." Certainly this holds true no less of the Americans. There are indeed several favourable circumstances which combine to make Romantic Love more ardent and more prevalent in the United States than in any other part of the world.

(1) The first is the intellectual culture of women just referred to, which they owe partly to the leisure they enjoy, partly to the fact that America has the best elementary schools in the world, so that their minds are aroused early from their dormant

state. As Bishop Spalding remarks: "Woman here in the United States is more religious, more moral, and more intelligent than man; more intelligent in the sense of greater openness to ideas, greater flexibility of mind, and a wider acquaintance with literature." Now the whole argument of this book tends to show that the capacity for feeling Romantic Love is dependent on intellectual culture, and increases with it; hence we might infer that there is more Love among the women of America than among those of any other country, even if this were not so patent from the greater number of Love-matches and various subtle signs known to international observers.

And as the sweetest pleasure and goad of Love lies in the conviction that it is really returned, man's Love is thus doubled in ardour through woman's responsive sympathy.

(2) That Courtship proper is longer than in England, and engagement shorter, is a circumstance in favour of America. For nothing adds so much to the ardour of Love as the uncertainty which prevails during Courtship; whereas, after engagment, all these alternate hopes and doubts, confidences and jealousies, are quieted, and the ship approaches the still waters of the harbour of matrimony, which may be quite as deep but are less sublime and romantic than mid-ocean, with its possibilities of storm and shipwreck.

Moreover, the longer the time of tentative Courtship, the fewer are the chances of a mistake being made in selecting a sympathetic spouse.

In Germany an engagement is so conclusive an affair that it is announced in the papers, and cards are sent out as at a wedding. In America we meet with the other extreme, for it is not very unusual for a couple to be engaged some time before even the parents know it. Though there is such a thing as breach of promise suits against fickle young men, such engagements, if unsatisfactory to either side, are commonly broken off amicably. And, as one of Mr. Howells's characters remarks in *Indian Summer:* "A broken engagement *may* be a bad thing in some cases, but I am inclined to think it is the very best thing that could happen in most cases where it happens. The evil is done long before; the broken engagement is merely sanative, and so far beneficent."

Were engagements less readily dissolved, divorces would be more frequent even than they are now.

(3) Parental dictation is almost unknown in America; nowhere else have young men and women such absolute freedom to choose their own soul-mate. Hence Individual Preference, on which the ardour of Love depends in the highest degree, has full sway. The comparative absence of barriers of rank and social grade also makes it easier for a man to find and claim his real *Juliet*.

(4) This dependence of Love on Individualisation gives it another advantage in America. For nowhere is there so great a mixture of nationalities as here; and, *away from home*, a national peculiarity of feature or manners has a sort of individualising effect. Till we get used to such national peculiarities through their constant recurrence we are apt to judge almost every woman in a new city attractive. From this point of view Love may be defined as an instinctive

longing to absorb national traits, and blend them all in the one cosmopolitan type of perfect Personal Beauty.

(5) There are beautiful women in all countries of the world, but no country has so many pretty girls as America. Money and rank find it hard to compete with such loveliness, hence Love has its own way. Here alone is it possible to find heiresses who have failed to get married through lack of Beauty. Personal Beauty is the great matchmaker in America; and thus it comes that Beauty is ever inherited and multiplied. For Love is the cause of Beauty as Beauty is the cause of Love.

One more characteristic of American Love remains to be noted—the most unique of all. American women are of all women in the world the most self-conscious, and have the keenest sense of humour. To these quick-witted damsels the sentimental sublimities of amorous Hyperbole, which may touch the heart of a naïve German or Italian girl, are apt to appear dangerously near the ludicrous; hence an American lover, if he is clever enough, deliberately covers the step which separates the sublime from the ridiculous. He gilds the gold of his compliments by using the form of playful exaggeration, which is the more easy to him because exaggeration is a national form of American humour. Mr. Howells's heroes often make love in this fashion. The lover in *The Lady of the Aroostook* spices his flatteries with open burlesque, and succeeds admirably with this new *Ars Amoris;* and Colville in *Indian Summer* says to Imogene: "Come, I'll go, of course, Imogene. A fancy-ball to please you is a very different thing from a fancy-ball in the abstract."

"Oh, what nice things you say! Do you know, I always admired your compliments? I think they're the most charming compliments in the world."

"I don't think they're half so pretty as yours; but they're more sincere."

"No, honestly. They flatter, and at the same time they make fun of the flattery a little; they make a person feel that you like them even while you laugh at them."

Perfect success in this form of flattery requires a talent for epigram. Not many, unfortunately, even in America, are poets and wits at the same time, like Mr. Howells; but there is an abundance of clever compliments nevertheless, and they are apt to assume the form of playful exaggeration.

SCHOPENHAUER'S THEORY OF LOVE

A first hasty perusal of Schopenhauer's brilliant essay on the "Metaphysics of Sexual Love" (in the second volume of his *Welt als Wille und Vorstellung*) will dispose most readers to agree with Dühring that the great pessimist "makes war on love." But a more careful consideration of his profound thoughts shows that this is not the case, notwithstanding his habitual cynical tone.

In the first place, his theory can do no possible harm, because, as he himself admits, no lover will ever believe in it. Secondly, the gist of Schopenhauer's theory is to show that a lover is the most noble and unselfish martyr in the world, because his usual attitude and fate is self-sacrifice.

LOVE IS AN ILLUSION

The fundamental truth which Schopenhauer claims to have discovered is that love is an illusion—an *instinctive* belief on the lover's part that his life's happiness absolutely depends on his union with his beloved; whereas, in truth, a love-match commonly leads to lifelong conjugal misery. The lover, on reaching the goal so eagerly striven for, finds himself disappointed, and realises, to his consternation, that he has been the dupe of a blind instinct. Quien se casa por amores, ha de vivir con dolores, says a Spanish proverb ("to marry for love is to live in misery"): and this doctrine Schopenhauer re-echoes in a dozen different forms: "It is not only disappointed love-passion that occasionally has a tragic end; successful love likewise leads more commonly to misery than to happiness." "Marriages based on love commonly end unhappily," etc.

INDIVIDUALS SACRIFICED TO THE SPECIES

The reason of this curious fact is given in this sentence: "Love-marriages are formed in the interest of the species, not of the individuals. True, the parties concerned imagine that they are providing for their own happiness; but their real [unconscious] aim is something foreign to their own selves—namely, the procreation of an individual whose existence becomes possible only through their marriage."

What urges a man on to this sacrifice of individual happiness to the welfare of his offspring is, as already intimated, a blind instinct known as Love.

The universal *Will* (Schopenhauer's fetish, or name for an impersonal deity underlying all phenomena) has implanted this blind instinct in man, for the same reason that it implants so many other instincts in various animals—to induce the parents to undergo any amount of labour, and even danger to life, for the sake of benefiting the offspring, and thus preserving the species. All these animals, like the lovers, are urged on blindly to sacrifice themselves in the belief that they are doing it for their own pleasure and benefit; whereas it is all in the interest of their offspring.

Why was the *Will* compelled to implant this blind instinct in man? Because man is so selfish wherever guided by reason, that it would have been unwise to entrust so important a matter as the welfare of coming generations to his intellect and prudence. Prudence would tell young people to choose not the most attractive and healthy partners, who would be able to transmit their excellence to the next generation, but the ones who are most liberally supplied with money and useful friends. That is, they would invariably look out first for "Number One," indifferent to the deluge that might come after them. It was to neutralise this selfishness that the *Will* created the instinct of Love, which impels a man to marry not the woman who will make *him* the most happy and comfortable, but whose qualities, combined with his own, will be likely to produce a harmonious, well-made group of children.

Schopenhauer's *Will*, it must be understood, is an æsthetic sort of a chap. He has his hobbies, and one of these hobbies is the desire to preserve the species in its typical purity and beauty. There are a thousand accidents of climate, vice, disease, etc., that tend to vitiate the type of each species; but Love strives for ever to restore a harmonious balance, by producing a mutual infatuation in two beings whose combined (and opposite) defects will neutralise one another in the offspring.

SOURCES OF LOVE

More definitely speaking, there are three ways in which the *Will* preserves the purity of its types—three ways in which it inspires the Love whose duty it is to achieve this result. Physical Beauty is the first thing desired by the lover, because that is the expression of typical perfection. Secondly, he may be influenced by such Psychic Traits as will blend well with his own; and thirdly, he will be attracted by perfections (or imperfections) which are the opposite of his own. These three sources must be considered briefly in detail.

(1) *Physical Beauty.*—The most important attribute of Beauty, in the lover's eye, is Youth. Men prefer the age from eighteen to twenty-eight in a woman; while women give the preference to a man aged from thirty to thirty-five, which represents the acme of his virility. Youth without Beauty may still inspire Love; not so Beauty without Youth.

Health ranks next in importance. Acute disease is only a temporary disadvantage, whereas chronic disease repels the amorous affections, for the reason that it is likely to be transmitted to the next generation.

A fine framework or skeleton is the third

desideratum. Besides age and disease, nothing proves so fatal to the chances of inspiring Love as deformity: "The most charming face does not atone for it; on the contrary, even the ugliest face is preferred if allied with a straight growth of the body."

A certain plumpness or fulness of flesh is the next thing considered in sexual selection; for this is an indication of Health, and promises a sound progeny. Excessive leanness is repulsive, and so is excessive stoutness, which is often an indication of sterility. "A well-developed bust has a magic effect on a man." What attracts women to men is especially muscular development, because that is a quality in which they are commonly deficient, and for which the children will accordingly have to rely on the father. Women may marry an ugly man, but never one who is unmanly.

Facial beauty ranks last in importance, according to Schopenhauer. Here too the skeleton is first considered in sexual selection. The mouth must be small, the chin projecting, "a slight curve of the nose, upwards or downwards, has decided the fate of innumerable girls; and justly, for the type of the species is at stake." The eyes and the forehead, finally, are closely associated with intellectual qualities.

(2) *Psychic Traits.*—What charms women in men is pre-eminently courage and energy, besides frankness and amiability. "Stupidity is no disadvantage with women: indeed, it is more likely that superior intellectual power, and especially genius, as being an abnormal trait, may make an

unfavourable impression on them. Hence we so often see an ugly, stupid, and coarse man preferred by women to a refined, clever, and amiable man." When women claim to have fallen in love with a man's intellect, it is either affectation or vanity. Wedlock is a union of hearts, not of heads; and its object is not entertaining conversation, but providing for the next generation. This part of Schopenhauer's theory is evidently an outcome of his doctrine that children inherit their intellectual qualities from the mother, and their character from the father. Hence the feeling that they are capable of supplying their children with sufficient intellect is part of the feminine Love-instinct, and makes women indifferent to the presence or absence of those qualities in men.

It does not follow from all this that a sensible man may not reflect on his chosen one's character, or she on his intellectual abilities, before marriage. Such reflection leads to marriages of reason, but not to Love-marriages, which alone are here under consideration.

(3) *Complementary Qualities.*—The physical and mental attributes considered under (1) and (2) are those which commonly inspire Love. But there are cases where perfect Beauty is less potent to inflame the passions than deviations from the normal type.

"Ordinarily it is not the regular perfect beauties that inspire the great passions," says Schopenhauer; and this seems to be borne out by the experience of Byron, who says: "I believe there are few men who, in the course of their observations on life, have not perceived that it is not the greatest female beauty who forms [inspires] the longest and the strongest passions."

How is this to be accounted for? By the anxiety of Nature (or the *Will*) to neutralise imperfections in one individual by wedding them to another's excesses in the opposite direction; as an acid is neutralised by combining it with an alkali. The greater the shortcoming the more ardent will be the infatuation if a person is found exactly adapted for its neutralisation. The weaker a woman is, for example, in her muscular system, the more apt will she be to fall violently in love with an athlete. Short men have a decided partiality for tall women, and *vice versâ*. Blondes almost always desire brunettes; and if the reverse does not hold true, this is owing to the fact, he says, that the original colour of the human complexion was not light but dark. A light complexion has indeed become second nature to us, but less so the other features; and "in love nature strives to return to dark hair and brown eyes, as the primitive type."

Again, persons afflicted with a pug-nose take a special delight in falcon-noses and parrot-faces; and those who are excessively long and slim, admire those who are abnormally short and even stumpy. So with temperaments; each one preferring the opposite to his or her own. True, if a person is quite perfect in any one respect, he does not exactly prefer the corresponding imperfection in another, but he is more readily reconciled to it.

Throughout his essay, Schopenhauer tacitly assumes that the parental peculiarities are fused or blended equally in the offspring, and that this blending is what the *Will* aims at. But on this point Mr. Herbert Spencer has some remarks, in his essay on "Personal Beauty," which directly contradict Schopenhauer, of whose theory, however, he does not seem to have been cognisant:—

"The fact," he says, "that the forms and qualities of any offspring are not a mean between the forms and qualities of its parents, but a mixture of them, is illustrated in every family. The features and peculiarities of a child are separately referred by observers to father and mother respectively—nose and mouth to this side; colour of the hair and eyes to that; this moral peculiarity to the first; this intellectual one to the second—and so with contour and idiosyncrasies of body. Manifestly, if each organ or faculty in a child was an average of the two developments of such organ or faculty in the parents, it would follow that all brothers and sisters should be alike; or should, at any rate, differ no more than their parents differed from year to year. So far, however, from finding that this is the case, we find not only that great irregularities are produced by intermixture of traits, but that there is no constancy in the mode of intermixture, or the extent of variations produced by it.

"This imperfect union of parental constitutions in the constitution of offspring is yet more clearly illustrated by the reappearance of peculiarities traceable to bygone generations. Forms, dispositions, and diseases, possessed by distant progenitors, habitually come out from time to time in descendants. Some single feature, or some solitary tendency, will again and again show itself after being apparently lost. It is notoriously thus with gout, scrofula, and insanity."

Again, unite a pure race " with another equally pure, but adapted to different conditions and having a correspondingly different physique, face, and morale, and there will occur in the descendants not a homogeneous mean between the two constitutions, but a seemingly irregular combination of characteristics of the one with characteristics of the other—one feature traceable to this race, a second to that, and a third uniting the attributes of both; while in disposition and intellect there will be found a like medley of the two originals."

The fact that the more remote ancestry must be taken into account besides the parents, in considering the traits of the offspring, is one which Mr. Galton has done much to emphasise, and which Schopenhauer completely ignores. It tells against the metaphysical part of his theory; for all the efforts of the *Will* to merge opposite characters into homogeneous traits must prove futile if a blue-eyed man, for instance, who marries a black-eyed girl, finds that their children have neither the father's blue nor the mother's black, but the grandmother's gray eyes.

Yet in the long run diverse traits of figure and physiognomy do tend to a harmonious fusion. Though a man with a prominent nose, which he inherited from his father, is likely to transmit it to his son, though his wife may have a snub-nose, yet there will be a slight modification even in the son's organ; and if the son keeps up the tradition of marrying a snub-nosed girl, and his children follow his example, the chances are that in a few generations the nose of that family will be a feature of moderate size and classic proportions. The very fact emphasised by Mr. Galton that all the ancestral influences count, will here aid the ultimate fusion. Conspicuous instances of the long-continued prevalence of a particular nose—or other feature—may be accounted for by the fact that other kinds of that organ were rare in the vicinity, or that marriage was decided by so many other considerations that the dimensions of one organ could not come into consideration, much as the bride or groom might have preferred an improvement in that respect.

So far as Schopenhauer's theory concerns only the fact that Love is apt to be based on complementary qualities, he is doubtless correct; but it needs no erratic metaphysical fetish, as a *deus ex machina*, to account for that fact. A simple application of psychologic principles explains the whole mystery.

In the first place, nothing could be more remote from the truth than the cynical notion that every woman considers herself a Venus. She may, on the whole, consider herself equal to the average of Beauty; but if she has any special fault—a mouth too large or too small, an upper lip too high, a nose too flat or too prominent, too much or too little flesh, excessive height or shortness—she is not only conscious of the defect, but morbidly conscious of it, and uses every possible device to conceal it. Thus constantly brooding over her misfortune her mind, by a natural reaction, will conceive a special admiration for an organ that exceeds the line of Beauty in the opposite direction. Every day one hears a *petite* girl admiring a specially tall woman; and this admiration will prompt her, other things being equal, to fall in love with a tall man.

Secondly, familiarity breeds indifference to one's own charms, and a disposition to admire what we lack ourselves.

Novelty comes into play. A Northern blonde among a nation of brunettes cannot fail to slay hearts by the hundred, while the mystic flashes of a Spanish woman's black eyes are fatal to every Northern visitor.

Nations, like individuals, admire and desire what they lack. The Germans and the English are deficient in grace—hence that quality is what chiefly charms them in the French, who have much more of it than of Beauty, and in the Spanish. Byron was so much smitten with the sun-mellowed complexions and the graceful proportions and gait of the Spanish maidens, that he became quite unjust to his own lovely countrywomen—

"Who round the North for paler dames would seek?
How poor their forms appear! How languid, wan, and weak!"

Were savages susceptible to Love, it might be suggested that their practice of exogamy, or marrying a woman from another tribe, had something to do with their admiration of novelty and complementary qualities; but we know that they do not admire such qualities, but only such typical traits as prevail among their own women, and these, moreover, in an exaggerated form. This is one reason why savages are so ugly. They have no Romantic

Love to improve their Personal Beauty by fusing heterogeneous defects into homogeneous perfections.

Thus we may freely endorse Schopenhauer's doctrine regarding the benefits derived by the offspring (ultimately, in several generations) from marriages based on complementary Love, without bowing down before his fetish—a fetish which appears doubly objectionable because it is old-fashioned; *i.e.* it strives to "maintain the type of the species in its primitive purity," whereas modern science teaches that this "primitive type" of human beauty had a very simian aspect.

Nor need we at all accept the pessimistic aspect of his theory—the notion that Love is an illusion, and that Love-marriages commonly end unhappily, the lover sacrificing himself for his progeny.

Mr. Herbert Spencer, in his *Sociology*, elaborates an idea which so curiously leads up to this phase of Schopenhauer's doctrine that it must be briefly referred to for its evolutionary suggestiveness.

Among the lowest animals—the microscopic protozoa—the individual, as he remarks, is sacrificed after a few hours of life, by breaking up into two new individuals, or into a number of germs which produce a new generation. The parents are here entirely sacrificed to the interests of the young and the species. As we ascend in the scale of life this sacrifice of parents to the young and the species becomes less and less prevalent. Among birds, for instance, "The lives of the parents are but partially subordinated at times when the young are being reared. And then there are long intervals between breeding-seasons, during which the lives of parents are carried on for their own sakes. . . . In proportion as organisms become higher in their structures and powers, they are individually less sacrificed to the maintenance of the species; and the implication is that in the highest type of man this sacrifice is reduced to a minimum."

Here is the point where Schopenhauer, had he been an evolutionist, might have dovetailed his theory with Spencer's, by saying that in man it is no longer the life of the individual, or most of his time, that is sacrificed, but merely his conjugal happiness, which the Love-instinct induces him unconsciously to barter for the superior physical and mental beauty of his offspring.

Unfortunately, Schopenhauer did not take any pains to verify his theory by testing it by vulgar facts. There are plenty of unhappy marriages, but no one who will search his memory can fail to come to the conclusion that the vast majority of them are cases where money or rank and not Love supplied the motive of an unsympathetic union. Though Conjugal Affection consists of a different group of emotions from Romantic Love, yet there is an affinity between them; and it is not likely that Conjugal Love will ever supervene where before marriage there was an entire absence of sympathy and adoration. Even an imprudent Love-match which leads to poverty—is it not preferable to a *mariage de convenance*, which leads to lifelong indifference and *ennui*? Is it not better to have one month of ecstatic bliss in life than to live and die without ever knowing life's highest rapture?

Again, the French marry for money and social

convenience, and their children are ugly; the Americans marry for Love, and have the most beautiful children in the world. Is it not more conducive to conjugal happiness to know that one has lovely children and that the race is increasing, than to have ugly children and to know that the race is dying out?

Love-matches would never end unhappily if the lovers would take proper care of their own happiness by transfusing the habits of Courtship into conjugal life, as elsewhere explained in this book.

Schopenhauer's whole argument is vitiated by the fact that it is chiefly the physical complementary qualities that inspire Love, not the mental—the latter, in fact, being barely noticed by him. Mental divergence might indeed occasionally lead to an unhappy marriage, but physical divergence—the fact that he is large and blond, she small and a brunette—cannot possibly lead to matrimonial discord. This knocks the whole bottom out of Schopenhauer's erotic pessimism. The only sense in which Love is an illusion is in its Hyperbolic phase—the notion that the beloved is superior to all other mortals; and that is a very harmless illusion.

Schopenhauer's pessimism, it should be added, is greatly mitigated by the poetic halo of martyrdom with which he invests the lover's head. Society and public opinion, he points out, applaud him for instinctively preferring the welfare of the next generation to his own comfort. "For is not the exact determination of the individualities of the next generation a much higher and nobler object than those ecstatic feelings of the lovers, and their super-sensual soap-bubbles?" It is this that invests Love with its poetic character. There is one thing only that justifies tears in a man, and that is the loss of his Love, for in that he bewails not his own loss but the loss of the species.

Apart from the suggestive details of his essay, Schopenhauer's merit and originality lies, first, in his having pointed out that Love becomes more intense the more it is individualised; secondly, in emphasising the fact that in match-making it is not the happiness of the to-be-married couple that should be chiefly consulted, but the consequences of their union to the offspring; thirdly, in dwelling on the important truth that Love is a cause of Beauty, because its aim always is either to perpetuate existing Beauty through hereditary transmission, or to create new Beauty by fusing two imperfect individuals into a being in whom their shortcomings mutually neutralise one another.

Love, however, is only one source of Personal Beauty. Personal Beauty has four sources; and these must now be considered in succession, in the order which roughly indicates their successive evolution—Health, Crossing, Love, and Mental Refinement.

The remainder of this work will be devoted exclusively to the subject of Personal Beauty, as it influences and is influenced by Romantic Love. And here, as in the preceding pages, I shall always cite the *ipsissima verba* of the greatest specialists who have written on any particular branch of this subject.

FOUR SOURCES OF BEAUTY
I.—HEALTH

Plants, Animals, Savages.—In two of the most exquisite passages, not only in his own works, but in all English literature, Mr. Ruskin has emphasised the dependence of physical beauty in plants on their healthy appearance, and the independence of this beauty on any idea of direct utility to man.

"It is a matter of easy demonstration," he says, "that, setting the characters of typical beauty aside, the pleasure afforded by every organic form is in proportion to its appearance of healthy vital energy; as in a rose-bush, setting aside all considerations of gradated flushing of colour and fair folding of line, which it shares with the cloud or the snow-wreath, we find in and through all this certain signs pleasant and acceptable as signs of life and enjoyment in the particular individual plant itself. Every leaf and stalk is seen to have a function, to be constantly exercising that function, and, as it seems, *solely* for the good and enjoyment of the plant. It is true that reflection will show us that the plant is not living for itself alone, that its life is one of benefaction, that it gives as well as receives, but no sense of this whatever mingles with our perception of physical beauty in its forms. Those forms which appear to be necessary to its health, the symmetry of its leaflets, the smoothness of its stalks, the vivid green of its shoots, are looked upon by us as signs of the plant's own happiness and perfection; they are useless to us, except as they give us pleasure in our sympathising with that of the plant, and if we see a leaf withered or shrunk or worm-eaten, we say it is ugly, and feel it to be most painful, not because it hurts *us*, but because it seems to hurt the plant, and conveys to us an idea of pain and disease and failure of life in *it*."

" The bending tree, waving to and fro in the wind above the waterfall, is beautiful because it is happy, though it is perfectly useless to us. The same trunk, hewn down and thrown across the stream, has lost its beauty. It serves as a bridge,—it has become useful ; it lives not for itself, and its beauty is gone, or what it retains is purely typical, dependent on its lines and colours, not its functions. Saw it into planks, and though now adapted to become permanently useful, its whole beauty is lost for ever, or to be regained only in part when decay and ruin shall have withdrawn it again from use, and left it to receive from the hand of Nature the velvet moss and varied lichen, which may again suggest ideas of inherent happiness, and tint its mouldering sides with hues of life."

In the animal world we find the same dependence of Beauty upon Health. As Mr. Wallace has shown, "colour and ornament are strictly correlated with health, vigour, and general fitness to survive." It is the superior vitality, vigour, and vivacity of certain male animals that leads the choicest females to prefer them to others less favoured ; and thus it happens that, thanks to the dependence of Beauty on Health, animals have become more and more beautiful. Moreover, it is Love in its primitive form that urges animals to prefer those that are most healthy. And thus we have the three great agents acting and reacting upon one another. Health produces Beauty, and together they inspire Love; while Love selects Health, and thus preserves and multiplies Beauty. But this whole subject has been so fully discussed in the chapter on Love among Animals that it is needless to recapitulate the facts here.

Concerning savages, there is a prevalent notion that, owing to their free and easy life in the forests, they are healthier on the average than civilised mankind. As a matter of fact, however, they are as inferior to us in Health as in Beauty. Their constant exposure and irregular feeding habits, their neglect and ignorance of every hygienic law, in conjunction with their vicious lives, their arbitrary mutilations of various parts, and their selection of inferior forms, prevent their bodies from assuming the regular and delicate proportions which we regard as essential to Beauty. They arrive at maturity at an earlier age, and lose their vitality sooner than we do. "Decrepitude," says Dr. Topinard, "shows itself sooner in some races than in others. The Australians and Bosjesmans are old men at a period when the European is in the full enjoyment of his faculties, both physical and intellectual. The Japanese the same, according to Dr. Krishaber, physician to the Japanese embassy."

Women everywhere pay less attention to the laws of Health than men. They have less exercise, less fresh air and sunshine than men. Hence, although the most beautiful women are more beautiful than the handsomest men, yet in probably every country of the world the average man is a more perfect specimen of masculine than the average woman of feminine Beauty. Concerning savages Mr. Spencer says: "Very generally among the lower races the females are even more unattractive in aspect than the males. It is remarked of the Puttooahs, whose men are diminutive and whose women are still more so, that 'the men are far from being handsome, but the palm of ugliness must be awarded to the women.' The latter are *hard-worked* and apparently *ill-fed*." Again, of the inhabitants of the Corea Gutzlaff says: "The females are very ugly, whilst the male sex is one of the best formed of Asia.... Women are *treated like beasts of burden*." Many similar cases are cited by Dr. Ploss in *Das Weib*.

Concerning modern civilised nations, a well-known art-critic has given his testimony to the effect that "Possibly owing to the fact that men are freer to follow their normal lives, I have found that in a majority of the countries I have visited there are more handsome men than beautiful women. This is peculiarly the case with the modern Greek, and was, if antique sculpture could be accepted as witness, with the ancient."

Greek Beauty.—In the preceding chapters of this work an attempt has been made to show that there is a general connection between the growth of Love and the growth of Beauty throughout the world. To some readers, no doubt, the thought has suggested itself, "How, if this be true, did the loveless Greeks succeed in reaching such uncommon physical beauty —beauty which artists of all times have admired?"

It must be borne in mind, however, that we are

very liable to exaggerate in our notions of Greek Beauty, because we are apt to generalise from the fine statues that have come down to us, and to imagine that they represent the common type of Greek Beauty. But it is well known that the Greeks idealised their statues according to certain physiognomic rules; and, moreover, as Winckelmann remarks, "Beauty was not a general quality even among the Greeks, and Cotta in *Cicero* says that, among the great numbers of young persons at Athens, there were only a few possessing true beauty."

Besides, it has not been claimed that Love is the *only* cause of Beauty. Taking into consideration the other sources of Beauty, it is easy enough to account for such physical attractiveness as the Greeks did possess. The intellectual culture which the men enjoyed gave them a great advantage over the women; and equally important, if not more so, was the attention which the men (and in some cases the women too) paid to Health. Their habitual life in the open air, while the women were locked up at home, combined with their daily gymnastic exercises in making their complexion healthy, their eyes sparkling, their limbs supple, vigorous, and graceful.

Other causes that tended to keep up an average of healthy bodily development were the refusal to bring up sickly and deformed infants, and the existence of numerous slaves, who did all the drudgery for the Greeks.

It is most characteristic that the author of a very old Greek ode formulates his wishes in this order: First, health; then, beauty; thirdly, wealth honestly got ; fourth, the privilege of being gay and merry with his friends.

First, Health; then, Beauty. There lies the secret, for they always go together ; and in aiming at one the Greeks got the other too.

There was every reason why Greek parents should have striven eagerly to follow those laws of Health which ensure beautiful children. In ancient Greece Beauty was a possession which led to national fame. Some persons, Winckelmann informs us, were even characterised by a particular name, borrowed from some specially fine feature. Thus Demetrius Poliorketes was named, from the beauty of his eyelids, χαριτοβλέφαρος, *i.e.* on whose lids the graces dwell.

"It appears, indeed," the same writer continues, "to have been a belief that the procreation of beautiful children might be promoted by the distribution of prizes for beauty, as there is reason to infer from the contests of beauty which were instituted in the remotest ages by Cypselus, King of Arcadia, in the time of the Heraclidæ, on the banks of the river Alpheus, in Elis ; and also from the fact that at the festival of the Philesian Apollo, a prize for the most exquisite kiss was conferred on the youthful. Its assignment was subject to the decision of a judge, as was probably also the case at Megara, at the tomb of Diocles.

"At Sparta, and at Lesbos, in the temple of Juno, and among the citizens of Parrhasia, the women contended for the prize of beauty. The regard for this quality was so strong that, as Oppian declares, the Spartan women placed in their sleeping-rooms an Apollo, or Bacchus, or Nereus, or Narcissus, or

Hyacinthus, or Castor and Pollux, in order that they might bear beautiful children."

Some hint as to what the Greeks regarded as beautiful is given by the epithets Homer bestows on Helen—" the well-rounded," " the white-armed," "fair-haired," " of the beautiful cheeks."

Mediæval Ugliness.—This is a topic which might as well be introduced under any of the other Sources of Beauty, for it is difficult to say which of these sources was most completely and deliberately choked up during the Dark Ages.

It is a curious irony of language that makes asceticism almost identical with æstheticism, of which it is the deadly enemy. As diseases are transmitted from generation to generation, so it seems that the fear of Beauty born of mediæval asceticism has not yet died out completely; for it is related that some years ago a pious dame in Boston seriously meditated the duty of having some of her daughter's sound teeth pulled out, so as to mitigate her sinful Beauty.

If this worthy lady had followed St. Jerome's injunction—" I entirely forbid a young lady to bathe ;" if she had taught her that it is unladylike to have a healthy appetite ; if she had locked her up in a house rendered pestilential by defective drainage ; allowed her mind to rot in fallow idleness ; taught her that to be really saintly and virtuous she must be pale and hysterical ; or imitated the lady who was praised by a bishop in the fourth century for " having brought upon herself a swarm of diseases which defied all medical skill to cure,"— if the worthy Boston lady had but followed this mediæval system, she would have succeeded in a short time in overcoming her daughter's sinful Beauty, and making her "ugly as a mud-fence," as they say out West.

That Personal Beauty cannot flourish where Health is regarded as a vice and Disease as a virtue is self-evident. And one needs only to look at mediæval pictures to note how coarse and void of refined expression are the men, how hard and masculine the women. The faces of the numerous mediæval women in Planché's *Cyclopædia of Costume* have almost all an expression approaching imbecility, and features as if they had been chiselled by a small boy trying his hand at sculpture for the first time. Thackeray does not hesitate to speak even of "those simpering Madonnas of Rafael." Mr. G. A. Simcox remarks that in manuscripts of the twelfth and thirteenth centuries (like the Harleian Gospels and Maccabees) we meet with "short, thickset figures, mostly with the long, square, horsey face, moving stiffly in small groups, in heavy dresses; and even the daughter of Herodias dances upon her head [*sic*] in a gown that might have stood alone. On the other hand, the faces are more set, more articulate, less flabby, though they are all mean, or almost all, and look askance out of the corners of their eyes" (*Art Journal*, 1874, p. 58).

There may be Oriental countries where woman is kept more closely under lock and key than she was in Europe during the Dark Ages; but nowhere else has man so well succeeded in reducing the pursuit of unhappiness to a science, in snubbing, scorning, abusing, maltreating woman. How all this must have tended to increase Personal Beauty is well brought out in the following advice given by Mr. Ruskin : "Do not think you can make a girl lovely if you do not make her happy. There is not one restraint you put on a good girl's nature—there is not one check you give to her instincts of affection or of effort—which will not be indelibly written on her features, with a hardness which is all the more painful because it takes away the brightness from the eyes of innocence, and the charm from the brow of virtue."

Modern Hygiene.—Disease is Beauty's deadliest enemy. Yet for the sake of gratifying a silly vanity —for the sake of being distinguished from ordinary mortals—a certain pallor and *blasé* languor have long been considered in certain influential circles as more *distingué* than ruddy cheeks and robust health. Yet even if pale cheeks were more beautiful than rosy cheeks, would it be worth while to purchase them at the cost of premature decay—of the certainty that a *few* years of pale cheeks will be followed by *many* years of sallow cheeks and lack-lustre eyes, deeply sunk into their orbits?

Though beauty is still of lamentably rare occurrence in every country, there is infinitely more of it than during the Middle Ages; and certainly not the least cause of this is the increased attention paid to Hygiene—public and personal. The difference in this respect between us and our ancestors is well brought out by the statistics regarding the average length of life. In ancient Rome, it is stated, "the average longevity among the most favoured classes was but thirty years, whereas to-day the average longevity among the corresponding class of people is fifty years. In the sixteenth century the average longevity in Geneva was 21.21 years. Between 1814 and 1833 it was 40.68, and as large a proportion now live to seventy as lived to forty-three three hundred years ago." Dr. Corfield, comparing the statistics of 1842 with those of 1884, states that the mean duration of life in London has increased from twenty-nine to thirty-eight years. "In the reign of Queen Elizabeth the death-rate of the metropolis as it then was amounted to 40 per thousand. In the reign of Queen Victoria, almost entirely by the reduction of mortality by means of improved drainage, ventilation, and water, it has often touched 15 and 14, and even fallen as low as 13 in the thousand," while " in many of the suburban districts, and in the fashionable region about Hyde Park, it ranges from 11 to 12."

In France, according to M. Topinard, the mean duration of life, which was twenty-nine at the close of the eighteenth century, and thirty-nine from 1817 to 1831, increased to forty from 1840 to 1859, thanks to the progress of sanitary science and civilisation.

As Hygiene is receiving more and more attention every year, it is possible that in course of time Dr. W. B. Richardson's ideal will be realised—a town ideally perfect in sanitary matters, having a death-rate of 9 per 1000, and 105 years the duration of a man's life.

As decrepitude and premature old age means a premature loss of Beauty, personal attractiveness would be correspondingly prolonged and increased with life itself.

Even at the present time not one house in a thousand is so constructed that every room has good ventilation. Architects are, however, less to blame than the people who will persist in their absurd old superstitution that draughts and night air are injurious. Professor Reclam, the distinguished hygienist, not long ago opened a crusade against the horror of night air and draughts which is especially prevalent among his countrymen. "Sleeping with open windows," he says, "is most unjustly decried among the people, as well as night air in general. But night air is injurious only in swampy regions, whereas on dry soil, in the mountains, and everywhere in the upper stories of a house it is *more salubrious than day air.* . . . Draughts are not injurious unless we are in a glow. To healthy persons they *cannot possibly do so much harm as the stagnant air in a close room.* The fear of draughts is entirely groundless, though it affects most people in a manner which is simply ludicrous."

Electricity, no doubt, will in less than a decade abolish horses from our cities, and with them the dust, foul odours, and sleep-murdering noise. The gain to Health, and through it to Beauty, from this alone, will be enormous. Doubtless one of the reasons why there is so much Beauty, so many fresh and sparkling eyes, in Venice, is because there are no horses in that city, and the inhabitants are not roused and half-roused from sleep every fifteen minutes during the night by a waggon rattling down the street.

It is not sufficiently known that street-noise may injure the Health even of those whom it does not entirely wake up. The restorative value of sleep lies in its depth and the absence of dreams. A noisy waggon interferes with the depth of sleep and starts a current of dreams, thus depriving it of half its potency.

"*Beauty sleep*" is an expression which rests on a real physiological truth. Sleep before midnight really is more health-giving and beautifying than after midnight, for the reason that in all towns and cities there is less noise in the early hours of the night than after four in the morning, wherefore sleep is deeper between ten and twelve than between six and eight o'clock. The reason why so many more proposals (by city folks) are made in the country than in the city is not only because there are more frequent opportunities of meeting at a summer hotel, but because the young folks retire early, and appear in the morning with an exuberance of Health, born of fresh air and sound sleep, which cannot fail to inspire Love.

Other matters of Hygiene will be discussed in connection with the organs which they specially concern.

II.—CROSSING

Darwin has proved experimentally that in the vegetable kingdom "cross-fertilisation is generally beneficial, and self-fertilisation injurious. This is shown by the difference in height, weight, constitutional vigour, and fertility of the offspring from crossed and self-fertilised flowers, and in the number of seeds produced by the parent plants." He also showed that "the benefit from cross-fertilisation depends on the plants which are crossed having been subjected during previous generations to somewhat different conditions."

Similarly, concerning animals, we read in Topinard, that "breeders who select their subjects with a definite object to breed *in and in*, that is to say, between near relations, rapidly obtain excellent results. They know, however, that fertility then diminishes, and that it will cease altogether if they do not have recourse from time to time to crossing, in order to *strengthen the race.*"

But both in the vegetable and the animal kingdom, as we have seen, superior Health also implies superior Beauty.

The inference is natural that the human race also must be benefited by marriages of individuals of different races, or of the same race, but brought up under different conditions of life. And the facts are entirely in favour of this supposition, as are the best authorities in Anthropology. Dr. Topinard gives the following instances among many others: "Immigration into the United States, which has taken so considerable a flight during the last thirty years, has already been enormous. Every variety of cross has been going on between English, Irish, Germans, Italians, French, etc., with the greatest possible success. We may also mention numberless Spaniards from the Peninsula, among whom are found the features of the Saracen invaders of the ninth century; then that population on the Barbary coast, called Moors, and which is a medley of races of every description, the Arab and Berber blood predominating. On tracing back the yellow races, we also discover a perfect eugenesis. . . . De Mas speaks in the highest terms of mixed breeds of Chinese and Mongolians, and MM. Mondières and Morice of those of Chinese and Annamites under the name of Minuongs. Dr. Bowring describes a race in the Philippine Islands, intermediate between the Malays and Chinese, as the principal agent of civilisation in these latitudes."

On the other hand, "it is undeniable that in Africa the Negro races do not cross to any great extent." Nor has any one ever accused the Negroes of an excessive amount of Beauty. Whereas in Lima, which has the finest women in South America, "there are twenty-three different names to designate the varieties of mixed breeds of Spaniards, Peruvians, and Negroes." "The number of mongrels on the face of the globe has been estimated at twelve millions, of whom no fewer than eleven millions are in South America." South American women are already famous for their Beauty, and there is reason to believe that when the fusion of all these elements is complete the race will be one of the finest in the world. What Beauty it has now seems to be owing chiefly to the magic of Crossing; for attention to Health there is little but what comes from life in the open air; while Romantic Love is perhaps as rare as Mental Refinement, inasmuch as Courtship is not so free and easy a matter as in North America. All the more honour to the potency of Crossing.

Take a few more cases. The African Negroes, as just stated, do not mix much, and are an ugly type. Among the Polynesians, on the other hand, there are many very fine types of human beauty;

and it is therefore not surprising to read that to-day in Polynesia, "mixed breeds are so numerous that it would be difficult to find among them any individuals of pure race."

Again, concerning the Magyars or Hungarians, Schweiger-Lerchenfeld remarks that "they are a splendid race, physically and intellectually.... The girls and young women are of most piquant charm, models of health in mind and body." But these Magyars, when they first came to Europe, were, as Waitz states, "of a repulsive ugliness in the eyes of all their neighbours." That they have mixed with the Indo-Germanic type is shown by their appearance, as well as by peculiarities of their language. "Where they have probably remained less mixed," Waitz continues, "and at the same time less cultivated, in some remote regions, especially in the mountains, the ugly primitive type may be found to the present day; in the plains may be found every transitional form from this to the nobler type; at Szegedin both are found face to face."

The Magyars, in turn, have, like the Slavo-Italians, Czechs, etc., assisted the Austrians in evolving a superior type of Beauty by fusing with them. That there is very much more Beauty in Vienna than in any purely German city is an almost proverbial commonplace; and the reason why may be found in the statistics: in Germany 31.80 per cent are blond, 14.05 brunet, 54.15 mixed; in Austria 19.59 per cent are blond, 23.17 brunet, and 68.04 mixed.

The European Turks have much nobler forms of the head and features than their Asiatic relatives;

and the inference seems inevitable that they owe these improvements to intermarriage with Circassian women.

A negative instance, showing the disadvantages of abstaining from Crossing, is given by the Jews. There are handsome Jews and, up to a certain age, very beautiful Jewesses. But the typical Jew is certainly not a thing of beauty. The disadvantages of Jewish separatism are shown not only in the long, thick, crooked nose, the bloated lips, almost suggesting a negro, and the heavy lower eyelid, but in the fact that the Jews "have proportionately more insane, deaf mutes, blind, and colour-blind" than other Europeans. From an intellectual and industrial point of view, the Jews are one of the finest races in the world, and their absorption by the natives of the countries in which they have settled could not but benefit both parties concerned. From this point of view there may be something said even in favour of the money-marriages, which are now so frequent between extravagant German officers and Jewish heiresses. Unfortunately, the Jews have kept apart so long from the rest of the world that they do not readily mix with non-Jews. Contrary to the general rule, mixed marriages of Jews and Christians are less fertile than pure Jewish unions.

The precise manner in which a mixture of races improves physical appearance is a question still open to debate. Professor Kollmann (*Plastische Anatomie*) thinks "the result of the crossing of two forms is comparable, not to a chemical, but to a mechanical mixture;" and this agrees with the view of Mr. Herbert Spencer, who endeavours to trace to this fact the frequent want of correspondence between intellectual and physical beauty. He believes, however, the time will come "when the present causes of incongruity will have worked themselves out," and intellectual beauty emerge in harmony with physical, in all details, as it no doubt exists in general.

, There is no lack of facts supporting the view that sexual fusion is a mere mechanical mixture. The "Bourbon nose" seems to defy mitigating circumstances for generations; and "M. de Quatrefages knew a great-grandson of the bailiff of Suffren who was a striking likeness of his ancestor after four generations, and who, nevertheless, bore no resemblance either to his father or his mother." A child may resemble its father, mother, aunt, uncle, grandparents, or several of them at once; and the resemblance may vary at different ages.

More extraordinary are the following cases cited by Topinard: "Sometimes the child possesses altogether the character of one or other parent: for example, the child of a European father and a Chinese mother, Dr. Scherzer says, is altogether a European or altogether a Chinese. A Berber with blue eyes and with the lobule of the ear absent, married to a dark Arab woman with a well-formed ear, had two children, one like himself, the other like his wife. An English officer, fair, with blue eyes and florid complexion, had several children by an Indian negress. Some were the image of the father, others exactly like the mother. . . . A decided negro, having had a white among his ancestors, has unexpectedly a child with a white skin by a negress."

Yet all these are exceptional cases, which, like

the winning number in a lottery, get a disproportionate amount of attention. Moreover, this "mechanical" form of assimilation seems to occur chiefly where very unrelated races are fused, and then especially in the first generation. In subsequent generations the union doubtless tends to become more and more chemical—no longer a negro character floating on a white one, like oil on water, but a mixture, as of wine and water.

Take the American quadroons, for instance, famous for their beauty of form and features. They are mongrels of the third generation, having one-eighth black, seven-eighths white blood in their veins. Surely these characters are not "mechanically" mixed in such a woman, but "chemically." That is, you do not find her with the eyes and nose of a negro, the lips and ears of a white, one part of her skin dark the other light: but in everything there is a fusion of the ancestral elements. Her nose is not flat like that of her ancestress, nor her lips swollen, but both are intermediate between those of her white and black ancestors. Her lip is still thicker than that of the whites, and that gives her a sensuous aspect, kiss-inviting. Her eyes, again, have lost the fierce glare and opaque blackness of the negro-grandmother, and assumed a more crystalline, tender lustre; while their form and surroundings have become more refined and expressive. All this is homogeneous fusion, not "heterogeneous mixture."

Finally, it is hardly correct to state dogmatically that a certain person resembles this or that ancestor. In nothing else do opinions vary so constantly and so ludicrously. No one who has ever been "trotted around" among his relatives in the "old country," can have failed to be amused at the countless resemblances to this and that uncle, aunt, or grand-parent discovered in him, until he came to the conclusion that he must be a veritable epitome of the whole genealogy. A man who at home is supposed to be absolutely unlike his brother, is elsewhere mistaken for him and addressed as such; while another man finds a friend who knew his father in his youth, and declares he is exactly like him; though a second friend who knew only the mother, claims a similar hereditary influence for her. All of which tends to show that there is more of both parents in each person than is commonly supposed; and that the reason why opinions differ so, is because the fusion is chemical rather than mechanical, which makes it difficult to put the finger on distinct points of resemblance.

It is in the more closely allied races, like the English and German, or Italian and Spanish, that "chemical" fusion is most readily attained, and Beauty most rapidly evolved. Such are the unions which take place on such a large scale in the United States and Canada; and this may account for the fact that there is more Beauty in North America than in South America, where the races that intermingle are less related. There is a golden mean here as in everything else.

III.—ROMANTIC LOVE

What Crossing does on a national scale, Love continues with individuals, by fusing dissonant, but complementary, parental qualities into a harmonious progeny. How this is done is sufficiently shown in the chapter on Schopenhauer.

This, however, is only one of the ways in which Love increases the amount of Beauty in the world. There are several others.

The second is that—apart from complementary considerations—Romantic Love always urges the choice of a mate who approaches nearest to the ideal type of Beauty. As Beauty is hereditary, and as a beautiful father and mother may have six or more beautiful children, this predilection for Beauty shown by Love necessarily preserves and multiplies it—

> "From fairest creatures we desire increase,
> That thereby Beauty's rose might never die,"

says Shakspere, anticipating the modern theory of heredity.

On this particular topic nothing more need be said here, because all the remainder of this book will be taken up with a consideration of those features of Personal Beauty for which the æsthetic taste which forms part of Romantic Love shows a decided preference.

The third way in which Love promotes the cause of Beauty is by the great attention it pays to Health in its choice. For though Health is not always synonymous with Beauty, it is the soil on which alone Beauty can germinate and flourish.

The fourth way is through the elimination of ugliness. Love, says Plato, is devotion to Beauty: "with the ugly Eros has no concern."

From the æsthetic point of view, ugliness is disease. Now there is a cast-iron Lykurgean law prevailing throughout Nature which eliminates the diseased and the ugly. It is a cruel agency, called Natural Selection, and has not the slightest regard for individuals, but provides only for the weal of the species, as Schopenhauer erroneously says is the case with Love. In a bed of plants, if there are more than can find sustenance, the stronger crowd out the weaker. Among animals, wherever there is competition, the best-developed, handsomest lion survives in combat, and the most fleet-footed, and consequently most graceful, deer escapes, while the clumsy, the ugly, and diseased perish miserably, inexorably. Savages leave the old and feeble to die, and weak or deformed children are either deliberately put out of the way or perish from want of proper care. Nor among the ancient civilised nations were such methods unknown. Plato and Aristotle, says Mr. Grote, agree in this point: "Both of them command that no child born crippled or deformed shall be brought up—a practice actually adopted at Sparta under the Lykurgean institutions, and even carried further, since no child was allowed to be brought up until it had been inspected and approved by the public nurses." The Romans, too, were legally permitted to expose deformed children.

Christianity, the religion of pity and charity, abhors such practices. Christianity is antagonistic to Natural Selection. One of its chief functions is the building of hospitals in which the cripples, the insane, the incurably diseased, are gratuitously and tenderly cared for, instead of being allowed to perish, as they would under the sway of Natural Selection.

This artificial preservation of disease and deformity, in and out of hospitals, due to Christian charity, might in the long run prove injurious to the welfare of the human race, were it not for the stepping in of Modern Love as a preserver of Health and Beauty. What formerly was left to the agency of Natural Selection is now done by Love, through Sexual Selection, on a vast scale.

From a moral point of view, the substitution of Sexual for Natural Selection is a great gain, in harmony with the spirit of Christianity. For Cupid does not *kill* those who do not come up to his standard of Health and Beauty, but simply ignores and condemns them to a life of single-blessedness.

IV.—MENTAL REFINEMENT

"After all," says Washington Irving, speaking of Spanish women, "it is the divinity *within* which makes the divinity *without;* and I have been more fascinated by a woman of talent and intelligence, though deficient in personal charms, than I have been by the most regular beauty."

It is one of the commonest commonplaces of conversation that in moments of intellectual or emotional excitement the features of plain people assume an aspect of exquisite beauty. Love transfuses a homely girl's countenance with a glow of angelic loveliness; and biographies are full of statements concerning the countenances of men of genius, which, ordinarily unattractive, assumed an expression of unearthly beauty while their minds were active and electrified the facial muscles.

"There is not any virtue the exercise of which, even momentarily, will not impress a new fairness upon the features," says Mr. Ruskin; and again, he speaks of "the operation of the intellectual powers upon the features, in the fine cutting and chiselling of them, and removal from them of signs of sensuality and sloth, by which they are blunted and deadened, and substitution of energy and intensity for vacancy and insipidity (by which wants alone the faces of many fair women are utterly spoiled and rendered valueless); and by the keenness given to the eye and fine moulding and development to the brow, of which effects Sir Charles Bell has well noted the desirableness and opposition to brutal types."

An English clergyman, the Rev. F. P. Lawson, diocesan inspector for Northamptonshire, issued a report not long ago concerning the results of his observations in 325 urban and rural schools during several years, regarding the effects of good education in improving the appearance of the children. "A school, thoroughly well taught, seldom failed to exhibit a considerable number of interesting little faces, and a striking absence of such faces might invariably be associated with poverty of tone and superficial instruction. Nothing struck him more forcibly in a school that has been suddenly lifted out of the mire by a firstrate teacher than the bright and thoughtful look which the children soon acquire."

Negative evidence to the same effect might also be cited by the volume, but one case may suffice. "It is unhappily a fact," says Mr. Galton, "that fairly distinct types of criminals *breeding true to their kind* have become established, and are one of the saddest disfigurements of modern civilisation."

The connection between culture and a superior type of Beauty is strikingly revealed in the following remarks on the far-famed Georgian women of the Caucasus, made by a great connoisseur of feminine beauty, the poet Bodenstedt: " In Europe the notion prevails that a Georgian woman is a tall, graceful being, of luscious form, clothed in wide, rich garments, with dense black hair, long enough to enchain all masculine hearts, an open, noble forehead, and a pair of eyes which contain within their dark, mysterious, magic circle all the secrets of human delight that come through the soul or the senses. Her gait is rapture. Joy precedes, and admiration follows her. . . . With such notions in their heads, strangers generally arrive in Georgia, and find themselves wofully disappointed. The tourists who come with such great expectations to visit this country, invested with the atmosphere of a fairyland by history and legend, either adhere stubbornly to their preconceived notions, or else they instantly go over to the opposite extreme, and find everything dirty, ugly, disgusting, dreadful.

" The truth lies between these extremes. The Georgians are, all in all, one of the handsomest nations on the earth. But although I am a great admirer of women, I am compelled in this case to award the prize to the men instead of the women. This opinion is endorsed by all educated inhabitants of Georgia who have eyes, taste, and an impartial judgment.

"I must add that of that higher beauty where

heart and intellect and soul are mirrored in the eye, I found few traces in the whole Caucasus, either among men or women. I have seen the greater number of the beauties which Georgia boasts, but not one face have I seen that satisfied me completely, though the picturesque native costume does much to heighten the charms of the women. The face entirely lacks that refined mental expression which makes a beautiful European woman such a unique enchantress. Such a woman may still inspire love and win hearts long after the time of her bloom; whereas in a Georgian *everything* fades with youth. The eyes, which, notwithstanding their apparent fire, never expressed anything but calm and voluptuous indolence, lose their lustre; the nose, which even in its normal relations exceeds the limits of beauty, assumes, in consequence of the premature hollowness of the cheeks, such abnormal dimensions that many people imagine that it actually continues to grow; and the bosom, which the national costume makes no effort to conceal, prematurely loses its natural firmness—all of which phenomena are observed in European women much less frequently, and in a less exaggerated form. If you add to this the habit, so prevalent among Georgians, young and old, of using white and red cosmetics, you will understand that such rude and inartistic arts of the toilet can only add to the observer's sense of dissatisfaction."

America affords many illustrations of the manner in which refinement of mind and manners increases Beauty in a single generation. There are in every city thousands of parents who began life as ordinary labourers, but soon got rich through industry or good luck. They bring up their children in houses where every attention is paid to sanitary rules; they send them to school and college; and when they come back you would hardly believe that those coarse-featured, clumsy-limbed, ungraceful persons could be their father and mother. The discrepancy is sometimes so great that when the young folks invite people of "their set" to their house, the old birds keep out of the way discreetly, either of their own accord or by filial dictation, which in America appears to be displacing parental authority.

But if there is such an intimate connection between culture and Beauty, how is it that we so often find plain features joined with a noble mind and fine features with a mean mind? Mr. Spencer has endeavoured to explain this apparent discrepancy by assuming that in such cases plain features are inherited severally and separately from ancestors of diverse physiognomies, which being merely mechanically mixed, not fused, fail to harmonise. There may be something in this, but a simpler explanation is at hand.

Noble minds are often the result of individual effort, and persistence in it. Many men of genius have had humble parents not specially gifted. From these parents and their ancestors they inherited their plain faces. Now individual effort, in the short period of a lifetime, is insufficient to alter the *proportions* of a face, which depend on its bony parts; but it does suffice to alter the *expression*, which depends on the movements of the soft, muscular parts. Hence every person, however plain-featured, may acquire a beautiful expression by cultivating his mind and refining his manners and temper. Whenever, therefore, we meet a man or woman whose features are less attractive at rest than when moved to expression of emotion, we may feel sure that they owe their mental refinement more to individual effort than to inherited capacity.

The children of such persons will be more beautiful than they are themselves, because they will inherit the parents' habit of expressive muscular action of the features. And owing to the fact that all the bony parts of the body are modified in accordance with the action of the muscles attached to them, the bony parts, the proportions, of the face will also be gradually modified and moulded into nobler shapes, through the continuance of refined emotional expression.

It is in this manner that intellectual growth and emotional refinement have gradually differentiated our features from those of our savage ancestors. Our lips have become more delicate, our mouths smaller, our jaws less gigantic, ponderous, and projecting, because civilisation has taught us to use the hands in preparing food, and to cut it instead of tearing it off the bone with the teeth, as savages and other wild animals do.

Use increases, disuse diminishes the size of an organ. Hence for the same reason that our jaws have become less projecting and heavy, our forehead has lost its backward slope and become straight and noble, owing to the growth of the brain. And similarly with other peculiarities of the face, indicating the connection between mental refinement and physical beauty. "Thus is it," says Mr. Spencer, "with depression of the bridge of the nose, which is a characteristic both of barbarians and of our babes, possessed by them in common with our higher quadrumana. Thus, also, is it with that forward opening of the nostrils, which renders them conspicuous in a front view of the face,—a trait alike of infants, savages, and apes. And the same may be said of widespread alæ to the nose, of great width between the eyes, of long mouth, of large mouth—indeed of all those leading peculiarities of feature which are by general consent called ugly."

EVOLUTION OF TASTE

SAVAGE NOTIONS OF BEAUTY

In all the preceding remarks concerning the connection between mental and physical beauty, the assumption has been made tacitly that what *we* consider beautiful is so in reality; and that our taste is a safe guide to follow. Yet this assumption may be challenged, and has, indeed, been often challenged. Every nation, every savage tribe, has its own standard of Beauty; what right, therefore, have *we* to claim dogmatically that we are infallible judges?

Ask the devil, says Voltaire, what is the meaning of τὸ καλὸν—the Beautiful—and he will tell you "Le beau est une paire de cornes, quatre griffes, et une queue"—a couple of horns, four claws, and a tail. Ask a North American Indian, says Hearne, what is Beauty, he will answer: "A broad, flat face, small eyes, high cheek-bones, three or four broad black lines across each cheek, a low forehead, a large, broad chin, a clumsy hook-nose, a tawny hide, and breasts hanging down to the belt." In the Chinese empire "those women are preferred who have ... a broad face, high cheek-bones, very broad noses, and enormous ears." "One of the titles of the Zulu king," says Darwin (who gives many other instances *à propos* in chapter xix. of the *Descent of Man*), "is 'You who are black.' Mr. Galton, in speaking to me about the natives of South Africa, remarked that their ideas of beauty seem very different from ours; for in one tribe two slim, slight, and pretty girls were not admired by the natives."

Darwin himself appears to have been staggered and puzzled by this diversity of taste, and to have partly inclined to the theory that Beauty is relative to the human mind (though elsewhere he repudiates it)—a theory which Jeffrey has so boldly formulated in the assertion that "All tastes are equally just and true, in as far as concerns the individual whose taste is in question; and what a man feels distinctly to be beautiful *is beautiful* to him, whatever other people may think of it."

Fiddlesticks! The Alison-Jeffrey school of Scotch æstheticians, having been among the first in the field, have done more to confuse the English mind on the subject of Beauty than several generations of other clever writers will be able to clear up again.

There are about half a dozen sound, square, solid, scientific reasons why we have a better right to our opinion concerning the nature of Beauty than a Hottentot or a North American Indian.

NON-ÆSTHETIC ORNAMENTATION

One of the things most commonly forgotten by those who wonder at the strange "taste" of savages is that many of their customs have nothing whatever to do with the sense of beauty. The habit of putting on "war-paint" originated not in a desire for ornamentation, but in the wish to make themselves frightful in appearance to the enemy. For the same reason heads are mutilated. As Waitz notes in speaking of Tahiti: "A very ugly mutilation is that to which most of the boys had to subject themselves. Immediately after birth their mothers compressed their forehead and the back of the head, so that the former became narrow and high, the latter flat; this was done to make their aspect more terrible, and thus turn them into more formidable warriors." Tattooing, likewise, was originally intended to be an easy sign of recognition, or of social or religious distinction, rather than an ornament of the body. And when we consider how prone the mind of our own fashionable ladies is to violate every canon of good taste in their wild effort to surpass one another in some novel extravagance just from Paris; when we note that if a Fifth Avenue lady wears a gull on her hat, her coloured cook will invest in a turkey or ostrich for her's, we understand at once that many of the mutilations approved by savages are the outcome of vanity and emulation, not of æsthetic taste.

PERSONAL BEAUTY AS A FINE ART

Yet there are undoubtedly a number of physiognomic and other peculiarities which savages admire while we consider them ugly; and some, again, which we admire and they dislike. Have we a right to consider them inferior to us in taste because they fail to admire what we adore?

Certainly; beyond the shadow of a doubt. It takes genius to fully appreciate genius; it takes a refined taste to appreciate refined beauty. This is what the savage lacks.

Look at any one of the fine arts. Why does the savage prefer his monotonous drumming and ear-piercing war-songs to a soft, beautiful, dreamy Chopin nocturne? Because he *cannot understand* the nocturne.

Why does he prefer his painted, clumsy, coarse-featured squaw to a civilised woman with delicate contours, refined features, graceful gait? Because he *does not understand* the beauty of the latter. It is too subtle for his coarse nerves, his feeble imagina tion. The smiles and manifold expressions that chase one another across her lovely features, like the subtly-interwoven melodies in a symphonic poem, are the visible signs of thoughts and emotions which he has never experienced, and therefore cannot understand. It is like giving him a page of Sanskrit to read.

It is for this reason that a negro never falls in love with a white woman, and that a peasant prefers his plump, crude country-girl to the fair, delicate city visitor. He requires more vigorous arms, broader features, than the city girl possesses, to make an impression on his callous nerves of touch and sight. And it is fortunate for the peasant girl that her lover does lack taste, else she would soon find him a fickle deserter.

The savage, in a word, prefers his style of "beauty" to ours for the same reason that he prefers a piece of raw liver and a glass of oil to the subtle flavours of French cookery and French wines. His senses are too coarse, his mind too vulgar, to perceive the poetry of refined features. Everything must be loud and exaggerated to make an impression on him — loud music, loud and glaring red and yellow colours, loud and coarse features.

This doctrine that differences of taste are merely due to differences in the degree of æsthetic culture, and that there is such a thing as an absolute standard of human beauty, derives further support from the facts (1) that the ideal of Beauty set up by the æsthetic Greeks two thousand years ago corresponds so remarkably with that of modern artistic minds; (2) that *e.g.* a Japanese student in the United States soon learns to prefer American female beauty to the Japanese variety; (3) that an English, Italian, or American audience who at first admire *Norma* and find *Lohengrin* tiresome, can in a few seasons be so educated as to prefer *Lohengrin* and actually scorn *Norma;* but not *vice versâ*, in either case (2) or (3).

Mr. Ruskin takes a similar view regarding differences of taste when he says that "Respecting what has been asserted of negro nations looking with disgust on the white face, no importance whatever is to be attached to the opinions of races who have never received any ideas of beauty whatsoever (these ideas being only received by minds under some certain degree of cultivation), and whose disgust arises naturally from what they suppose to be a sign of weakness or ill-health."

That this consideration of health does affect the negro's judgment regarding the beauty of the white complexion, is also shown by what Mr. Winwood Reade told Mr. Darwin, namely, that the negro's "horror of whiteness may be attributed . . . partly to the belief held by most negroes that demons and spirits are white, and partly to their thinking it a sign of ill-health."

But of all the theoretical truths emphasised in the *Modern Painters* none is so important as this: "That not only changes of opinion take place in consequence of experience, but that those changes are from *variation* of opinion to *unity* of opinion,—that whatever may be the difference of estimate among unpractised or uncultivated tastes, there will be unity of taste among the experienced; and that, therefore, the result of repeated trial and experience is to arrive at principles of preference in some sort common to all, and which are part of our nature."

Let us now see what are those principles of Beauty that may be considered independent of a more or less crude and undeveloped taste. Some are negative, some positive.

NEGATIVE TESTS OF BEAUTY

(*a*) *Animals.*—"It has been argued," says Darwin (by Schaffhausen), "that ugliness consists in an approach to the structure of the lower animals, and no doubt this is partly true with the more civilised nations, in which intellect is highly appreciated; but this explanation will hardly apply to all forms of ugliness."

Curiously enough, savages themselves use animals as a negative test of beauty. Thus we read that "the Indians of Paraguay eradicate their eyebrows and eyelashes, saying that they do not wish to be like horses." "On the Eastern coast, the negro boys, when they saw Burton, cried out, 'Look at the white man; does he not look like a white ape?'" "A man of Cochin China 'spoke with contempt of the wife of the English ambassador—that she had white teeth like a dog, and a rosy colour like that of potato-flowers.'"

A few centuries ago it was a favourite pastime of physiognomists to draw elaborate parallels between men and animals. Thus, in 1593, there appeared a work, *De Humana Physiognomia*, with numerous illustrations, in which always a human face was matched with some animal's head. Professor Wundt thus sums up the essence of this book: "A broad forehead, we are told, indicates fearfulness, because the ox with his broad head lacks courage. A long forehead, on the other hand, indicates erudition, as is shown by means of an intelligent dog who has the honour of serving as a pendant to Plato's profile. Persons with shaggy hair are good-natured, as they resemble the lion. He whose eyebrows are turned inwards, towards the nose, is uncleanly like the pig, which this resembles. The narrow chin of the ape signifies malice and envy. Long ears and thick lips, such as the donkey possesses, are signs of stupidity. A person who has a nose crooked from the forehead inclines, like the raven, to theft, etc.

These animal-physiognomists appear to have favoured a thoroughly pessimistic view of man's capacities, inasmuch as for every creditable resemblance they find at least ten discreditable ones."

Apart from these puerilities, it is in most cases simply absurd to compare man with animals. Except in the case of apes there are no proper terms of comparison, because the types are so distinct; and, moreover, from the point of view of its own type, the average animal of any species is more beautiful than the average man or woman from the human point of view. This assertion is indirectly corroborated by Mr. Galton's testimony, that "our human civilised stock is far more weakly through congenital imperfection than that of any other species of animals, whether wild or domestic."

Schopenhauer considered animals beautiful in every way, and suggested that whenever we do find an animal ugly it is due to some irrelevant, inevitable association of ideas, as when a monkey suggests a man, or a toad mud. And Mr. Ruskin pertinently suggests that "That mind only is fully disciplined in its theoretic power which, when it chooses, throwing off the sympathies and repugnancies with which the ideas of destructiveness or of innocence accustom us to regard the animal tribes, as well as those meaner likes and dislikes which arise, I think, from the greater or less resemblance of animal powers to our own, can pursue the pleasures of typical beauty down to the scales of the alligator, the coils of the serpent, and the joints of the beetle."

When Sir Charles Bell intimated that in Greek sculpture the guiding principle was remoteness from the animal type, he stated only one side of the truth, of which the other is thus noted by Winckelmann: among the Greeks, he says, "The study of artists in producing ideal beauties was directed to the nature of the nobler beasts, so that they not only instituted comparisons between the forms of the human countenance and the shape of the head of certain animals, but they even undertook to adopt from animals the means of imparting greater majesty and elevation to their statues . . . especially in the heads of Hercules." Jupiter's head "has the complete aspect of the lion, the king of beasts, not only in the large, round eyes, in the fulness of the prominent, and, as it were, swollen forehead, and in the nose, but also in the hair, which hangs from his head like the mane of the lion, first rising upward from the forehead, and then, parting on each side into a bow, again falling downward."

So that we may safely reject the theory that ugliness consists in an approach to the structure of the lower animals, whatever savages and Chinamen may think on this subject. Coarse minds little suspect what exquisite beauty is to be found in the head of a cow or a donkey, a puppy or a lamb—beauty which, like a lovely melody, may bring tears to the eyes of one who is sensitive to æsthetic impressions. Objectively considered, even the destructive emotions do not appear ugly in an animal. The ferocity of a lion does not make him appear vicious, because ferocity is his nature. He knows no better; can only live by fighting. But a man *is* disfigured by ferocity because he does know better; he *can* live without fighting; and it is *the consciousness of his selfish meanness* that puts the stamp of ugliness on his distorted features.

In apes alone does fierceness seem ugly and brutal instead of sublime. For apes bear so much resemblance to us, and have a brain so superior in structure to that of other animals, that we feel justified in applying the human standard. Hence apes alone afford us a negative test of beauty. Their heads and faces are cast in our mould, and therefore afford the means of direct comparison. In looking at their massive, brutal jaws, their receding foreheads, their undifferentiated hands and feet, their coarse, hairy skin, their clumsy, inexpressive, gigantic mouths, their flat noses and nostrils open to the view, we are justified in calling them ugly, compared with ourselves, and in feeling proud that civilisation has gradually raised us so far above our country cousins, in beauty as in everything else, except the art of climbing trees.

(*b*) *Savages* are valuable as negative tests of beauty for the same reason : they enable us to see what progress we have made in refining our features into harmonious proportions, and making them susceptible of diverse emotional expression. It should be noted that Nature constantly endeavours to make primitive mankind beautiful, as it does with all other animals. Tourists constantly note the occurrence of remarkable instances of Personal Beauty among the young in most tribes. But this natural Beauty is not appreciated by the vulgar taste of savages, as we saw a few pages back in a case mentioned by Mr. Galton. Beauty must be distorted and exaggerated before it pleases the savage's taste. Paint must be laid on an inch thick, the nose perforated and "adorned" with a ring, and ditto the abnormally lengthened lips. This corrects the notion that savage hideousness is a product of Nature. Nature may blunder, but never so sadly as in the appearance of a savage belle or warrior; and in scorning these we do not therefore scorn Nature, but merely the artificial products of the vulgar taste of primitive man.

(*c*) *Degraded Classes.*—Poverty, suffering, want of leisure for mental culture, want of money for sanitary modes of living, have, unfortunately, produced in all countries a large class in whom Personal Beauty occurs only as an accident. That such unhappy mortals afford a negative test of Beauty is seen by the fact that, just as savages are intermediate between monkeys and them, so they stand between savages and refined men in features and expression.

Poverty alone does not produce this vulgar type of personal appearance; it is intellectual indolence, moral vice, and hygienic indifference that are responsible for it. Hence this third negative test of Beauty is not at all difficult to find in any sphere of society, from the hod-carrier to the aristocrat with a pedigree of a hundred generations. In every scale of the social ladder may be found "features seamed by sickness, dimmed by sensuality, convulsed by passion, pinched by poverty, shadowed by sorrow, branded with remorse; bodies consumed with sloth, broken down by labour, tortured by disease, dishonoured in foul uses; intellects without power, hearts without hope, minds earthly and devilish" (Ruskin).

(*d*) *Age and Decrepitude.*—It is not true, as a famous Frenchwoman has remarked, that age and beauty are incompatible terms. Even age and Love are not incompatible, as we saw in the chapter on Genius in Love; and Byron has remarked that Love, like the measles, is most dangerous when it comes late in life.

There is a special variety of Beauty for every period of life, and the Beauty of old age certainly is not the least attractive of these varieties. What could be more majestic, more admirable, than the head of a Longfellow in his last days? Provided health of mind and body has been maintained, even the folds in the cheeks, the wrinkles on the forehead of old age, are not unbeautiful. But when senility means decrepitude, brought on by a neglectful or otherwise vicious life, then it is positively ugly. The loveliest thing in the world is a fair and amiable maiden; the ugliest a vicious old hag—savages and apes *not* excepted.

(*e*) *Disease.*—Temperance preachers and other hygienic reformers commonly dwell too exclusively on the dangers to health, domestic peace, moral progress, and refinement which the indulgence in various vices entails. If they would insist with equal, or even greater, emphasis on the havoc which diseases brought on by intemperance and neglect of the laws of Health make on Personal Beauty, they would double their influence on their audiences or readers. For in woman's heart the desire to be beautiful is and always will be the strongest motive to action or non-action; nor are men, as a rule, much less interested in the matter of preserving a handsome appearance. It may make *some* impression on a man to tell him that if he takes ice-water before breakfast, or "cock-tails" at various odd hours on an empty stomach, he will ruin his digestion ; but the impression will be six times as deep if you can convince him that he will ere long look like that confirmed dyspeptic Jones, with lack-lustre eyes, sallow complexion, and a general expression of premature senility, which accounts for the fact that he has been twice already refused by the girl he adores.

Or take that girl over there who never takes a walk, always sleeps with her windows hermetically closed, and never allows a ray of sunshine to touch any part of her body. Tell her she is ruining her health and she may be momentarily alarmed by this vague warning, and walk half a mile for a week or so, until she has forgotten it. But make it clear to her what is the exact consequence of such neglect of the primal laws of health—namely, the premature loss of every trace of Personal Beauty and youthful charm, with old-maidenhood inevitably staring her in the face, owing to her apathetic appearance and gait, her sickly complexion, her features distorted by frequent headaches, brought on by lack of fresh, cool air— each of which leaves its permanent trace in the form of an addition to a wrinkle or subtraction from the plumpness of her cheeks,—tell her all this, and that her eyes will soon sink into their sockets and have blue rings like those of an invalid, and a ghastly stare—and she will, perhaps, be sufficiently roused to save her Health for the sake of her Beauty.

We are now confronted with the question, Why

is it that disease is a mark of ugliness, health a mark of Beauty? The old Scotch school of æstheticians think it is all a matter of association. We consider certain forms characteristic of health as beautiful simply because we associate with them various emotions of affection, the pleasures of love, etc., and conversely with disease and vice. According to Stendhal, "La beauté n'est que la promesse du bonheur," or, in American, Beauty is simply the promise of a "good time." But it is Lord Jeffrey who, to use another appropriate American expression, "goes the whole hog" in this matter, by practically denying the existence of such a thing as a pure, disinterested, æsthetic sense. Suppose, he says, "that the smooth forehead, the firm cheek, and the full lip, which are now so distinctly expressive to us of the gay and vigorous periods of youth—and the clear and blooming complexion, which indicates health and activity—had been, in fact, the forms and colours by which old age and sickness were characterised; and that, instead of being found united to those sources and seasons of enjoyment, they had been the badges by which Nature pointed out that state of suffering and decay which is now signified to us by the livid and emaciated face of sickness, or the wrinkled front, the quivering lip, and hollow cheek of age; if this were the familiar law of our nature, can it be doubted that we should look upon these appearances, not with rapture, but with aversion, and consider it as absolutely ludicrous or disgusting to speak of the beauty of what was interpreted by every one as the lamented sign of pain and decrepitude?

"Mr. Knight himself, though a firm believer in the intrinsic beauty of colours, is so much of this opinion that he thinks it entirely owing to those associations that we prefer the tame smoothness and comparatively poor colours of a youthful face to the richly fretted and variegated countenance of a pimpled drunkard."

Bosh! and a hundred times bosh! One feels that these men lived at a time when port was drunk by the bottle, like claret, and when variegated noses were to a certain extent fashionable.

Though every reader feels the sophistry and absurdity of the above argumentation, it is not easy to refute it. Professor Blackie declaims against it, Ruskin sneers at it, but nowhere have I been able to find a definite, direct refutation of the thesis. The following suggestions may, therefore, be of some value.

In the first place, Jeffrey's supposition is equivalent to saying that if black were white, white would be black. For if all the phenomena of human nature were reversed, our taste, being also a "phenomenon," would be reversed too. If health meant emaciation, then a lover would not be happy unless he could kiss a pair of leathery lips and embrace a skeleton. Hence his sense of touch, like his sight, would have to be the reverse of what they are now; and that being the case, æsthetic taste, which is based on the senses, would of course be reversed too. But that is simply saying that if you stand a man on his head his feet will be in the air.

Secondly, Lord Jeffrey's argument involves the old fallacy that the useful and the beautiful are identical

—that we only consider those things beautiful which afford us some utilitarian gratification. If this theory were correct, a coal-boat would be more beautiful than a yacht; a savage's big jaw-bone more beautiful than our delicate ones; a clumsy, dirty, coarse-featured labourer more beautiful than a society belle.

No, we have, thank heaven, an æsthetic sense which enables us to see and admire beauty quite independently of any "associations" which it may have with our utilitarian cravings. It is possible, however, and even probable, that the æsthetic sense was originally *developed* from utilitarian associations. On this subject Mr. Grant Allen has some exceedingly valuable remarks in his interesting work on the Colour-Sense. He there eloquently sets forth the view that it was the bright tints of luscious fruits that first taught primitive man to derive pleasure from the sight of coloured objects. This gradually led to a "predilection for brilliant dyes and glistening pebbles; till at last the whole series culminates in that intense and unselfish enjoyment of rich and pure tints which make civilised man linger so lovingly over the hues of sunset and the myriad shades of autumn. . . . The *disinterested* affection can only be reached by many previous steps of utilitarian progress." But—and here lies the kernel of the argument—"fruit-eaters and flower-feeders derive pleasure from brilliant colours . . . not because those colours have mental associations with their food, but because the structures which perceive them have been continually exercised and strengthened by hereditary use," until at last they formed a special nervous or cerebral apparatus which presides over impressions of beauty, and takes a special pleasure in its own activity, apart from all utilitarian considerations.

Lord Jeffrey apparently lacked this special æsthetic sense, as shown by his whole argument, and by his inability, which he shared with Alison, of finding beauty in Nature, unless it was in some way associated with man's presence and man's mean utilities.

How different this from the feelings of the man who of all writers on Beauty has the most highly developed æsthetic sense—Mr. Ruskin, who has just told us in his *Autobiography* that his love of Nature, ardent as it is, depends entirely on the *wildness* of the scenery—its remoteness from human influences and associations.

It is this specially-developed æsthetic taste that would prevent man from calling flabby cheeks, sallow complexions, pimpled noses, and sunken eyes beautiful, if by some miracle they should be changed into signs of health. For this sense of beauty was first educated not by the sight of human beauty, but of beauty in Nature—fruits, pebbles, shells, lustrous metals, etc.; and the notions of beauty thus obtained have been gradually transferred to human beings as standards of attractiveness. It can be shown that what the best judges pronounce the highest human beauty, is so because it partakes of certain characteristics which we find beautiful throughout Nature. And conversely, what we consider ugly in the human form and features would also be called ugly in external objects; in both cases, be it distinctly understood, without any direct reference to utilitarian considerations, and sometimes even in opposition to them, as in our admiration of a beautiful poisonous plant or snake, or a tiger.

It is these universal characteristics of Beauty, found in man as in animals, that we now have to consider. They are the *positive* criteria of Beauty, and may be regarded as a new set of "overtones" or leading motives for the remainder of this volume, although the old ones will occasionally reappear and combine with them.

POSITIVE TESTS OF BEAUTY

Of these there are at least eight—Symmetry, Curvature, Gradation, Smoothness, Delicacy, Colour, Lustre, Expression, including Variety and Individuality.

(*a*) *Symmetry.* — "In all perfectly beautiful objects," says Mr. Ruskin, "there is found the opposition of one part to another, and a reciprocal balance obtained; in animals the balance being commonly between opposite sides (note the disagreeableness occasioned by the exception in flat fish, having the eyes on one side of the head); but in vegetables the opposition is less distinct, as in the boughs on opposite sides of trees, and the leaves and sprays on each side of the boughs, and in dead matter less perfect still, often amounting only to a certain tendency towards a balance, as in the opposite sides of valleys and alternate windings of streams. In things in which perfect symmetry is, from their nature, impossible or improper, a balance must be at least in some measure expressed before they can be beheld with pleasure. . . . Symmetry is the *opposition* of *equal* quantities to each other. Proportion the *connection* of *unequal* quantities with each other. The property of a tree in sending out equal boughs on opposite sides is symmetrical. Its sending out shorter and smaller towards the top, proportional. In the human face its balance of opposite sides is symmetry, its division upwards, proportion."

Mr. Darwin thus gives his testimony as to the prevalence of symmetry in Nature: "If beautiful objects had been created solely for man's gratification, it ought to be shown that before man appeared there was less beauty on the face of the earth than since he came on the stage. Were the beautiful volute and cone shells of the Eocene epoch, and the gracefully sculptured ammonites of the Secondary period, created that man might ages afterwards admire them in his cabinet? Few objects are more beautiful than the minute silicious cases of the diatomaceæ: were they created that they might be examined and admired under the higher powers of the microscope? The beauty in this latter case, and in many others, is apparently wholly due to symmetry of growth" (*Origin of Species*, chap. vi.)

In the floral world, again, the natural tendency is always towards symmetry. Wind-fertilised flowers are symmetrical in form; and "as Mr. Darwin has observed, there does not appear to be a single instance of an irregular flower which is not fertilised by insects or birds" (Lubbock), and therefore modified in form in the effort to adapt itself to useful insects and to exclude pirates.

Throughout the animal kingdom, including man, this law of symmetry is true. Hence it is not likely that we should ever admire a lame leg, a crooked nose, bent on one side, eyes that are not mates, or a face several inches longer on one side than the other, owing to paralysis—as *beautiful*, even if, as Jeffrey would have it, Madame Nature should suddenly take it into her head to associate such abnormalities with health instead of with disease.

(*b*) *Gradation.*—On this law of Nature Mr. Ruskin again has spoken at once more scientifically and poetically than any other writer on æsthetics: "What curvature is to lines, gradation is to shades and colours.... For instances of the complete *absence* of gradation we must look to man's work, or to his *disease* and *decrepitude*. Compare the gradated colours of the rainbow with the stripes of a target, and the gradual concentration of the youthful blood in the cheek with an abrupt patch of rouge, or with the sharply-drawn veining of old age.

"Gradation is so inseparable a quality of all natural shade and colour that the eye refuses in art to understand anything as either which appears without it; while, on the other hand, nearly all the gradations of nature are so subtile, and between degrees of tint so slightly separated, that no human hand can in any wise equal, or do anything more than suggest the idea of them."

The following remarks which the same writer makes in another place concerning Gradation show at the same time how asinine it is for a savage or any other person of uncultivated taste to set himself up as a judge of Personal Beauty, as good as any one else, on the plea that it is all "a matter of taste" and *de gustibus non est disputandum* :—

"When the eye is quite uncultivated, it sees that a man is a man, and a face is a face, but has no idea what shadows or lights fall upon the form or features. Cultivate it to some degree of artistic power, and it will then see shadows distinctly, but only the more vigorous of them. Cultivate it still further, and it will see light within light, and shadow within shadow, and will continually refuse to rest in what it has already discovered, that it may pursue what is more removed and more subtle, until at last it comes to give its chief attention and display its chief power on *gradations which to an untrained faculty are partly matters of indifference and partly imperceptible.*"

The words italicised enable us to appreciate what Sokrates must have had in his mind when he distinguished between that which *is* beautiful and that which only *appears* beautiful. Æsthetic training enables us to see things as they are, instead of as they appear through inattention, through ignorance, or through clouds of national prejudice, or individual utilitarianism.

The way in which æsthetic training enables us to see gradations of beauty previously imperceptible can be most strikingly illustrated in the case of music. There are thousands of intelligent folks who cannot tell the difference between a superb Steinway Grand, just tuned for a concert, and a harsh, clangy, mountain-hotel piano that has not been tuned for two years. But give these persons a thorough musical education, and they will soon be able to smile at Jeffrey's notion that the tone of the hotel-piano was quite as beautiful as that of the Steinway, because it *seemed* so to them. It is not only the imagination but the senses themselves that require training. A Hottentot or any unmusical person cannot tell the difference between two consecutive tones on the piano, whereas a skilled musician can detect all the gradations from one tone to another, down to the sixty-fourth part of a semitone!

"It is all a matter of taste!" Precisely. Of good taste and bad taste.

Examples of gradation in the human form are the gradual tapering of the limbs and the fingers, the exquisite line from the female neck to the shoulders and the bosom, the blushes on the cheeks, so long as they do not assume the form of a hectic flush, and the delicate tints of the complexion in general, varying with emotional states, according as the veins and arteries are more or less filled with the vital fluid.

Is it then "entirely owing to their associations" with health or disease that we prefer the complexion of a youthful face to the hideous daubs of red which Knight refers to as the "richly fretted and variegated countenance of a pimpled drunkard?" Is it owing to such associations that we prefer the delicately gradated blushes of coloured marble to the richly bedaubed countenance of a pimpled brickbat? But it would be a waste of time to refer again to the crude anti-æsthetic notions of Messrs. Knight, Alison, and Jeffrey.

One more exquisite illustration of subtle gradation in the human form divine may be cited from Winckelmann :—

"The soul, though a simple existence, brings

forth at once, and in an instant, many different ideas; so it is with the beautiful youthful outline, which appears simple, and yet at the same time has infinitely different variations, and that soft tapering which is difficult of attainment in a column, is still more so in the diverse forms of the youthful body. Among the innumerable kinds of columns in Rome some appear pre-eminently elegant on account of this very tapering; of these I have particularly noted two of granite, which I am always studying anew: just so rare is a perfect form, even in the most beautiful youth, which has a stationary point in our sex still less than in the female."

(*c*) *Curvature.*—" That all forms of acknowledged beauty are composed exclusively of curves will," Mr. Ruskin believes, " be at once allowed; but that which there will be need more especially to prove, is the subtility and constancy of curvature in all natural forms whatsoever. I believe that, except in crystals, in certain mountain forms admitted for the sake of sublimity or contrast (as in the slope of debris), in rays of light, in the levels of calm water and alluvial land, and in some few organic developments, there are no lines or surfaces of nature without curvature, though, as we before saw in clouds, more especially in their under lines towards the horizon, and in vast and extended plains, right lines are often suggested which are not actual. Without these we should not be sensible of the value of contrasting curves; and while, therefore, for the most part, the eye is fed in natural forms with a grace of curvature which no hand nor instrument can follow, other means are provided to give beauty to those surfaces which are admitted for contrast, *as in water by its reflection of the gradations which it possesses not itself.*"

In a footnote to the last edition of the *Modern Painters* he adds regarding the apparent exceptions named: "Crystals are indeed subject to rectilinear limitations, but their real surfaces are continually curved; the level of calm water is only right lined when it is shoreless."

On the other hand, "Generally in all ruin and disease, and interference of one order of being with another (as in the cattle line of park trees), the curves vanish, and violently opposed or broken and unmeaning lines take their place." I feel tempted to cite another most admirable passage on curvature throughout Nature—even where it is least looked for, and the untrained eye cannot see it—in the shattered walls and crests of mountains which "seem to rise in a gloomy contrast with the soft waves of bank and wood beneath." But it is too long to quote, and I can only advise the reader most earnestly to look it up in chapter xiv. vol. iv.

"Straight lines," Professor Bain observes, "are rendered artistic only by associations of power, regularity, fitness, etc." "In some situations straight lines are æsthetic. . . . In the human figure there underlies the curved outline a certain element of rigidity and straightness, indicating strength in the supporting limbs and spine. Whenever firmness is required, there must be a solid structure, and straightness of form is a frequent accompaniment of solidity. The straight nose and the flat brow are subsidiary to the movement and the stability of the face."

Yet even our straight limbs follow in their motions the law of curvature. And to this fact that they move more easily and naturally in a curved than in a straight line, which requires laborious adjustment, Bain traces part of our superior pleasure in rounded lines.

What infinite subtlety and variety Curvature is capable of is vividly brought before the eyes by Winckelmann : "The forms of a beautiful body are determined by lines the centre of which is constantly changing, and which, if continued, would never describe circles. They are, consequently, more simple, but also more complex, than a circle, which, however large or small it may be, always has the same centre, and either includes others or is included in others. This diversity was sought after by the Greeks in works of all kinds ; and their discernment of its beauty led them to introduce the same system even into the form of their utensils and vases, whose easy and elegant outline is drawn after the same rule, that is, by a line which must be found by means of several circles, for all these works have an elliptical figure, and herein consists their beauty. The greater unity there is in the junction of the forms, and in the flowing of one out of another, so much the greater is the beauty of the whole."

Masculine and Feminine Beauty.—The universality of curvature as a form of beautiful objects throughout nature and art is of importance in helping us to determine the question which is the more beautiful form, a perfect man or a perfect woman—an Apollo or a Venus? A Venus, no doubt. In those qualities which are subsumed under the terms of the sublime or the characteristic—in strength, manly dignity, intellectual power, majesty—the masculine type, no doubt, is superior to the feminine. But in Beauty proper—in the roundness and delicacy of contours, in the smoothness of complexion and its subtle gradations of colour, in the symmetrical roundness and lustrous expressiveness of the eyes—the feminine type is pre-eminent.

"Woman," says Professor Kollmann, "is smaller, more delicate, but also softer and more graceful (*schwungvoller*) in form, in her breasts, hips, thighs, and calves. No line on her body is short and sharply angular; they all swell, or vault themselves in a gentle curve. . . . The neck and the rounded shoulders are connected by gracefully curved lines, whereas a man's neck is placed more at a right angle to the more straight and angular shoulders. . . . The hair is softer, the skin more tender and transparent. All the forms are more covered over with adipose tissue, and connected by those gradual transitions which produce the gently rounded outlines; whereas in a man everything—muscles, sinews, blood-vessels, bones—is more conspicuous."

Schopenhauer, accordingly, was clearly in the wrong when he endeavoured to make out that man is vastly superior to woman in physical beauty,— a notion which Professor Huxley, too, does not appear to disapprove of very violently. At the same time it is, no doubt, true that there are more good specimens of masculine beauty in most countries than of feminine beauty; true also that man's beauty lasts much longer than woman's. A boy is more beautiful than a girl under sixteen, for the very reason that his form is more like that of an adult woman than a girl's is. From eighteen to twenty-five woman is more beautiful than man; while after thirty, owing to the almost universal neglect of the laws of health—women are apt to become either too rotund, which ruins their grace and delicacy, or too angular—more angular than a man under fifty.

(*d*) *Delicacy and Grace.*—The difference between masculine and feminine beauty and the superiority of the latter is also indirectly brought out in Burke's remarks on Delicacy, which, though open to criticism in one or two points, are on the whole admirable and exhaustive :—

"An air of robustness and strength is very prejudicial to beauty. An appearance of delicacy, and even of fragility, is almost essential to it. Whoever examines the vegetable or animal creation will find this observation to be founded in nature. It is not the oak, the ash, or the elm, or any of the robust trees of the forest which we consider as beautiful; they are awful and majestic, they inspire a sort of reverence. It is the delicate myrtle, it is the orange, it is the almond, it is the jasmine, it is the vine, which we look on as vegetable beauties. It is the flowery species, so remarkable for its weakness and momentary duration, that gives us the liveliest idea of beauty and elegance. Among animals the grey-hound is more beautiful than the mastiff, and the delicacy of a jennet, a barb, or an Arabian horse, is much more amiable than the strength and stability of some horses of war or carriage.

"I need here say little of the fair sex, where I believe the point will be easily allowed me. The beauty of women is considerably owing to their weakness or delicacy, and is even enhanced by their timidity, a quality of mind analogous to it. I would not here be understood to say that weakness betraying very bad health has any share in beauty; but the ill effect of this is not because it is weakness, but because the ill state of health, which produces such weakness, alters the other conditions of beauty; the parts in such a case collapse, the bright colour, the *lumen purpureum juventæ* is gone, and the fine variation is lost in wrinkles, sudden breaks, and right lines."

Delicacy is a quality closely related to grace, or beauty in motion and attitude. "Grace," says Dr. J. A. Symonds, "is a striking illustration of the union of the two principles of similarity and variety. For the secret of graceful action is that the symmetry is preserved through all the varieties of position." This is well put; but the *first* condition and essence of grace is that there must be an exact correspondence between the work done and the limb which does it. The attitude of an oak-trunk, with nothing on the top but a geranium bush, however symmetrical, would always be ungraceful, owing to the ludicrous disproportion between the support and the thing supported. Conversely, a weak fern-stalk, trying to support a branch of heavy cactus leaves, would be equally ungraceful; for there must be neither a waste of energy nor a sense of effort. Part of this feeling may perhaps be traced to sympathy—thus showing how various emotions enter into our æsthetic judgments, sometimes weakening, sometimes strengthening them. As Professor Bain remarks, *à propos:* "We love to have removed from our sight every aspect of suffering, and none more so than the suffering of toil."

Grace is almost as powerful to inspire Love as Beauty itself. Women know this instinctively, and in order to acquire the Delicacy which leads to grace, they deprive their bodies of air and sunshine and strengthening sleep, hoping thereby to acquire artificially, through ill-health, what Nature has denied them. Fortunately such violations of the laws of health always frustrate their object. Delicacy conjoined with Health inspires Love, but delicacy born of disease inspires only pity—a feeling which may inspire in a woman what she imagines is Love, but in a man *never.*

(*e*) *Smoothness* is another attribute of Beauty on which Burke was the first to place proper emphasis: It is, he says, "a quality so essential to beauty that I do not recollect anything beautiful that is not smooth. In trees and flowers, smooth leaves are beautiful; smooth slopes of earth in gardens; smooth streams in the landscape; smooth coats of birds and beasts in animal beauties; in fine women, smooth skins; and in several sorts of ornamental furniture, smooth and polished surfaces. . . . Any ruggedness, any sudden projection, any sharp angle, is in the highest degree contrary to the idea of beauty."

Though there are exceptions to this rule of smoothness—including such a marvel of beauty as the moss-rose, as well as various leaves covered with down, etc.—yet, on the whole, Burke is right. Certainly the smooth white hand of a delicate lady is more beautiful than the rough, horny "paws" of a bricklayer; and the inferior beauty of a man's arm is owing as much to its rough scattered hairs as to the prominence of the muscles, in contrast to the smooth and rounded arm of woman. In animals, however, hairs on the limbs are not unbeautiful, because they are dense enough to overlap, and thus form a hairy surface admirable alike for its soft smoothness, its gloss, and its colour.

(*f*) *Lustre and Colour.*—Lustrous, sparkling eyes, glossy hair, pearly teeth,—where would human beauty be without them—without the delicate tints and blushes of the skin, the brown or blue iris, the golden or chestnut locks, the ebony eyebrows and lashes?

Yet the greatest art-critics incline to the opinion that, on the whole, colour is a less essential ingredient of beauty than form. "Colour assists beauty," says Winckelmann, but "the essence of beauty consists not in colour but in shape." "A negro might be called handsome when the conformation of his face is handsome." "The colour of bronze and of the black and greenish basalt does not detract from the beauty of the antique heads," hence "we possess a knowledge of the beautiful, although in an unreal dress and of a disagreeable colour."

Similarly Mr. Ruskin, who remarks of colour that it "is richly bestowed on the highest works of creation, and the eminent *sign and seal of perfection in them;* being associated with *life* in the human form, with *light* in the sky, with purity and hardness in the earth,—death, night, and pollution of all kinds being colourless. And although if form and colour be brought into complete opposition, so that it should be put to us as a stern choice whether we should have a work of art all of form, without colour (as an Albert Dürer's engraving), or all of colour, without form (as an imitation of mother-of-pearl), form is beyond all comparison the more precious of the two . . . yet if colour be introduced at all, it is necessary that, whatever else may be wrong, *that* should be right," etc.

Again : " An oak is an oak, whether green with spring or red with winter ; a dahlia is a dahlia, whether it be yellow or crimson ; and if some monster-hunting botanist should ever frighten the flower blue, still it will be a dahlia ; but let one curve of the petals—one groove of the stamens—be wanting, and the flower ceases to be the same. Let the roughness of the bark and the angles of the boughs be smoothed or diminished, and the oak ceases to be an oak ; but let it retain its inward structure and outward form, and though its leaves grew white, or pink, or blue, or tri-colour, it would be a white oak, or a pink oak, or a republican oak, but an oak still."

" If we look at Nature carefully, we shall find that her colours are in a state of perpetual confusion and indistinctness, while her forms, as told by light and shade, are invariably clear, distinct, and speaking. The stones and gravel of the bank catch green reflections from the boughs above ; the bushes receive grays and yellows from the ground ; every hairbreadth of polished surface gives a little bit of the blue of the sky, or the gold of the sun, like a star upon the local colour ; this local colour, changeful and uncertain in itself, is again disguised and modified by the hue of the light or quenched in the gray of the shadow; and the confusion and blending of tint is altogether so great that were we left to find out what objects were by their colours only, we would scarcely in place distinguish the boughs of a tree from the air beyond them or the ground beneath them. I know that people unpractised in art will not believe this at first; but if they have accurate powers of observation, they may soon ascertain it for themselves; they will find that, while they can scarcely ever determine the *exact* hue of anything, except when it occurs in large masses, as in a green field or the blue sky, the form, as told by light and shade, is always decided and evident, and the source of the chief character of every object."

Professor Bain remarks on this topic that "Among the several kinds of beauty, the eye takes most delight in colour.... For this reason we find the poets borrowing more of their epithets from colours than from any other topic."

This view seems to be confirmed by the fact that lovers in expatiating on the beauty of their Dulcineas seem to have much more to say about their brown or golden locks, their light or dark complexion, their blue or black eyes, than about the shape of their features. This, however, partly finds its explanation in the fact that colour, being a sensuous quality, is more easily and more directly appreciated than form, the perception of which is a much more complicated matter, being a translation into intellectual terms of remembered impressions of touch, associated with certain colours, lights, and shades which recall them; and partly in the greater ease with which peculiarities of colour are referred to than peculiarities of form. In the days of ancient Greece the nomenclature of colours was equally undeveloped, and is so vague in Homer that Gladstone and Geiger actually set up the theory that Homer's colour-sense was imperfect, and that that sense has been gradually developed within historic times,—a theory which I have confuted on anatomical grounds in *Macmillan's Magazine*, Dec. 1879.

That as regards human beauty colour is of less importance than form is shown, moreover, in this, that a girl with regular features and a freckled complexion will much sooner find a lover than one with the most delicately-coloured complexion, conjoined with a big mouth, irregular nose, or sunken cheeks. And a beautifully-shaped eye is sure to be admired by all, no matter whether blue, gray, or brown; whereas an eye that is too small or otherwise defective in form can never be redeemed by the most beautiful colour or brilliancy.

On the other hand, there are several things to be said in favour of colour that will mitigate our judgment on this point. In the first place, colour is more perfect in its way than form, so that it is impossible ever to improve on it by idealising, as it is often with form. As Mr. Ruskin remarks, "Form may be attained in perfection by painters, who, in their course of study, are continually altering or idealising it; but only the sternest fidelity will reach colouring. Idealise or alter in that, and you are lost. Whether you alter by debasing or exaggerating, by glare or by decline, one fate is for you —ruin. . . . Colour is sacred in that you must keep to facts. Hence the apparent anomaly that the only schools of colour are the schools of realism."

Again, looking at Nature with an artist's eye, Ruskin discovered and frequently alludes to the "apparent connection of brilliancy of colour with vigour of life," and Mr. Wallace, looking at Nature with a naturalist's eye, established this "apparent connection" as a scientific fact. The passage in which he sums up his views has been once already quoted; but it is of such extreme importance in enforcing the lesson that beauty is impossible without health, that it may be quoted again:—

"The colours of an animal usually fade during disease or weakness, while robust health and vigour adds to its intensity. . . . In all quadrupeds a 'dull coat' is indicative of ill-health or low condition; while a glossy coat and sparkling eye are the invariable accompaniments of health and energy. The same rule applies to the feathers of birds, whose colours are only seen in their purity during perfect health; and a similar phenomenon occurs even among insects, for the bright hues of caterpillars begin to fade as soon as they become inactive, preparatory to their undergoing transformation. Even in the Vegetable Kingdom we see the same thing; for the tints of foliage are deepest, and the colours of flowers and fruits richest, on those plants which are in the most healthy and vigorous condition."

(*g*) *Expression, Variety, Individuality.*—Besides the circumstances that colour is more uniformly perfect in Nature than form, and that it is always associated with Health, without which Beauty is impossible, another peculiarity may be mentioned in its favour. The complexion is a kaleidoscope whose delicate blushes and constant changes of tint, from the ashen pallor of despair to the rosy flush of delight, are the fascinating signs of emotional expression. And herein lies the superior beauty of the human complexion over all other tinted objects: it reflects not only the hues of surrounding external bodies, but all the moods of the soul within.

Form without colour is form without expression. But form without expression soon ceases to fascinate, for we constantly crave novelty and variety; and form is one, while expression is infinitely varied and ever new. Herein lies the extreme importance of expression as a test of Beauty. Colour, of course, is only one phase of expression. The soul not only changes the tints of the complexion, but liquifies the facial muscles so that they can be readily moulded into forms characteristic of joy, sadness, hope, fear, adoration, hatred, anger, affection, etc.

Why is the portrait-painter so infinitely superior to the photographer? Because the photographer—paradoxical as this may seem—gives you a less realistic picture of yourself than the artist. He only gives you the fixed form, or at most a transient expression which, being fixed permanently, loses its essence, which is motion—and thus becomes a caricature—an exaggeration in duration. But the artist studies you by the hour, makes you talk, notes the habitual forms of expression most characteristic of your individuality; and, blending these into a sort of "typical portrait" of your various individual traits, makes a picture which reveals all the advantages of art over mere solar mechanism or photography.

This explains why some of the most charming persons we know never appear well in a photograph, while others much less charming do. The beauty of the latter lies in form, of the former in expression. But expression is much more potent to inspire admiration and Love than mere beauty of features; and not without reason, for beautiful features, being a lucky inheritance, may be conjoined with unamiable individual traits, whereas beautiful expression is the infallible index of a beautiful mind and character; and promises, moreover, beautiful sons and daughters, because "expression is feature in the making." It is by such subtle signs and promises that Love is unconsciously and instinctively guided in its choice.

Formal Beauty alone is external and cold. It is those slight variations in Beauty and expression which we call individuality and character that excite emotion: so much so that Love, as we have seen, is dependent on individuality, and a man who warmly admires all beautiful women is in love with none.

Speaking of the Greeks, Sir Charles Bell says: "In high art it appears to have been the rule of the sculptor to divest the form of expression. . . . In the Venus, the form is exquisite and the face perfect, but there is *no expression* there; it has no human softness, *nothing to love.*" "All individuality was studiously avoided by the ancient sculptors in the representation of divinity; they maintained the beauty of form and proportion, but without expression, which, in their system, belonged exclusively to humanity."

But inasmuch as the Greeks attributed to their deities all the various emotions which agitate man, why did they refuse them the signs of expression? One cannot but suspect that the Greeks did not sufficiently appreciate the beauty of expression. Had they valued it more they would not have allowed their women to vegetate in ignorance like flowers, one like the other, but would have educated them and given them the individuality and expression which alone can inspire Love.

Again, if the Greeks had been susceptible to the superior charms of emotional expression, is it likely that they would have been so completely absorbed in the two least expressive and emotional of the arts—architecture and sculpture?

We cannot avoid the conclusion that the Greeks were as indifferent to the charms of individual expression as to Romantic Love, which is dependent on it. In their statues, as Dr. Max Schasler remarks, a mouth or eye has no more significance as a mark of beauty than a well-shaped leg. Whereas in modern, and even sometimes in mediæval art, what a world of expression in a mouth, a pair of eyes!

Leaving individual exceptions (like Homer) aside, it may be said that the arts have been successively developed to a climax in the order of their capacity for emotional expression, viz.—Architecture, Sculpture, Painting, Poetry, and Music. Poetry precedes music, because though its emotional scope is wider, it is less intense. To-day music is the most popular and universal of all the arts because it stirs most deeply our feelings. And just as the discovery of harmony, by individualising the melodies, has increased the power and variety of music a thousandfold; so the individualisation of Beauty and character through modern culture has made Romantic Love a blessing accessible to all—the most prevalent form of modern affection.

Individuality is of such extreme importance in Love that a slight blemish is not only pardoned but actually adored if it increases the individuality. Bacon evidently had this in his mind when he said that "there is no excellent beauty which has not some strangeness in its proportion." Seneca, as well as Ovid, noted the attractiveness of slight shortcomings; and the following anecdote shows that though the Persians, as a nation, have ever been strangers to Romantic Love, their greatest poet, Háfiz, understood the psychology of the subject in its subtlest details :—

"One day Timur (fourteenth century) sent for Háfiz and asked angrily: 'Art thou he who was so bold as to offer my two great cities Samarkand and Bokhara for the black mole on thy mistress's cheek?' alluding to a well-known verse in one of his odes. 'Yes, sire,' replied Háfiz, 'and it is by such acts of generosity that I have brought myself to such a state of destitution that I have now to solicit your bounty.' Timur was so pleased with the ready wit displayed in this answer that he dismissed the poet with a handsome present."

To sum up: the reason why

> "The rose that lives its little hour
> Is prized beyond the sculptured flower"

is not, as Bryant implies, the transitoriness of the rose, but the fact that the marble flower, like the wax-flower, is dead and unchangeable, while the short-lived rose beams with the expression of happy vitality after a shower, or sadly droops and hangs its head in a drouth. It has life and expression, subtle gradations of colour, and light and shade, which are the signs of its vitality and moods, varying every day, every hour. And so with all the higher forms of life, those always being most beautiful and highly prized which are most capable of expressing subtle variations of health, happiness, and mental refinement.

There is no part of the human body which does not serve as a mark of expression—

"In many's looks the false heart's history
Is writ in moods and frowns and wrinkles strange."

" There's language in her eye, her cheek, her lip,
Nay, her foot speaks."—SHAKSPERE.

It will not do, therefore, to neglect any part of the body. As it is the last straw which breaks the camel's back, so Cupid's capricious choice is often determined by some minor point of perfection, when the balance is otherwise equal. Suppose there are two sisters whose faces, figures, and mental attractions are about equal; then it is possible that one of them will die an old maid simply because the other had a smaller foot, a more graceful gait, or longer eyelashes.

But though every organ has its own beauty, there is an æsthetic scale of lower and higher which corresponds pretty accurately with the physical scale from down upwards—from the foot to the eye and forehead. It is in this order, accordingly, that we shall now proceed to consider the various parts of the human form, and those peculiarities in them which are considered most beautiful and most liable to inspire Romantic Love.

THE FEET

SIZE

There is hardly anything concerning which vain people are so sensitive as their feet. To have large feet is considered one of the greatest misfortunes that can befall a woman. Mathematically stated, the length of a woman's skirts is directly proportional to the size of her feet; and women with large feet are always shocked at the frivolity of those who have neat ankles and coquettishly allow them to be seen on occasion; nor do they see any beauty in Sir John Suckling's lines—

> "Her feet beneath her petticoat
> Like little mice stole in and out,
> As if they feared the light."

Nor are men, as a rule, sufficiently free from pedal vanity to pose as satirists. Byron found a mark of aristocracy in small feet, and he was rendered almost as miserable by the morbid consciousness of his own defects as Mme. de Staël (who had very ugly feet, yet once ventured to assume the *rôle*, in private theatricals, of a statue) was offended by Talleyrand's witticism, that he recognised her by the *pied de Staël*.

There is a *ben trovato*, if not true, story of a clever wife who objected to her husband's habit of spending his evenings away from home, and who reformed him by utilising his vanity. By insisting that his boots were too large, she repeatedly induced him to buy smaller ones, which finally tortured him so much that he was only too glad to stay at home and wear his slippers.

FASHIONABLE UGLINESS

How universal is the desire to have, or appear to have, small feet is shown by the fact that everybody blackens his shoes or boots; for, owing to a peculiar optical delusion, black objects always appear smaller than white ones; which is also the reason why too slim and delicate ladies never appear to such advantage in winter as they do in summer, when they exchange their dark for light dresses.

To a certain point the admiration of small feet is in accordance with the canons of good Taste, as will be presently shown. But Taste has a disease which is called Fashion. It is a sort of microbe which has the effect of distorting and *exaggerating* everything it takes hold of. Fashion is not satisfied with small feet; it wants them *very* small, unnaturally small, at the cost of beauty, health, grace, comfort, and happiness. Hence for many generations shoemakers have been compelled to manufacture instruments of torture so ruinous to the constitution of man and woman, that an Austrian military surgeon has seriously counselled the enactment of legal fines to be imposed on the makers of noxiously-shaped shoes, similar to those imposed on food-adulterators.

Most ugly and vulgar fashions come from France; but as regards crippled feet the first prize has to be yielded to the Chinese, even by the Parisians. The normal size of the human foot varies, for men, from $9\frac{1}{2}$ to 13; for women from $5\frac{1}{2}$ to 9 inches, man's feet being longer proportionately to the greater length of his lower limbs. In China the men value the normal healthy condition of their own feet enough to have introduced certain features of elasticity in their shoes which we might copy with advantage; but the women are treated very differently. "The fashionable length for a Chinese foot," says Dr. Jamieson, "is between $3\frac{1}{2}$ and 4 inches, but comparatively few parents succeed in arresting growth so completely." When girls are five years old their feet are tightly wrapped up in bandages, which on successive occasions are tightened more and more, till the surface ulcerates, and some of the flesh, skin, and sometimes even a toe or two come off. "During the first year," says Professor Flower, "the pain is so intense that the sufferer can do nothing but lie and cry and moan. For about two years the foot aches continually, and is subject to a constant pain, like the pricking of sharp needles." Finally the foot becomes reduced to a shapeless mass, void of sensibility, which "has now the appearance of the hoof of some animal rather than a human foot, and affords a very insufficient organ of support, as the peculiar tottering gait of those possessing it clearly shows."

The difference between the Chinese belle and the Parisian is one of degree merely. The former has her torturing done once for all while a child, whereas the latter allows her tight, high-heeled shoes to torture her throughout life. The English are the only nation that have recognised the injuriousness and vulgarity of the French shoe, and substituted one made on hygienic principles; and as England has in almost everything else displaced France as the leader in modern fashion, it is reasonable to hope that ere long other nations will follow her in this reform. American girls are, as a rule, much less sensible in this matter than their English sisters; one need only ask a clerk in a shoe store to find out how most of them endeavour to squeeze their small feet into shoes too small by a number.

Fashions are always followed blindly, without deliberation. But would it not be worth while for French, American, and German women—and many men too—to ask themselves what they gain and what they lose by trying to make their feet appear smaller than they are? The disadvantages outweigh the advantages to an almost ludicrous extent.

On the one side there is absolutely nothing but the gratification of vanity derived from the fact that a few acquaintances admire one's "pretty feet"; and even this advantage is problematical, because a person who wears too tight shoes can hardly conceal them from an observer, and is therefore apt to get pity for her vain weakness in place of admiration.

On the other hand are the following disadvantages:—

(1) The constant torture of pressure (not to mention the resulting corns and bunions), which alone must surely outweigh a hundred times the pleasure of gratified vanity at having a Chinese foot.

(2) The unconscious distortion of the features and furrowing of the forehead in the effort to endure

and repress the pain,—and wrinkles, be it remembered, when once formed are ineradicable.

(3) The discouragement of walking and other exercise, involving a general lowering of vitality, sickly pallor, and premature loss of the bloom of youth.

(4) The wasting of the calf of the leg to dimensions characteristic of savagedom, disease, and old age, not to speak of the numerous maladies resulting to women from the use of hard high heels of fashionable shoes, every contact of which with the ground sends a shock through the spinal column to the brain and produces obscure disorders in various parts of the organism.

(5) The mutilation of one of the most beautiful and characteristically human parts of the body. As the author of Harper's *Ugly Girl Papers* remarks: " One's foot is as proper an object of pride and complacency as a shapely hand. But where in a thousand would a sculptor find one that was a pleasure to contemplate like that of the Princess Pauline Bonaparte, whose lovely foot was modelled in marble for the delight of all the world who have seen it ? "

(6) Finally, and most important of all, the loss of a graceful gait, of the poetry of motion, which is a thousand times more calculated to inspire admiration—æsthetic or erotic—than a small foot.

Man is said to be a reasoning animal; and man embraces woman. But surely in matters of fashion woman is not a reasoning being. Very large feet being properly regarded as ugly, she draws the inference that the smaller they can be made the more will they be beautiful; forgetting that Beauty is a matter of proportion, not of absolute size. A foot may, like a waist, as easily appear ugly from being too small as from being too large. A large woman with very small feet cannot but make a disagreeable impression, like a bust on an insecure pedestal or a leaning tower.

TESTS OF BEAUTY

According to Schopenhauer, the great value which all attach to small feet "depends on the fact that small feet are an essentially human characteristic, since in no animal are the tarsus and metatarsus together so small as in man, which peculiarity is connected with his erect attitude: he is a plantigrade." But it is difficult to see any force in this reasoning, since not one person in a hundred thousand knows what the bones called tarsus and metatarsus are, nor cares whether they are larger in man or in animals; while, as regards the upright position, large feet would appear more suitable for maintaining it than small ones.

If smallness were the test of beauty in man, why should we not feel ashamed to have larger heads than animals, or envy the elephant, who, for his size, has the smallest foot of all animals?

Those who believe that human beauty consists in the degree of remoteness from animal types, will derive satisfaction from the fact that apes have feet that are larger than ours. Topinard gives these figures showing the relative sizes: man, 16.96; gorilla, 20.69; chimpanzee, 21.00; orang, 25. But why should man feel a special pride in the fact that his feet are somewhat smaller than those of his nearest relatives, whom, until recently, he did not even acknowledge as such?

It is, moreover, unscientific to compare man's foot with the ape's too closely, because they have different functions—being used by man for walking, by the ape for climbing—and therefore require different characteristics. It is only in those organs that have a like function—as the jaws, teeth, nose, eyes, and forehead—that a direct comparison is permissible, and a progress noted in our favour.

Again, as M. Topinard tells us, "The hand and the foot of man, although shorter than those of the anthropoid ape, do not vary among races according to their order of superiority, as we should have supposed. *A long hand or foot is not a characteristic of inferiority.*"

The same is true among individuals of the same race. Mme. de Staël was one of the most intelligent women the world has ever seen, yet her feet were very large; and conversely, some of our silliest girls have the smallest feet.

Since, then, there is no obvious connection between small feet and superior culture, it follows that the beauty of a foot is not to be determined by so simple a matter as its length. There are other peculiarities, of greater importance, in which the laws of Beauty manifest themselves. First, in the arched instep, which is not only attractive because it introduces the beauty-curve in place of the straight, flat line of the sole, but which is of the utmost importance in increasing the foot's capacity for carrying its burden, just as architects build arches under bridges, etc., for the sake of the greater strength and more equable distribution of pressure thus obtained. Secondly, in the symmetrical correspondence of the toes and contours of one foot with those of its partner; in the gradation of the regularly shortened toes, from the first to the fifth; in the delicate tints of the skin which, moreover, is smooth and not (as in apes) covered with straggling hairs and deep furrows, which would have concealed the delicate veins that variegate the surface and give it the colour of life.

Professor Carl Vogt, in his *Lectures on Man*, vividly illustrates the principles on which our judgment regarding beauty in feet is based, by comparing a negro's foot with that of civilised man: "The foot of the negro, says Burmeister, produces a disagreeable impression. Everything in it is ugly; the flatness, the projecting heel, the thick, fatty cushion in the inner cavity, the spreading toes. . . . The character of the human foot lies mainly in its arched structure, in the predominance of the metatarsus, the shortening and equal direction of the toes, among which the great toe is remarkably long, but not, like the thumb, opposable. . . . The toes in standing leave no mark, but do so in progression. The whole middle part of the foot does not touch the ground. Persons with flat feet, in whom the middle of the sole touches the ground, are bad pedestrians, and are rejected as recruits. . . . The negro is a decided flat foot . . . the fat cushion on the sole not only fills up the whole cavity, but projects beyond the surface."

Inasmuch as it is the custom among all civilised peoples to cover the foot entirely, many of its aspects of beauty are rendered invisible permanently, so that it is perhaps not to be wondered at that in their absence Fashion should have so eagerly fixed on the two visible features—size and arched instep—and endeavoured to exaggerate them by Procrustean dimensions and stiltlike high heels. Yet in this matter even modern Parisians represent a progress over the mediæval Venetian ladies, who, according to Marinello, at one time wore soles and heels over a foot in height, so that on going out they had to be accompanied by several servants to prevent them from falling. *Mais que voulez vous?* Fashion is fashion, and women are women.

By the ancient Greeks the feet were frequently exposed to view; hence, says Winckelmann, "in descriptions of beautiful persons, as Polyxena and Aspasia, even their beautiful feet are mentioned." Possibly in some future age, when Health and Beauty will be more worshipped than vulgar Fashion fetishes, a clever Yankee will invent an elastic, tough, and leathery, but transparent substance that will protect the foot while fitting it like a glove and showing its outlines. This would put an end to the mutilations resorted to from vanity guided by bad taste, and would add one more feature to Personal Beauty. And the foot, as Burmeister insists, has one advantage over every other part of the body. Beauty in all these other features depends on health and a certain muscular roundness. But the foot's beauty is independent of such variations, as it lies mainly in its permanent bony contours and in its fat cushion, which alone of all adipose layers resists the ravages of disease and old age. Hence a beautiful foot is a thing of beauty and a joy for ever, long after all other youthful charms have faded and fled.

A GRACEFUL GAIT

So long as the foot remains entirely covered, its beauty is, on the whole, of less importance than the grace of its movements. Grace, under all circumstances, is as potent a love-charm as Beauty itself—of which, in fact, it is only a phase; and if young men and women could be made to realise how much they could add to their fascinations by cultivating a graceful gait and attitudes, hygienic shoemakers, dancing-masters, and gymnasiums would enjoy as great and sudden a popularity as skating-rinks, and a much more permanent popularity too.

It is the laws of Grace that chiefly determine the most admirable characteristics of the foot. The arched instep is beautiful because of its curved outlines; but its greatest value lies in the superior elasticity and grace it imparts to the gait. The habitual carrying of heavy loads tends to make the feet flat and to ruin Grace; hence the clumsy gait of most working people, and, on the other hand, the graceful walk of the "aristocratic" classes.

The proper size of the foot, again, is most easily determined with reference to the principles of Grace. Motion is graceful when it does not involve any waste of energy, and when it is in accordance with the lines of Beauty. There must be no disproportion between the machinery and the work done—no locomotive to pull a baby-carriage. Too large feet are ugly because they appear to have been made for carrying a giant; too small ones are ugly because seemingly belonging to a dwarf. What are the exact proportions lying between "too large" and "too small" can only be determined by those who have educated their taste by the study of the laws of Beauty and Grace throughout Nature.

From this point of view Grace is synonymous with *functional fitness*. A monkey's foot is less beautiful than a man's, but in *climbing* it is more graceful; whereas in *walking* man's is infinitely more graceful. Apes rarely assume an erect position, and when they do so they never walk on the flat sole. "When the orang-outang takes to the ground," says Mr. E. B. Tylor, "he shambles *clumsily* along, generally putting down the outer edge of the foot and the bent knuckles of the hand."

I have italicised the word "clumsily" because it touches the vital point of the question. Man owes his intellectual superiority largely to the fact that he does not need his hands for walking or climbing, but uses them as organs of delicate touch and as tools. To acquire this independence of the hands he needed feet, which enabled him to stand erect and walk along, not "clumsily," but firmly, naturally, and therefore gracefully. Hence in course of time, through the effects of constant use, there was developed the callous cushion of the heel and toes; while, through discontinuance of the habit of climbing, the toes became reduced in size. In the ape's foot, it is well known, the toes are almost as long as the fingers of the hand: a fact which led Blumenbach and Cuvier to classify apes as quadrumana or four-*handed* animals. But Professor Huxley showed that this classification was based on erroneous reasoning. The resemblance between the hands and feet of apes is merely *physiological* or functional—

because hands and feet are used alike for climbing. But *anatomically*, in its bones and muscles, etc., the monkey's apparent hind "hand" is a true foot no less than man's. If the *physiological* function, *i.e.* the opposability of the thumb to the other fingers, were taken as a ground of classification, then birds, who have such toes, would have no feet at all but only wings and hands.

There is a limit, however, beyond which the size of man's toes cannot be reduced without injuring the foot's usefulness and the grace of gait. The front part of the foot is distinguished for its yielding or elastic character. Hence, says Professor Humphrey, "in descending from a height, as from a chair or in walking downstairs, we alight upon the balls of the toes. If we alight upon the heels—for instance, if we walk downstairs on the heels—we find it an uncomfortable and rather jarring procedure. In walking and jumping, it is true, the heels come first in contact with the ground, but the weight then falls obliquely upon them, and is not fully borne by the foot till the toes also are upon the ground."

One of the reasons why Grace is more rare even than Beauty on this planet is that the toes are cramped or even turned out of their natural position by tight, pointed, fashionable shoes, and are thus prevented from giving elasticity to the step. Instances are not rare (and by no means only in China) where the great toe is almost at right angles to the length of the foot. In walking, says Professor Flower, "the heel is first lifted from the ground, and the weight of the body gradually transferred through the middle to the anterior end of the foot, and the final push or impulse given with the great toe. It is necessary then that all these parts should be in a straight line with one another."

It is a mooted question whether the toes should be slightly turned outward, as dancing-masters insist, or placed in straight parallel lines, as some physiologists hold. For the reason indicated in the last paragraph, physiologists are clearly right. With parallel or almost parallel great toes, a graceful walk is more easily attained than by turning out the toes. Even in standing, Dr. T. S. Ellis argues, the parallel position is preferable : "When a body stands on four points I know of no reason why it should stand more firmly if those points be unequally disposed. The tendency to fall forwards would seem to be even increased by widening the distance between the points in front, and it is in this direction that falls most commonly occur."

EVOLUTION OF THE GREAT TOE

Perhaps the most striking difference between the feet of men and apes lies in the relative size of the first and second toes. In the ape's foot the second toe is longer than the first, whereas in modern civilised man's foot the first or great toe is almost always the longer. Not so, however, with savages, who are intermediate in this as in other respects between man and ape ; and there are various other facts which seem to indicate that the evolution of the great toe, like that of the other extreme of the body—the head and brain—is still in progress.

There is a notion very prevalent among artists that the second toe should be longer than the first.

This idea, Professor Flower thinks, is derived from the Greek canon, which in its turn was copied from the Egyptian, and probably originally derived from the negro. It certainly does not represent what is most usual in our race and time. "Among hundreds of bare, and therefore undeformed, feet of children I lately examined in Perthshire, I was not able to find one in which the second toe was the longest. Since in all apes—in fact, in all other animals—the first toe is considerably shorter than the second, a long first toe is a specially human attribute; and instead of being despised by artists, it should be looked upon as a mark of elevation in the scale of organised beings."

Mr. J. P. Harrison, after a careful examination of the unrestored feet of Greek and Roman statues in various museums and art galleries, wrote an article in the *Journal of the Anthropological Institute of Great Britain* (vol. xiii. 1884), in which he states that he was "led to the conviction that it was from Italy and not Greece that the long second toe affected by many English artists had been imported." Among the Italians a longer second toe is common, as also among Alsatians; in England so rarely that its occurrence probably indicates foreign blood. Professor Flower, as we have seen, found no cases at all; Paget examined twenty-seven English males, in twenty-four of whom the great toe was the longer. "In the case of the female feet, in ten out of twenty-three subjects the first or great toe was longest, and *in ten females it was shorter* than the second toe. In the remaining three instances the first and second toes were of equal length."

Bear these last sentences in mind a moment, till we

have seen what is the case with savages. Says Dr. Bruner: "A slight shortening of the great toe undoubtedly exists, not merely amongst the Negro tribes, but also in ancient and modern Egyptians, and even in some of the most beautiful races of Caucasian *females*." And Mr. Harrison found this to be, with a few exceptions, a general trait of savages. The great toe was shorter than the second in skeletons of Peruvians, Tahitians, New Hebrideans, Savage islanders, Ainos, New Caledonians.

Must we therefore agree with Carl Vogt when he says, "We may be sure that, whenever we perceive an approach to the animal type, the female is nearer to it than the male?"

Perhaps, however, we can find a solution of the problem *somewhat* less insulting to women than this statement of the ungallant German professor.

It is *Fashion*, the handmaid of ugliness, that has thus apparently caused almost half the women to approximate the simian type of the foot; *Fashion*, which, by inducing women for centuries to thrust their tender feet into Spanish boots of torture, has taken from their toes the freedom of action requisite for that free development and growth which is to be noticed in almost all the men.

Considering the great difference between the left and the right foot, it appears almost incredible, but is a sober fact, that until about half a century ago "rights and lefts" were not made even for the men, who now always wear them. But even to-day "they are not, it is believed, made use of by women, except in a shape that is little efficacious," says Mr. Harrison; and concerning the Austrians Dr. Schaffer remarks, similarly, that "the like shoe for the left and right foot is still in use in the vast majority of cases." No wonder women are so averse to taking exercise, and therefore lose their beauty at a time when it ought to be still in full bloom. For to walk in such shoes must be a torture forbidding all unnecessary movement.

Once more be it said—it is Fashion, the hand-maid of ugliness, that is responsible for the inferior beauty of the average female foot, by preventing the free development and play of the toes which are absolutely necessary for a graceful walk.

To what an extent the woful rarity of a graceful gait is due to the shape of "fashionable" shoes is vividly brought out in a passage concerning the natives of Martinique, which appeared in a letter in the New York *Evening Post:* "Many of the quadroons are handsome, even beautiful, in their youth, and all the women of pure black and mixed blood walk with a lightness of step and a graceful freedom of motion that is very noticeable and pleasant to see. I say all the women; but I must confine this description to those who go shoeless, for when a negress crams her feet into even the best-fitting pair of shoes her gait becomes as awkward as the waddle of an Indian squaw, or of a black swan on dry land, and she minces and totters in such danger of falling forward that one feels constrained to go to her and say, 'Mam'selle Ebène or Noirette, do, I beseech you, put your shoes where you carry everything else, namely, on the top of your well-balanced head, and do let me see you walk barefoot again, for I do assure you that neither your Chinese cousins nor your European mistresses can ever hope to imitate your goddess-like gait until they practise the art of walking with their high-heeled, tiny boots nicely balanced on *their* heads, as you so often are pleased to do.'"

There is another lesson to be learned from this discussion, namely, that in trying to establish the principles of Beauty, it is better to follow one's own taste than adhere blindly to Greek canons, and what are supposed to be Greek canons. The longer second toe, as we have seen, is not a characteristic of Greek art, but due apparently to restorations made in Italy where this peculiarity prevails. The Greeks, indeed, never hesitated to idealise and improve Nature if caught napping; and there can be little doubt that if in their own feet the first toe had been shorter than the second, they would have made it longer all the same in their statues, following the laws of gradation and curvature which a longer second toe would interrupt. For it is undeniable that, as Mr. Harrison remarks, "a model foot, according to Flaxman, is one in which the toes follow each other imperceptibly in a graceful curve from the first or great toe to the fifth."

NATIONAL DIFFERENCES

The statement made above regarding the prevalence among Italians of a longer second toe enables us also to qualify the remark made in the *Westminster Review* (1884), that "Even at the present day it is a fact well known to all sculptors that Italy possesses the finest models as regards the female hands and feet in any part of Europe; and that to the eye of an Italian the wrists and ankles of most English women would not serve as a study even for those revivalisms of the antique which are to be purchased in our streets for a few shillings." Whatever may be true of wrists and ankles, the toes must be excepted, at least if a larger percentage of Italian than of English women have the second toe longer.

Although in matters where so many individual differences exist it is hazardous to generalise, the following remarks on national peculiarities in feet, made by a reviewer of Zachariae's *Diseases of the Human Foot*, may be cited for what they are worth: "The French foot is meagre, narrow, and bony; the Spanish foot is small and elegantly curved, thanks to its Moorish blood. . . . The Arab foot is proverbial for its high arch; 'a stream can run under his foot,' is a description of its form. The foot of the Scotch is large and thick—that of the Irish flat and square—the English short and fleshy. The American foot is apt to be disproportionately small."

BEAUTIFYING HYGIENE

Walking, running, and dancing are the most potent cosmetics for producing a foot beautiful in form and graceful in movement. It is possible that much walking does slightly increase the size of the foot, but not enough to become perceptible in the life of an individual; and it has been sufficiently shown that the standard of Beauty in a foot is not smallness but curved outlines, litheness, and grace of gait, these qualities being a thousand times more powerful "love-charms" than the smallest Chinese foot. Moreover, it is probable that *graceful* walking has no tendency to enlarge the foot as a whole, but only the great toe; and a well-developed great toe is a distinctive sign of higher evolution.

It is useless for any one to try to walk or dance gracefully in shoes which do not allow the toes to spread and act like two sets of elastic springs. One of the most curious aberrations of modern taste is the notion that the shape of the natural foot is not beautiful—that it will look better if made narrowest in front instead of widest. Even were this so, it would not pay to sacrifice all grace to a slight gain in Beauty. But it is not so. It is only habit, which blunts perception, that makes us indifferent to the ugliness of the pointed shoes in our shop-windows, or even in many cases prefer them to naturally-shaped shoes. Were we once accustomed to properly-shaped hygienic boots, in which no part of the foot is cramped, our present shoes, with their unnatural curves where there should be none, and the absence of curves where they should be ("rights and lefts"), would seem as "awful" and "horrid" as the old crinoline does to the eyes of the present generation. As Professor Flower remarks: "The fact that the excessively pointed, elongated toes of the time of Richard II., for instance, were superseded by the broad, round-toed, almost elephantine, but most comfortable shoes seen in the portraits of Henry VIII. and his contemporaries, shows that there is nothing in the former essential to the gratification of the æsthetic instincts of mankind. Each form was, doubtless, equally admired in the time of its prevalence."

The Germans claim that it was one of their countrymen, Petrus Camper, who first called attention, about a hundred years ago, to another objectionable peculiarity of the modern shoe—its high heels—ruinous alike to comfort, grace, and health (a number of female diseases being caused by them); yet they admit that Camper's advice was hardly heeded by the Germans, and that it therefore serves them right that quite recently the modern hygienic shoe, with low, broad heels, has been introduced in Germany as the " English form," the English having proved themselves less obtuse and conservative in this matter.

The heel is, however, capable of still further improvement. It is not elastic like the cushion of the heel, after which it should be modelled; and Dr. Schaffer's suggestion that an elastic mechanism should be introduced in the heel is certainly worthy of trial. Everybody knows how much more lightly, gracefully, as well as noiselessly, he can walk in rubbers than in leather shoes; and this gain is owing to the superior elasticity of the heel and the middle part of the shoe, covering the arch, which should be especially elastic. It is pleasanter to walk in a meadow than on a stone pavement; but if we wear soles that are both soft and elastic we need never walk on a hard surface; for then, as Dr. Schaffer remarks, "we have the meadow in our boots."

As the left foot always differs considerably from the right, it is not sufficient to have one measure taken. The fact that shoemakers do take but one measure shows what clumsy bunglers most of them are. As a rule, it is easier to get a fit from a large stock of ready-made boots than at a shoemaker's.

The stockings, as well as the shoes, often cramp and deform the foot ; and Professor Flower suggests that they should never be made with pointed toes, or similar forms for both sides. Digitated stockings, however, are a nuisance, for they hamper the free and elastic action of the toes. Woollen stockings are the best both for summer and winter use. No one who has ever experienced the comfort of wearing woollen socks (and underclothes in general), will ever dream of reverting to silk, cotton, or any other material.

Soaking the feet in water in which a handful of salt has been dissolved, several times a week, is an excellent way of keeping the skin in sound condition. For perfect cleanliness it does not suffice to change the socks frequently. As the author of the *Ugly Girl Papers* remarks, " The time will come when we will find it as shocking to our ideas to wear out a pair of boots without putting in new lining as we think the habits of George the First's time, when maids of honour went without washing their faces for a week, and people wore out their linen without the aid of a laundress."

DANCING AND GRACE

Among the ancients dancing included graceful gestures and poses of all parts of the body, as well as facial expression. In Oriental dancing of the present day, likewise, graceful movements of the arms and upper part of the body play a more important *rôle* than the lower limbs. Modern dancing, on the contrary, is chiefly an affair of the lower extremities. It is pre-eminently an exercise of the toes; and herein lies its hygienic and beautifying value, for, as we have seen, grace of gait depends chiefly on the firm litheness and springiness of the toes, especially the great toe. By their grace of gait one can almost always distinguish persons who have enjoyed the privilege of dancing-lessons, which have strengthened their toes and, by implication, many other muscles, not forgetting those of the arm, which has to hold the partner.

There are thousands of young women who have no opportunities for prolonged and exhilarating exercise except in ballrooms. In the majority of cases, unfortunately, Fashion, the handmaid of Ugliness and Disease, frustrates the advantages which would result from dancing by prescribing for ballrooms not only the smallest shoes, but the tightest corsets and the lowest dresses, which render it impossible or imprudent to breathe fresh air, without which exercise is of no hygienic value, and may even be injurious. But what are such trifling sacrifices as Health, Beauty, and Grace compared to the glorious consciousness of being fashionable?

DANCING AND COURTSHIP

The ballroom is Cupid's camping ground, not only because it facilitates the acquisition of that grace by which he is so easily enamoured, but because it affords such excellent opportunities for Courtship and Sexual Selection. And this applies not only to the era of modern Romantic Love, but, from its most primitive manifestations in the animal world, dancing, like song, has been connected with love and courtship.

Darwin devotes several pages to a description of the love-antics and dances of birds. Some of them, as the black African weaver, perform their love-antics on the wing, " gliding through the air with quivering wings, which make a rapid whirring sound like a child's rattle"; others remain on the ground, like the English white-throat, which "flutters with a fitful and fantastic motion"; or the English bustard, who "throws himself into indescribably odd attitudes whilst courting the female"; and a third class, the famous Bower-birds, perform their love-antics in bowers specially constructed and adorned with leaves, shells, and feathers. These are the earliest *ballrooms* known in natural history; and it is quite proper to call them so, for, as Darwin remarks, they "are built on the ground for the sole purpose of courtship, for their nests are formed in trees."

Passing on to primitive man, we again find him inferior to animals in not knowing that the sole proper function of dancing is in the service of Love, courtship, and grace. Savages have three classes of dance, two being performed by the men alone, the third by men and women. First come the War-Dances, in which the grotesquely-painted warriors brandish their spears and utter unearthly howls, to excite themselves for an approaching contest. Second, the Hunters' Dances, in which the game is impersonated by some of the men and chased about, which leads to many comic scenes; though there is a serious undercurrent of superstition, for they believe that such dances—a sort of saltatorial prayer—bring on good luck in the subsequent real chase. Third, the Dance of Love, practised *e.g.* by the Brazilian Indians, with whom "men and women dance a rude courting dance, advancing in lines with a kind of primitive polka step" (Tylor). That there is as little refinement and idealism in the savage's dances as in his love-affairs in general is self-evident.

The civilised nations of antiquity, as we have seen, had no prolonged Courtship, and therefore no Romantic Love. Since young men and women were not allowed to meet freely, dancing was of course not esteemed as a high social accomplishment. It was therefore commonly relegated to a special class of women (or slaves), such as the Bayaderes of India and the Greek flute girls. Notwithstanding that even the Greek gods are sometimes represented as dancing, yet this art came to be considered a sign of effeminacy in men who indulged in it; and as for the Romans, their view is indicated in Cicero's anathema: "No man who is sober dances, unless he is out of his mind, either when alone or in decent society, for dancing is the companion of wanton conviviality, dissoluteness, and luxury."

In ancient Egypt, too, the upper classes were not allowed to learn dancing. And herein, as in so many things in which women are concerned, the modern Oriental is the direct descendant of the ancients. "In the eyes of the Chinese," says M. Letourneau, "dancing is a ridiculous amusement by which a man compromises his dignity."

Plato appears to have been the first who recognised the importance of dancing as affording opportunities for Courtship and prematrimonial acquaintance. But his advice remained unheeded by his countrymen. A view regarding dancing similar to Plato's was announced by an uncommonly liberal theologian of the sixteenth century in the words, as quoted by Scherr, that "Dancing had been originally arranged and permitted with the respectable purpose of teaching manners to the young in the presence of many people, and enabling young men and maidens to form honest attachments. For in the dance it was easy to observe and note the habits and peculiarities of the young."

Thus we see that, with the exception of the savage's war-dances and hunting pantomimes, the art of dancing has at all times and everywhere been born of love; even the ancient religious dances having commonly been but a veil concealing other purposes, as among the Greeks. But all ceremonial dancing, like ceremonial kissing, has been from the beginning doomed to be absorbed and annihilated by the all-engrossing modern passion of Romantic Love.

True, as a miser mistakes the means for the end and loves gold for its own sake, so we sometimes see girls dance alone—possibly with a vaguely coy intention of giving the men to understand that they can get along without them. But their heart is not in it, and they never do it when there are men enough to go round. As for the men, they are too open and frank ever to veil their sentiments. They never dance except with a woman.

To-day our fashion and society papers are eternally complaining of the fact that the young men—especially the *desirable* young men—seem to have lost all interest in dancing. But who is to blame for this? Certainly not the men. It is *Fashion* again, and the mothers who sacrifice the matrimonial prospects of their daughters—as well as their Health, Beauty, and Individuality—to this hideous fetish. It is the late hours of the dance, prescribed by Fashion, that are responsible for the apparent loss of masculine interest in this art. Formerly, when aristocracy meant laziness and stupidity, the habit of turning night into day was harmless or even useful, because it helped to rid the world prematurely of a lot of fools. But to-day the leading men of the community are also the busiest. Aristocracy implies activity, intellectual and otherwise. Hence there are few men in the higher ranks who have not their regular work to do during the day. To ask them after a day's hard labour to go to a dance beginning at midnight and ending at four or five is to ask them to commit suicide. Sensible men do not believe in slow suicide, hence they avoid dancing-parties as if such parties were held in small-pox hospitals.

Let society women throw their stupid conservatism to the winds. Let them arrange balls to begin at eight or nine and end at midnight or one, and "desirable" men will be only too eager to flock to assemblies which they now shun. The result will be a sudden and startling diminution in the number of old maids and bachelors.

It is the *moral duty* of mothers who have marriageable daughters to encourage this reform. Maternal love does not merely imply solicitude for the first twenty years of a daughter's life, but careful provision for the remainder of her life, covering twice that period, by enabling her to meet and choose a husband after her own heart.

EVOLUTION OF DANCE-MUSIC

Did space permit, it would be interesting to study in detail the dances of various epochs and countries, coloured, like the Love which originated them, by national peculiarities—the Polish mazourka and polonaise, the Spanish fandango, the Viennese waltz, the Parisian cancan, etc. Suffice it to note the great difference between the dances of a few generations ago and those of to-day, as shown most vividly in the evolution of dance-music.

The earliest dance-tunes are vocal, and were sung by the (professional) dancers themselves, in the days when the young were not yet allowed to meet, converse, and flirt and dance. Subsequently, the transference of dance-music to instruments played by others gave the dancers opportunity to perform more complicated figures, and made it possible to converse. But even as late as the eighteenth century dancing and dance-music were characterised by a stately reserve, slowness, and pompous dignity which showed at once that they had nothing to do with Romantic Love. It was not the fiery, passionate youths who danced these solemnly stupid minuets, gavottes, sarabandes, and allemandes, but the older folks, whose perruques, and collars, and frills, and bloated clothes would not have enabled them to execute rapid movements even if the warm blood of youth had coursed in their veins.

How all this artificiality and snail-like pomp has been brushed away by triumphant Romantic Love, which has secured for modern lovers the privilege of dancing together before they are married and cease to care for it! True, we still have the monotonous soporific quadrille, as if to remind us of bygone times; but the true modern dance is the round dance, which differs from the stately mediæval dance as a jolly rural picnic does from a formal morning call.

The difference between the mediæval and the modern dance is thus indicated by F. Bremer:—

"Peculiar to modern dance-music is the round dance, especially the waltz; and it is in consequence warmer than the older dance-music, more passionate in expression, in rhythm and modulation more sharply accented. As its creator we must regard Carl Maria von Weber, who, in his *Invitation to Dance*, struck the keynote through which subsequently, in the music of Chopin, Lanner, Strauss, Musard, etc., utterance was given to the whole gamut of dreamy, languishing, sentimental, ardent passion. The consequence was the displacement of the stately, measured dances by impetuous, chivalrous forms; and in place of the former naïve sentimentality and childish mirth, it is the *rapture of Love* that constitutes the spirit of modern dance-music."

Not to speak of more primitive dance-tunes, what a difference there is between the slow and dreary monotony of eighteenth century dances and a Viennese waltz of to-day! The vast superiority of a Strauss waltz lies in this—that it is no longer a mere rhythmic noise calculated to guide the steps, and skips, and bows, and evolutions of the dancers, but *the symphonic accompaniment to the first act in the drama of Romantic Love*. It recognises the fact that Courtship is the prime object of the dance. Hence, though still bound by the inevitable dance rhythm, Strauss is ever trying to break loose from it, to secure that freedom and variety of rhythm which is needed to give full utterance to passion. Note the slow, pathetic introductions; the signs in the score indicating an accelerated or retarded tempo when the waltz is played at a concert, where the uniformity of ballroom movement is not called for; note what subtle use he makes of all the other means of expressing amorous feeling—the wide melodic intervals, the piquant, stirring harmonies, the exquisitely melancholy flashes of instrumental colouring, alternating with cheerful moments, showing a subtle psychologic art of translating the Mixed Moods of Love into the language of tones.

In the waltzes, mazourkas and polonaises of Chopin we see still more strikingly that the true function of dance-music is amorous. Even as Dante's Love for Beatrice was too super-sensual, too ethereal for this world, so Chopin's dance-pieces are too subtle, too full of delicate *nuances* of *tempo* and Love episodes, to be adapted to a ballroom with ordinary mortals. Graceful fairies alone could dance a Chopin waltz; mortals are too heavy, too clumsy. They can follow an amorous Chopin waltz with the imagination alone, which is the abode of Romantic Love. To a Strauss waltz a hundred couples may make love at once, hence he writes for the orchestra; but Chopin wrote for the parlour piano, because the feelings he utters are too deep to be realised by more than two at a time—one who plays and one who listens, till their souls dance together in an ecstatic embrace of Mutual Sympathy.

THE DANCE OF LOVE

It is at Vienna, which has more feminine grace and beauty to the square mile than any other city in the world, that the art of dancing is to be seen in its greatest perfection. No wonder that it is the home of the Waltz-King, Johann Strauss; and that a Viennese feuilletonist has shown the deepest insight into the psychology of the dance in an article from which the following excerpts are taken:—

"The waltz has a creative, a rejuvenating power, which no other dance possesses. The skipping polka is characterised by a certain stiffness and angularity, a rhythm rather sober and old-fashioned. The galop is a wild hurricane, which moves along rudely and threatens to blow over everything that comes in its way; it is the most brutal of all dances, an enemy of all tender and refined feelings, a bacchanalian rushing up and down. . . .

"The waltz, therefore, remains as the only true and real dance. Waltzing is not walking, skipping, jumping, rushing, raving; it is a gentle floating and flying; from the heaviest men it seems to take away some of their materiality, to raise the most massive women from the ground into the air. True, the Viennese alone know how to dance it, as they alone know how to play it. . . .

"The waltz insists on a personal monopoly, on being loved for its own sake, and permits no vapid side-remarks regarding the fine weather, the hot room, the toilets of the ladies; the couple glide along hardly speaking a word; except that she may beg for a pause, or he, indefatigable, insatiable, intoxicated by the music and motion, the fragrance of flowers and ladies, invites her to a new flight around the hall. And yet is this mute dance the most eloquent, the most expressive and emotional, the most sensuous that could be imagined; and if the dancer has anything to say to his partner, let him mutely confide it to her in the sweet whirl of a waltz, for then the music is his advocate, then every bar pleads for him, every note is a *billet-doux*, every breath a declaration of love. Jealous husbands do not allow their wives to waltz with another man. They are right, for the waltz is the Dance of Love."

BALLET-DANCING

There is one more form of dancing which may be briefly alluded to, because it illustrates the hypocrisy of the average mortal as well as the rarity of true æsthetic taste. Solo ballet-dancing is admired not only by the bald-headed old men in the parquet, but there are critics who seriously discuss such dancing as if it were a fine art; generally lamenting the good old times of the great and graceful ballet-dancers. The truth is that ballet-dancing *never can be graceful*, as now practised. To secure graceful movement it is absolutely necessary to make use of the elasticity of the toes—to touch the ground at the place where the toes articulate with the middle foot, and to give the last push with the yielding great toe. Ballet-dancers, however, walk on the tips of their stiffened toes, the result of which is, as the anatomist, Professor Kollmann, remarks, that "their gait is deprived of all elasticity and becomes stiff, as in going on stilts."

It speaks well for the growing sensibility of mankind that this form of dancing is gradually losing favour. Like the vocal tight-rope dancing of the operatic *prime donne* with whom ballet-dancers are associated, their art is a mere circus-trick, gaped at as a difficult *tour de force*, but appealing in no sense to æsthetic sentiments.

These strictures, of course, apply merely to solo-dancing on tiptoe. The spectacular ballet, which delights the eye with kaleidoscopic colours and groupings, is quite another thing, and may be made highly artistic.

THE LOWER LIMBS

MUSCULAR DEVELOPMENT

The assumption by man of an erect attitude has modified and improved the appearance of his leg and thigh quite as marvellously as his feet. "In walking," says Professor Kollmann, "the weight of the body is alternately transferred from one foot to the other. Each one is obliged in locomotion to take its turn in supporting the whole body, which explains the great size of the muscles which make up man's calf. The ape's calf is smaller for the reason that these animals commonly go on all fours." Professor Carl Vogt gives these details: "No ape has such a cylindrical, *gradually diminishing* thigh; and we are justified in saying that man alone possesses thighs. The muscles of the leg are in man so accumulated as to form a calf, while in the ape they are more equally distributed; still, transitions are not wanting, since one of the greatest characteristics of the negro consists in his calfless leg." And again: "Man possesses, as contrasted with the ape, a distinctive character in the strength, *rotundity*, and length of the lower limb; especially in the thighs, which in most animals are shortened in proportion to the leg."

The words here italicised call attention to two of the qualities of Beauty—gradation and the curve of rotundity—which the lower limbs in their evolution are thus seen to be gradually approximating. Other improvements are seen in the greater smoothness, the more graceful and expressive gait resulting from the rounded but straight knee, etc.

The implication that savages are in the muscular development of their limbs intermediate between apes and civilised men calls for further testimony and explanation. Waitz states that "in regard to muscular power Indians are commonly inferior to Europeans;" and Mr. Herbert Spencer has collected much evidence of a similar nature. The Ostyaks have "thin and slender legs"; the Kamtchatdales "short and slender legs"; those of the Chinooks are "small and crooked"; and the African Akka have "short and bandy legs." The legs of Australians are "inferior in mass of muscle"; the gigantic Patagonians have limbs "neither so muscular nor so large-boned as their height and apparent bulk would induce one to suppose." Spencer likewise calls attention to the fact that relatively-inferior legs are "a trait which, remotely simian, is also repeated by the child of the civilised man"—which thus individually passes through the several stages of development that have successively characterised its ancestors.

Numerous exceptions are of course to be found to the rule that the muscular rotundity and plumpness of the limbs increases with civilisation. The lank shins which may be seen by the hundred among the bathers at our sea-coast resorts contrast disadvantageously with many photographs of savages; and tourists in Africa and among South American Indians and elsewhere have often enough noted the occurrence of individuals and tribes who would have furnished admirable models for sculptors. But this only proves, on the one hand, that "civilised" persons who are uncivilised in their neglect of the laws of Health, inevitably lose certain traits of Beauty which exercise alone can give; while, on the other hand, those "savages" who lead an active and healthy life are *in so far* civilised, and therefore enjoy the superior attractions bestowed by civilisation. Moreover, as Mr. Spencer suggests, " In combat, the power exercised by arm and trunk is limited by the power of the legs to withstand the strain thrown on them. Hence, apart from advantages in locomotion, the stronger-legged nations have tended to become, other things equal, dominant races."

"Rengger," says Darwin, "attributes the thin legs and thick arms of the Payaguas Indians to successive generations having passed nearly their whole lives in canoes, with their lower extremities motionless. Other writers have come to a similar conclusion in analogous cases."

Although savages have to hunt for a living and occasionally go to war, they are essentially a lazy crew, taking no more exercise than necessary; which accounts for the fact that, with the exceptions noted, their muscular development is inferior to that of higher races.

BEAUTIFYING EXERCISE

One of the most discouraging aspects of modern life is the growing tendency toward concentration of the population in large cities. Not only is the air less salubrious in cities than in the country, but the numerous cheap facilities for riding discourage the habit of walking. London is one of the healthiest cities, and the English the most vigorous race, in the world; yet it is said that it is difficult to trace a London family down through five generations. Few Paris families can, it is said, be traced even through three generations. Without constant rural accessions cities would tend to become depopulated.

The enormous importance of exercise for Health and Beauty, which are impossible without it, is vividly brought out in this statement of Kollmann's: "Muscles which are thoroughly exercised do not only retain their strength, but increase in circumference and power, in man as in animals. The flesh is then firm, and coloured intensely red. In a paralysed arm the muscles are degenerated, and have lost a portion of one of their most important constituents—albumen. Repeated contractions strengthen a muscle, because motion accelerates the circulation of the blood and the nutrition of the tissues. What a great influence this has on the whole body may be inferred from the fact that the organs of locomotion—the skeleton and muscles—make up more than 82 per cent of the substance of the body. With this enormous proportion of bone and muscle, it is obvious that exercise is essential to bodily health."

Exercise in a gymnasium is useful but monotonous; and too often the benefits are neutralised by the insufficient provision for fresh air, without which exercise is worse than useless. Hence the superiority of open-air games—base-ball, tennis, rowing, riding, swimming, etc., to the addiction to which the English owe so much of their superior physique. Tourists in Canada invariably notice the wonderful figures of the women, which they owe largely to their fondness for skating. "Beyond question," says the *Lancet*, "skating is one of the finest sports, especially for ladies. It is graceful, healthy, stimulating to the muscles, and it develops in a very high degree the important faculty of balancing the body and preserving perfect control over the whole of the muscular system, while bringing certain muscles into action at will. Moreover, there is this about it which is of especial value: it trains by exercise the power of intentionally inducing and maintaining a continuous contraction of the muscles of the lower extremity The joints, hip, knee, and ankle are firmly fixed or rather kept steadily under control, while the limbs are so set by their muscular apparatus that they form, as it were, part of the skate that glides over the smooth surface. To skate well and gracefully is a very high accomplishment indeed, and perhaps one of the very best exercises in which young women and girls can engage with a view to healthful development."

For the acquisition of a graceful gait women need such exercise more even than men; and while engaged in it they should pay especial attention to exercising the left side of the body. On this point Sir Charles Bell has made the following suggestive remarks:—

"We see that opera-dancers execute their more difficult feats on the right foot, but their preparatory exercises better evince the natural weakness of the left limb; in order to avoid awkwardness in the public exhibitions, they are obliged to give double practice to the left leg; and if they neglect to do so an ungraceful preference to the right side will be remarked. In walking behind a person we seldom see an equalised motion of the body; the tread is not so firm upon the left foot, the toe is not so much turned out, and a greater push is made with the right. From the peculiar form of woman, and from the elasticity of her step, resulting from the motion of the ankle rather than of the haunches, the defect of the left foot, when it exists, is more apparent in her gait."

Those who wish to acquire a graceful gait will find several useful hints in this extract from Professor Kollmann's *Plastische Anatomie*, p. 506:—

"Human gait, it is well known, is subject to individual variations. Differences are to be noted not only in rapidity of motion, but as regards the position of the trunk and the movements of the limbs, within certain limits. For instance, the gait of very fat persons is somewhat vacillating; other persons acquire a certain dignity of gait by bending and stretching their limbs as little as possible while taking long steps; and others still bend their knees very much, which gives a slovenly character to their gait. And as regards the attitude of the trunk, a different effect is given according as it is inclined backwards or forwards, or executes superfluous movements in the same direction or to the sides. All these peculiarities make an impression on our eyes, while our ears are impressed at the same time by the differences in rapidity of movement, so that we learn to recognise our friends by the sound of their walk as we do by the quality of their voice."

Bell states that "upwards of fifty muscles of the arm and hand may be demonstrated, which must all consent to the simplest action." Walking is a no less complicated affair, to which the attention of men of science has been only quite recently directed. The new process of instantaneous photography has been found very useful, but much remains to be done before the mystery of a graceful gait can be considered solved. If some skilled photographer would go to Spain and take a number of instantaneous pictures of Andalusian girls, the most graceful beings in the world, in every variety of attitude and motion, he might render most valuable service to the cause of personal æsthetics.

The time will come, no doubt, when dancing masters and mistresses will consider the teaching of the waltz and the lancers only the crudest and easiest part of their work, and when they will have advanced classes who will be instructed in the refinements of movement as carefully and as intelligently as professors of music teach their pupils the proper use of the parts and muscles of the hand, to attain a delicate and varied touch. The majority of women might make much more progress in the art of gracefulness than they ever will in music ; and is not the poetry of motion as noble and desirable an object of study as any other fine art ?

FASHIONABLE UGLINESS

It is the essence of fashion to exaggerate everything to the point of ugliness. Instead of trying to remedy the disadvantages to their gait resulting from anatomical peculiarities (just referred to in a quotation from Bell), women frequently take pains to deliberately exaggerate them. As Alexander Walker remarks : "The largeness of the pelvis and the approximation of the knees influence the gait of woman, and render it vacillating and unsteady. Conscious of this, women, in countries where the nutritive system in general and the pelvis in particular are large, affect a greater degree of this vacillating unsteadiness. An example of this is seen in the lateral and rotatory motion which is given to the pelvis in walking by certain classes of the women in London."

The Egyptians and Arabians consider this ludicrous rotatory motion a great fascination, and have a special name for it—Ghung.

But Fashion, the handmaid of ugliness, is not content with aping the bad taste of Arabians and Egyptians. It goes several steps lower than that, down to the Hottentots. The latest hideous craze of Fashion, against which not one woman in a hundred had taste or courage enough to revolt—the bustle or "dress-improver"(!)—was simply the milliner's substitute for an anatomical peculiarity natural to some African savages.

"It is well known," says Darwin, "that with many Hottentot women the posterior part of the body projects in a wonderful manner; they are steatopygous; and Sir Andrew Smith is certain that this peculiarity is greatly admired by the men. He once saw a woman who was considered a beauty, and she was so immensely developed behind, that when seated on level ground she could not rise, and had to push herself along until she came to a slope. Some of the women in various negro tribes have the same peculiarity; and, according to Burton, the Somal men 'are said to choose their wives by ranging them in a line, and by picking her out who projects farthest *a tergo*. Nothing can be more hateful to a negro than the opposite form.'"

Evidently "civilised" and savage women do not differ as regards Fashion, the handmaid of ugliness. But the men do. While the male Hottentots admire the natural steatopyga of their women, civilised men, without exception, detest the artificial imitation of it, which makes a woman look and walk like a deformed dromedary.

THE CRINOLINE CRAZE

The bustle is not only objectionable in itself as a hideous deformity and a revival of Hottentot taste, but still more as a probable forerunner of that most unutterably vulgar article of dress ever invented by Fashion—the crinoline. For we read that when, in

1856, the crinoline came in again, it was preceded by the "inelegant bustle in the upper part of the skirt"; and it is a notorious fact that cunning milliners are making strenuous efforts every year to reintroduce the crinoline.

In their abhorrence of the crinoline men do not stand alone. There are several refined women to-day who would absolutely refuse to submit to the tyranny of Fashion if it should again prescribe the crinoline. One of these is evidently Mrs. Haweis, who in *The Art of Beauty* remarks that "The crinoline superseded all our *attention to posture;* whilst our long trains, which can hardly look inelegant [?] even on clumsy persons, make small ankles or thick ones a matter of little moment. We have become inexpressibly slovenly. We no longer study how to walk, perhaps the most difficult of all actions to do gracefully. Our fashionable women stride and loll in open defiance of elegance," etc. And again : "This gown in outline simply looks *like a very ill-shaped wine-glass upside down.* The wide crinoline entirely *conceals every natural grace of attitude."*

Another lady, writing in the *Atlantic Monthly* (1859), remarks concerning the crinoline : "A woman in this rig hangs in her skirts *like a clapper in a bell ;* and I never meet one without being tempted to take her by the neck and ring her."

About 1710, says a writer in the *Encyclopædia Britannica,* "as if resolved that their figures should rival their heads in extravagance, they introduced the hooped petticoat, at first worn in such a manner as to give to the person of the wearer below her very tightly-laced waist a contour *resembling the letter V inverted*—Λ. The hooped dresses, thus introduced, about 1740 attained to an enormous expansion; and being worn at their full circumference immediately below the waist, they in many ways emulated the most outrageous of the fardingales of the Elizabethan period."

"About 1744 hoops are mentioned as so extravagant," says Chambers's *Encyclopædia*, "that *a woman occupied the space of six men.*" .George IV. had the good taste to abolish them by royal command, but they were revived in 1856. The newspapers of two decades ago daily contained accounts of accidents due to the idiotic crinoline. "The *Spectator* dealt out much cutting, though playful, raillery at the hoops of his day, but apparently with little effect; and equally unavailing are the satires of *Punch* and other caricaturists of the present time against the hideous fashion of crinoline. . . . Owing to its prevalence, church-pews that formerly held seven are now let for six, and yet feel rather crowded. The hoops are sometimes made with a *circumference of four or even five yards.*"

It is universally admitted that the human form, in its perfection, is Nature's *chef d'œuvre*—the most finished specimen of her workmanship. Yet the accounts of savage taste given by travellers and anthropologists show that the savage is never satisfied with the human outlines as God made them, but constantly mars and mutilates them by altering the shape of the head, piercing the nose, filing or colouring the teeth, enlarging the lips to enormous dimensions, favouring an adipose bustle, etc. This is precisely what modern Fashion, the handmaid of ugliness, does. We have just seen how fashionable women, unable to comprehend the beauty of the human form, have for several generations endeavoured to give it the shape of "a very ill-shaped wine-glass, upside down," "a clapper in a bell," or "the letter V inverted." And concerning Queen Elizabeth the *Atlantic* writer already quoted says very pithily: "What with stomachers and pointed waist and fardingale, and sticking in here and sticking out there, and ruffs and cuffs, and ouches and jewels and puckers, she looks *like a hideous flying insect* with expanded wings, seen through a microscope —not at all like a woman."

Fortunately, for the moment, the crinoline, like the fardingale, is not "in fashion." But, as already stated, there is considerable danger of a new invasion every year; and, should Fashion proclaim its edict, no doubt the vast majority of women would follow, as they did a decade or two ago. In the interest of good taste, as of common sense, it is therefore necessary to speak with brutal frankness on this subject. There is good evidence to show that the crinoline originated in the desire of an aristocratic dame of low moral principles to conceal the evidences of a crime. Hence the original French name for the crinoline—*Cache-Bâtard.* Will respectable and refined women consent once more to have the fashion set for them by a courtesan?

THE WAIST

THE BEAUTY CURVE

In a well-shaped waist, as in every other part of the body, the curved line of Beauty, with its delicate gradations, exercises a great charm. Examination of a Greek statue of the best period, male or female, or of the goddess of beauty in the Pagoda at Bangalur, India, shows a slight inward curve at the waist, whereas in early Greek and Egyptian art this curve is absent. The waist, therefore, like the feet and limbs, appears to have been gradually moulded into accordance with the line of Beauty—a notion which is also supported by the following remarks in Tylor's *Anthropology:* "If fairly chosen photographs of Kaffirs be compared with a classic model such as the Apollo, it will be noticed that the trunk of the African has a somewhat wall-sided straightness, wanting in the inward slope which gives fineness to the waist, and in the expansion below, which gives breadth across the hips, these being two of the most noticeable points in the classic model which our painters recognise as an ideal of manly beauty."

In woman, owing to the greater dimensions of her pelvis, this curvature is more pronounced than in man; yet even in woman it must be slight if the laws of Health and Beauty are to suffer no violation. "*Moderation*" is the one word which Mr. Ruskin says he would have inscribed in golden letters over the door of every school of art. For "the least appearance of violence or extravagance, of the want of moderation and restraint, is," as he remarks, " destructive of all beauty whatsoever in everything—colour, form, motion, language, or thought—giving rise to that which in colour we call glaring, in form inelegant, in motion ungraceful, in language coarse, in thought undisciplined, in all unchastened; which qualities are in everything most painful, because the signs of disobedient and irregular operation. And herein we at last find the reason of that which has been so often noted respecting the subtility and almost invisibility of natural curves and colours, and why it is that we look on those lines as least beautiful which fall into wide and far license of curvature, and as most beautiful which approach nearest (so that the curvilinear character be distinctly asserted) to the government of the right line, as in the pure and severe curves of the draperies of the religious painters," etc.

THE WASP-WAIST MANIA

But Fashion, the handmaid of ugliness, too vulgar to appreciate the exquisite beauty of slight and subtle curvature, makes woman's waist the most maltreated and deformed part of her body. There is not one woman in a hundred who does not deliberately destroy twenty per cent of her Personal Beauty by the way in which she reduces the natural dimensions of her waist. There is, indeed, ground to believe that the main reason why the bustle, and even the crinoline, are not looked on with abhorrence by all women is because they aid the corset in making the waist look smaller by contrast. The Wasp-waist Mania is therefore the disease which most imperatively calls for cure. But the task seems almost hopeless; for, as a female writer remarks, it is almost as difficult to cure a woman of the corset habit as a man of intemperance in drink.

"The injurious custom of tight lacing," says Planché in his *Cyclopædia of Costumes*, "'a custom fertile in disease and death,' appears to have been introduced by the Normans as early as the twelfth century; and the romances of the Middle Ages teem with allusions to and laudations of the wasp-like waists of the dames and demoiselles of the period.... Chaucer, describing the carpenter's wife, says her body was 'gentyll and small as a weasel'; and the depraved taste extended to Scotland. Dunbar, in *The Thistle and the Rose*, describing some beautiful women, observes—

"'Their middles were as small as wands.'

And to make their middles as small as possible has been ever since an unfortunate mania with the generality of the fair sex, to the detriment of their health and the distortion of their forms."

Ever since 1602, when Felix Plater raised his voice against the corset, physicians have written against tight lacing. But not only has it been found impossible to cure this mania, even its causes have remained a mystery to the present day. Certainly no man can understand the problem. Is it simply the average woman's lack of taste that urges her thus to mutilate her Personal Beauty? Is it the admiration of a few vulgar "mashers" and barber's pets—since educated men detest wasp-waists? Or is it simply the proverbial feminine craze for emulating one another and arousing envy by excelling in some extravagance of dress, no matter at what cost? This last suggestion is probably the true solution of the problem. The only satisfaction a woman can get from having a wasp-waist is the envy of other silly women. What a glorious recompense for her æsthetic suicide, her invalidism, and her humiliating confession that she considers the natural shape of God's masterwork—the female body—inferior in beauty to the contours of the lowly wasp!

With this ignoble pleasure derived from the envy of silly women and the admiration of vulgar men, compare a few of the disadvantages resulting from tight lacing. They are of two kinds—hygienic and æsthetic.

Hygienic Disadvantages.—Surely no woman can look without a shudder at a fashionable Parisian figure placed side by side with the Venus of Milo in Professor Flower's *Fashion in Deformity*, in Mrs. Haweis's *Art of Beauty*, or in Behnke and Brown's *Voice, Song, and Speech;* or look without horror at the skeletons showing the excessive compression of the lower ribs brought about by fashionable lacing, and the injurious displacement, in consequence, of some of the most important vital organs. Nor can any young man who does not desire to marry a foredoomed invalid, and raise sickly children, fail to be cured for ever of his love for any wasp-waisted girl if he will take the trouble to read the account of the terrible female maladies resulting from lacing, given in Dr. Gaillard Thomas's famous treatise on the *Diseases of Women*, in the chapter on "Improprieties in Dress." To cite only one sentence: Women, he says, subject their waist to a "constriction which, in autopsy, will sometimes be found to have *left the impress of the ribs upon the liver, producing depressions corresponding to them.*"

Says Dr. J. J. Pope: "The German physiologist, Sömmering, has enumerated no fewer than *ninety-two diseases* resulting from tight lacing. . . . 'But I do not lace tightly,' every lady is ready to answer. No woman ever did, if we accept her own statement. Yet stay. Why does your corset unclasp with a snap? *And why do you involuntarily take a deep breath directly it is loosened?*" Young ladies who imagine they do not wear too tight stays, inasmuch as they can still insert their hand, will find the fallacy and danger of this reasoning exposed in Mr. B. Roth's *Dress: its Sanitary Aspect.*

The last line which I have italicised is of extreme significance. Perhaps the greatest of all evils resulting from tight lacing is that it discourages or *prevents deep breathing*, which is so absolutely essential to the maintenance of health and beauty. The "heaving bosom" of a maiden may be a fine poetic expression, but it indicates that the maiden wears stays and breathes at the wrong (upper) end of her lungs. "The fact of a patient breathing in this manner is noted by a physician as a grave symptom, because it indicates mischief of a vital nature in lungs, heart, or other important organ." Healthy breathing should be chiefly costal or abdominal; but this is made impossible by the corset, which compresses the lower ribs, till, instead of being widely apart below, they meet in the middle, and thus prevent the lungs from expanding and receiving the normal share of oxygen, the only true elixir of life, youth, and beauty.

This wrong breathing, due to tight lacing, also causes "congestion of the vessels of the neck and throat. . . . gasping, jerking, and fatigue in inspiration, and unevenness, trembling, and undue vibration in the production and emission of vocal tone."

Further, as the *Lancet* points out, " tight stays are a common cause of so-called 'weak' spine, due to weakness of muscles of the back." Lacing prevents the abdominal muscles from exercising their natural functions—alternate relaxation and contraction : " A tight-laced pair of stays acts precisely as a splint to the trunk, and prevents or greatly impedes the action of the chief back muscles, which therefore become weakened. The unfortunate wearer feels her spine weaken, thinks she wants more support, so laces herself still tighter ; she no doubt does get some support in this way, but at what a terrible cost !"

In regard to tight corsets, as another physician has aptly remarked, women are like the victims of the opium habit, who also daily feel the need of a larger dose of their stimulant, every increment of which adds a year to their age, and brings them a few steps nearer disease and ugly decrepitude.

Æsthetic Disadvantages.—Among the æsthetic disadvantages resulting from the Wasp-waist Mania, the following may be mentioned, besides the loss of a clear, mellow, musical voice already referred to :—

(1) A stiff, inflexible waist, with a coarsely exaggerated contour, in place of the slight and subtle curvature so becoming to woman. In other words, a violation of the first law of personal æsthetics— imposing the shape of a vulgar garment on the

human form, instead of making the dress follow the outlines of the body.

(2) A sickly, sallow complexion, pale lips, a red nose, lack of buoyancy, general feebleness, lassitude, apathy, and stupidity, resulting from the fact that the compression of the waist induces an oxygen-famine. The eyes lose their sparkle and love-inspiring magic, the features are perceptibly distorted, the brow is prematurely wrinkled, and the expression and temper are soured by the constant discomfort that has to be silently endured.

(3) Ugly shoulders. A woman's shoulders should be sloping and well rounded, like every other part of her body. Regarding the common feminine deformity of square shoulders Drs. Brinton and Napheys remark, in their work on *Personal Beauty*, that "in four cases out of five it has been brought about by too close-fitting corsets, which press the shoulder-blades behind, and collar-bones in front, too far upwards, and thus ruin the appearance of the shoulders."

(4) An ugly bust. Tight lacing "flattens and displaces the breasts."

(5) Clumsiness. The corset is ruinous to grace. "Almost daily," says Dr. Alice B. Stockham (*Tokology*), "women come to my office [in Chicago] burdened with bands and heavy clothing, every vital organ restricted by dress. It is not unusual to count from *sixteen to eighteen thicknesses of cloth* worn tightly about the pliable structure of the waist." And Dr. Lennox Browne advances the following crushing *argumentum ad feminam* :—

"It is impossible for the stiffly-corseted girl to be other than inelegant and ungraceful in her movements. Her imprisoned waist, with its flabby muscles, has no chance of performing beautiful undulatory movements. In the ballroom the ungraceful motions of our stiff-figured ladies are bad enough; there is no possibility for poetry of motion; but nowhere is this more ludicrously and, to the thoughtful, painfully manifest than in the tennis court. Let any one watch the movements of ladies as compared with those of male players, and the absolute ugliness of the female figure, with its stiff, unyielding, deformed, round waist, will at once be seen. Ladies can only bend the body from the hip-joint. All that wonderfully contrived set of hinges, with their connected muscles, in the elastic column of the spine, is unable to act from the shoulders downwards; and their figures remind one of the old-fashioned modern Dutch doll."

CORPULENCE AND LEANNESS

Many women consider the corset necessary as a figure-improver, especially if they suffer from excessive fatness. They will be surprised to hear that the corset is one of the principal causes of their corpulence. Says Professor M. Williams: "There is one horror which no lady can bear to contemplate, viz. fat. What is fat? It is an accumulation of unburnt body-fuse. How can we get rid of it when accumulated in excess? Simply by burning it away—this burning being done by means of the oxygen inhaled by the lungs. If, as Mr. Lennox Browne has shown, a lady with normal lung capacity of 125 cubic inches, reduces this to 78 inches by means of her stays, and attains 118 inches all at once on leaving them off, it is certain that her prospects of becoming fat and flabby as she advances towards middle age are greatly increased by tight lacing, and the consequent suppression of natural respiration."

Thus corpulence may be put down as a sixth—or rather seventh—æsthetic disadvantage resulting from the use of corsets.

The reason why women, although inferior to men in muscular development, have softer and rounder forms, is because there is a greater natural tendency in women than in men towards the accumulation of fatty tissue under the skin. The least excess of this adipose tissue is, however, as fatal as emaciation to that admiration of Personal Beauty which constitutes the essence of Love. Leanness repels the æsthetico-amorous sense because it obliterates the round contours of beauty, exposes the sinews and bones, and thus suggests old age and disease. Corpulence repels it because it destroys all delicacy of form, all grace of movement, and in its exaggerated forms may indeed be looked upon as a real disease imperatively calling for medical treatment; as Dr. Oscar Maas shows most clearly and concisely in his pamphlet on the "Schwenninger Cure," which should be read by all who suffer from obesity.

Although the very "father of medicine," Hippokrates, studied the subject of corpulence, and formulated rules for curing it, doctors still disagree regarding some of the details of its treatment. Some forbid all fatty food, others prescribe it in small quantities, and Dr. Ebstein specially recommends fat viands and sauces as preventives; but the preponderance of the best medical opinion is against him. Dr. Say recommends the drinking of very large quantities of tea, while Professor Oertel urges the diminution of fluids in the body, first by drinking little, and secondly by inducing copious perspiration, either artificially (by hot air and steam baths, etc.), or, what is much better, by brisk daily exercise. Dr. Schwenninger, who secured so much fame by reducing Bismarck's weight about 40 pounds, forbids the taking of liquids during or within an hour or two of meal-time; in other words, he counsels his patients not to eat and drink at the same time.

On the two most important points all authorities are practically agreed. They are that the patient must avoid food which contains large quantities ot starch and sugar (such as cake, pastry, potatoes, bread, pudding, honey, syrup, etc.); and secondly, that he must take as much exercise as possible in the open air, because during walking the bodily fat is consumed as fuel, to keep the machine going.

The notorious Mr. Banting, who reduced his weight in a year from 202 to 150 pounds, "lived on beef, mutton, fish, bacon, dry toast and biscuit, poultry, game, tea, coffee, claret, and sherry in small quantities, and a night-cap of gin, whisky, brandy, or wine. He *abstained* from the following articles: pork, veal, salmon, eels, herrings, sugar, milk, and all sorts of vegetables grown underground, and nearly all fatty and farinaceous substances. He daily drank 43 ounces of liquids. On this diet he kept himself for seven years at 150 pounds. He found, what other experience confirms, that *sugar was the most powerful of all fatteners*" (Dr. G. M.

Beard, in *Eating and Drinking*, a most entertaining and useful little volume).

Lean persons wishing to increase their weight need only reverse the directions here given as regards the choice or avoidance of certain articles of food. Not so, however, with regard to exercise. If you wish to reduce your corpulence, take exercise; if you wish to increase your weight, again take exercise. The apparent paradox lurking in this rule is easily explained. If you are too fat and walk a great deal, you burn up the superfluous *fat* and lose weight. If you are too lean and walk a great deal you increase the bulk of your *muscles*, and thus gain weight. Moreover, you greatly stimulate your appetite, and become able to eat larger quantities of sweet and starchy food—more than enough to counteract the wear and tear caused by the exercise.

Muscle is the plastic material of beauty. Fat should only be present in sufficient quantity to prevent the irregular outlines of the muscles from being too conspicuously indicated, at the expense of rounded smoothness. What the ancient Greeks thought on this subject is vividly shown in the following remarks by Dr. Maas: "According to the unanimous testimony of Thukydides, Plato, Xenophon, the gymnastic exercises to which the Greeks were so passionately addicted, and which constituted, as is well known, a very essential part of the public education of the young, had for their avowed object the prevention of undue corpulence, since an excessive paunch did not only offend the highly-developed æsthetic sense of this talented nation, but was justly regarded as an impediment to bodily activity. In order, therefore, to make the youths not only beautiful, but also vigorous and able to resist hardship, and thus more capable of serving their country, they were, from their childhood, and uninterruptedly, exercised daily in running, wrestling, throwing the discus, etc.; so that the prevention of corpulence was practically raised to a formal state-maxim, and as such enforced occasionally with unyielding persistence."

The ruinous consequences of an exaggerated abdomen to the harmonious proportions of the body, and to grace of attitude and gait, are so universally known that it would be superfluous to apply any of our negative tests of Beauty—such as the facts that apes and savages are commonly characterised by protuberant bellies, and that intemperance and gluttony have the same disastrous effect on Personal Beauty. In civilised communities, indolence and beer-drinking are the chief causes predisposing to corpulence. In Bavaria, where enormous quantities of beer are consumed, almost all the men are deformed by obesity; but in other countries, as a rule, women suffer more from this anomaly than men, because they lead a less active life.

It may be stated as a general rule that girls under eighteen are too slight and women over thirty too heavy—"fat and forty." This calamity is commonly looked on as one of the inevitable dispensations of Providence, whereas it is simply a result of indolence and ignorance. With a little care in dieting, and two or three hours a day devoted to walking, rowing, tennis, swimming, dancing, etc., any young lady can add ten to fifteen pounds to her weight in one summer, or reduce it by that amount, as may be desired. But as the consumption of enormous quantities of fresh air by the unimprisoned lungs is the absolute condition of success in this beautifying process, it is useless to attempt it without laying aside the corset.

The plea that corsets are needed to hold up the heavy clothing is of no moment. Women, like men, should wear their clothing suspended from the shoulder, which is a great deal more conducive to health, comfort, and gracefulness than the clumsy fashion of attaching everything to the waist.

Still less weight can be attached to the monstrous argument that women need stays for support. What an insulting proposition to assert that civilised woman is so imperfectly constructed that she alone of all created beings needs artificial surgical support to keep her body in position! If there are any women so very corpulent or so very lean that they need a corset as a figure-improver or a support, then let them have it for heaven's sake, and look upon themselves as subjects ripe for medical treatment. What is objected to here is that strong, healthy, well-shaped girls should deform themselves deliberately by wearing tight, unshapely corsets, rankly offensive to the æsthetic sense.

THE FASHION FETISH ANALYSED

Once more the question must be asked, "Why do women wear such hideous things as crinolines, bustles, and corsets, so universally abhorred by men?" Is it because they are inferior to men in æsthetic taste? Is Schopenhauer right when he says that "women are and remain, on the whole, the most absolute and incurable Philistines?" They are deficient in objectivity, he adds: "hence they have no real intelligence or appreciation for music or poetry, or the plastic arts; and if they make any pretences of this sort, it is only apish affectation to gratify their vanity. Hence it would be more correct to call them the *unæsthetic* than the beautiful sex."

The pessimistic woman-hater no doubt exaggerates. Yet—without alluding to the paucity of women who have distinguished themselves in the fine arts—is it credible that the average woman would so readily submit to a repulsive fashion like the bustle, or a hat "adorned" with the corpse of a murdered bird, if she had even a trace of æsthetic feeling? If women had the refined æsthetic taste with which they are commonly credited, is it conceivable that they would voluntarily adopt the African bustle, because fashionable, in preference to a more becoming style? Have you ever heard that a person of acknowledged musical taste, for example, gave up his violin or piano to learn the African banjo, because that happened to be the fashionable instrument?

Yet there are, no doubt, many women whose eyes even custom cannot blind to the hideousness of most Parisian fashions. But they have not the courage to show their superior taste in their dresses, being overawed and paralysed in presence of a monstrous idol, the Fashion Fetish.

Never has a stone image, consecrated by cunning priests, exercised a more magic influence on a superstitious heathen's mind than the invisible Fashion Fetish on the modern feminine intellect. It is both amusing and pathetic to hear a woman exclaim: "Our women are most blind and thoughtless followers of fashions still imposed upon them, *Heaven knows wherefore and by whom*" (Mrs. Haweis).

So great is the awe in which this Fetish is held that no one has yet dared to lay violent hands on it. Yet if we now knock it on the head, we shall find it hollow inside; and the fragments, subjected to chemical analysis, show that they consist of the following five elements:—

(1) *Vulgar Display of Wealth.*—A certain number of rich people, being unable to distinguish themselves from poorer mortals in any other way, make a parade of their money by constantly introducing changes in the fashion of their apparel which those who have less income are unable to adopt at once. This, and not the love of novelty, is the real cause of the minute variations in styles constantly introduced. Of course it is generally understood that to boast of your wealth is as vulgar as to boast of your wit or wisdom; but this makes no difference, for Fashion in its very essence is vulgar.

(2) *Milliners' Cunning.*—Milliners grow fat on fashionable extravagance. Hence it is the one object of their life to encourage this extravagance. So they constantly invent new styles, to prevent women from wearing the same dress more than one season. And every customer is slyly flattered into the belief that nothing was ever so becoming to her as the latest style, though it probably makes her look like a fright. As a little flattery goes a great way with most women, the milliner's hypocrisy escapes detection. "The persons who devise fashions

are not artists in the best sense of the word, nor are they persons of culture or taste," as Mr. E. L. Godkin remarks: "their business is not to provide beautiful costumes but new ones."

It is to such scheming and unscrupulous artisans that women entrust the care of their personal appearance. And they will continue doing so until they are more generally taught the elements of the fine arts and a love of beauty in Nature.

To make sure of a rich harvest, milliners, when a new fashion has appeared, manufacture all their goods in that style, so that it is almost impossible to buy any others, all of which are declared "bad form." And their poor victims meekly submit to this tyranny!

(3) *Tyranny of the Ugly Majority.*—This is another form of tyranny from which ladies suffer. Most women are ugly and ungraceful, and resent the contrast which beautiful women, naturally and becomingly attired, would present to their own persons: hence they favour the crinolette, the bustle, the corset, the long, trailing dresses, the sleeve-puffs at the shoulders, etc., because such fashionable devices make all women look equally ugly and ungraceful.

Mrs. Armytage throws light on the origin of some absurd fashions when she refers to the cases of "the patches first applied to hide an ugly wen; of cushions carried to equalise strangely-deformed hips; of long skirts to cover ugly feet; and long shoes to hide an excrescence on the toe."

Surely it is sufficient to expose the origin of such fashions to make sensible women turn away from them in disgust. There are indeed indications that the handsome women have at last begun to find out the trick which the ugly majority have been playing on them; and many are now dressing in such a way as to show their personal beauty to advantage, undaunted by the fact that ugly women pretend to be shocked at short dresses which allow a pretty ankle to be seen, and jerseys which reveal the outlines of a beautiful bust and waist.

(4) *Cowardice.*—Many women adopt a fashion which they dislike simply because they do not dare to face the remark of a rival that they are not in fashion. As one of them frankly confesses: "We women dress not to be simple, genuine, and harmonious, or even to please you men, but *to brave each other's criticism.*" A noble motive, truly!

One is often tempted to doubt the old saying that the first desire of women is to be considered beautiful, on observing how ready they are to sacrifice fifty per cent or more of their beauty for the sake of being in fashion. Last summer, for instance, the edict seems to have gone forth that the hair was no longer to be allowed to form a graceful fringe over the forehead, but was to be combed back tightly. So back it was combed, and beautiful faces became rarer than ever. Leigh Hunt had written in vain that the hair should be brought over large bare foreheads "as vines are trailed over a wall." Théophile Gautier, "the most perfect poet in respect of poetical form that France has ever produced" (Saintsbury), agreed with Schopenhauer regarding woman's æsthetic sense: "Women," he says, "have only the sense of fashion and not that of beauty. A woman will always find beautiful the most abominable fashion if it is the *genre suprême* to wear that style." He commends the women of Granada for their good taste in preferring their lovely mantillas to the hideous French hats, and hopes Spain may never be invaded by French fashions and milliners.

(5) *Sheepishness.*—It may seem ungallant to apply this term to the conduct of a woman who imitates the habits of a sheep; but, after all, which is the more gallant action: to applaud a woman's self-chosen ugliness, or, at least, to ignore it for fear of offending her; or, on the other hand, to restore her beauty by boldly holding up the mirror and allowing her to see herself as others see her? It is the nature of a flock of sheep to jump into the sea without a moment's hesitation if their leader does so. It is the nature of fashionable women to commit æsthetic suicide if their leader sets the example. Where is the difference?

It is surprising that Darwin did not refer to Fashion as furnishing a most convincing proof of his theory that men are descended from apelike ancestors. One of the ape's most conspicuous traits is imitativeness—blind, silly, slavish imitation: hence the verb "to ape." Blind, silly, slavish imitation is also the essence of Fashion. Imitativeness implies a low order of mind, a lack of originality. The more a man is intellectually removed from the ape, the less is he inclined to imitate blindly. Men of genius are a law unto themselves, while inferior minds can only re-echo or plagiarise. Just so the prevalent anxiety to be in fashion is a tacit confession of mental inferiority, of insufficient independence of taste and originality to choose a style suited to one's individual requirements.

INDIVIDUALISM *VERSUS* FASHION

Fashion is a deadly enemy of Romantic Love, not only because it makes women sacrifice their Beauty to unhealthful garments and habits, but because it obliterates *individuality*, on which the ardour of Love depends. " Why don't girls marry ? " asks Mrs. Haweis. " Because the press is great, and girls are undistinguishable in the crowd. The distinguishable ones marry —those who are beautiful or magnetic in some way, whose characters have some definite colouring, and who can make their *individuality* felt. I would have said—who can make themselves in any way conspicuous, but that the word has been too long associated with an *undesirable* prominence. Yet after all, prominence is the thing needed—prominence of character, or *individuality*. Men, so to speak, pitch upon the girls they can see: those who are completely negative, unnoticeable, colourless, formless, invisible, are left behind."

Women, in their eagerness to sacrifice their individuality to Fashion, forget that *fashion leaders are never in fashion*, *i.e.* that *they* always adopt a new style as soon as the crowd has aped them : wherefore it is doubly silly to join the apes.

Mlle. Sarah Bernhardt never allows a corset to deform her figure and mar her movements : and who has not had occasion to admire the inimitable grace of this actress ? But how many women have the courage thus to sacrifice Fashion to Grace and Beauty ?

Yet, notwithstanding the continuance of the corset and the bustle mania and Parisian hats, it may be asserted that women are just at present more sensibly dressed than they have been for some generations, and there is *some* disposition to listen to the artistic and hygienic advice of reformers. Unfortunately, the history of Fashion does not tend to confirm any optimistic hopes that may be based on this fact. There have been periods heretofore when women became comparatively sensible, only to relapse again into utter barbarism. Thus we read that "after the straight gown came the fardingale, which in turn developed into the hoop with its concomitants of patches, paint, and high-heeled shoes." Then came the reaction: "Short waists and limp, clinging draperies came in to expose every contour; stays and corsets were for a time discredited, only to be reintroduced, and with them the whole cycle of fashions which had once already had their day."

Experience shows that argumentation, ridicule, malicious or good-natured, and satire, are equally powerless against Fashion. Progress can only be hoped for in two ways—by instructing women in the elementary laws of beauty in nature and mankind, and by destroying the superstitious halo around the word *Fashion*. It has just been shown that a disposition to imitate a fashion set by others is always a sign of inferior intellect and rudimentary taste; and the time no doubt will come when this fact will be generally recognised, and when it will be considered anything but a compliment to have it said that one follows the flock of fashionable imitators.

The progress of democratic institutions and sentiments will aid in emancipating women from the slavery of Fashion. Empresses who can set the fashion for two continents are becoming scarce; and the woman of the future will no doubt open her eyes wide in astonishment on reading that in the nineteenth century most women allowed some mysterious personage to prescribe what they should wear. "Can it be *possible*," she will exclaim, "that my poor dear grandmothers did not know that what is food for one person is poison for another, and that any fashion universally followed means æsthetic suicide for nine-tenths of the women who adopt it? *I am my own fashion-leader*, and wear only what is becoming to my *individual* style of beauty. What a preposterous notion to proclaim that any particular colour or cut is to be exclusively fashionable this year for all women, for blondes and brunettes, for the tall and the short, the stout and the slim alike! What *could* have induced those women thus to annihilate their own beauty deliberately? And not only their beauty, but their comfort as well. For I see that in New York, Fashion used to decree that women must exchange their light, comfortable summer clothes for heavier autumn fabrics exactly in the middle of September, although the last two weeks of September are often the hottest part of the year. And the women, almost without exception, obeyed this decree!

"And then those long trailing dresses! How they must have added to their ease and grace of movement in the ballroom, tucked up clumsily or held in the hand! And it seems that these trails were even worn in the dirty streets, for I see that at one time the Dresden authorities forbade women to sweep the streets with their dresses; and in one of Mr. Ruskin's works I find this advice to girls: 'Your walking dress must never touch the ground at all. I have lost much of the faith I once had in the common sense, and even in the personal delicacy, of the present race of average English women, by seeing how they will allow their dresses to sweep the streets if it is *the fashion to be scavengers.*'"

MASCULINE FASHIONS

In his emancipation from Fashion man has made much more progress than woman. There is still a considerable number of shallow-brained young "society men" who naïvely and minutely accept the slight variations introduced every year in the cut and style of cravats, shirts, and evening-dress by cunning tailors, in order to compel men to throw away last season's suits and order new ones. But much larger is the number of men who disregard such innovations, and laugh at the silly persons who meekly accept them, even when their taste is offended by such new fashions as the hideous collars and hats with which the market is occasionally flooded.

There was a time when men spent as much time and money on dress in a week as they now do in a year; a time when men were as strictly ruled by capricious, cunning Fashion as women are to-day. Lord March, we read, "laid a wager that he would make fashionable the most humiliating dress he could think of. Accordingly, he wore a blue coat with crimson collar and cuffs—a livery, and not a tasteful livery—but he won his bet." After the battle of Agincourt, it is said, "the Duc de Bourbon, in order to ransom King John, sold his overcoat to a London Jew, who gave no more than its value, we may be pretty sure, but nevertheless gave 5200 crowns of gold for it. It seems to have been a mass of the most precious gems." The Duke of Buckingham " had twenty-seven suits of clothes made, the richest that embroidery, lace, silk, velvet, silver, gold, and gems could contribute ; one of which was a white uncut velvet, set all over, both suit and cloak, with diamonds valued at fourscore thousand pounds, besides a great feather stuck all over with diamonds, as were also his sword, girdle, hat, and spurs."

Mr. Spencer cites two amusing instances of masculine subjection to fashion in Africa and mediæval Europe. Among the Darfurs in Africa, " If the sultan, being on horseback, happens to fall off, all his followers must fall off likewise ; and should any one omit this formality, however great he may be, he is laid down and beaten." " In 1461, Duke Philip of Burgundy, having had his hair cut during an illness, issued an edict that all the nobles of his states should be shorn also. More than five hundred persons sacrificed their hair."

So far as men are still subject to the influence of ugly fashions, they differ from women in at least frankly acknowledging the ugliness of these fashions. Whereas most women admire, or pretend to admire, corsets, high-heeled boots, crinolettes, bustles, etc., there are few men who do not detest *e.g.* the unshapely, baggy trousers, which were so greatly abhorred by the æsthetic sense of the ancient Greeks; and most men to-day (except those who have ugly legs) would gladly wear knee-breeches, if they could do so without making themselves too conspicuous. Herein lies the greatest impediment to dress reform. To make oneself very conspicuous is justly considered a breach of good manners; and few have the courage, like Mr. Oscar Wilde, to make martyrs and butts of ridicule of themselves.

But if individuals are comparatively powerless, clubs of acknowledged standing might make themselves very useful to the cause of Personal Beauty, as affected by dress, if they would vote to adopt in a body certain reforms as regards trousers, hats, and evening-dress. Then it would no longer be said of a man rationally dressed that he is eccentric, but that he belongs to the X—— Club; and many outsiders would immediately follow suit for the coveted distinction of being taken for members of that club. Thus both the wise and the foolish would be gratified.

As showing how invariably and consistently Fashion is the handmaid of ugliness, it is curious to note that the several styles of dress worn by men are fashionable in proportion to their ugliness. For the greatest occasions the swallow-tail or evening-dress is prescribed. Next in rank is the ugly frock coat, for morning calls. Of late, it is true, the more becoming "cut-away" has been tolerated in place of the frock coat; but the sack-coat, which alone follows the natural outlines of the body, and neither has a caudal appendage, like the evening-dress, nor, like the frock coat, gives the impression that a man's waist extends down to his knees, is altogether tabooed at social gatherings, except those of the most informal kind.

Man's evening-dress is so uniquely unæsthetic and ugly that fashionable women have of course long been eyeing it with envy, and have gradually adopted some of its features. One of these is the chimney-pot hat, the cause of so much premature baldness and discomfort. But women are not quite so foolish as men in this matter; for they do not wear tall hats at evening-parties and the opera, but only when out riding, where the necessity of dodging about to keep them on against the force of the wind and the blows of overhanging boughs, compels them to go through all sorts of grotesque gymnastics with neck and head. If they wore a more rational and becoming head-dress on horseback they might easily look pretty and graceful, which would be fatal to their chances of being considered fashionable.

In comparing masculine and feminine fashions, we must note that trousers and swallow-tailed coats, though ugly, are harmless; while high-heeled shoes, corsets, chignons, etc., are as fatal to health as to Personal Beauty.

It is sometimes claimed in behalf of Fashion that, though it often favours ugliness, it establishes a rule and model for all; whereas, if everything were left to individual taste, the result might be still more disastrous. Nonsense. Rare as good taste is among women, a modicum is commonly present; and there are extremely few who, if not overawed by the Fashion Fetish, would ever invent or adopt such hideous irrepressible monstrosities as bustles, crinolines, chignons, trailing dresses, Chinese boots, bird-corpse hats, etc.

A protest must, finally, be made against the horrible figures which in our fashion papers are constantly offered as models of style and appearance. Even in the best of them, such as Harper's *Bazar*, which frequently points out the injuriousness of tight lacing, female figures are printed every week with hideously narrow waists, such as no woman could possibly possess unless she were in the last stages of consumption, or some other wasting disease.

CHEST AND BOSOM
FEMININE BEAUTY

Burke, in his chapter on "Gradual Variation" as a characteristic of Beauty, begs us to "observe that part of a beautiful woman where she is perhaps the most beautiful, about the neck and breasts; the smoothness, the softness, the easy and insensible swell; the variety of the surface, which is never for the smallest space the same; the deceitful maze through which the unsteady eye slides giddily, without knowing where to fix, or whither it is carried. Is not this a demonstration of that change of surface, continual, and yet hardly perceptible at any point, which forms one of the greatest constituents of beauty?"

There is reason to believe that the beautifully-rounded form of the female bosom is a result of æsthetico-sexual selection; for primitive human tribes resemble in this respect the lower animals.

Says the famous anatomist Hyrtl: "It is only among the white and yellow races that the breasts, in their compact virginal condition, have a hemispheric form, while those of negresses of a corresponding age and physique are more elongated, pointed, turned outwards and downwards; in a word, more like the teats of animals." Even the Arabian poets sing of the charms of a goatlike breast. In the Soudan older women, when at work, sometimes throw their breasts over the shoulder to prevent them from being in the way; and "the women of the Basutos, a Kaffir tribe, carry their children on the back, and pass the breast to them under the arm."

It is a very interesting and important fact that not only do we find more beauty among the higher than among the lower races of mankind, but the superior beauty of civilised races is also *of a more permanent kind*. This truth is admirably illustrated in the following remarks by Dr. Peschuel Lœschke: The breasts of the Loango negress, he says, "approach the conic rather than the hemispheric form; they often have a too small and insufficiently gradated basis, and in rare extreme cases have almost the appearance of teats, besides being unequally developed. Breasts of such a shape are naturally much more easily affected by the law of gravitation, and soon become changed into the pendent bags which we find so ugly, especially among Africans, although they also occur among other tribes, and are not unknown among civilised peoples. The superior form, with a broad basis, is naturally the more enduring, and remains in many cases an ornament of women of a more advanced age."

Savages and Orientals, being deficient in æsthetic taste, admire an excessively-developed bust. Europeans, on the other hand, long ago recognised the connection between such a bust and clumsy, unhealthy corpulence, suggesting advanced age. The same appears to have been true of the most refined nations of antiquity. Says Professor Kollmann: "The ancient as well as the modern inhabitants of the Nile region appear, in the majority of cases, like those of India, to possess hemispheric breasts, for neither in the sphinxes or other superhuman beings, nor in the images of human beauties, do we come across pointed breasts. . . . The Romans did not consider large bosoms a mark of beauty. Among European women the Portuguese are said to have the largest busts, the Castilians the smallest. To judge by Rubens's nude figures, the Netherland women appear to rival the Portuguese in exuberant bosoms."

In Greek works of art, says Winckelmann, "the breast or bosom of female figures is never exuberant." "Among ideal figures, the Amazons alone have large and fully-developed breasts." "The form of the breasts in the figures of divinities is virginal in the extreme, since their beauty was made to consist in the moderateness of their size. A stone, found in the Island of Naxos, was smoothly polished and placed upon them for the purpose of repressing an undue development."

Modern Fashion, for a wonder, endorses the Greek standard of beauty as regards a moderately-developed bust. But it was not always thus. It is Fashion that induces some savages whose breasts are naturally long and hanging to use bandages which make them still more hanging and elongated in form. In Spain, during the sixteenth and seventeenth century, and in other parts of Europe, on the contrary, Fashion prescribed flat chests. Plates of lead were tied on the breasts of young girls with such force that sometimes the natural form was replaced by an actual depression where "love's pillows" should have been. In some parts of South Germany and the Tyrol a similar fashion prevails to the present day among the lower classes, the result being not only a sacrifice of beauty, but a great mortality among the children, that have to be reared artificially in consequence of it.

But if modern Fashion has a correct standard of taste in this matter, it nevertheless encourages practices which lead to as disastrous results as the Spanish fashions of three centuries ago. " The horrible custom of wearing pads," says the author of the *Ugly Girl Papers*, " is the ruin of natural figures, by heating and pressing down the bosom. . . . A low, deep bosom, rather than a bold one, is a sign of grace in a full-grown woman, and a full bust is hardly admirable in an unmarried girl. Her figure should be all curves, but slender, promising a fuller beauty when maturity is reached. One is not fond of over-ripe pears. . . . Due attention to the general laws of health always has its effect in restoring the bust to its roundness. . . . Weakness of any kind affects the contour of the figure, and it is useless to try to improve it in any other way than by restoring the strength where it is wanting."

The same author, whose book is brimful of useful advice, not only to "ugly girls," but to those who have beauty and wish to preserve it, also recommends battledore, swinging the skipping-rope over the shoulder, swinging by the hand from a rope, as well as playing ball, "bean bags," pillow fights, and especially daily vocal exercises, with corset off and lungs deeply inflated—as excellent means of improving the bust.

If women could be made to realise how rarely they succeed, even with the aid of the cleverest milliner, in counterfeiting a properly developed chest, they would, perhaps, be more willing to submit to the exercise or regimen requisite for the acquirement and preservation of Personal Beauty. Flat chests are a consequence of insufficient muscular exercise, insufficient fresh air, and insufficient food. The main reason why the majority of girls in the world are over-delicate and fragile is because they do not get enough properly-cooked food in which *fat is introduced in such a way as to be palatable and digestible.* The adipose layer between the skin and the muscles contributes so much to the undulating roundness of contour peculiar to feminine beauty, that Kollmann places it among the differentiating sexual characteristics.

Too exuberant busts, on the other hand, are the result of too much indulgence in fattening food, combined with lack of exercise in the open air, which would consume the fat. Maternity, with proper hygienic precautions, is never fatal to a fine bust.

That savages, like their civilised brethren and sisters, owe their deformed chests entirely to their indolence and neglect of the laws of health, is shown by the fact that there are notable exceptions—energetic tribes living healthy lives, and therefore blessed with beautiful figures. Thus Mr. A. R. Wallace tells us regarding some of the Amazon valley Indians that "their figures are generally superb; and I have never felt so much pleasure in gazing at the finest statue as at these living illustrations of the beauty of the human form. The development of the bust is such as I believe never exists in the best-formed European, exhibiting *a splendid series of convex undulations, without a hollow in any part of it.*" And what he says in another place regarding a neighbouring tribe explains the secret of this Beauty: "Though some of them were too fat, most of them had splendid figures, and many of them were very pretty. Before daylight in the morning all were astir and came to the river to wash. It is the chilliest hour of the twenty-four, and when we were wrapping our sheet or blanket more closely around us, we could hear the plunges and splashings of these early bathers. Rain or wind is all alike to them: their morning bath is never dispensed with."

MASCULINE BEAUTY

Winckelmann remarks that, among the ancient Greeks, "a proudly-arched chest was regarded as a universal attribute of beauty in male figures. The father of the poets describes Neptune with such a chest, and Agamemnon as resembling him; and such a one Anakreon desired to see in the image of the youth whom he loved."

"A prominent, *arched* chest," says Professor Kollmann, "is an infallible sign of a vigorous, *healthy* skeleton; whereas a narrow, *flat*, and, still more, a bent thorax is a physical index of bodily weakness and inherited *decrepitude*. An arched chest imparts to a man's whole figure an aspect of physical perfection, not to say sublimity, as may be seen in the ancient statues of gods, in which the chest is intentionally made more prominent than it ever can be in a man, presumably in order to weaken the impression of the chest's more *animal* neighbour, the abdomen. There is a deep meaning in our phraseology which localises courage, boldness, martial valour, in a man's vigorous breast."

I have italicised several words in this quotation, because they tersely show how writers on art are guided both by the positive and negative tests of Beauty formulated in another part of this volume.

MAGIC EFFECT OF DEEP BREATHING

Indolence is the mother of ugliness. No one who realises the absolute necessity to Health of a sufficient supply of fresh air can wonder at the rarity of Beauty in the world, if he considers that nineteen people out of every twenty are *too lazy to breathe properly*.

It is estimated that there are from 75 to 100 cubic inches of air which always remain in a man's lungs. About an equal amount of "supplemental" air remains after an *ordinary* expiration; and only

20 to 30 inches of what Professor Huxley calls "tidal air" passes in and out. But this "tidal air" can be largely increased in amount by the habit of breathing deeply and *slowly*, whereby an additional supply of oxygen is supplied to the lungs, which is a thousand times better for the health than quinine, iron pills, or any other tonic. There are few persons whose health and personal appearance would not be improved vastly if they would take *several daily meals* of fresh air—consisting of 20-50 deep inspirations in a park or some other place where the air is pure and bracing. Slowly inhale as much air as you can get into the lungs without discomfort (avoiding a strain), and then exhale again just as slowly. After a while the habit will be formed of *constantly* breathing more deeply than formerly, both awake and asleep; thus bringing into regular use a larger part of the lungs' surface. It is the slight sense of fatigue at first accompanying deep breathing which prevents most people from enjoying its benefits; but when once this natural indolence is overcome the reward of deep breathing is analogous to the delicious exhilaration which follows a brisk walk or a cold bath.

It is important to note that all breathing, whether deep or ordinary, should be done through the nose, as thus the air is warmed before it reaches the delicate lungs, and the mucous membranes remain moist, thus preventing those disagreeable enemies of refreshing sleep—a dry mouth and snoring.

Habitual deep breathing adds to Personal Beauty not only by exercising the muscles of the chest, which thus becomes more arched and prominent relatively to the abdomen, but also by throwing back the neck and head and compelling the whole body to assume a straight, military attitude. We are all taught as children, says Professor Kollmann, to hold ourselves straight; but rarely is the information added that the best way to secure an erect, manly bearing and a dignified gait is by cultivating the habit of deep breathing. "It is worthy of notice that forcible breathing, such as results from a correct bearing, from prolonged sojourn and exercise in the open air, in hunting, gymnastic exercises, riding, etc., not only increases the chest for the moment, but permanently. . . . There are proofs in abundance that even with young persons of eighteen to twenty years, the whole circumference of the chest is capable of considerable widening under such circumstances."

A medical writer, referring to the fact that children frequently become round-shouldered from sitting for hours and bending over a desk, makes these very sensible suggestions:—

"In the first place, the lungs should be fully expanded by drawing in all the air that is possible; this process will be aided by throwing the shoulders well back, and you should encourage your children to do this frequently in the open air when going to and coming from school. Children are easily bribed, and we would suggest to school teachers a simple and effective way of accomplishing this desirable end. This forcible expansion of the lungs will enlarge the chest and increase its circumference. Then let the teacher, at the beginning of the session, measure each child's chest and record the circumference, then explain and demonstrate to them how to forcibly fill the lungs, and offer a premium at the end of the session to the child who shall have most increased the circumference of his chest; make it worth their while to expand their lungs, as much so as we now do for them to expand their minds, and the result will be wonderful."

A MORAL QUESTION

An eminent authority on the physiology of the vocal organs, Dr. Lennox Browne, remarks (in *Voice, Song, and Speech*) that "respiratory exercises, and subsequently lessons in reading, reciting, and singing, are oftentimes of the greatest use in strengthening a weak chest; and, indeed, it is not too much to say, *in arresting consumption.*" Another excellent authority, Mr. A. B. Bach, points out (in his *Musical Education and Vocal Culture*, which should be consulted by all who wish to learn the art of Deep Breathing) that "very few vocalists die of consumption," owing to the fact that they properly exercise their lungs and chests.

This brings us face to face with a moral question of enormous importance, to which writers on ethics have by no means as yet given the attention it loudly clamours for. Consumption, we read, "is a disease of great frequency and severity, which, in the civilised nations of Europe, produces from *one-sixth to one-tenth of the total mortality*, in ordinary times." Now if, as we have just seen, consumption can be arrested and cured by proper exercise of the lungs and chest in pure air, does it not follow that the neglect of such exercises makes certain parties criminally responsible for the greater number of deaths from consumption? It is "proved by careful inquiries that the workshops of tailors, printers, and other businesses carried on in close, ill-ventilated apartments, by large numbers of workmen, are, in a very aggravated sense, *nurseries of consumption.* Cotton and linen factories have also been shown, when ill-regulated, to be largely responsible for the death of their inmates from this disease."

Why should not the owners of factories who refuse to ventilate their buildings be held responsible for the ill-health, the early decrepitude and death of many of the workers, and the workers' weakly, consumptive children who die young? As England alone has over three hundred thousand women engaged in cotton manufacture, the amount of ill-health, early senility, ugliness, consumption, etc., bred by criminal neglect of hygienic precautions, is appalling to the imagination. A case was mentioned in the American papers a few years ago, where the windows in a factory were *nailed fast* to prevent the poor, suffocating girls from opening them. And, strange to say, the owner of that factory was not immediately lynched. Surely, if ever a monster deserved to be hanged to the nearest tree, it was the man who ordered those windows to be nailed down.

But factory owners are by no means the only persons who are thus responsible for indirect manslaughter by foul-air poisoning. Thousands of loving mothers and fathers blaspheme their Creator in attributing the early death of their children to a "dispensation of Providence," when the plain truth, brutally expressed, is that they killed them with the poisoned air, indigestible food, and insufficient exercise that brought on the fatal consumption. To say that the disease was hereditary is only to shift the hygienic crime on to the shoulders of the grandparents.

In human courts of justice ignorance of the law is not considered an excuse for the commission of crime. If the same principle holds true in some future world where human actions will be judged, what terrible indictments will be brought against some parents for crimes committed against the health and life of their children and grandchildren, for neglecting to learn the laws of health, as laid down in physiological and hygienic textbooks!

Inasmuch as Personal Beauty is the flower and symbol of perfect Health, it might be shown, by following out this argument, that *ugliness is a sin, and man's first duty the cultivation of Beauty.*

NECK AND SHOULDER

Nowhere are the æsthetic laws of Gradation and gentle Curvature more beautifully illustrated than in the neck—the column of the head. Note how a lovely woman's neck repeats on a small scale the delicate contours of the trunk—widened at the base and at the top, with a subtle inward slope towards the middle. Note, also, how imperceptibly it passes into the shoulders, which continue the gentle curve in a downward slope, unless prevented by the deforming corset.

Man's neck is less cylindrical than woman's, and

presents four slightly flattened surfaces; while his shoulders are not sloping, but square. We not only pardon, but even admire and demand this conformation in man; because in judging masculine beauty we are guided by dynamic as much as by æsthetic considerations, while the fair sex is judged by the laws of beauty alone. A masculine neck is in good form if it shows traces of the sinews and muscles which give it strength; but in a woman's neck the feminine adipose layer under the skin must obliterate all such traces of masculinity,—especially the bones at the junction of neck and breast, the prominence of which suggests emaciation and disease.

In the face of such considerations, how can any one maintain that man is more beautiful than woman? He may show more character, more individuality, more originality than a fine woman, but more beauty *never*. And the fact that in Sexual Selection women have always been chiefly guided by dynamic considerations—*i.e.* vigour, boldness, "manliness"—whereas men have been fascinated by beauty alone, explains why, as Schopenhauer asserts, women are the "unæsthetic sex," and why their taste for Personal Beauty, not being exercised, like that of man, in the selection of a mate, is so lamentably callous to the deformities resulting from corsets and other instruments of torture.

The neck being the pivot on which the head executes its movements, it is evident that it requires attention from the point of view of Grace as well as of Beauty. To how many women has it ever occurred that as the feet are taught to dance lithely, the arms to execute eloquent gestures, so the neck should be trained to naturally assume graceful attitudes? Great paintings and famous actresses should be studied from this point of view. Always bear in mind that grace of movement often excels beauty of form in the power of inspiring Romantic Love. And remember that any pains you take to acquire grace will not only multiply your own charms, but will establish a habit of graceful movement in your muscles which will be inherited by your children. It is owing to this circumstance that the children of truly refined families are born with an ease, grace, and dignity of movement and mien which it is impossible for "self-made" persons to acquire in a lifetime, because they are not born with an inherited *talent* for graceful movement.

ARM AND HAND

EVOLUTION AND SEXUAL DIFFERENCES

One of the redeeming features of what is ironically called "full-dress" is the opportunity it gives of admiring a woman's shapely neck, shoulders, and arms—if she has such. No healthy woman of the well-to-do classes need have an ill-favoured arm if she has a sensible mother, who compels her from her childhood to exercise her muscles. The great preponderance of leathery, angular, bony arms at ballrooms shows, therefore, how shamefully the hygienic arts of personal adornment are neglected in our best society. The stifling heat which commonly prevails at social gatherings suggests the thought that many ladies are indifferent to the display of their bony arms on the grounds given in Sydney Smith's exclamation: " Heat, ma'am! it was so dreadful here that I found there was nothing left for it but to take off my flesh and sit in my bones."

A meagre, skinny arm is objectionable not only because it offends against all the conditions of Beauty—plump roundness, softness, fresh colour, smoothness, gradual tapering to the wrist—but because it is associated with the aspect of old age and disease; and again, because it suggests man's lowly origin by its approximation to the appearance of the arms in our simian country cousins.

Man's arm has become differentiated from the ape's not only in the matter of greater muscular rotundity and smoothness, *i.e.* loss of hair, but also in regard to length. An ape's arms are much longer than a white man's, the negro's being intermediate. Says Mr. Tylor: "In an upright position and reaching down with the middle finger, the gibbon can touch its foot, the orang its ankle, the chimpanzee its knee, while man only reaches partly down his thigh. . . . Negro soldiers standing at drill bring the middle finger-tip an inch or two nearer the knee than white men can do, and some have been even known to touch the knee-pan." Taking this in connection with the fact that the arms of sailors, who use them constantly in climbing, are longer than those of soldiers, we may safely infer that man's arms have gradually become shorter because he has ceased to climb trees; while the greater muscular rotundity, especially of the forearm, has been acquired through the varied activity and movements of the hand and fingers: a circumstance almost self-evident on physiological principles, and furthermore corroborated by the fact that negroes, unskilled in trades which call for manipulation of the separate fingers, again occupy an intermediate position. "Even in muscular negroes the arms are less rotund," says Professor Carl Vogt; and, according to Van der Hœven, the skin between the fingers reaches up higher in the negro, which must impede activity.

The peculiar arrangement of the hair on man's arm has been referred to by Wallace and Darwin as one of the countless signs arguing our descent from apelike ancestors. On the arm of man, as of most anthropoid apes, the hair "tends to converge from above and below to a point at the elbow." Now it is known that the gorilla, as well as the orang, "sits in pelting rain with his hands over his head"; and Mr. Wallace, therefore, suggests that the present inclination of the hair on man's arms is simply a survival of the time when his arboreal ancestors used to sit in that fashion, the hair having gradually assumed the direction which would most easily allow the rain to run off.

The evolution theory that the hair on the arm, as on the body in general, was lost through Sexual Selection, is corroborated by the fact that woman's arm has made more progress toward complete smoothness than man's, owing to the circumstance that man is in Sexual Selection more guided by æsthetic, woman by dynamic, considerations. Yet there can be no doubt that a hairy arm and hand are always ugly, in man as in woman, not only on account of their simian suggestiveness, but because they cover the smooth skin and its delicate tints, and, moreover, especially if black, are very apt to make the arm and hand look as if they needed a good scrubbing. Hair on the hand may sometimes be permanently removed by passing the hand quickly and repeatedly through a large flame—a much less painful process than the use of pincers.

The *muscular* deviations from the lines of beauty are much more pardonable in a man's arm than the hair, although it is evident that a professional athlete's excessively muscular arm is æsthetically objectionable, however much it may be admired on other grounds. To feminine beauty, and the chances of inspiring Love, an arm which is so muscular as to obliterate the lines of beauty is absolutely fatal. Among the labouring classes there are many women whose arms are so hard and sinewy that the very bones to which they are attached have become heavy and masculine, so that it becomes difficult to tell a woman's from a man's skeleton, which ordinarily is very easy.

CALISTHENICS AND MASSAGE

It is, however, hardly necessary to refer to these facts as a warning to girls not to use their arms too much. The danger almost always lies the other way, and what girls need is a set of intelligent directions for securing a shapely arm. If the arm is too plump the method discussed in preceding pages for the general reduction of corpulence will also affect the arm. If too thin, which is much more frequently the case in young women, don't be afraid that exercise will make them thinner—on the ground that hard labourers are commonly meagre. It is only *excessive* exercise that produces leanness, by burning away all the fat. Moderate exercise develops the muscles — the plastic material of beauty—and stimulates the appetite, so that the fat-cushion under the skin also increases in depth, covering up the angular outlines of bones, muscles, and sinews.

It is a suggestive fact that the word calisthenics— "the art of promoting the health of the body by exercise"—comes from two Greek words meaning "beautiful" and "strength."

So many books have been written on calisthenics that it is needless to repeat here minute directions for training the muscles of the arm or any other part of the body. One bit of sensible advice may, however, be quoted from the *Ugly Girl Papers:* "Throwing quoits and sweeping are good exercises to develop the arms. There is nothing like three hours of housework a day for giving a woman a good figure, and if she sleep in tight cosmetic gloves, she need not fear that her hands will be spoiled. The time to form the hand is in youth, and with thimbles for the finger-tips, and close gloves lined with cold cream, every mother might secure a good hand for her daughter."

It is an ill wind that blows no man good. The incessant piano-banging and violin-scraping of thousands of unmusical young ladies has at least one thing to be said in its favour: it helps to round and beautify the arms of these young players.

Active exercise is the surest and quickest way of securing muscular rotundity. But in cases where, owing to some infirmity, long-continued spontaneous exertion is out of the question, *massage*, which has been defined as "passive exercise," may be resorted to as of calisthenic value. It should only be performed by an expert, and always centripetally, *i.e.* in the direction of the heart. It facilitates the flow of the venous current, which in the arms and lower limbs has to struggle upwards against the force of gravitation ; and to this is partly due its refreshing effect. As Americans are the most nervous and sensitive people in the world, it seems probable that the feeling of ease following the facilitating of the venous flow has taught them instinctively to assume that peculiar position, with the feet on a chair or table, which has been so often ridiculed by Europeans.

THE "SECOND FACE"

"The beauty of a youthful hand," says Winckelmann, "consists in a moderate degree of plumpness, and a scarcely observable depression, resembling a soft shadow, over the articulations of the fingers, where, if the hand is plump, there is a dimple. The fingers taper gently towards their extremities, like finely-shaped columns ; and, in art, the articulations are not expressed. The fore part of the terminating joint is not bent over, nor are the nails very long, though both are common in the works of modern sculptors."

Balzac pointed out that "men of superior intellect almost always have beautiful hands, the perfection of which is the distinctive indication of a high destination. . . . The hand is the despair of sculptors and painters when they wish to express the changing labyrinth of its mysterious lineaments."

A fine hand is, indeed, a sign of superior intelligence in a much more comprehensive sense than that which Balzac had in mind. The difference between the simian and human faces is hardly greater than the progress from an ape's hand to a man's in beauty of outline, smoothness of surface, grace of movement, and varied utility. The ape's hand is hairy on the upper surface, hard and callous on the lower. Except in climbing, its movements are clumsy. The fingers have adapted themselves to the need of climbing, and have become permanently bent in front, so that when the animal goes on all fours it cannot walk on the palm, but only on the bent knuckles.

A step higher we have the negro's hands, in which the fingers are less independent and nimble, and the palmar fat-cushions less developed and sensitive, than in our hands. These fat-cushions serve to protect the blood-vessels as well as the delicate nerves, which make the hand the principal organ of touch. The muscles of the hand are more easily and instantaneously obedient to the will than those of any other part of the body, except those of the mouth and eyes; and hence it is that the hands are almost as good an index of a man's character, habits, and profession as his face, and have been aptly called his "second face."

Division of labour is the index of progress in the evolution of organs. To the fact that his feet have become exclusively adapted to locomotion, leaving the hands free to serve as tools, man chiefly owes his superiority to other animals. For what would superior intellect avail him without the implements needed to carry out its schemes? Feeling, grasping, handling, writing, sewing, playing an instrument, squeezing, caressing,—these are a few of the innumerable functions of the human hand; while the ape's is good for little but climbing. The finger language of deaf mutes shows to what subtle intellectual uses the hands can be put; and as for emotional expression, are there any facial muscles which can indicate finer shades of feeling than the infinitely varied touch with which a pianist or violinist gives utterance to every mood and phase of human passion?

No wonder that, just as the face has had its physiognomists and phrenologists, so the hand its chiromancers, who pretended, by looking at its lines, not only to read character, but even to foretell one's fate. Books on this subject are indeed still published, which shows that the race of fools is in no immediate danger of extinction. Wrinkles in the face do bear some relation to character and experience; but surely no one needs to be told that the palmar lines are purely accidental—caused by the manner in which the skin is folded when we close the hand.

FINGER-NAILS

Our nails are modified claws—modified to their advantage. When properly cared for, they are one of the greatest personal ornaments—beginning and ending as they do with a delicate curve, rounded on the surface, suffused with a gentle blush, and smooth as ivory. They may also serve as a mode of expression and index of nationality, as seen in these remarks by Mr. E. B. Tylor: "In the Southern

United States, till slavery was done away a few years ago, the traces of Negro descent were noted with the utmost nicety. Not only were the mixed breeds regularly classed as mulattos, quadroons, and down to octoroons, but even where the mixture was so slight that the untrained eye noticed nothing beyond a brunette complexion, the intruder, who had ventured to sit down at a public dinner-table, was called upon to show his hands, and the African taint detected by the dark tinge at the root of the finger-nails."

Becker remarks that among the ancient Greeks "it was considered very unseemly to appear with nails unpared"; nor did the Greeks consider it beneath their dignity, like the Romans, to pare their own nails.

The Greeks, being an æsthetic nation, were guided in the treatment of their nails by the sense of beauty. Elsewhere, however, the idiotic notion that laziness is aristocratic led to a different treatment of the nails. Mr. Tylor, in his *Anthropology*, gives an illustration of the hand of a Chinese ascetic whose finger-nails are five or six times as long as his fingers. " Long finger - nails," he remarks, " are noticed even among ourselves as showing that the owner does no manual labour, and in China and neighbouring countries they are allowed to grow to a monstrous length as a symbol of nobility, ladies wearing silver cases to protect them, or at least as a pretence that they are there."

Useless hands, with elongated nails, reverting to a claw-like character, as "symbols of nobility!" The study of evolution throws much sarcastic light on the fashionable follies of mankind.

MANICURE SECRETS

According to the New York *Analyist*: "There are not nearly as many secrets in manicure as people imagine. A little ammonia or borax in the water you wash your hands with, and that water just lukewarm, will keep the skin clean and soft. A little oatmeal mixed with the water will whiten the hands. Many people use glycerine on their hands when they go to bed, wearing gloves to keep the bedding clean; but glycerine don't agree with every one. It makes some skins harsh and red. These people should rub their hands with dry oatmeal and wear gloves in bed. The best preparation for the hands at night is white of egg, with a grain of alum dissolved in it. . . . The roughest and hardest hands can be made soft and white in a month's time by doctoring them a little at bedtime, and all the tools you need are a nail-brush (avoid metal), a bottle of ammonia, a box of powdered borax, and a little fine white sand to rub the stains off, or a cut of lemon. Manicures use acids in their shops, but the lemon is quite as good, and isn't poisonous, while the acids are."

In the *Ugly Girl Papers* the following recipes are given:—

"To give a fine colour to the nails, the hands and fingers must be well lathered and washed with scented soap; then the nails must be rubbed with equal parts of cinnabar and emery, followed by oil of bitter almonds. To take white specks from the nails, melt equal parts of pitch and turpentine in a small cup; add to it vinegar and powdered sulphur. Rub this on the nails and the specks will soon disappear. Pitch and myrrh melted together may be used with the same results."

But, after all, what is the use of beautifying one's hands as long as ladies bow to the Fashion Fetish, which compels them to conceal them in the skins of animals? To wear gloves on going out, as a protection against rough weather and for the sake of cleanliness, is rational enough; but to wear them at social gatherings is almost as absurd as the compulsory impenetrable veils of Turkish women; for does not the hand rank next to the face as an index of character?

Another stupidity of fashion is our enforced and cultivated right-handedness. Despite the force of inherited habit, children show a natural inclination toward using both their hands equally; but they are constantly scolded and punished, until they have succeeded, like their parents, in reducing one hand to a state of imbecility, so to speak, which is constantly betrayed in awkward, ungraceful action. Practising on a musical instrument, with special attention to the left hand, has a tendency to correct this awkwardness. Indeed, is there any part of the body that music does not benefit? Dancing to a Strauss waltz gives elasticity to the limbs and grace to the gait; singing is the most useful kind of lung-gymnastics, and develops the chest; a musically-trained ear modulates the voice to sweeter expression; while equally skilled and graceful hands are acquired by practice on a musical instrument. So that the word music, though much less comprehensive than among the ancient Greeks, has lost none of the magic, beautifying power they ascribed to it.

Much of the ugliness in the world is due to the neglect of parents in properly supervising the actions of their children, to prevent the formation of bad habits, which ruin beauty irretrievably. As an instance of what can be done in this direction may be cited the following remark by a Philadelphia surgeon: "The school-girl habit of biting the nails must be broken up at once. If in children, rub a little extract of quassia on the finger-tips. This is so bitter that they are careful not to taste it twice. Not only the nails, but the whole finger and hand is often forfeited by neglect in this respect."

By travelling from the shoulder down to the finger-tips we have apparently interrupted our steady progress from toe to tip of the body. But we shall see in a moment that the interruption is only apparent, for our subject leads naturally "from Hand to Mouth."

JAW, CHIN, AND MOUTH

HANDS *VERSUS* JAWS

Just as among some male ruminants the growth of horns as a means of defence has apparently led to the disappearance of the canine teeth, so man's erect attitude, by leaving his hands free to do much of the work which inferior animals do with their jaws and teeth, has gradually modified the appearance of his face, greatly to its advantage. "The early male forefathers of man," says Darwin, "were probably furnished with great canine teeth; but as they gradually acquired the habit of using stones, clubs, or other weapons, for fighting with their enemies or rivals, they would use their jaws and teeth less and less. In this case the jaws, together with the teeth, would become reduced in size, as we may feel almost sure from innumerable analogous cases." And in another place he remarks : " As the prodigious difference between the skulls of the two sexes in the orang and gorilla stands in close relation with the development of the immense canine teeth in the males, we may infer that the reduction of the jaws and teeth in the early progenitors of man must have led to a most striking and favourable change in his appearance."

Why a "favourable" change ? No doubt a male gorilla, if it could be taught to pronounce an æsthetic judgment, would indignantly scout the notion that our weak, delicate jaw is preferable to its own massive bones ; nor would a prognathous or " forward-jawed " African or Australian admit that he is less beautiful than the orthognathous or " upright-jawed " European. What right, then, have we to claim that we alone have beautiful faces ? Must we not admit, with the Jeffrey-Alison school, that it is all " a matter of taste," and that in so far as a heavy, projecting jaw *appears* beautiful to a gorilla or a savage, it *is* beautiful to them ?

The general answer to such questions as these has already been given in another part of this volume. We need therefore only say in brief *résumé* that a heavy, projecting, clumsy, brutal jaw probably appears to a gorilla or a Hottentot *neither ugly nor beautiful*. The æsthetic sense—as we can see among ourselves

—is the last and highest product of civilisation. Monkeys are apparently excited by brilliant *colours*, but to beauty of *form* neither apes nor the lower races and classes of man appear to be susceptible.

Should a negro, however, on having his attention called to this matter, claim that his prognathous face is more beautiful than our orthognathous face, the retort simple would be that his imagination is not sufficiently educated to understand our more refined and delicate beauty ; just as an Esquimaux prefers a rotten egg to a fresh one, a working man a glass of fusil oil to one of tokay—simply because their senses of taste and smell are not sufficiently refined to appreciate *or even detect* the delicate flavour of a fresh egg and the subtle bouquet of wine.

Of the positive tests of beauty, Delicacy is the one which most emphatically condemns the heavy, prognathous jaw and the accompanying big mouth. Massive bones and clumsy movements are everywhere the signs of excessive toil, fatal to beauty, as may be seen on comparing the angular and almost masculine skeleton of a labouring woman with the delicately-articulated joints of a "society woman" ; or the heavy structure of a dray-horse with the fine contours of a race-horse ; showing that Delicacy is always associated with the other elements of beauty —Curvature, Gradation, Expression, etc.

On the manner in which the beauty of the mouth is proportioned to its capability for Expression, Mr. Ruskin has made the following interesting observations : " Taking the mouth, another source of expression, we find it ugliest where it has none, as mostly in fish ; or perhaps where, without gaining much in expression of any kind, it becomes a formidable destructive instrument, as again in the alligator ; and then, by some increase of expression, we arrive at birds' beaks, wherein there is much obtained by the different ways of setting on the mandibles (compare the bills of the duck and the eagle); and thence we reach the finely-developed lips of the carnivora (which nevertheless lose their beauty in the actions of snarling and biting) ; and from these we pass to the nobler, because gentler and more sensitive, of the horse, camel, and fawn, and so again up to man : only the principle is less traceable in the mouths of the lower animals, because they are only in slight measure capable of expression, and chiefly used as instruments, and that of low function ; whereas in man the mouth is given most definitely as a means of expression, beyond and above its lower functions. . . . The beauty of the animal form is in exact proportion to the amount of moral or intellectual virtue expressed by it."

Shakspere, by the way, seems to differ from Ruskin's theory implied in this last sentence. According to Ruskin, animals "lose their beauty in the actions of snarling and biting." But man has an action similar to snarling, namely, what Bell calls " that arching of the lips so expressive of contempt, hatred, and jealousy." It is to this that Shakspere refers in these lines—

> " O what a deal of scorn looks beautiful
> In the contempt and anger of his lip."

But the word "beautiful" is here evidently taken by Shakspere in the wider sense of interesting and characteristic, and not in the special æsthetic sense of formal and emotional beauty.

Delicacy and the capacity for varied and subtle Expression—these, we may conclude, are the chief criteria of beauty in the lower part of the face. Anatomically, it may be well to state here, the word "face" does not include the forehead, but only extends from the chin to the eyebrows. The upper and posterior part is called the cranium or skull. It seems odd at first not to include the forehead in the face, but there are scientific grounds for making such a division, for a discussion of which the reader must be referred to some anatomical textbook (*vide* Kollmann, pp. 82-85).

To a certain extent the face and the cranium are independent of one another in development and physiognomic significance. And it should be noted that, contrary to the general impression, in estimating the degree of intelligence and refinement, the face is a safer guide than the cranium; for there are many powerful brains in low and even receding foreheads, whereas a large projecting jaw is almost invariably a sign of vulgarity or lack of delicate feeling. We do not find a dog ugly because of his receding forehead; but we do find that the most infallible way of giving a man's picture a brutal expression is by enlarging the jaw and mouth. It is the deadliest weapon of the caricaturist.

What makes a gorilla so frightfully ugly is the prominence and massive preponderance of his face over his cranium. It is his monstrous jaws, with their "simply brutal armature" of teeth, that give him such a repulsive appearance. The gorilla's mouth, as Professor Kollmann remarks, is a caricature even from the animal point of view. How much more delicate and refined are a dog's or cat's jaws and teeth in comparison! Unfortunately, while man is a savage, or when he relapses into brutal habits, it is the gorilla's mouth and teeth that his resemble, and not the cat's or the dog's.

A small face being therefore a test of refined beauty, we have here another proof of the superiority of feminine over masculine beauty. For although woman has a smaller cranium than man, it is larger than man's relatively to the face. In other words, women have smaller and less massive faces than men, both absolutely and relatively to their size. Kollmann, who is not an evolutionist, endeavours to account for this difference on the ground that men are more addicted to the pleasures of the table than women. But surely, though women eat less than men, they do not make much less use of their teeth; and for any deficiency in this respect they more than make up by the constant wagging of their jaws in small-talk. It is infinitely more probable that Darwin is right in attributing the massiveness of the masculine jaws to the accumulated, inherited effects of constant use in fighting with enemies and rivals—contests from which the passive females have as a rule been exempt.

It is the assumption by the hands of many of the former functions of the teeth that has led to the decrease in the size of the teeth, and, in consequence, of the jaw-bones to which they are attached. Some writers have even claimed that the wisdom-teeth are becoming rudimentary, and will ultimately disappear, because there will be no room for them in our gradually diminishing jaws. We may feel confident, however, that if this reduction in the size of the jaws tended to go *too* far, the sense of beauty and Sexual Selection, *i.e.* Love, would step in to arrest the process, by favouring the survival of those who gave their teeth sufficient exercise to prevent the lower part of the face from becoming too much reduced in size. Our sense of beauty demands that the distance from tip of chin to nose should be about the same as the length of the nose and the height of the forehead. Should these proportions be violated, Love will restore the balance; for no lover would ever select a face in which the chin almost touches the nose, as in infants, whose teeth and jaws are not yet developed, or as in old men and women, in whom the loss of the teeth has led to a collapse of the jaws, resulting in a loss of proportion, clumsy movements, and prognathism.

DIMPLES IN THE CHIN

An oval, well-rounded chin is one of the most important elements of formal beauty, and is a characteristic trait of humanity; for man is the only animal that has a chin. Lavater distinguishes three principal varieties of chin: the receding chin, which is peculiar to lower races and types; the chin which does not project beyond a line dropped from the lips; and the chin which does project beyond that line. Of all parts of the face the chin has the least variety of form and capability of emotional expression. Physiognomists have expended much ingenuity in attempting to trace a connection between various forms of the chin and traits of character; but their generalisations have no scientific value. It is probable that often a very small, weak chin indicates weak desires and a vacillating character, while an energetic chin, like Richard Wagner's, indicates the iron will of a reformer. But the connection between the development of the brain and special modifications of the bones of the chin is too remote to permit a safe inference in individual cases.

In ancient Egyptian art, as Winckelmann points out, "the chin is always somewhat small and receding, whereby the oval of the face becomes imperfect."

One of the most essential conditions of beauty in a chin, if we may judge by the descriptions of novelists, is a dimple. Yet it is doubtful whether a dimple can ever be accepted as a special mark of beauty. Temporary dimples (for the production of which there seems to be a special muscle) are interesting as a mode of transient emotional expression. But permanent dimples interrupt the regular gradation of the beauty-curve, and too often indicate that the plump roundness, so fascinating in a woman's face, has passed the line which indicates corpulence and obliterates the delicate lines of expression.

Dimples occur not only in the chin, but also in the cheek, at the elbow-joints, on the back, and in plump female hands at the knuckles. They are caused by a dense tissue of fibres, blood-vessels, and nerves holding down the skin tightly in one place, and thus preventing such an accumulation of fat between the skin and muscles as is seen in the surrounding parts.

Tommaseo (quoted by Mantegazza) probably had in mind the connection between corpulence and mental indolence when he said that "a dimple in the chin indicates more physical than mental grace."

"As a dimple—by the Greeks termed νύμφη—is an isolated and somewhat accidental adjunct to the chin, it was not," says Winckelmann, "regarded by the Greek artists as an attribute of abstract and pure beauty, though it is so considered by modern writers." With a few unimportant exceptions, it is not found in "any beautiful ideal figure which has come down to us." And although Varro prettily calls a dimple in a statue of Bathyllus an impress from the finger of Cupid, Winckelmann thinks that when dimples do occur in Greek art works they must be attributed to a conscious deviation from the highest principles of art for the sake of personal portraiture. "In images whose beauties were of a lofty cast, the Greek artists never allowed a dimple to break the uniformity of the chin's surface. Its beauty, indeed, consists in the rounded fulness of its arched form, to which the lower lip, when full, imparts additional size."

REFINED LIPS

Whereas the beauty of the chin is purely physical, its neighbour, the mouth, has the emotional charm of expression besides the formal beauty of outline. When we come to speak of the ears we shall find that some animals have five times as many muscles as man, wherewith they can execute expressive movements with those organs. But in the number and delicacy of the muscles of the mouth no animal approaches man, in whom they are more numerous even than those which serve for the varied expression of the eyes. Great as is the difference between an animal's forefoot and man's hand, it is not so great as the difference between an animal's and a man's mouth. Chewing and sucking are almost the only functions of the animal's mouth, while man moulds his lips into a thousand shapes in singing, whistling, pouting, blowing, speaking, smiling, kissing, etc. From being a mere mechanism for masticating food, it has become the most delicate instrument for intellectual and emotional expression.

Sir Charles Bell's testimony that "the lips are, of all the features, the most susceptible of action, and the most direct index of the feelings," has already been quoted in the chapter on Kissing. Could Rubinstein himself express a wider range of emotions, by subtle variations of pianistic touch, than our lips can express degrees and varieties of affection in the family, friendly, conjugal, and love kisses? And can we find, even in the music of Chopin and Wagner, harmonic changes more infinitely varied than the countless subtle modulations of the human lips, as revealed in the fact that deaf mutes can be taught to understand what we say to them merely by watching the movements of our lips?

"The mouth, which is the end of love" (Dante), is also the seat of Love's smiles; "and in her smile Love's image you may see." We often read of smiling eyes, and the eyes *do* partake in the expression of smiling, by increased brightness and the wrinkling of the surrounding muscles. But that the mouth is a more important factor in this expression can be shown by painting the face of a man with a sad expression, and then pasting on a smiling mouth, which will give the man at once a happy expression, notwithstanding the unchanged eyes. In life the muscles of the mouth and eyes execute certain movements in harmony. "In all exhilarating emotions," says Bell, "the eyebrows, the eyelids, the nostril, and the angle of the mouth are raised. In the depressing emotions it is the reverse."

For the execution of these diverse movements, which make it the most expressive organ of the body, the mouth employs more than a dozen important groups of muscles, some of which originate in the chin, some in the cheeks, some in the lips themselves, enabling them to execute independent movements.

While surpassing the eyes in expressiveness, the mouth rivals them in beauty of form and colour. "The lips answer the purpose of displaying a more brilliant red than is to be seen elsewhere," says Winckelmann. "The under lip should be fuller than the upper." In Greek divinities the lips are not always closed: "and this is especially the case with Venus, in order that her countenance may express the languishing softness of desire and love." At the same time, "very few of the figures which have been represented laughing, as some Satyrs or Fauns are, show the teeth." This is natural enough, for the long-continued exposure of the teeth would only result in a grimace. It is only in the transient smile that the teeth may peep forth; and then what a charming contrast their ivory curve and lustrous colour presents to the full-blooded, soft, pink lips!

> "Lillies married to the rose,
> Have made her cheek the nuptial bed;
> Her lips betray their virgin red,
> As they only blushed for this,
> That they one another kiss."

Health, Beauty, and Love—everywhere we see them inseparably associated. Who could ever fall in love with a pair of thin, pallid lips that have lost their pink and plump loveliness through anæmic indolence, or disease, or tight lacing? The very teeth, though the hardest substance of the body, lose their natural colour and beauty in ill-health. Not only do they decay and become blackish, but "in bilious people they become yellow, and in consumptive patients they show occasionally an unnaturally pearly and translucent whiteness" (Brinton and Napheys).

Negroes have, normally, teeth of a dazzling whiteness, which is often regarded as a racial peculiarity, but is due, according to Waitz, to the use of chalk or vegetal fibres. But various savages are dissatisfied with the natural form and colour of their teeth, and disfigure them in various ways. "In different countries the teeth are stained black, red, blue, etc., and in the Malay Archipelago it is thought shameful to have teeth like those of a dog" (Darwin).

"In Macassar the women spend a part of the day in painting their teeth red and yellow, in such a way that a red tooth follows a yellow one, and alternately." In Japan, Fashion compels married women to blacken their teeth, not, however, as an ornament, but to make them ugly and save them from temptation.

Some African tribes knock out two or more of their front teeth, on the ground that they do not wish to look like brutes. The Batokas "think the presence of incisors most unsightly, and on beholding some Europeans, cried out, 'Look at the great teeth!' . . . In various parts of Africa, and in the Malay Archipelago, the natives file the incisors into points like those of a saw, or pierce them with holes, into which they insert studs."

In case of the lips, primitive Fashion prescribes still more atrocious mutilations. One would think that a negro's swollen lips were ugly enough to suit even a devotee of African Fashion; but no! Her lips being naturally large, the fashionable negro belle considers it incumbent on her to exaggerate them into additional hideousness, just as European and American fashionable women exaggerate the slight and beautiful natural curve of their waist into the atrocious hour-glass shape.

"Among the Babines, who live north of the Columbia River," says Sir John Lubbock, "the size of the under lip is the standard of female beauty. A hole is made in the under lip of the infant, in which a small bone is inserted; from time to time the bone is replaced by a larger one, until at last a piece of wood, three inches long and an inch and a half wide, is inserted in the orifice, which makes the lip protrude to a frightful extent. The process appears to be very painful."

"In Central Africa," says Darwin, "the women perforate the lower lip and wear a crystal, which, from the movement of the tongue, has 'a wriggling motion indescribably ludicrous during conversation.' The wife of the chief of Latooka told Sir S. Baker that Lady Baker 'would be much improved if she would extract her four front teeth from the lower jaw, and wear the long pointed polished crystal in her under lip.' Further south, with the Makalolo, the upper lip is perforated, and a large metal and bamboo ring, called a *pelelé*, is worn in the hole. This caused the lip to project in one point two inches beyond the tip of the nose; and when the lady smiled, the contraction of the muscles elevated it over the eyes. 'Why do the women wear these things?' the venerable chief Chinsurdi was asked. Evidently surprised at such a stupid question, he replied, 'For beauty! They are the only beautiful things women have; men have beards, women have none. What kind of a person would she be without a *pelelé*? She would not be a woman at all, with a mouth like a man but no beard.'"

In New Zealand, according to Tylor, "it was considered shameful for a woman not to have her mouth tattooed, for people would say with disgust, 'She has red lips.'"

Compare these two pictures for a moment: on the one side, the protuberant mouth-borders of the negro woman, swollen as by disease or an insect's sting, enlarged, in smiling, to the very ears, and showing not only the teeth but the gums, the tongue and the unæsthetic œsophagus; on the other side, the full but delicate cherry lips of civilised woman, capable of an infinite variety of subtle, graceful movements, a keyboard on which the whole gamut of human feelings finds expression, and revealing, in a smile, only the tips of the pearly, undeformed teeth. Shall we say, with Alison and Jeffrey, that it is all a matter of taste, and that the negro has as much right to his taste as we have to ours? Or have we not plentiful reasons for claiming that Personal Beauty is a fine art, and that the reason why the negro prefers his coarse mouth to our refined lips is because he *does not understand* our highly-developed and specialised Beauty?

There are cogent scientific reasons for believing that, just as the skull has been modified and developed from the upper part of the spinal column, and the brain from its contents, so the facial muscles are all developed from the broad muscle of the neck. In the orang, according to Professor Owen, we find already all the important facial muscles which man uses to express emotions. But, as Darwin remarks, "distinct uses, independently of expression, can . . . be assigned with much probability for almost all the facial muscles."

On the other hand, the facial muscles "are, as is admitted by every one who has written on the subject, very variable in structure; and Moreau remarks that they are hardly alike in half a dozen subjects. They are also variable in function. Thus the power of uncovering the canine tooth on one side differs much in different persons. The power of raising the wings of the nostrils is also, according to Dr. Piderit, variable in a remarkable degree; and other such cases could be given."

The facts that the facial muscles blend so much together that their number has been variously estimated at from nineteen to fifty-five, and that they vary so much in details of structure and function in individuals, are of extreme significance. For, in the first place, this variableness allows Love—or Sexual Selection—to favour the survival of those modifications of the features which are most in harmony with the laws of Beauty; and, secondly, it affords the means of further specialisation and increased accuracy in the modes of emotional expression.

When we see a friend reading a letter, we fancy his face a perfect mirror, reflecting every mood touched upon in its contents. Yet many of our expressions are vague, and there is much room for improvement in definiteness. Darwin, in the introduction to his work on the *Expression of Emotions in Man and Animals*, has remarked how difficult it often is to name the exact emotion intended to be expressed in a picture of a man, unless we regard the accessories by which the painter illustrates the situation; and how apt people are to disagree in naming the emotions expressed by a series of physiognomic portraits. With monkeys, he says, "the expression of slight pain, or of any painful emotion, such as grief, vexation, jealousy, etc., is not easily distinguished from that of moderate anger."

Savages, as we saw in a previous chapter, are strangers to many of the tender emotions which enter into our daily life; hence it would be absurd to look for muscles specially trained to express them. And even with Europeans the refined emotions are of such recent development that, as just stated, they are capable of much further specialisation. To take only one case: it is probable that, whereas in the present stage of human evolution, it is almost impossible, without accessories, to distinguish the facial expression of feminine Romantic Love from that of maternal love, future generations will have specially modified muscles for those modes of expression. Duchenne has pointed out on the side of the nose a series of transient folds expressive of amorous desire. As Romantic Love displaces coarse passion, may not these or another set of muscles be pressed into the special service of refined Love as a sign of encouragement to lovers about to propose? Coquettes, of course, would immediately cultivate this expression, as a new wile or "wrinkle."

Between the facial muscles that are thus utilised for the expression of emotions and other muscles of the body, there is one difference which is of the utmost importance from the point of view of Personal Beauty. The function of ordinary muscles is to move bones, whereas the muscles of expression in the face are only concerned with the movements of the skin. Hence they do not enlarge the bones of the face, which would destroy its delicacy. Their exercise gives elasticity and plump roundness to the outlines of the face; and as they are subtly subdivided in function, they cannot easily become too plump from exercise.

Individual peculiarities of expression are of course due to the frequent exercise of certain sets of muscles, leading gradually to a fixed physiognomic aspect; for form is merely crystallised expression. Hence no one can be beautiful without being good. Vice soon destroys Personal Beauty. If the muscles of anger, envy, jealousy, spite, cruelty, etc., are too frequently called into exercise, the result is a face on which the word *vicious* is written as legibly and in as many corners as the numerals X and 10 are printed on a United States banknote.

One of the reasons why Fashion encourages the *blasé, nil admirari* attitude, and the stolid suppression of emotional expression, is to hide these signs of moral and hygienic sins.

Oliver Wendell Holmes, anatomist and poet, says of Emerson that he had "that look of refinement centring about the lips which is rarely found in the male New Englander, unless the family features have been for two or three cultivated generations the battlefield and the playground of varied thoughts and complex emotions, as well as the sensuous and nutritive port of entry."

Dr. Holmes need not have limited his generalisation to "male New Englanders." Refined mouths are rare in every country, among women as well as among men. As a writer in the *Victoria Magazine* exclaims: "It is wonderful how far more common good foreheads and eyes are amongst us than good mouths and chins." Yet there is a special reason for singling out the average male New Englander as a "warning example." He inherits the thin, famished, pale, stern, forbidding lips of his Puritan ancestors, whose sins are thus visited on later generations. Sins? Yes, sins against health. Without cheerfulness there can be no sound health, and the Puritans made the systematic pursuit of unhappiness the chief object of their life. They made cruel war on all those innocent pursuits and amusements which bring the bloom of health and beauty to the youthful cheek, and exercise the lips in the expression of refined æsthetic emotion. Even music, the most innocent of the arts, was included in their fanatic ostracism, to which historians also trace the rarity of musical taste of the highest order in England.

There is reason to believe that it is especially æsthetic culture which betrays itself in the refined contours and expression of the lips. Men of genius, though their cast of features is not always handsome, commonly have finely-cut mouths. Among German women addicted to music and love of nature, though beauty is comparatively rare—owing to causes which will be considered in a later chapter—good mouths are more common than in some other countries which boast a higher general average of Personal Beauty. Among Americans in general, all the features are apt to be finely cut, hence the lips also partake of this advantage.

But it is among Spanish maidens that perhaps the most inviting, full-blooded yet delicate, soft, and refined lips are to be sought. True, the Spanish maiden seems to lack refined feelings when she goes, as commonly supposed, to be thrilled by a bull-fight. Yet it is well known that the upper classes of women in Spain do not commonly attend these spectacles; and if they did, would they be more cruel than our fashionable women? Which is the more glaring evidence of callous emotions, to voluntarily witness the slaughter of an infuriated, dangerous beast, or to wear on one's hat the painted corpses of innocent song-birds?

The following passage in one of Washington

Irving's works shows that the Spanish have genuine æsthetic feeling and taste :—

"'How near the Sierra looks this evening!' said Mateo; 'it seems as if you could touch it with your hand, and yet it is many leagues off.' While he was speaking a star appeared over the snowy summit of the mountain, the only one yet visible in the heavens, and so pure, so large, so bright and beautiful as to call forth ejaculations of delight from honest Mateo.

"'Que lucero hermoso!—que clara y limpio es!—no pueda ser lucero mas brillante.' (What a beautiful star! how clear and lucid!—no star could be more brilliant!)

"I have often remarked this sensibility of the common people of Spain to the charms of natural objects. The lustre of a star—the beauty or fragrance of a flower—the crystal purity of a fountain, will inspire them with a kind of poetical delight—and then what euphonious words their magnificent language affords with which to give utterance to their transports!"

Possibly the constant pronouncing of these "euphonious words" is one of the causes of the beauty of Spanish lips. But one need not go into such subtle details for an explanation of the phenomenon. Sexual Selection accounts for it sufficiently. The admiration of Beauty is the strongest factor in Romantic Love. The Spaniard's sense of Beauty is refined through his love of Beauty in natural objects. Hence in Sexual Selection he is guided by a taste which abhors equally the coarse, protuberant lips suggestive of mere animality, and the leathery, lifeless lips indicating neglect of the laws of health and a lack of lusty vitality. For true labial refinement consists not in ascetic elimination of sensuous fulness, but in æsthetic harmony between sense and intellect. The lips, like all other parts of the body, are naturally plump and full-blooded in Southern nations, saturated with sunshine and fresh air; and when this plumpness is checked by mental refinement and the exigencies of varied expression, then it is that lips become ideally beautiful.

It is with the lips as with Love, of which they are the perch. Neither Zola nor Dante are the true painters of the romantic passion, but Shakspere, who pays respect to flesh and blood as well as to emotion and intellect.

COSMETIC HINTS

Although the size and shape of the lips afford an index of coarse or refined ancestry, the mouth is commonly the most self-made feature in the countenance, because it is such an important seat of individual expression. Herein lies a soothing balm to those who, owing to the stupidly irregular and incalculable laws of heredity, have inherited an ugly mouth from a grandfather or a more remote ancestor.

A pleasing impression, oft repeated, leaves its traces on the facial muscles. Kant gives this advice to parents: "Children, especially girls, must be accustomed early to smile in a frank, unconstrained manner; for the cheerfulness and animation of the features gradually leave an impression on the mind itself, and thus create a disposition towards gaiety, amiableness, and sociability, which lay an early foundation for the virtue of benevolence."

So Kant evidently believed that we can beautify the soul by beautifying the body. And the reverse is equally true. As Mr. Ruskin remarks: "There is not any virtue the exercise of which, even momentarily, will not impress a new fairness upon the features. . . . On the gentleness and decision of just feeling there follows a grace of action which by no discipline may be taught or obtained."

If educators and parents would thoroughly impress on the minds of the young the great truth that good moral behaviour and the industry which leads to intellectual pre-eminence are magic sources of youthful and permanent Personal Beauty, they would find it the most potent of all civilising agencies, especially with women.

Drs. Brinton and Napheys, in their work on *Personal Beauty* (1870), which is especially valuable from the point of view of medical and surgical cosmetics, but which is unfortunately out of print, offer the following suggestions as to how the shape and expression of the mouth may be improved:—

"For cosmetic reasons, immoderate laughter is objectionable. It keeps the muscles on the stretch, destroys the contour of the features, and produces wrinkles. It is better to cultivate a 'classic repose.'

"Still more decidedly should the habit of 'making mouths' be condemned, whether it occur in conversing in private or to express emotions. It never adds to the emphasis of the discourse, never improves the looks, and leads to actual malformations.

"Children sometimes learn to suck and bite their lips. This distorts these organs, and unless they are persuaded to give it up betimes, a permanent deformity will arise.

"When the lips have once assumed a given form, it is difficult to change them. Those that are too thin can occasionally be increased by adopting the plan of sucking them. This forces a large quantity of blood to the part, and consequently a greater amount of nutriment. When too large, compresses can sometimes, but not always, be used with effect. We have employed silver plates connected by a wire spring, or a mould of stiff leather. Either may be worn at night, or in the house during the day."

It is astonishing to note how many persons are utterly unconcerned regarding the appearance of their mouths in talking, smiling, and laughing, sometimes revealing the whole of the teeth and even the gums, like savages, or as if they were walking tooth-powder advertisements. Self-observation before a mirror is the best antidote against such grimaces.

Chapped lips sometimes call for constitutional treatment, but ordinarily they can be easily cured by obtaining a lip-salve of some reputable chemist. Glycerine is almost always adulterated and injurious, and should only be used on any part of the skin when chemically pure.

Pale lips are commonly an indication of ill-health, and therefore call for exercise, tonics, or other medical treatment. And the colour of the lips is an index of emotion as well as of health—

"Whispering, with white lips, 'The foe! They come! They come!'"—BYRON.

That sound teeth, though they should never be

seen except in glimpses, are an extremely important element in facial beauty, may be seen by the fact that the loss of a few front teeth makes a person look ten years older at once. The art of dentistry has reached such marvellous perfection that there is no excuse for having unsightly teeth. They may be easily preserved to a good age, if properly exercised on solid food—bread crusts, etc. Very hot and very cold food and drink is injurious, especially if cold and hot things are taken in immediate succession. The teeth should be cleaned twice a day, on rising and before retiring. The brush should not be too hard, and a harmless powder, wash, or soap should be obtained of a trustworthy chemist for the threefold purpose of whitening the teeth by removing tartar, of killing the numerous microbes in the mouth, and purifying the breath. An offensive breath is shockingly common, probably owing to the fact that many brush only the outside surface of their teeth. They should be brushed inside as well, and on the top, and the tooth wash or soap should be brought into contact with every corner and crevasse of the mouth and teeth. An offensive breath ought to be good cause for divorce, and certainly it is a deadly enemy of Romantic Love.

THE CHEEKS

HIGH CHEEK-BONES

When we look at a Mongolian, the flat nose and oblique eyes at once attract our attention, but hardly to such a degree as his high and prominent cheek-bones. The North American Indians, who are probably the descendants of Mongolians, resemble them in their prominent cheek-bones; and the Esquimaux likewise possess these in a most exaggerated form. "The Siamese," says Darwin, "have small noses with divergent nostrils, a wide mouth, rather thick lips, a remarkably large face, with very high and broad cheek-bones. It is therefore not wonderful that 'beauty, according to our notion, is a stranger to them. Yet they consider their own females to be much more beautiful than those of Europe.'"

Here is another "matter of taste," which is decided in our favour by the general laws of Beauty, positive and negative.

High, prominent cheek-bones are ugly, in the first place, because they interfere with the regularly graded oval of the face. Secondly, because, like projecting bones and angles in any other part of the body, they interrupt the regular curve of Beauty. Thirdly, because they are coarse and inelegant, offending the sense of delicacy and grace, like big, clumsy ankles and wrists. Fourthly, because they suggest the decrepitude of old age and disease. In the healthy cheek of youth and beauty there is a large amount of adipose tissue, both under the skin and between the subjacent muscles. When age or disease makes fatal inroads on the body, this fat disappears and leaves the impression of starvation. "Famine is in thy cheeks," exclaims Shakspere; and again—

"Meagre were his looks,
Sharp misery had worn him to the bones."

When the malar bones are too high, the fleshy cheeks, instead of including them in a plump curve, are made by contrast to appear hollow, thus simulating and suggesting the appearance of disease to those whose imagination is sufficiently awake to notice such suggestions. And besides emaciation, hollow cheeks suggest another sign of age and decrepitude—the loss of the teeth, which on the sides of the jaws help to give youthful cheeks their plump outlines.

Finally, prominent cheek-bones are objectionable because they are concomitants of the large, clumsy, brutal jaws which characterise savages and apes. To the cheek-bones the upper jaw-bone is directly attached; hence the larger the teeth are, and the more vigorously they are exercised in fighting and picking bones, the more massive must be the cheek-bones, to prevent the upper jaw from being pushed out of position. Moreover, there is attached to the cheek-bones a powerful muscle which connects it with the lower jaw, and by its contraction brings the two jaws together; and this is a second way in which violent exercise of the jaws tends to enlarge the cheek-bones, for all bones become enlarged if the muscles attached to them are much exercised.

At a recent meeting of the British Association, Sir George Campbell advanced the theory that the Aryan race, to which we belong, originally had prominent cheek-bones, like those of lower races. On general evolutionary grounds this is indeed a foregone conclusion; as is the corollary that our cheek-bones have become smaller, for the same reason that our jaws have become more delicate;

viz. because we no longer use them to fight and tear our food like wild beasts, but to masticate soft cooked food, to talk, etc. Thus does the progress of civilisation enhance our Personal Beauty.

An excessive diminution in the size of the cheek-bones, as of the jaws, will be prevented by Romantic Love (Sexual Selection), which ever aims at establishing and preserving those proportions and outlines of the features which are most in harmony with the general laws of beauty.

Among the lower animals cruel Natural Selection eliminates those individuals who are ugly, *i.e.* unnatural, unhealthy, clumsy. With mankind charity and pity have checked the operation of this cruel though beneficial law, and progress in the direction of refinement and Beauty would therefore be fatally impeded were it not that Sexual Selection, or Love guided by the sense of Beauty, steps in to eliminate the ill-favoured, who bear in their countenance too conspicuously the marks of their savage and animal ancestry. Perhaps Mr. Wallace had some such thought in his mind when he anticipated the time when man's selection shall have supplanted natural selection.

Yet there are thousands of good people who still profess to believe that "beauty is only skin deep," and that Romantic Love and æsthetic culture are of no practical importance, but mere gaudy soap-bubbles to delight our vision for a transient moment!

In future ages, when æsthetic refinement will be more common, and Romantic Love, its offspring, less impeded by those considerations of rank and money and imaginary " prudence " which lead parents to *sacrifice the physique and wellbeing of their grandchildren* to the illusive comfort of their sons and daughters (in " marriages of reason ")—what an impetus will then be given to the development of Personal Beauty! Refined mouths and noses, rosy cheeks, sparkling eyes, plump and graceful healthy figures, now so lamentably rare, will then become as plentiful as blackberries in the autumn.

COLOUR AND BLUSHES

Although the heart's warm blood is not carried to the cheeks in so dense a network of arteries, nor so near the surface as in the lips, yet the cheeks come next to the lips in delicate sensibility—a fact which Love has discovered instinctively; for a kiss on the cheeks is still a kiss of love, whereas a kiss on the forehead or eyelids indicates less ecstatic forms of affection or esteem.

What makes the cheeks so sensitive is the great delicacy of their transparent skin, which readily allows the colour of the blood to be seen as through a veil, not only in blushing, but in the natural rosy aspect of youth and health.

Though the cheeks may not vie with the lips and teeth, the hair and the eyes, in lustrous depth of colour, they have an advantage in their chamæleonic variety and changes of tint, and their delicious gradations. Even the delicate blushes on an apple or a peach, caused by the warm and loving glances of the sun, what are they compared to the luscious, mellow tints on a maiden's ripe cheeks? Nor is it possible to find in the leaves of an autumnal

American forest more endless individual *nuances* and shades of red and rose and pink than in the cheeks of lovely girls—unless indolence or other sins against health have painted them with ghastly repulsive pallor, or the hideous Hottentot habit of bedaubing them with brutal paint has ruined their translucent delicacy.

Says the author of the *Ugly Girl Papers:* " Some cheeks have a winelike, purplish glow, others a transparent saffron tinge, like yellowish-pink porcelain; others still have clear, pale carmine; and the rarest of all, that suffused tint like apple-blossoms."

At summer resorts where girls drink in daily draughts of the elixir of youth and beauty, commonly known as fresh air, one of their greatest love-charms is these colour-symphonies on their cheeks, changing their melody with every pulse-beat. These charms they might possess all the year round did not their parents commonly convert their dwelling-houses into hothouses, reeking with stagnant, enervating air.

If, therefore, we read that Africans prefer the opaque, inky, immutable ebony of their complexion to the translucent, ever-changing tints, eloquent of health and varied emotions, in a white maiden's face, we—well, we simply smile, on recalling the fact that even among ourselves a cheap, gaudy chromo is preferred by the great multitude to the work of a great master which they do not understand. The slow growth of æsthetic refinement is illustrated by the fact that it is only a few years since Fashion has set its face against the use of vulgar paints and powders, which ensure a most questionable temporary advantage at the expense of future permanent defacement.

The colours of the cheeks, so far under consideration, are to a certain extent subject to our will and skill; for no one who cultivates the complexion and has plenty of pure air need be without these blooming buccal roses. But the "thousand *blushing apparitions*" that start into our faces are, as Shakspere's well-chosen words imply, as independent of our will and control as any other apparitions.

Are blushes ornamental or useful? That is, were they developed through Sexual or through Natural Selection? Such Shaksperian expressions as "Bid the cheek be ready with a blush, modest as morning;" "Thy cheeks blush for pure shame to counterfeit our roses;" and "To blush and beautify the cheek again," suggest the notion that the great poet regarded blushes as beautiful; while the following permit a different interpretation: "Her blush is guiltiness, not modesty;" "Blushing cheeks by faults are bred, and fears by pale white shown;" "You virtuous ass, you bashful fool, must you be blushing?" "His treasons will sit blushing in his face."

Let us see if any light is thrown on the problem by going back to the beginning, and tracing the development of the habit of blushing. That blushing is a comparatively recent human acquisition is made apparent from the facts that it is not seen in animals, nor in very young children, nor in idiots, as a rule; while among savages the faculty of blushing seems to be dependent on the presence of a sense of shame, which is almost, if not entirely, unknown to the lowest tribes.

That animals never blush, Darwin thinks, is almost certain. "Blushing," he says, "is the most peculiar and the most human of all expressions. Monkeys redden from passion, but it would require an overwhelming amount of evidence to make us believe that any animal could blush." Concerning children he says: "The young blush much more freely than the old, but not during infancy, which is remarkable, as we know that infants at a very early age redden from passion. I have received authentic accounts of two little girls blushing at the ages of between two and three years; and of another sensitive child, a year older, blushing when reproved for a fault."

"In the dark-brown Peruvian," says Mr. Tylor, "or the yet blacker African, though a hand or a thermometer put to the cheek will detect the blush by its heat, the somewhat increased depth of colour is hardly perceptible to the eye." Dr. Burgess repeatedly had occasion to observe that a scar in the face of a negress "invariably became red whenever she was abruptly spoken to, or charged with any trivial offence." And Darwin was assured by several trustworthy observers "that they have seen on the faces of negroes an appearance resembling a blush, under circumstances which would have excited one in us, though their skins were of an ebony-black tint. Some describe it as a blushing brown, but most say that the blackness becomes more intense."

Now evidence has already been quoted in a previous chapter showing that negroes admire a black skin more than a white one (vide *Descent of Man*, 1885, p. 579). Is it likely, therefore, that the blush was admired by negroes, and became a ground of selection, because it intensified the blackness of the skin? It hardly seems probable that the coarse negro can be influenced in his amorous choice by any such subtle, almost imperceptible difference; and even the great originator of the theory of Sexual Selection does not believe that it accounts for the origin of blushes: "No doubt a slight blush adds to the beauty of a maiden's face; and the Circassian women who are capable of blushing invariably fetch a higher price in the seraglio of the Sultan than less susceptible women. But the firmest believer in the efficacy of sexual selection will hardly suppose that blushing was acquired as a sexual ornament. This view would also be opposed to what has just been said about the dark-coloured races blushing in an invisible manner."

On the other hand, it seems equally difficult to account for the origin of blushing on utilitarian grounds. No one likes to be caught blushing; on the contrary, every one tries to conceal such a state by lowering or averting the face. How could such an unwelcome, embarrassing habit prove of advantage to us? Sir Charles Bell's remarks on the subject may serve as a clue to the answer. That blushing "is a provision for expression may be inferred," he says, "from the colour extending only to the surface of the face, neck, and breast—the parts most exposed. . . . The colour caused by blushing gives brilliancy and interest to the expression of the face. In this we perceive an advantage possessed by the fair family of mankind, and which must be lost to the dark; for I can hardly believe that a blush may be seen in the negro. . . . Blushing assorts well with youthful and with effeminate features, while nothing is more hateful than a dog-face that exhibits no token of sensibility in the variations of colour."

The poet Young tells us that "the man that blushes is not quite a brute"; and Darwin quotes from Humboldt a sneer of the Spaniard, "How can those be trusted who know not how to blush?" Darwin's remark that some idiots, "*if not utterly degraded*, are capable of blushing," also accords with Bell's notion that blushing is a provision for expression. Bell's assertion that it is "indicative of excitement" is, however, not sufficiently definite. What is it that a blush expresses? Evidently nervous sensibility, a moral sense, modesty, innocence. The Circassian who can blush is more highly valued than another, because the blush is eloquent of maiden modesty and heart untainted. The fact that there is also a blush of violated modesty, a blush of shame, and of guilt, does not argue against this view, any more than the fact that we blush if, though innocent, we are accused of guilt. It is the association of ideas and of emotions that evokes the blush in such cases.

We may therefore conclude that a blush is useful on account of its *moral beauty, i.e.* its expressiveness of presumptive innocence, or at least of a desire to be considered innocent; whereas the unblushing front and cheek indicate a brutal, callous indifference to virtue. We admire a blush as "the most peculiar and the most human of all expressions." And we admire it also, to some extent, on purely æsthetic grounds, if not exaggerated. A slight blush has a rosy charm of its own, and it is only when it becomes a too diffused and deep facial aurora borealis that it loses its charm, because suggestive of the hectic or fever flush, or the redness caused by anger, heat, violent exertion, etc., which has a physiological origin distinct from that of blushing.

According to Bell, "the colour which attends exertion or the violent passions, as of rage, arises from general vascular excitement, and differs from blushing. Blushing is too sudden and too partial to be traced to the heart's action." Darwin endeavours to find the explanation of blushing in the intimate sympathy which exists between the capillary circulation of the surface of the head and face, and that of the brain, which would account for the mental confusion of shyness, modesty, etc., being so immediately photographed on the face. He sums up his theory in these words :—

"I conclude that blushing—whether due to shyness—to shame for a real crime—to shame from a breach of the laws of etiquette—to modesty from humility—to modesty from an indelicacy—depends in all cases on the same principle; this principle being a sensitive regard for the opinion, more particularly for the depreciation of others, primarily in relation to our personal appearance, especially of our faces; and secondarily, through the force of association and habit, in relation to the opinion of others on our conduct."

He gives various illustrations showing how by directing our attention to certain parts of the body we can increase their sensitivity and activity in a manner analogous to that postulated by the theory of blushing. But for these the reader must be referred to his essay on this subject in the Expression of Emotions—a masterpiece of physiological and psychological analysis. One more passage, however, may be cited, as it helps to justify this long discussion of blushing by showing its special relations to Romantic Love and Personal Beauty :—

"It is plain to every one that young men and women are highly sensitive to the opinion of each other with reference to their personal appearance; and they blush incomparably more in presence of the opposite sex than in that of their own. A young man, not very liable to blush, will blush intensely at any slight ridicule of his appearance from a girl whose judgment on any important subject he would disregard. No happy pair of young lovers, valuing each other's admiration and love more than anything else in the world, probably ever courted each other without many a blush. Even the barbarians of Tierra del Fuego, according to Mr. Bridges, blush 'chiefly in regard to women, but certainly also at their own personal appearance.'"

THE EARS

A USELESS ORNAMENT

The shell of the ear appears to be the only part of man's visible body which has ceased to be useful and become purely ornamental. "Persons whose ears have been cut off hear just as well as before," says Professor Haeckel. Dr. J. Toynbee, F.R.S., "after collecting all the evidence on this head, concludes that the external shell is of no distinct use;" and Darwin was informed by Professor Preyer that after experimenting on the functions of the shell of the ear he had come to nearly the same conclusion.

To infer from this that our external ears have been developed, through Sexual Selection, for purely ornamental purposes, would not be in accord with scientific analogies. For, often as existing organs (horns, feathers, etc.) are *modified* for ornamental purposes, there are no known instances of any that have been specially developed for that purpose; even the facial muscles of expression being, as we have seen, in this predicament. Hence we are led to conclude that man has inherited the shell of his ear from a remote apelike ancestor, to whom it was of use in catching faint sounds, and who consequently had the power, common to other animals, not only of directing the ears as a whole to different points of the compass, but of temporarily altering its shape. Indeed, one of the strongest proofs of our descent from lower animals lies in the fact that man still possesses, in a rudimentary form, the muscles needed to move the ears. Some savage tribes have considerable control over these muscles. The famous physiologist, Johannes Müller, after long and patient efforts, succeeded in recovering the power of moving his ears; and Darwin writes: "I have seen one man who could draw the whole ear forwards; other men can draw it upwards; another who could draw it backwards; and from what one of these persons told me, it is probable that most of us, by often touching our ears, and thus directing our attention towards them, could recover some power of movement by repeated trials."

Ordinary monkeys still possess the power to move their ears; but the manlike or anthropoid apes resemble us in the rudimentary condition of their ear-muscles; and Darwin was assured by the keepers in the London Zoological Gardens that these animals never move or erect their ears. He suggests two theories to account for the loss of this power: first, that, owing to their arboreal habits and great strength, these apes were not exposed to much danger, and thus gradually, through disuse, lost control over these organs, just as birds on oceanic islands where they are not subject to attacks have lost the use of their wings; secondly, that the freedom with which they can move the head in a horizontal plane enabled them to dispense with mobile ears.

The remarkable variability of the ears—greater, by the way, in men than in women—is another reason for regarding them as rudimentary organs, inherited from remote semi-human ancestors, to whom they were useful; for great variability is a characteristic of all rudimentary organs. Haeckel facetiously suggests that " at large assemblies, where our interest is not sufficiently enchained, nothing is more instructive and entertaining than a comparative study of the countless variations in the form of the ears." The ancient Greek artists were aware of this variability, for Winckelmann speaks of "the infinite variety of forms of the ear on heads modelled from life." "It was customary with the ancient artists to elaborate no portion of the head more diligently than the ears." "In portrait figures, when the countenance is so much injured as not to be recognised, we can occasionally make a correct conjecture as to the person intended, if it is one of whom we have any knowledge, merely by the form of the ear; thus we infer a head of Marcus Aurelius from an ear with an unusually large inner opening."

If we compare a man's ears with those of a dog or horse, differences of shape appear no less conspicuous than differences in mobility. Two points are especially characteristic of man—the folded upper margin and the lobule. Our cousins, the anthropoid apes, are the only other animals which have the margin of the ear thus folded inwards, the lower monkeys having them simple and pointed, like other animals. The sculptor, Mr. Woolner, called Darwin's attention to "a little blunt point, projecting from the inwardly-folded margin or helix." Darwin, on investigating the matter, came to the conclusion that these points "are vestiges of the tips of former erect and pointed ears"; being led to think so "from the frequency of their occurrence, and from the general correspondence in position with that of the tip of a pointed ear."

The lobule is still more peculiar to man than the folded margin, since he does not even share it with the anthropoid apes, although, according to Professor Mivart, "a rudiment of it is found in the gorilla." An intermediate stage between man and ape is occupied by some savage tribes in whom the lobule is scantily developed or even absent.

COSMETICS AND FASHION

The lobule of the human ear has been presumably developed through the agency of Sexual Selection, as it is an ornament the absence of which is at once felt. And there are other ways in which this organ has been gradually brought into harmony with the laws of beauty. Thus the loss of the hair (of which rudiments are still occasionally present) made visible the soft skin and the delicate tint of the ear, which, like that of the cheeks, may be momentarily heightened by a blush, and thus become an index of emotional expression. A permanently-heightened colour of the ear, however, caused by exposure to extreme cold or by rough treatment, is almost as great a blemish as a red nose or pallid lips. If boxers are anxious to deform their ears, no one has a right to object; but children have a right to ask of their parents and teachers not to redden their ears permanently by pulling or boxing them. That a delicate and important sense-organ like the ear should be so frequently chosen as a place to inflict punishment, shows the necessity of a general diffusion of hygienic knowledge. It may not be superfluous to add a caution to lovers, that the ears should never be taken as an osculatory substitute for the lips or cheeks, as cases are known in medical practice where the tympanum, and consequently the hearing, has been destroyed by a vigorous kiss implanted by a foolish lover on his sweetheart's ears.

An ear to be beautiful should be about twice as long as broad. It should be attached to the head almost straight, or slightly inclined backwards, and should almost touch the head with the back of its upper point. Many poor girls are deformed for life through the ignorance of their mothers, who allow them to wear their hair or bonnets in such a way as to make the ears stand out obliquely. As the ears contain no bones, but consist entirely of cartilages and skin, they can be, more readily even than the nose, moulded into a fine shape at an early age. As Drs. Brinton and Napheys remark, "Even when the ear is in part or altogether absent, the case is not desperate. An 'artificial ear' can be made of vulcanised rubber, or other material, tinted the colour of the flesh, and attached to the side of the head with such deftness that its character will escape every ordinary eye." There is therefore no excuse for having badly-shaped or wrongly-inclined ears in these days of cosmetic surgery.

In the most beautiful ears the lobe is free, and not attached to the head in its lower part. Heavy earrings, which have a tendency to unduly enlarge the lobules, are now tabooed by Fashion; but very small jewels in the ear may be looked on, like small finger-rings, necklaces, and bracelets, as unobjectionable from an æsthetic point of view, though real beauty unadorned is adorned the most.

Formerly Fashion maltreated the poor ears quite as badly as it still does the waist and the feet. Lubbock remarks that the East Islanders enlarge their ears till they come down to the shoulders; and Darwin, after referring to liberties taken with the nose, says that "the ears are everywhere pierced and similarly ornamented, and with the Botocudos and Lenguas of South America the hole is gradually so much enlarged that the lower edge touches the shoulder."

Among the Greeks, as Becker remarks, "it was considered a dishonour, or a token of foreign manners, for men to have their ears bored.... Women and girls, however, not only used earrings, ἐνώτια, ἐλλόβια, ἑλικτῆρες, which are seen perpetually in vases, but also wore numerous articles of jewellery about the neck, the arms, and on the leg above the ankle."

The ancients, too, had heard of the malformed ears of primitive peoples. "It is possible," says Tylor, "that there may be some truth in the favourite wonder-tale of the old geographers, about the tribes whose great ears reached down to their shoulders, though the story had to be stretched a good deal when it was declared they lay down on one ear and covered themselves with the other for a blanket."

Such blanket-ears would be the æsthetic equivalent of modern bustles, crinolettes, and wasp-waists.

PHYSIOGNOMIC VAGARIES

Ever since the days of ancient Greek philosophy ingenious attempts have been made to find a special meaning for this or that particular form of the ear. According to Aristotle, a long ear indicates a good memory, whereas modern physiognomists incline to the opinion that a long ear shows a man's mental relationship to a certain unjustly-maligned animal. Small ears, Lavater thinks, are a sign of an active mind, while a deep shell indicates a thirst for knowledge.

As a matter of fact, the ears have no connection whatever with intellectual or emotional expression, except that a well-shaped ear indicates in a general way that its possessor comes of a stock in which the laws of cosmetic hygiene have been observed during many generations. To many of the lower animals the ears are a means of emotional expression. What, for instance, could be more expressive and droll than the way a dog expresses mild surprise or expectation by pricking up his ears? Or what a more certain sign of viciousness in a horse than the drawing back of the ears?—a movement of which Darwin has found the reason in the fact that all animals that fight with their teeth retract their ears to protect them; whence, through habit and association, it comes that they draw them back whenever a fighting mood comes over them. Man, on the other hand, never uses his ears for emotional expression, because they are the least mobile part of the body. Now form is merely crystallised expression: and the absence of special movements for emotional expression necessarily prevents individual alterations indicative of character. Hence the absurdity of trying to use the ears as a basis for physiognomic distinctions.

NOISE AND CIVILISATION

What is the cause of the folding of the margin of the human ear, which distinguishes it from that of all other animals? Darwin remarks that it "appears to be in some manner connected with the whole external ear being permanently pressed backwards;" but this does not explain the mysterious phenomenon.

After many hours of profound meditation on this subject I have come to the conclusion that this slight folding of the ear's margin is the beginning of a new phase of human evolution. In course of time —this cannot be disproved—the fold of the margin will become larger and larger, until finally the shells of the ear will have been transformed into mobile lids for shutting out at will disagreeable noises, even as the eyelids have been developed to shut out glaring light. This would account for the providential preservation of the rudimentary ear-muscles referred to above. When this process of evolution is completed men coming home late will no longer have to listen to curtain-lectures. The innovation will tend to make them polite, for instead of telling the lecturer to "shut up," they will shut up themselves.

Seriously speaking, such movable ear-lids are very much needed in this transition stage of civilisation. The present age of steam will by future historians be classified as the age of noise. It is almost impossible to find a place within ten miles of a city where one can rest without having one's sleep constantly disturbed, or at least *deprived of its refreshing depth*, by the blowing of railway and factory whistles. Both are unnecessary, inasmuch as railway signals would be quite as effective if not so murderously loud and prolonged, while factory whistles are either blown at the moment when the operatives go to work, when a simple bell would do as well, or they are blown an hour earlier to wake up the workmen,—a most outrageous proceeding, as everybody else sleeping within a radius of a mile or more is thus waked up at six o'clock.

The fact that these nuisances have so long been tolerated shows how primitive is as yet the æsthetic development of the average human ear. Some people even smile at you for being so "nervous," and boast of their indifference to such hideous, brain-racking noises. The Esquimaux and Chinese would doubtless assume a similar attitude regarding their indifference to noisome stenches. In mediæval times, Europeans in general were quite as indifferent to the emanations from their gutters as they still are to the hideous noises in the streets. It has often been noted with surprise that the death-rate in London and the general aspect of health should be so much more favourable than that of continental cities, which are free from the depressing London fogs. The reason, doubtless, lies chiefly in the facts that there are no vile sewer odours in London to poison the atmosphere, and that the pavement of the streets is of such a nature that one can sleep soundly at night, provided there are no steam whistles near. London, too, does not tolerate the brutal whip-cracking which transforms French, German, and Swiss towns and cities into Bedlams of noise. In this respect New York resembles London; but here the comparison ends. New York pavements are the noisiest, roughest, and dirtiest in the world. I have known of invalids who were advised to drive in the Central Park, but could not do so because they could not bear on their way to drive even up Fifth Avenue,—a street lined with the houses of millionaires. And to walk on Broadway for twenty minutes, talking to a friend, makes one as hoarse as delivering a two-hour lecture.

There can be no doubt that a horror of useless noise grows with the general refinement of the senses and the mind. Goethe's aversion to noise, especially at night, is well known. It led him to poison dogs that disturbed him. The delicate hearing of Franz, the great song composer, was ruined by the whistle of a locomotive. And Schopenhauer has put the whole matter into a nutshell in these admirable words: "Intellectual persons, and all in general who have much *esprit*, cannot endure noise. Astounding, on the other hand, is the insensibility of ordinary people to noise. The quantity of noise which any one can endure without annoyance is really related inversely to his mental endowments, and may be regarded as a pretty accurate measure of them."

A MUSICAL VOICE

It is self-evident that indifference to ear-splitting noises implies a lack of appreciation for the exquisite clang-tints of music; for whenever the acoustic nerve is sufficiently refined to appreciate such subtle tints, it is affected as painfully by harsh sounds as the artistic eye is by glaring colours and flickering light. And an ear which is indifferent to the sweetness of musical sounds is of course indifferent also to the musical charm of the speaking voice. But a sweetly modulated voice is one of the most conspicuous attributes of Personal Beauty—for Beauty refers to sounds as well as to sights—

> " Her voice was ever soft,
> Gentle and low, an excellent thing in woman."—SHAKSPERE.

There *is* as much variety in voices as in faces; and in estimating a person's general refinement, the voice is perhaps a safer guide than the face; because the quality of the voice is largely a matter of individual training, whereas in reading faces the judgment is warped by the presence of inherited features speaking of traits which have not been modified by individual effort and culture.

Many young men and women live in absolute indifference to the quality of their speaking voice, till one day Cupid arouses them from their unæsthetic slumber with his golden arrows, and makes them eager not only to brush up their hats and improve their personal appearance, but also to modulate their voices into sweet, expressive accents. But the vocal cords, like a violin, can only be made to yield mellow sounds after long practice; hence the usual result of a sudden effort to speak in love's sweet accents is a ridiculous lover's falsetto.

THE NOSE

SHAPE AND SIZE

"The fate of innumerable girls has been decided by a slight upward or downward curvature of the nose," says Schopenhauer; and Pascal points out that if Cleopatra's nose had been but a trifle larger, the whole political geography of this planet might have been different. Owing to the fact that the nose occupies the most prominent part of the face, Professor Kollmann remarks that "the partial or complete loss of the nose causes a greater disfigurement than a much greater fault of conformation in any other part of the face." And Winckelmann thus bears witness to the importance of the nose as an element of Personal Beauty: "The proof, easy to be understood, of the superiority of shape of the Greeks and the present inhabitants of the Levant lies in the fact that we find among them no flattened noses, which are the greatest disfigurement of the face."

Yet here again we find that "tastes differ." Thus we read in Darwin "that the ancient Huns during the age of Attila were accustomed to flatten the noses of their infants with bandages, 'for the sake of *exaggerating a natural conformation*'" [note the stamp of Fashion]; that, "with the Tahitians, to be called *long-nose* is considered as an insult, and they compress the noses and foreheads of their children for the sake of beauty"; and that "the same holds true with the Malays of Sumatra, the Hottentots, certain Negroes, and the natives of Brazil." But the *ne-plus-ultra* of nasal ugliness is found among the Tartars and Esquimaux. "European travellers in Tartary in the Middle Ages," says Tylor, "described its flat-nosed inhabitants as having no noses at all, but breathing through holes in the face." And among the Esquimaux, as Mantegazza remarks, a rule can be placed on both the cheeks at once without touching the nose. Flat noses, says Topinard, "are either depressed as a whole, as among Chinese, or only in the lower half, as among Malays. Negroes have both forms."

The yellow and black races, who naturally have flat noses, consider it fashionable to have them *very* flat. The same is true with our modern Fashion regarding wasp-waists and feet. But in regard to the face the white races—including even the women —have emancipated themselves from the tyranny of fashionable exaggeration. Hence, though we admire prominent noses, we do not admire them more and more in proportion to their size. On the contrary, every one looks upon the very large Jewish nose as ugly. The reason is that in judging of the face Fashion has been displaced by æsthetic Taste, whose motto is Moderation, and which is based on a knowledge of the cosmic laws of beauty. Savages have Fashion but no Taste. We have both; but Taste is gradually demolishing Fashion, like other relics of barbarism.

Sometimes our estimate of the nose, as of other features, may be influenced by non-æsthetic considerations—by prejudices of race, aristocracy, etc. "In Italy," says Mantegazza, "we call a long nose aristocratic (especially if it is aquiline) perhaps because conquerors with long noses, Greeks and Romans, have subjected the indigenous small-nosed inhabitants." But the Italians are not the only people who, if asked to choose between a nose too large or one too small, would ask for the former. And the cause of this preference is suggested very forcibly in these remarks of Grose: "Convex faces, prominent features, and large aquiline noses, though differing much from beauty, still give an air of dignity to their owners; whereas concave faces, flat, snub, or broken noses, always stamp a meanness and vulgarity. *The one seems to have passed through the limits of beauty, the other never to have arrived at them.*"

EVOLUTION OF THE NOSE

The flat, irregular nose of savages and semi-civilised peoples, with its visible nostrils and imperfectly developed bridge, being intermediate between the ape's nose and our own, we are naturally led to infer that the nose has been gradually developed into the shape now regarded as most perfect by good judges of Beauty. To what are we indebted for this favourable change—to Natural or to Sexual Selection? In other words, is the present perfected shape of the nose of any use to us, or is it purely ornamental?

It appears that both these laws have acted in subtle combination to improve our nasal organ. The nose is a sort of funnel for warming the air on its way to the sensitive lungs. In cold latitudes a long nose would therefore be an advantage favoured by Natural Selection; and it is noteworthy that in general the flat-nosed peoples live in warm climes. There are exceptions, however—notably the Esquimaux—showing that this hypothesis does not entirely cover the facts.

Let us examine, therefore, the second function of the nasal organ. The external nose is a sort of filter for keeping organic impurities out of the lungs. At the entrance of the nostrils there are a number of fine hairs which serve to keep out the dust. If any particles manage to get beyond this first fortress, they are liable to be arrested by the rows of more minute, microscopic hairs, or *cilia*, which line the mucous membrane and keep up a constant downward movement, by means of which dusty intruders are expelled and the air filtered. Esquimaux living in snowfields, and savages in the forests and grass-carpeted meadows, do not need these filters so much as we do in our dusty cities and along dusty country roads ; hence their noses have remained more like those of the arboreal apes, while ours have grown larger, so as to yield a larger surface of sifting hairs and cilia. When we think of the dusty American prairies and the African and Asian deserts, can we wonder, accordingly, that the American Indians, as well as the nomadic Arabs and Jews, have such immense noses ? The theory seems fanciful, if not grotesque ; but perhaps there is more in it than appears at first sight.

Even if both these hypotheses should prove untenable, there is a third consideration which alone suffices to account for the development of the European nose. The nose has a most important *musico-philological* function. The language of savages often consists of only a few hundred words, while ours is so complicated that it requires the co-operation of the vocal cords, and the cavities of the mouth and the nose to produce the countless modifications of speech and song which make us listen with so much pleasure to an eloquent speaker or a great singer. The subject is far too complicated with anatomical details to be fully explained here, and the reader must be referred to a full discussion (not from the evolutionary point of view, however) to Professor Georg Hermann von Meyer's elaborate treatise on *The Organs of Speech*, chap. iii.

A few points, however, must be noted here. The nasal air-passage, " with its two narrow openings and intermediate greater width, possesses the general form of a resonator, and there can be no doubt but that it has a corresponding influence, and that the tones with which the air passing through it vibrates are strengthened by its resonance. The larger the nasal cavity the more powerful the resonance, and, consequently, the reinforcement experienced by the tone. . . . In consequence of the peculiarity of the walls of the nasal cavity, it appears that sounds uttered with the nasal resonance, particularly the nasal vowels, are fuller and more ample than the same sounds when strengthened by the resonance of the cavity of the mouth. The general impression of fulness and richness conveyed by the French language arises from its wealth in nasal vowels; and it is for this reason that second-rate tragic actors like to give a nasal resonance to all the vowels in the pathetic speeches of their heroic parts."

Further, it is of great importance to bear in mind "*that the resonance of the nasal cavity also plays a part in the formation of non-nasal articulate sounds*," appearing here as a mere reinforcement of the resonance of the cavity of the mouth, and free from the nasal twang. Indeed, paradoxical as it may seem, an infallible way to make our speech sound "nasal" is to keep the air out of the nose by clasping it tightly; whereas if the nasal passage remains open the nasal twang is replaced by an agreeable resonance. What could more forcibly illustrate the importance of a well-developed nose?

Now there are several groups of muscles attached to the lower cartilages of the nose,—parts which are imperfectly developed in apes and negroes. The constant exercise of these, during many generations, in the service of speech, in expressing several emotions, and in heavy breathing, suffice to account, on accepted physiological principles, for the gradual enlargement of the resonant tube which we call the nose.

So much for Natural or Utilitarian Selection. But Sexual Selection or Romantic Love plays also a most important *rôle* in the development of the nose. The quotations from Pascal and Schopenhauer made at the beginning of this chapter show that the efficacy of Sexual Selection was recognised long before Darwin had coined the term. As soon as a refined æsthetic taste appears, it rejects ugly forms of the nose. It rejects, for instance, open, visible nostrils, because they are a scavenging apparatus, unæsthetic to behold, though the savage, having no taste, is not thus offended. It gives the preference, in the second place, to the long nose, on musical grounds, because its owner has a more sonorous speech. It scorns the snub-nose because of its simian suggestiveness, and dislikes the excessively large and aquiline nose because it is an exaggerated form, which has passed beyond the delicate dimensions and subtle curves of beauty.

GREEK AND HEBREW NOSES

This checking of excessive development in the direction at first prescribed by the cosmic laws of beauty is indeed one of the main functions of Sexual Selection, without which our mouths would gradually become too small, our eyes and noses too large, our foreheads too high, our hair too scant, etc.

Why, for instance, have the Jews such large noses compared with the Greeks? Evidently because Taste—which, though commonly associated with Romantic Love, may, in a highly æsthetic nation, act independently of it—did not restrain the excessive development of the Jewish nose. The ancient Hebrews were not an æsthetic nation, like the Greeks. The finest works of sculpture ever created were made by the Greeks, while the Hebrews practically had no sculpture at all—not even such works as were produced by Assyrians and Egyptians. And if any further proof were needed of the statement that the ancient Hebrews had little taste for beauty it might be found in the fact that Solomon, esteemed a great judge of feminine charms, compares his love's nose to "the tower of Lebanon, which looketh toward Damascus."

The admission which I have just made that there may be a sort of æsthetic selection independent of real Romantic Love, does not militate against the general thesis of this book: that Love is the cause of Beauty, as Beauty is the cause of Love. For though the Greek artists knew what the shape and size of a beautiful nose should be, there are cogent reasons for believing that "Greek noses" were rare even among the ancient Greeks, thanks to their habit of sacrificing Romantic Love to the dragon chaperon. Hear what Ruskin has to say, in his *Aratra Pentelici*, about the Greek features in general: "Will you look again at the series of coins of the best time of Greek art which I have just set before you? Are any of these goddesses or nymphs very beautiful? Certainly the Junos are not. Certainly the Demeters are not. The Siren and Arethusa have well-formed and regular features; but I am quite sure that if you look at them without prejudice, you will think neither reaches even the average standard of pretty

English girls. The Venus Urania suggests at first the idea of a very charming person, but you will find there is no real depth nor sweetness in the contours, looked at closely. And remember, these are chosen examples; the best I can find of art current in Greece at the great time; and even if I were to take the celebrated statues, of which only two or three are extant, not one of them excels the Venus of Melos; and she, as I have already asserted in *The Queen of the Air*, has nothing notable in feature except dignity and simplicity. Of Athena I do not know one authentic type of great beauty; but the intense ugliness which the Greeks could tolerate in their symbolism of her will be convincingly proved to you by the coin represented in Plate VI. You need only look at two or three vases of the best time to assure yourselves that beauty of feature was, in popular art, not only unattained, but unattempted; and finally—and this you may accept as a conclusive proof of the Greek insensitiveness to the most subtle beauty—there is little evidence, even in their literature, and none in their art, of their having ever perceived any beauty in infancy or early childhood."

Nevertheless, it was to the contours of childhood that the Greek artists apparently went for their ideal of the divine nose. Greek beauty was youthful masculine beauty; and the "Greek nose" is one which not only is straight in itself, but forms a straight line with the forehead. In other words, there is no hollow at the root of the nose, where it meets the forehead. Now the absence of this cavity is characteristic of youth, and is owing to the imperfect development of the brain cavities. Later in life these cavities bulge forwards and produce the hollow, which, therefore, is an indication of superior cranial development and higher intellectual powers. Hence, as Professor Kollmann suggests, the object of the Greek artists in making the nose of their deities form a straight line with the forehead, was probably to give them the stamp of eternal youth ; which would thus appear to have been considered a more important attribute even than the expression of superior *masculine* intellectual power, which we associate with the hollow at the junction of nose and forehead, and for which reason we do not admire it in women if too pronounced. Nevertheless, even in women the cosmic laws of Beauty call for a gentle curve instead of a perfectly straight line; but the more subtle the curve the greater is its beauty ; whereas the nose itself may be perfectly straight on its upper edge, because it forms a dividing line of the face into two symmetric halves, and by its contrasting straightness heightens the beauty of the surrounding facial curves.

To sum up : the Greek's admiration of such features as are naturally associated with youthful masculine beauty no doubt led him, in choosing a wife, to give the preference to similar features, including the "Greek" nose. Yet in the absence of opportunities for courtship, Sexual Selection could not operate very extensively ; hence it is probable that ungainly noses, though not so extravagant as among the Semitic races, were common enough in Greece as in Rome. In the Dark Ages hideous noses must have prevailed everywhere, as might be inferred from the facts that Romantic Love was unknown, and physical beauty looked on as a sinful possession, even if the painted and sculptured portraits did not prove it to our eyes in most instances.

Regarding modern noses it may be said that the nose is such a prominent feature that more has been done for its improvement, through the agency of Love or Sexual Selection, than for the mouth or any other feature, excepting the eye. The average Englishman's nose of to-day, for example, is a tolerably shapely organ, and yet his ancestors were not exactly distinguished for nasal beauty, according to a close observer and student of portraiture, Mr. G. A. Simcox, who remarks that "sometimes both Danes and Saxons had their fair proportions of snub-noses and pug-noses, but when they escaped that catastrophe the Danish nose tended to be a beak (rather a hawk's beak than an eagle's), while the Saxon nose tends to be a proboscis."

Yet even at this date perfect noses are rare, and it is easy to see why. In the first place, it takes many generations to wipe out entirely the ugliness inherited from our unæsthetic ancestors; secondly, Romantic Love, based on æsthetic admiration, is still very commonly ignored in the marriage market in favour of considerations of rank and wealth; and thirdly, a lover, infatuated by his sweetheart's fascinating eyes, is apt to overlook her large nose or mouth—till after the honeymoon.

FASHION AND COSMETIC SURGERY

Inasmuch as the civilised races of Europe have so long been indifferent to their ugly noses, we can hardly wonder that barbarians should not only disregard their nasal caricatures, but even exaggerate their grotesqueness deliberately. We have already seen how certain tribes habitually flatten their already flat noses. Moreover, " in all quarters of the world the septum, and more rarely the wings, of the nose are pierced; rings, sticks, feathers, and other ornaments being inserted into the holes." "In Persia one still finds the nose-ring through one side of a woman's nostril;" and Professor Flower states that such rings are often worn by female servants who accompany English families returning from India.

Captain Cook, in the account of his first voyage, says of the east-coast Australians: "Their principal ornament is the bone which they thrust through the cartilage which divides the nostrils from each other. . . . As this bone is as thick as a man's finger, and between five and six inches long, it reaches quite across the face, and so effectually stops up both the nostrils that they are forced to keep their mouths wide open for breath, and snuffle so when they attempt to speak that they are scarcely intelligible even to each other."

This last sentence bears out our assertion regarding the philological or conversational importance of the nose. And there is another lesson to be learned from these barbarian mutilations of the nose. If Huns, Tahitians, and Hottentots are able to make their noses as delightfully ugly as they please, why should not we utilise the plastic character of the nasal cartilages for beautifying ourselves? Says a specialist: " Much can be done by an ingenious surgeon in restoration and improvement. A nose that is too flat can be raised, one with unequal apertures can be modified, one too thin can be expanded. Cosmetic surgery is rich in devices here, all of which are very available in children and young persons, less so when years have hardened and stiffened the cartilages and bones."

Thus may Cupid employ a medical artist as an assistant in his efforts at improving the physical beauty of mankind. Needless to add that only a first-class surgeon should ever be allowed to meddle with the features.

Cosmetic surgery has already reached such perfection that it can even make "a good, living, fleshly nose. It will transplant you one from the arm or the forehead, Roman or Grecian, à volonté; it will graft it adroitly into the middle of the face, with two regular nostrils and a handsome bridge; and it will almost challenge Nature herself to improve on the model" (Brinton and Napheys).

Medical men are daily complaining in a more clamorous chorus that their profession is overcrowded. Why don't some of them in every city and town make a specialty of cosmetic surgery and hygienic advice? Why leave this remunerative field entirely in the hands of dangerous quacks who alone have enterprise and sense enough to advertise?

As illustrations of what may be done in this direction, two points may be noted. A French surgeon, Dr. Cid, noticed that persons who wear eyeglasses are apt to have long and thin noses. The thought occurred to him that this might be due to the compression of the arteries which carry blood to the nose, by the springs of the glasses; so he constructed a special apparatus for compressing these arteries, and by attaching it to a young girl's large and fleshy nose, succeeded in reducing its size. Why should people worry themselves and frighten others with ugly noses when they can be so easily improved?

The second point is still more simple. It is important that the nose should occupy exactly the middle of the face, so as to secure bilateral symmetry. Yet Welcker, who made a number of accurate observations on skulls, plaster casts of the dead, as well as on the living countenance, noted that perfect symmetry is very rarely found. The obliqueness is sometimes at the root, sometimes at the tip of the nose, and the cause of the deviation from a straight line is attributed to the habit most persons have of sleeping exclusively on one side,—a practice which is also objectionable on other grounds. Mantegazza, however, suggests that, as he has found the deviation almost always toward the right side, it may be due to our habit of always taking our handkerchief in the right hand; and the same view is held by Drs. Brinton and Napheys. So that we have here an additional argument in favour of ambidexterity.

The New York *Medical and Surgical Reporter* for November 1, 1884, prints a lecture by Dr. J. B. Roberts on "The Cure of Crooked Noses by a New Method," which, as it is not conspicuous and hardly leaves a scar, may be commended to the attention of those afflicted with nasal deformities. The pin method, he says, is applicable "even to those slight deformities whose chief annoyance is an æsthetic and cosmetic one. I leave the pins in position for about two weeks."

Red noses, if due to exposure, can be readily whitened by one of the methods to be discussed in the chapter on the complexion. If due to disease, they call for medical treatment; if to intemperance or tight lacing, moral and æsthetic reform is the only possible cure.

NOSE-BREATHING AND HEALTH

Owing to its tendency toward unsightly redness and malformation, the nose is very apt to be looked at from a comic point of view. Wits and caricaturists fix on it habitually for their nefarious purposes, as if it were a sort of facial clown. Indeed, ninety-nine persons in a hundred, if questioned regarding the functions of the nose, would know no answer but this: that it is sometimes ornamental, and is remotely connected with the "almost useless" sense of smell.

We have seen, however, that besides being ornamental *per se*, the nose plays a most important æsthetic—as well as utilitarian—*rôle* in giving sonority and variety to human speech; and that it is, further, of great use as an apparatus for warming, moistening, and filtering the air before it enters the lungs. Hence the importance of nose-breathing. Professor Reclam states that city people at the age of thirty usually have *a whole gramme of calcareous dust in their lungs*, which they can never again get rid of, and which may at any time engender dangerous disease. This is one of the bad results of mouth-breathing, but by no means the only one.

"The continued irritation from dry, cold, and unfiltered air upon the mucous membrane of the upper air tract soon results," says Dr. T. R. French, "in the establishment of catarrhal inflammation, the parts most affected being the tongue, pharynx, and larynx.... The habit of breathing through the mouth interferes with general nutrition. The subjects of this habit are usually anæmic, spare, and dyspeptic."

That mouth-breathing at night leaves a disagreeable taste in the mouth and leads to snoring, thus interfering with refreshing sleep, has already been stated. It also injures the teeth and gums by exposing them all night to the dry air. And in the daytime it compels one to keep the mouth wide open, which imparts a rustic if not semi-idiotic expression to the face. Moreover, think of the filthy dust you swallow in walking along the street with your mouth open. However, it is useless to advise people on such matters. An attempt is made for a day or two to reform, and then—the whole matter is forgotten. These points are therefore noted here not with any missionary intentions, but merely for their scientific interest.

COSMETIC VALUE OF ODOURS

We come now to the fourth important function of the nose—the sense of smell. What has this to do with Personal Beauty? A great deal. In the first place, is not the flower-like fragrance of a lovely maiden a personal charm that has been sung of by a thousand poets, of all times? "The fragrant bosom of Andromache and of Aphrodite finds a place in Homer's poetry," as Professor Bain remarks; and an eccentric German professor, Dr. Jäger of Stuttgart, even wrote a book a few years ago on the *Discovery of the Soul*, in which he endeavoured to prove that the whole mystery of Love lies in the intoxicating personal perfumes.

It is not with such fancies, however, that we are concerned here. It can be shown on purely scientific grounds that the cause of Personal Beauty would gain an immense advantage if people would train and refine their olfactory nerves systematically, as they do their eyes and ears. Unfortunately, Kant's absurd notion, expressed a century ago, that it is not worth while to cultivate the sense of smell, has been countenanced to the present day by the erroneous views held by the leading men of science, including Darwin, who wrote that "the sense of smell is of extremely slight service" to man.

In an article on the "Gastronomic Value of Odours," which appeared in the *Contemporary Review* for November 1886, I pointed out that this undervaluation of the sense of smell is explained by the fact that the sense of taste has hitherto been credited with all the countless flavours inherent in food, whereas, in fact, taste includes only four sensations of gastronomic value—sweet, sour, bitter, and saline, all other "flavours" being in reality odours; as is proved by the fact that by clasping the nose we cannot distinguish between a lime and a lemon, different kinds of confectionary, of cheese, of nuts, of meat, etc.

Now it is well known that most people show a most amazing tolerance to insipid, badly-cooked food, gulping it down as rapidly as possible; and why? Simply because they do not know that in order to enjoy our meals we must eat slowly, and, while masticating, *continually exhale the aroma-laden air through the nose* (mind, not inhale but *exhale*). This is what epicures do unconsciously; and look at the results! No dyspepsia, no anæmia and sickly pallor, no walking skeletons;—and surely a slight *embonpoint* is preferable to leanness from the point of view of Personal Beauty.

If this gastronomic secret were generally known, people would insist on having better cooked food; dyspepsia, and leanness, and a thousand infirmities hostile to Beauty would disappear, and in course of time everybody would be as sleek and handsome and rosy-cheeked as a professional epicure.

Nor is this the only way in which refinement of the sense of smell would benefit Personal Beauty. In consequence of the criminally superstitious dread of night air, the atmosphere in most bedrooms is as foul, compared to fresh air, as a street puddle after a shower compared to a mountain brook. I have seen well-dressed persons in America and Italy take into their mouths the shamefully filthy and disease-soaked banknotes current in those countries; and I have seen others shudder at this sight who, if their smell were as refined as their sight, would have shuddered equally at the foul air in their bedrooms, which diminishes their vital energy and working power by one-half. Architects, of course, will make no provision for proper ventilation as long as they are not compelled to do so. Why should they? They don't even care, in building a theatre, how many hundreds of people will some day be burnt in it, in consequence of their neglect of the simplest precautions for exit.

One more important consideration. When you leave the city for a few weeks everybody will exclaim on your return, " Why, how well you look! where have you been?" But wherein lies this cosmetic magic of country air? Not in its oxygen, for it has been proved, by accurate chemical tests, that in regard to the quantity of oxygen there is not the slightest difference between city and country air. What, then, is the secret?

I am convinced, from numerous experiments, that the value of country air lies partly in its tonic fragrance, partly in the *absence of depressing, foul odours*. The great cosmetic and hygienic value of deep-breathing has been proved in the chapter on the Chest. Now the tonic value of fragrant meadow or forest air lies in this—that it causes us involuntarily to breathe deeply, in order to drink in as many mouthfuls of this luscious aerial Tokay as possible; whereas in the city the air is—well, say unfragrant and uninviting; and the constant fear of gulping down a pint of deadly sewer gas discourages deep breathing. The general pallor and nervousness of New York people have often been noted. The cause is obvious. New York has the dirtiest streets of any city in the world, except Constantinople and Canton; and, moreover, it is surrounded by oil-refineries, which sometimes for days poison the whole city with the stifling fumes of petroleum, so that one hardly dares to breathe at all. No wonder that, by universal consent, there is more

Fashion than Beauty in New York. And no wonder that it is becoming more and more customary, for all who can afford it, to spend six to eight months of the year in the country.

THE FOREHEAD
BEAUTY AND BRAIN

It has been stated already that, anatomically considered, the forehead is not a part of the face but of the cranium. From an artistic and popular point of view, however, the forehead is a part of the face, and a most important one. Modern taste fully endorses the ancient law of facial proportion, which makes the height of the forehead equal to the length of the nose, and to the distance from the tip of the nose to the tip of the chin. "Foreheads villainous low" are objectionable, because associated with a vulgar unintellectual type of man, and too vividly suggestive of our simian ancestors. Foreheads abnormally high, though preferable to the other extreme, displease, because they violate the law of facial proportion. We excuse them in men, because they are commonly expressive of intellectual power. But in women a high forehead is always objectionable, because it gives them a masculine appearance. Hence Romantic Love, which cannot exist without sexual contrasts, and which aims at making woman a perfect embodiment of the laws of Beauty, eliminates girls with too high foreheads. Yet at the command of Fashion thousands of maidens deliberately prevent men from falling in love with them by combing back their hair and giving their foreheads a masculine appearance, instead of coyly hiding it under a fringe or "bang."

The fact that the feminine forehead, though more perpendicular than the masculine at the lower part, slants backward in its upper part in a more pronounced angle, is another reason why women should cover up this part of their forehead, which Sexual Selection has not yet succeeded in moulding into perfect shape. For the receding forehead is universally recognised as a sign of inferior culture. Everybody knows what is meant by Camper's facial angle, which is formed by a horizontal line drawn from the opening of the ear to the nasal spine, and a perpendicular line touching the most prominent parts of the forehead and front teeth. In adult Europeans Camper's angle rarely exceeds 85 degrees. The average in the Caucasian race is 80°; in the yellow races 75°; in the negro 60° to 70°; in the gorilla 31°. In antique Greek heads the angle is sometimes over 90°. Says Camper: "If I cause the facial line to fall in front, I have an antique head; if I incline it backwards, I have the head of a negro; if I cause it to incline still further, I have the head of a monkey; inclined still more, I have that of a dog, and, lastly, that of a goose."

It appears, however, that this angle has more value as a test of beauty than as an absolute gauge of intellect. Generally speaking, there is no doubt a correlation between a bulging forehead and a superior intellect; but individual exceptions to this rule are not infrequent. Nor is it at all difficult to account for them. For intellectual power does not depend so much on the size and shape of the skull as on the convoluted structure of the brain.

Our brain consists of two kinds of matter—the white, which is inside, and the gray, which covers it. The white substance is a complicated telegraphic network for conveying messages which are sent from the external gray cells. It has been proved, by comparing the brains of man and various animals, that the amount of intelligence depends not so much on the absolute size of the brain, as on the abundance of this gray matter. And, what is of extreme importance from a cosmetic point of view, the gray cells are increased in number, not by an addition to the absolute size or circumference of the brain, but by a system of furrows and convolutions which increase the surface lining of the brain without enlarging its visible mass. For the benefit of those who have never seen a human brain, it may be very roughly compared to the convoluted kernel of an English walnut.

Wherein lies the æsthetic significance of this mode of cerebral evolution? It prevents our head from becoming too large. Have you ever considered why infants appear so ugly to every one but their mothers? One of the principal reasons is that their heads are twice as large in proportion to the rest of the body as those of adults. A child's stature is equal to four times the height of its head, an adult's to eight heads. If our heads continued to grow larger as our mind's expanded, from generation to generation, all the proportions of human stature would ultimately be violated. But thanks to the peculiar mode of cerebral evolution just described,

Romantic Love may continue to "select" in accordance with our present standards of beauty, without thereby favouring the survival of lower intellectual types.

This view of the question also solves a difficulty which has staggered even such a leading evolutionist as Mr. Wallace, viz., the fact that the oldest prehistoric skulls that have been found "surpass the average of modern European skulls in capacity." But if it is the easiest thing in the world to find an ordinary stupid man in our streets with a larger skull than that of many a clever brain-worker, why should we attach so much importance to those prehistoric skulls? Had their brains been examined, they would doubtless have been found as scantily furrowed as those of a big-headed modern anarchist.

FASHIONABLE DEFORMITY

That the intellectual powers are to a large extent independent of the particular conformation of the skull is shown further by the circumstance that so many savage tribes have for centuries followed the fashion of artificially shaping their heads, without any apparent effect on their minds. Man's brain incites him, as Topinard remarks, "to the noblest deeds, as well as to the most ridiculous practices, such as cutting off the little finger, scorching the soles of the feet, extracting the front teeth, or deforming the head, *because others have done so before him.*" But of all silly Fashions hostile to Beauty, that of deforming the head has found the largest number of followers—always excepting, of course, the modern Wasp-Waist Mania.

Deformed skulls have been found in the Caucasus, the Crimea, Hungary, Silesia, France, Belgium, Switzerland, in Polynesia, in different parts of Asia, etc. "But the classic country in which these deformations are found is America," says Topinard. "M. Gosse has described sixteen species of artificial deformation, ten of which were in American skulls." "Sometimes the infant was fastened on a plank or a sort of cradle with leather straps; or they applied pieces of clay, pressing them down with small boards on the forehead, the vertex, and the occiput. .... Sometimes the head was kneaded with the hands or knees, or, the infant being laid on the back, the elbow was pressed on the forehead. Circular bands were sometimes employed to support the sides of the head."

"Many American Indians," says Darwin, "are known to admire a head so extremely flattened as to appear to us idiotic. The natives of the north-western coast compress the head into a pointed cone;" while the inhabitants of Arakhan "admire a broad, smooth forehead, and in order to produce it, they fasten a plate of lead on the head of the new-born children."

"The genuine Turkish skull is of the broad Tartar form," says Mr. Tylor, "while the nations of Greece and Asia Minor have oval skulls, which gives the reason why at Constantinople it became the fashion to mould the babies' skulls round, so that they grew up with the broad head of the conquering race. Relics of such barbarism linger on in the midst of civilisation, and not long ago a French physician surprised the world by the fact that nurses in Normandy were still giving the children's heads a sugar-loaf shape by bandages and a tight cap, while in Brittany they preferred to press it round. No doubt they are doing so to this day."

"Failure properly to mould the cranium of her offspring," says Bancroft, "gives to the Chinook matron the reputation of a lazy and undutiful mother, and subjects the neglected children to the ridicule of their young companions, *so despotic is fashion.*"

Food for thought will also be found in these remarks by Darwin. Ethnologists believe, he says, "that the skull is modified by the kind of cradle in which infants sleep;" and Schaffhausen is convinced that "in certain trades, such as that of a shoemaker, where the head is habitually held forward, the forehead becomes more round and prominent." If this is true, then we have one reason, at least, why authors have such large foreheads.

WRINKLES

Wrinkles in the face are signs of advanced age, or disease, or habits of profound meditation, or frequent indulgence in frowning and grief. The wrinkles on a thinker's forehead do not arouse our disapproval, because they are often eloquent of genius, which excuses a slight sacrifice of the smoothness of skin that belongs to perfect Beauty. In women, however, we apply a pure and strict æsthetic standard, wherefore all wrinkles are regarded as regrettable inroads on Personal Beauty. Old women, of course, form an exception, because in them we no longer look for youthful Beauty, and are therefore gratified at the sight of wrinkles and folds as stereotyped forms of expression bespeaking a life rich in experiences, and associated with the veneration due to old age. Such wrinkles are characteristic, but not beautiful; and it may be stated, by the way, that Alison's whole book on Taste is vitiated by the ever-recurring argument in which he forgets that we may take a personal and even an artistic interest in a thing which is characteristic without being beautiful.

In youth, while the skin is firm and elastic, the wrinkles on the forehead or around the eyes, caused by a frown or smile, pass away, leaving no more trace than the ripples on the surface of a lake. With advancing age the skin becomes looser and less elastic, so that frequent repetition of those movements which produce a fold in the skin finally leaves an indelible mark on the furrowed countenance. Woman's skin, being commonly better "padded" with fat than man's, is not so liable to wrinkles, provided attention is paid to the laws of health. Mantegazza suggests that the simplest antidote for wrinkles would be to distend the folded skin again by fattening up. The daily use of *good* soap and slight friction helps to ward off wrinkles by keeping the facial muscles toned up and the skin elastic.

The (voluntary) mobility of the skin of the forehead, to which we owe our wrinkles, affords an interesting illustration of the way in which facial muscles, once "useful," have been modified for mere purposes of expression. "Many monkeys have, and frequently use, the power of largely moving their scalps up and down." This may be of use in shaking off leaves, flies, rain, etc. But man, with his covered head, needs no such protection; hence most of us have lost the power of moving our scalps. A correspondent wrote to Darwin, however, of a youth who could pitch several heavy books from his head by the movement of the scalp alone; and many other similar cases are on record, attesting our simian relationship. But lower down on the forehead, our skin has universally retained the power of movement, as shown in frowning and the expression of various emotions.

At first sight it is somewhat difficult to understand why meditation should wrinkle the skin; but Darwin explains it by concluding that frowning (which, oft repeated, results in wrinkles) "is not the expression of simple reflection, however profound, or of attention, however close, but of something difficult or displeasing encountered in a train of thought or in action. Deep reflection can, however, seldom be long carried on without some difficulty, so that it will generally be accompanied by a frown."

Fashionable women sometimes endeavour (unsuccessfully) to distend the skin and remove wrinkles by pasting court-plaster on certain spots in the face. But the repulsive fashion of wearing patches of court-plaster all over the face as an ornament ("beauty-spots!"), doubtless had its origin in the desire of some aristocratic dame to conceal pimples or other skin blemishes. At one time women even submitted to the fashion of pasting on the face and bosom paper flies, fleas, and other loathsome creatures.

The African monkeys who held an indignation meeting when they first heard of Darwin's theory of the descent of man, had probably just been reading a history of human Fashions.

THE COMPLEXION

WHITE *VERSUS* BLACK

"The charm of colour, especially in the intricate infinities of human flesh, is so mysterious and fascinating, that some almost measure a painter's merit by his success in dealing with it," says Hegel; and again: "Man is the only animal that has flesh in its display of the infinities of colour." "No loveliness of colour, even of the humming birds or the birds of Paradise, is living, is glowing with its own life, but shines with the lustre of light reflected, and its charm is from without and not from within" (*Æsthetics*, Kedney's edition).

For a metaphysician, trained to scornfully ignore facts, the difference between man and animals is in these sentences pointed out with commendable insight. Regard for scientific accuracy, it is true, compels us to qualify Hegel's generalisation, for not only have monkeys bare coloured patches in their faces, and elsewhere, which are subject to changes, but the plumage of birds, too, is dulled by ill-health and brightened by health, reaching its greatest brilliancy in the season of Courtship, thus showing a connection between internal states and external appearances. Nevertheless, these correspondences in animals are transient and crude; and man is the only being whose nude skin is sufficiently delicate and transparent to indicate the minute changes in the blood's circulation brought about by various phases of pleasure and pain.

To understand the exact nature of these tints of the complexion, which are so greatly admired—though different nations, as usual, have different standards of "taste"—it is necessary to bear in mind a few simple facts of microscopic anatomy.

To put the matter graphically, it may be said that our body wears two tight-fitting physiological coats, called the epidermis or overskin, and the cutis or underskin.

The overskin is not simple, but consists of an outside layer of horny cells, such as are removed by the razor on shaving, and an inside mucous layer, as seen on the lips, which have no horny covering.

The underskin contains nerves, fat cells, hair-bulbs, and numerous blood-vessels, some as fine as a hair, all embedded in a soft, elastic network of connective tissue.

The overskin has none of these blood-vessels; but as it is very delicate and transparent, it allows the colour of the blood to be seen as through a veil. In the extremely blond races of the North nothing but the blood can be seen through this veil; but in the coloured races the lower or mucous layer of the overskin contains a number of black, brown, or yellowish pigment cells. The colours of these cells blend with that of the blood, thus producing, according to their number and depth of coloration, the brunette, black, yellow, or red complexion. The palm of the negro's hand is whiter than the rest of his body, because there the horny epidermis is so thick that the black pigmentary matter cannot be seen through it. And the reason why every negro is born to blush unseen is because the pigmentary matter in his skin is so deep and abundant that it neutralises the colour of the blood.

Now, why do the races of various countries differ so greatly in the colour of their skin? This is the most vexed and difficult question in anthropology, on which there are almost as many opinions as writers.

The oldest and most obvious theory is that the sun is responsible for dark complexions. Are not those parts of our body which are constantly exposed to sunlight—the hands, face, and neck—darker than the rest of the body? and does not this colour become darker still if we spend a few weeks in the country or make a trip across the Atlantic? Do we not find in Europe, as we pass from the sunny South to the cloudy North, that complexion, hair, and eyes grow gradually lighter? And not only are the Spaniards and Italians darker than the Germans, but the South Germans are darker than the North Germans, and the Swedes and Norwegians lighter still than the Prussians.

The same holds true not only of South America as compared to North America, but of the southern United States compared to the northern. It also holds true of the East, where, as Waitz tells us, "The Chinese from Peking to Canton show every shade from a light to a dark copper colour, while in the Arabians, from the desert down to Yemen, we find every gradation from olive colour to black." Moreover, aristocratic ladies in Japan and China are almost or quite white, whereas the labouring classes, as with us, are of a darker tint.

These and numerous similar facts, taken in connection with the circumstance that the blackest of all races lives in the hottest continent, and that Jews may be found of all colours according to the country they inhabit, lead almost irresistibly to the conclusion that it is the sun who paints the complexion dark.

Nevertheless there are numerous and striking exceptions to the rule that the warmer the climate the darker the complexion. To obviate this difficulty, Heusinger in 1829, Jarrold in 1838, and others after them have endeavoured to show that the moisture and altitude, as well as the direct action of the sun, had to be taken into consideration. But since " D'Orbigny in South America, and Livingstone in Africa, arrived at diametrically opposite conclusions with respect to dampness and dryness," Darwin excogitated the theory (which, he subsequently found, had already been advanced in 1813 by Dr. Wells), that inasmuch as "the colour of the skin and hair is sometimes correlated in a surprising manner with a complete immunity from the action of certain vegetable poisons, and from the attacks of parasites . . . negroes and other dark races might have acquired their dark tints by the darker individuals escaping from the deadly influence of the miasma of their native countries, during a long series of generations."

The testimony on this point being, however, conflicting and unsatisfactory, Darwin gave up this notion too, and fell back on the theory that differences in complexion are due to differences in taste, and were created through the agency of Sexual Selection. "We know," he says, "from the many facts already given that the colour of the skin is regarded by the men of all races as a highly important element in their beauty; so that it is a character which would be likely to have been modified through selection, as has occurred in innumerable instances with the lower animals. It seems at first sight a monstrous supposition that the jet-blackness of the negro should have been gained through sexual selection; but this view is supported by various analogies, and we know that negroes admire their own colour."

Doubtless there is some truth in Darwin's view, but it does not cover the whole ground. Natural as well as Sexual Selection has been instrumental in producing the diverse colours of various races. Hitherto the trouble has been that no one could understand how a black skin could be useful to an African negro. It ought to make him feel uncomfortably hot—for is it not well known that black absorbs heat more than any other colour? and do we not feel warmer in summer if we wear black than if we wear white clothes?

No doubt whatever. But it so happens that the skin is not made of dead wool or felt. It contains, among various other ingenious arrangements, a vast number of minute holes or pores, through which, when we are very warm, the perspiration leaks, and, in changing into vapour, absorbs the body's heat and leaves it cool, or even cold. Now, in a negro's skin these pores are both larger and more numerous than in ours, which partly accounts for his indifference to heat, and the fact that his temperature is lower than ours. Yet it does not solve the problem in hand;

for there is no visible reason why Natural Selection should not succeed in enlarging the number and size of the pores in a white skin as easily as in a black one.

A year or two ago Surgeon-Major Alcock sent a communication to *Nature* in which, as I believe, he for the first time suggested the true reason why tropical man is black, and why his blackness is useful to him. He pointed out that since the pigment-cells in the negro's skin are placed in front of the nerve terminations, they serve to lessen the intensity of the nerve vibrations that would be caused in a naked human body by exposure to a tropical sun; so that the pigment plays the same part as a piece of smoked glass held between the sun and the eyes.

This ingenious theory at once explains some curious and apparently anomalous observations communicated to *Nature* by Mr. Ralph Abercrombie from Darjeeling. They are that "In Morocco, and all along the north of Africa, the inhabitants blacken themselves round the eyes to avert ophthalmia from the glare off hot sand;" that "In Fiji the natives, who are in the habit of painting their faces with red and white stripes as an ornament, invariably blacken them when they go out fishing on the reef in the full glare of the sun;" and that "In the Sikkim hills the natives blacken themselves round the eyes with charcoal to palliate the glare of a tropical sun on newly-fallen snow."

How, on the other hand, are we to account for the white complexion of northern races? It is well known that there is a tendency among arctic animals to become white. This, in many cases, can be accounted for by the advantage white beasts of prey, as well as their victims, thus gain in escaping detection. But it is probable that another agency comes into play, first suggested by Craven in 1846, and thus summarised by a writer in *Nature*, 2d April 1885: "It is well known that white, as the worst absorber, is also the worst radiator of all forms of radiant energy, so that *warm-blooded* creatures thus clad would be better enabled to withstand the severity of an arctic climate—the loss of heat by radiation might, in fact, be expected to be less rapid than if the hairs or feathers were of a darker colour."

This argument, which may be applied to man as well as to animals, is greatly strengthened by a circumstance which at first appears to oppose it—the fact, namely, that insects in northern regions, instead of being light-coloured, show a tendency toward blackness. But this apparent anomaly is easily explained. Insects, being cold-blooded, cannot lose any bodily heat through radiation; whereas a black surface, by absorbing as much solar heat as possible while it lasts, adds to their comfort and vitality.

The question now arises, Which was the original colour of the human race, white or black? This question, too, we are enabled to answer with the aid of a principle of evolution which, so far, has stood every test,—the principle that the child's development is an epitome of the evolution of his race. Before birth there is no colouring matter at all in the skin of a negro child. "In a new-born child the colour is light gray, and in the northern parts of the negro countries the completely dark colour is not attained till towards the third year," says Waitz; and again, in speaking of Tahiti : " The children are here (as everywhere in Polynesia) white at birth, and only gradually assume their darker colour under the influence of sunlight ; covered portions of their bodies remain lighter, and since women wear more clothes than men, and dwell more in the shade, they too are often of so light a colour that they have red cheeks and blush visibly."

So we are entitled to infer that primitive man was originally white, or whitish. As he moved south, Natural Selection made him darker and darker by continually favouring the survival of those individuals whose colour—owing to the spontaneous variation found throughout Nature—was of a dark shade, and therefore better able to dull the ardour of the sun's rays. In the north, on the contrary, a light complexion was favoured for its quality of retaining the body's heat. The yellow and red varieties need not be specially considered, for it has been shown that the different tints of the iris are merely due to the greater or less quantity of the same pigmentary matter ; and as the colouring matter of the complexion and the hair is similar to that of the eye, it is probable that the same holds true of different hues of the skin ; so that yellowish, brown, and reddish tints may be looked upon as mere intermediate stages between white and black. A trace of pigment, indeed, is found even in our skins ; and I believe that the reason why we become brown on exposure to the sun is that the skin, when thus exposed and irritated, secretes a larger amount of this colouring matter, to serve, like a dimly-smoked glass, as a protection against scorching rays.

From all these considerations we may safely infer that the particular hue of man's skin in each climate is useful to him, and not merely an ornamental product of "taste," as Darwin believed. Yet to some extent Sexual Selection, doubtless, does come into play in most cases. At a low stage of culture each race likes its special characteristics in an exaggerated form,—a trait which would lead the more vigorous men to persistently select the darkest girls as wives, and thus cause their gradual predominance over the others; while the men, too, would, of course, inherit a darker tint from their mothers. But a still more important consideration is this, that, as Dr. Topinard points out, " Dark colour in the negro is *a sign of health*,"—naturally, since the darker the dermal pigment, the better are the nerves of temperature protected against the enervating solar rays. Concerning the Polynesians, too, Ellis (cited by Waitz) " notes expressly that a dark colour was more admired and desired because it was looked upon as a sign of vigour."

These facts yield us a most profound insight into the methods of amorous selection. The erotic instinct, whose duty is the preservation of the species, is above all things attracted by Health, because without Health the species must languish and die out. In a climate where—under the circumstances in which negroes live—a light complexion is incompatible with Health, it is bound to be eliminated.

Fortunately, the negro's taste is not sufficiently refined to make him feel the æsthetic inferiority of the ebony complexion imposed on him by his climate. Wherein this æsthetic inferiority consists is graphically pointed out in these words of Figuier: " The colour of the skin takes away all charm from the negro's countenance. What renders the European's face pleasing is that each of its features exhibits a particular shade. The cheeks, forehead, nose, and chin of the white have each a different tinge. On an African visage, on the contrary, all is black, even the eyebrows, as inky as the rest, are merged in the general colour; scarcely another shade is perceptible, except at the line where the lips join each other."

Nor is this all. Not only do we look in vain, in the monotonous blackness of the negro's face, for those varied tints which adorn a white maiden's face, borrowing one another's charms by insensible gradations, but also for those subtle emotional changes which, even if they existed in the negro's mind, could not paint themselves so delicately on his opaque countenance, betraying every acceleration or retardation in the heart's beats, indicating every *nuance* of hope and despair, of pleasure or anguish.

In our own latitude, luckily, Natural Selection favours, in the manner indicated, the survival of the translucent white complexion. And what Natural Selection leaves undone, Sexual Selection completes. Romantic Love is the great awakener of the sense of Beauty, and in proportion as Love is developed and unimpeded in its action, does the complexion become more beautiful and more appreciated. Savages, blind to the delicate tints of a transparent skin, daub themselves all over with mixtures of grease and paint. The women of ancient Greece had taste enough to feel the ugliness of the pallor caused by being constantly chaperoned and locked up, but not enough to know that no artificial paint can ever replace the natural colour of health. Hence, as Becker tells us, "painting was almost universal among Grecian women." Perhaps they did not use any rouge at home, but it "was resumed when they were going out, or wished to be specially attractive." The men, apparently, had better taste, for we read that "Ischomachos counselled his young wife to take exercise, that she might do without rouge, which she was accustomed constantly to use."

Coming to more recent times, we find men still protesting in vain against the feminine fashion of bedaubing the face with vulgar paint. More than two centuries ago La Bruyère informed his countrywomen pointedly that "If it is the men they desire to please, if it is for them that they paint and stain themselves, I have collected their opinions, and I assure them, in the name of all or most men, that the white and red paint renders them frightful and disgusting; that the red alone makes them appear old and artificial; that men hate as much to see them with cherry in their faces, as with false teeth in their mouth and lumps of wax in the jaws."

It is needless to say that women who paint their faces put themselves on a level with savages; for they show thereby that they prefer hideous opaque daubs to the charm of translucent facial tints. Masculine protestation, combined with masculine amorous preference for pure complexions, has at last succeeded in banishing paint from the boudoir of the most refined ladies; and this, combined with compulsory vaccination against smallpox, accounts for the increasing number of good complexions in the world.

But, the important question now confronts us, Is there no limit to the evolution of whiteness of complexion? Will Sexual Selection continue to favour the lighter shades until the hyperbolic " milk and blood " complexion will have been universally realised?

An emphatic " No " is the answer. An exaggerated white is as objectionable as black,—more so, in fact, because, whereas the deepest black indicates good health, *extreme* whiteness suggests the pallor of ill-health, and will therefore always displease Cupid, the supreme judge of Personal Beauty. Moreover, in a very white face the red cheek suggests the confusing blush or the hectic flush rather than the subtle tints of health and normal emotion. And again, the Scandinavian rose-and-lily complexion is inferior to the delicate and slightly-veiled tint of the Spanish brunette, because the latter suggests *the mellowing action of the sun's rays, which promises more permanence of beauty*. Hence it is that in the marriage market a decided preference is shown for the brunette type, as we shall see in the chapter on Blondes and Brunettes.

COSMETIC HINTS

We are now in a position to understand the extreme importance of the complexion from an amorous point of view, and to see why the care of the complexion has almost monopolised the attention of those desiring to improve their personal appearance, as shown by the fact that the word "cosmetic," in common parlance, refers to the care of the skin alone.

Books containing recipes for skin lotions, ointments, and powders are so numerous, that it is not worth while to devote much space to the matter here. As a rule, the best advice to those about to use cosmetics is *Don't*. Every man whose admiration is worth having will infinitely prefer a freckled, or even a pallid or smallpox-marked, face to one showing traces of powder or greasy ointments, or lifeless, cadaverous enamel, opaque as ebony blackness.

If a woman's skin is so morbidly sensitive as to be injured by ordinary water and good soap, it is a sign of ill-health which calls for residence in the country and the mellowing rays of the sun. Where this is unattainable, the water may be medicated by the addition of a slice of lemon, cucumber, or horse-radish, to all of which magic effects are often attributed. The black spots on the sides of the nose may be removed in a few weeks by the daily application (with friction) of lemon juice. For pimples and barber's itch a camphor and sulphur ointment, which may be obtained of any chemist, is the simplest remedy. For a shiny, polished complexion, and excessive redness of the nose, cheeks, and knuckles, the following mixture is recommended by a good authority:—Powdered borax, one half ounce; *pure* glycerine, one ounce; camphor-water, one quart. Borax, indeed, is as indispensable a toilet article as soap or a nail-brush. After washing the face, exposure to the raw air should always be avoided for ten or fifteen minutes.

"A certain amount of friction applied to the face daily will do much," says Dr. Bulkley, "to keep the pores of the sebaceous glands open; and, by stimulating the face, to prevent the formation of the black specks and red spots so common in young people, I generally direct that the face be rubbed to a degree short of discomfort, and that the towel be not too rough." Slight friction also helps to ward off wrinkles.

Two or three weekly baths—hot in winter, cold in summer—are absolutely necessary for those who wish to keep their skin in a healthy condition; and no elixir of youth and beauty could produce such a sparkling eye and glow of rosy health as a daily morning sponge bath, followed by friction—care being taken, in a cold room, to expose only one part of the body at a time. The importance of keeping open the pores of the skin by bathing is seen by the fact that if a man were painted with varnish he would suffocate in a few hours; for the skin is a sort of external lung, aiding its internal colleague in removing effete products, dissolved in the perspiration, from the system.

The debris and oily matter brought to the surface of the skin and deposited there by the perspiration cannot be completely removed without soap. Unfortunately, this article has done more to ruin complexions than almost any other cause, except smallpox and the superstitious dread of sunshine. Many people have a peculiar mania for economising in soap. If they can buy a piece of soap for a farthing, they consider themselves wonderfully clever, regardless of the fact that it may not only ruin their complexion, but produce a repulsive skin disease which it will cost much gold to cure. Do they ever realise that these soaps, which they thus smear over the most delicate parts of their body every day, are made of putrid carcasses of animals, rancid fat, and corrosive alkalies? Has no one ever told them that if a soap is both cheap and highly perfumed it is *certain* to be of vile composition, and injurious to the skin? After washing yourself wait a moment till the soap's artificial odour has disappeared, and then smell your hands. That vile rancid odour which remains—if you knew its source, you would immediately run for a Turkish bath to wash off the very epidermis to which that odour has adhered.

What has ruined so many complexions is not soap itself, but bad soap. A famous specialist, Dr. Bulkley, says that "there is no intrinsic reason why soap should not be applied to the face, although there is a very common impression among the profession, as well as the laity, that it should not be used there. . . . The fact is, that many cases of eruptions upon the face are largely due to the fact that soap has *not* been used on that part; and it is also true that, if properly employed, and *if the soap is good*, it is not only harmless, but beneficial to the skin of the face, as to every other part of the body."

" A word may be added in reference to the so-called 'medicated soaps,' whose number and variety are legion, each claiming virtues far excelling all others previously produced. . . . Now all or most of this attempt to 'medicate' soap is a perfect farce a delusion, and a snare to entrap the unwary and uneducated. . . . Carbolic soap is useless and may be dangerous, because the carbolic acid may possibly become the blind beneath which a cheap, poor soap is used; for in all these advertised and patented nostrums the temptation is great to employ inferior articles that the pecuniary gain may be greater. The small amount of carbolic acid incorporated in the soap cannot act as an efficient disinfectant."

FRECKLES AND SUNSHINE

Soap is not the only cosmetic that has been tabooed in the face because of illogical reasoning. There is a much more potent beautifying influence—viz., the mellowing rays of the sun—of which the face has long been deprived, chiefly on account of an unscientific prejudice that the sun is responsible for freckles. In his famous work on skin diseases Professor Hebra of Vienna, the greatest modern authority in his specialty, has completely disproved this almost universally accepted theory. The matter is of such extreme importance to Health and Beauty that his remarks must be quoted at length :—

" It is a fact that lentigo (freckles) neither appears in the newly-born nor in children under the age of 6–8 years, whether they run about the whole day in the open air and exposed to the bronzing influence of the sun, or whether they remain confined to the darkest room; it is therefore certain that neither light nor air nor warmth produces such spots in children. . . .

" If we examine the skin of an individual who is said to be affected with the so-called freckles only in the summer, at other seasons of the year with sufficient closeness in a good light, and with the skin put on the stretch by the finger, we shall detect the same spots, of the same size but of somewhat lighter colour than in summer. In further illustration of what has just been said, I will mention that I have repeatedly had the opportunity of seeing lentigines on parts of the body that, as a rule, are never exposed to the influence of the light and sun. . . .

"*A priori*, it is difficult to understand how ephelides can originate from the influence of sun and light in the singular form of disseminated spots, since these influences act not only on single points, but uniformly over the whole surface of the skin of the face, hands, etc. The pigmentary changes must appear, therefore, in the form of patches, not of points. Moreover, it is known to every one that, if the skin of the face be directly exposed, even for only a short time, to a rough wind or to intense heat, a tolerably dark bronzing appears, which invades the affected parts uniformly, and not in the form of disseminated, so-called summer-spots (freckles). It was, therefore, only faulty observation on the part of our forefathers which induced them to attribute the ephelides to the influence of light and sun."

But the amount of mischief done by this "faulty observation of our forefathers" is incalculable. To it we owe the universal feminine horror of sunshine, without which it is as impossible for their complexion to have a healthy, love-inspiring aspect, as it is for a plant grown in a cellar to have a healthy green colour. How many women are there who preserve their youthful beauty after twenty-five—the age when they ought to be in full bloom? They owe this early decay partly to their indolence, mental and physical, partly to their habit of shutting out every ray of sunlight from their faces as if it were a rank poison instead of the source of all Health and Beauty. If young ladies would daily exercise their muscles in fresh air and sunshine, they would not need veils to make themselves look younger. Veils may be useful against very rough wind, but otherwise they should be avoided, because they injure the eyesight. Parasols are a necessity on very hot summer afternoons, but "the rest of the year the complexion needs all the sun it can get."

Were any further argument needed to convince us that the sun has been falsely accused of creating freckles, it would be found in the fact that southern brunette races, though constantly exposed to the sun, are much less liable to them than the yellow and especially the red-haired individuals of the North. Professor Hebra regards freckles as "a freak of Nature rather than as a veritable disease," and thinks they are "analogous to the piebald appearances met with in the lower animals." As has just been noted, they exist in winter as well as in summer. All that the summer heat does is to make them visible by making the skin more transparent. As the heat itself causes them to appear any way, it is useless to taboo the direct sunlight as their source.

Inasmuch as freckles appear chiefly among northern races, whose skin has been excessively bleached and weakened in its action by constant indoor life, it seems probable, notwithstanding Dr. Hebra's opinion, that they are the result of an unhealthy, abnormal action of the pigment-secreting apparatus which exists even in the white skin. If this be so, then proper care of the skin continued for several generations would obliterate them. The reason why country folks are more liable to freckles than their city cousins would then be referable, not to the greater amount of sunlight in the country, but to the rarity of bath-tubs, good soap, and friction-towels. My own observation leads me to believe that freckles are rarer in England than on the continent, and the English are proverbially enamoured of the bath-tub and open-air exercise.

For those who, without any fault of their own, have inherited freckles from their parents, there is this consoling reflection that these blemishes reside in a very superficial layer of the skin, and can therefore be removed. Several methods are known; but as no one should ever use them without medical assistance, they need not be described here (see Hebra's *Treatise*, vol. iii.) Any one who wishes to temporarily conceal skin-blemishes may find this citation from Hebra of use: " Perfumers and apothecaries have prepared from time immemorial cosmetics whose chief constituent is *talcum venetum,* or *pulvis aluminis plumosi* (Federweiss), which, when rubbed in, in the form of a paste, with water and alcohol, or a salve with lard, or quite dry, as a powder, gives to the skin an agreeable white colour, and does not injure it in the least, even if the use of the cosmetic be continued throughout life."

It is probable that electricity will play a grand *rôle* in future as an agent for removing superfluous hairs, freckles, moles, port-wine marks, etc. Much has already been done in this direction, and the only danger is in falling into the hands of an unscrupulous quack. In vol. iii. No. 4 of the *Journal of Cutaneous and Venereal Diseases*, Dr. Hardaway has an interesting article on this subject.

THE EYES

In one of the Platonic dialogues Sokrates points out the relativity of standards of Beauty. "Is not," he asks in effect, "the most beautiful ape ugly compared to a maiden? and is not the maiden, in turn, inferior in beauty to a goddess?"

Regarding most of the human features it may be conceded that Sokrates is right in his second question. To find a human forehead, nose, or mouth that could not be improved in some respect, is perhaps impossible. But *one* feature must be excepted. There are human eyes which no artist with a goddess for a model could make more divine. And of these glorious orbs there are so many, in every country, that one cannot help concluding that Schopenhauer made a great mistake in placing the face, with the eyes, so low down in his list of love-inspiring human qualities. On the contrary, I am convinced that no feminine charm so frequently and so fatally fascinates men as lovely eyes, and that it is for this reason that Sexual Selection has done more to perfect the eyes than any other part of the body.

When Petruchio says of Katharina that "she looks as clear as morning roses newly washed with dew," he compliments her complexion; but when the Persian poet compares "a violet sparkling with dew" to "the blue eyes of a beautiful girl in tears," the compliment is to the violet. A woman's eye is the most beautiful object in the universe; and what made it so is man's Romantic Love.

Putting poetry aside, we must now consider a few scientific facts and correct a few misconceptions regarding the eye, its colour, lustre, form, and expression.

COLOUR

To say of any one that he has gray, blue, brown, or black eyes, is vague and incorrect from a strictly scientific point of view, inasmuch as there are no really gray or black eyes, and, as a matter of fact, every eye, if closely examined, shows at least five or six different colours.

There is, first, the tough sclerotic coat or *white* of the eye, which covers the greater part of the eyeball, and is not transparent, except in front where the coloured *iris* (or rainbow membrane) is seen through it. This central transparent portion of the sclerotic coat is called the cornea, and is slightly raised above the general surface of the eyeball, like the middle portion of some watch-glasses.

The white of the eye is sometimes slightly tinged with blue or yellow, and sometimes netted with inflamed blood-vessels. All these deviations are æsthetically inferior to the pure white of the healthy European, because suggestive of disease, and conflicting with the general cosmic standards of beauty. The bluish tint is a sign of consumption or scrofulous disorders, being caused by a diminution of the pigmentary matter in the choroid coat which lines the inside of the sclerotic. The yellowish tint, in the European, is indicative of jaundice, dyspepsia, or premature degeneracy of the white of the eye. It is normal, on the other hand, in the healthy negro; but if a negro should claim that, inasmuch as a yellowish sclerotic is to him not suggestive of disease, he has as much right to consider it beautiful as we our white sclerotic, the simple retort would be, that we are guided in our æsthetic judgment by positive as well as negative tests. Disease is the negative test; the positive lies in the fact that in inanimate objects, where disease is altogether out of the question—as in ivory ornaments (which no one associates with an elephant's tusk)—we also invariably, prefer a pure snowy white to a muddy uncertain yellow. It is these two tests in combination which have guided Sexual Selection in its efforts to eliminate all but the pure white sclerotic,—a tint which, moreover, throws into brighter relief the enchanting hues of the " sunbeamed " iris.

More objectionable still than a yellowish or bluish sclerotic is a bloodshot eye, not only because the inflamed blood-vessels which swell and flood the white surface of the eye deface the marble purity of the sclerotic (in a manner not in the least analogous to marble "veins"), but because the red, watery blear-eye generally indicates the ravages of intemperance or unrestrained passions. However, a bloodshot eye may be the result of mere overwork, or reading in a flickering light, or lack of sleep; hence it is not always safe to allow the disagreeable æsthetic impression given by inflamed eyes to prognosticate moral obliquity. But, after all, the intimate connection between æsthetic and moral judgments is in this case based on a correct, subtle instinct; for is not a man who ruins the health and beauty of his eyes by intemperance in drink or night-work sinning against himself? If attempts at suicide are punished by law, why should not minor offences against one's Health at least be looked upon with moral disapproval? If this sentiment could be made universal, there would be fifty per cent more Beauty in the world after a single generation.

In the centre of the white sclerotic is the membrane which gives the eyes their characteristic variations of colour,—the iris or rainbow curtain. If we look at an eye from a distance of a few paces, it seems to have some one definite colour, as brown or blue. But on closer examination we see that there are always several hues in each iris. The colour of the iris is due to the presence of small pigment granules in its interior layer. These granules are *always* brown, in blue and gray as well as in brown eyes; and the greater their number and thickness, the darker is the colour of the iris. Blue eyes are caused by the presence, in front of the pigment-layer, of a thin, almost colourless membrane, which absorbs all the rays of light except the blue, which it reflects, and thus causes the translucent iris to appear of that colour.

The Instructions de la Société d'Anthropologie, says Dr. Topinard, " recognise four shades of colour,— brown, green, blue, and gray ; each having five tones —the very dark, the dark, the intermediate, the light, and the very light. The expression "brown" does not mean pure brown ; it is rather a reddish, a yellowish, or a greenish brown, corresponding with the chestnut or auburn colour, the hazel and the sandy, made use of by the English. The gray, too, is not pure; it is, strictly speaking, a violet more or less mixed with black and white."

"The negro, in spite of his name, is not black but deep brown," as Mr. Tylor remarks; and what is true of his complexion is also true of his eyes; "what are popularly called black eyes are far from having the iris really black like the pupil; eyes described as black are commonly of the deepest shades of brown or violet."

The pupil, however, is always jetblack, not only in negroes, but in all races. For the pupil is simply a round opening in the centre of the iris which allows us to see clear through the lens and watery substance of the eyeball to the black pigment which lines its inside surface. The iris, in truth, is nothing but a muscular curtain for regulating the size of the pupil, and thus determining how much light shall be admitted into the interior of the eye. When the light is bright and glaring, a little of it suffices for vision, hence the iris relaxes its fibres and the pupil becomes smaller; whereas, in twilight and moonlight, the eye needs all the light it can catch, so the muscles of the iris-curtain contract and enlarge the pupil-window. This mechanism of the iris in diminishing or enlarging the pupil can be neatly observed by looking into a mirror placed on one side of a window. If the hand is put up in such a way as to screen the eye from the light, the pupil will be seen to enlarge; and if the hand is then suddenly taken away, it will immediately return to its smaller size. For the muscles of the iris have the power, denied to other unstriped or involuntary muscles, of acting quite rapidly.

Thus we find in the eyeball three distinct zones of colour—the white of the eye, sometimes slightly tinted blue, yellow, or red; the iris, which has various shades of brown, green, blue, and gray, commonly two or three in each eye; and the central black pupil. Add to this the flesh-colour of the eyelid and surrounding parts, and the light or dark lashes and eyebrows, and we see that the eye in itself is a perfect colour-symphony.

Can we account for the existence of all these colours? The easiest thing in the world, with the aid of the principles of Natural and Sexual Selection. There are reasons for believing that the sense of sight is merely a higher development from the sense of temperature, adapted to vibrations so rapid that the nerves of temperature can no longer distinguish them. In its simplest form, among the lowest animals, the sense of sight is represented by a mere pigment spot. And in the highest form of sight, after the development of the various parts of our complicated eye, we still find this pigment as one of the most essential conditions of vision. Its function, however, is not the same as that of the pigment in the human skin. There it is interposed between the sun and the underskin, in order to protect the nerves of temperature. The optic nerve needs no such protection; for the heat-rays of the sun cannot but be cooled on passing through the membranes, the lens, and the watery substance in the eye, before reaching the optic nerve, spread out on the retina. Consequently the eye-pigment, instead of being placed in front of the nerves, is put behind them; and their function is to absorb any excess of light that enters the eye. Were the membrane which contains this pigment whitish, all the light would be reflected back, and create such a glare and confusion that no object could be seen distinctly.

This view regarding the function of the pigment is strikingly supported by the anomalous case of Albinos. "The pink of their eyes (as of white rabbits) is caused by the absence of the black pigment," says Mr. Tylor, "so that light passing out through the iris and pupil is tinged red from the blood-vessels at the back; thus their eyes may be seen to blush with the rest of the face."

Bearing these facts in mind, it is obvious why it is an advantage in a sunny country to have as much pigmentary matter as possible in the eye, and why, therefore, Natural Selection makes the eyes blacker the nearer we approach the tropics. And, as with the complexion, so here, it is fortunate for the negro that he has not sufficient taste to feel the æsthetic inferiority of the monotonous black thus imposed on him by Natural Selection. "The iris is so dark," says Figuier, "as almost to be confounded with the black of the pupil. In the European, the colour of the iris is so strongly marked as to render at once perceptible whether the person has black, blue, or gray eyes. There is nothing similar in the case of the negro, where all parts of the eye are blended in the same hue. Add to this that the white of the eye is always suffused with yellow in the Negro, and you will understand how this organ, which contributes so powerfully to give life to the countenance of the

White, is invariably dull and expressionless in the Black Race."

To the Esquimaux, living in the constant glare of ice and snowfields, a protective pigment is quite as necessary as to an African savage; hence their eyes are equally black. But among other northern races, who are less constantly exposed to the blinding rays of the sun, it suffices to have coal-black pigment in the back part of the eye, as seen through the pupil, while the iris need not be so absolutely opaque. This leaves room for the action of Sexual Selection in giving the preference to eyes less monotonously black. Our æsthetic sense craves variety and contrasts in colour; and as the sense of Beauty originally stood in the service of Love almost exclusively, it is to Cupid's selective action that we doubtless owe the diverse hues of the modern iris.

To what kind of an iris does modern Love or æsthetic selection give the preference? Doubtless to that which has the deepest and most unmistakable colour—to dark brown, or deep blue, or violet. One reason why we care less for the lighter, faded tints of the iris is because they present a less vivid contrast to the white of the eye; and another reason, as Dr. Hugo Magnus suggests, lies in the disagreeable impression produced in us by the difficulty of making out the exact character of the various indistinct shades of gray, yellow, green, or blue.

The consideration of the question whether amorous selection shows any further preference for one of its two favourite colours—dark brown and deep blue—must be deferred to the chapter on Blondes and Brunettes.

LUSTRE

But Cupid is not guided by colour alone in his choice. However beautiful the colour of an eye, it loses half its charm if it lacks lustre. A bright, sparkling eye is the most infallible index of youthful vigour and health, whereas the lack-lustre eyes of ill-health can never serve as windows from which Cupid shoots his arrows. No wonder that the poets have searched all nature for analogies to the lustre of a maiden's eye, comparing it to sun and stars, to diamonds, crystalline lakes, the light of glow-worms, glistening dewdrops, etc.

What is the source of this light which shines from the eye and intoxicates the lover's senses? Several answers to this question have been suggested. Twenty-five hundred years ago Empedokles taught that "there is in the eye a fine network which holds back the watery substance swimming about in it, but the fiery particles penetrate through it like the rays of light through a lantern" (Ueberweg). And a notion similar to this, that there is a kind of magnetic or nervous emanation which beams from the eye and is a direct efflux of the soul, was entertained in recent times by Lavater and Carus. It was apparently supported by the peculiar light which may be seen occasionally in the eyes of cats, dogs, and horses in the twilight; but this has been proved to be a purely physical phenomenon of reflection, due to an anatomical peculiarity in the eyes of these animals.

Some writers have attempted to account for the lustrous fire of the eye by attributing it to the increased tension of the eyeball brought about through certain joyous and exciting emotions. Dr. Hugo Magnus, however, denies that these emotions ever increase the tension of the eyeball: " We know from numerous exceedingly minute measurements that there is no such thing whatever as a rapid change of tension in the eye, as long as it is in a healthy condition." In some diseases, especially in cataract or glaucoma, such an increased tension does occur, indeed, but it does not in the least impart to the eye the sparkle of joyous excitement. Hence Professor Magnus concludes that "the mimic significance of the eye cannot be conditioned by changes in the form of the eyeball, through tension or pressure on it."

His own theory (as developed in his two interesting pamphlets, *Die Sprache der Augen* and *Das Auge in seinen aesthetischen und culturgeschichtlichen Beziehungen*) is that the greater or less brilliancy of the eyes depends entirely on the movements of the eyelids. Instead of calling the eye the window of the soul, it is more correct to say that the cornea is a mirror which, like any other mirror, reflects the light that falls on it. The higher the eyelids are raised the larger becomes the mirror, and the more light is therefore reflected. Now it is well known that exciting emotions like joy, enthusiasm, anger, and pride have a tendency to raise the eyelids, while the sad and depressing emotions cause them to sink and partially cover the eyeball; hence joy makes the eyes sparkling, while grief renders them dull and lustreless.

The old poetic and popular notion that the lustre

of the eye is a direct emanation of the human soul must therefore be abandoned. The sparkling eye is a mere physical consequence of the involuntary raising of the eyelids brought about through exhilarating or exciting emotions.

This theory of Dr. Magnus doubtless comes nearer the truth than the others referred to; and the fact that snakes' eyes, though small, are proverbially glistening, apparently because they are lidless, may be used as an additional argument in his favour, which he overlooked. Yet his view does not cover the whole ground; for it does not explain why, after weeping, or when we are weary or ill, we may open our eyes as widely as we please without making them appear lustrous.

This difficulty suggested to me the theory that, though partly dependent on the movements of the eyelids, the lustre of the eyes is due originally to the tension and moisture of the *conjunctiva*.

The *conjunctiva*, though consisting of 6–8 layers of cells, is an extremely thin and highly sensitive, transparent membrane, which lines the surface of the eyeball as well as the inside of the eyelids. In this membrane is located the pain which we feel if dust, etc. flies into our eyes. In order to wash out any particles that may get into the eye, and to prevent the lid from sticking to the eyeball, the lachrymal glands constantly secrete the water which, during an emotional shower, consolidates into teardrops.

Now, just as "the rose is sweetest washed with morning dew," so the eye is brightest and most fascinating which glistens in an ever fresh supply of lachrymal fluid. After weeping, this supply is temporarily exhausted, hence not only are the eyes "sticky" and the lids difficult to raise, but even if they are raised there is no lustre: you look in vain for "Cupid's bonfires burning in the eye." But when we wake up from refreshing sleep in the morning, or when we take a walk in the bracing country air, the eye sparkles its best and "emulates the diamond," because at such a time all the vital energies, including of course those of the lachrymal glands, are incited to fresh activity, which they lose again after prolonged use of the eye, thus making it appear duller in the evening.

Thus we can readily account for those lights in the eye "that do mislead the morn." Yet it is probable that (although in a less degree than dewy moisture) the tension and translucency of the conjunctiva are also concerned in the production of a liquid, lustrous expression. Though the eyeball itself may not undergo any changes in tension, the conjunctiva doubtless does. The eyeball rests on a bed of fatty tissue which shrinks after death, owing to the emptying of the blood-vessels and the consolidation of the fat, which makes a corpse appear "hollow-eyed." The same effect, to a slighter degree, is caused by disease and excessive fatigue, making the eyes sink into their sockets. This sinking must diminish the tension of the conjunctiva, both under the eyelids and on the surface of the eyeball; and in shrinking it becomes less transparent and glistening.

The following observations of Professor Kollmann indirectly support my theory that the conjunctiva is the source of the eye's lustre: "After death this transparent membrane (the conjunctiva) becomes turbid, the eye loses its lustre and becomes veiled. The surface reflects but a faint degree of light, the eye is 'broken.'" The loss of lustre extends to the white of the eye, but is less noticeable, perhaps because there lustre does not blend with colour, as in the iris region.

Fashionable young ladies who dance throughout the night several times a week may well be disgusted with the *blue* rings which appear around their sunken eyes. These rings are a warning that they need "beauty sleep" and fresh air to fill up the sockets again with healthy fat and *red* blood, so as to increase the tension of the conjunctiva and stimulate the flow of dewy moisture on which the lustre of the eye depends. There are tears of Beauty as well as of anguish and joy.

FORM

Of the beauty of the eye as conditioned by its form, Dr. Magnus has made such an admirable and exhaustive analysis that I can do little more than summarise his observations. He points out, in the first place, that the form of the eyeball itself is of subordinate importance. The differences in the size and shape of eyeballs are insignificant, and are, moreover, liable to be concealed by the shape of the eyelids; hence it is to the lids and brows that the eye chiefly owes its formal beauty.

"The form of the eye is conditioned exclusively by the cut of the lids and the size of the aperture between them. . . . The countless individual differences in this aperture give to the eyeballs the most diverse shapes, so that we speak of round eyes, wide eyes, almond-shaped, elongated, and owl eyes, etc."

The first condition of beauty in an eye is size. Large eyes have been extolled ever since the beginnings of poetry. The Mahometan heaven is peopled with "virgins with chaste mien and large black eyes," and the Arabian poets never tire of comparing their idols' eyes to those of the gazelle and the deer. The Greeks appear to have considered large eyes an essential trait of beauty as well as of mental superiority; hence Sokrates as well as Aspasia are described as having had such eyes; and who has not read of Homer's ox-eyed Juno? Juvenal specially mentions small eyes as a blemish.

Large eyes, however, are not beautiful if the aperture between the lids is too wide, or if the white can be seen above the iris. They must owe their largeness to the graceful curvature of the upper eyelid. As Winckelmann remarks, "Jupiter, Apollo, and Juno have the opening of their eyelids large and vaulted, and less elongated than is usual, so as to make the arch more pronounced."

At the same time we are sufficiently catholic in taste to admire eyes which are not quite round but somewhat elongated. One favourite variety is that in which "the upper lid shows, in the margin adjoining the inner corner of the eye, a rather decided curvature, which, however, diminishes toward the outer corner in an extremely graceful and pleasing wavy line. As the lower lid has a similar, though less decided, marginal curve, the eyeball which appears within this aperture assumes a unique oval form, which has been very aptly and characteristically named 'almond-shaped.' The Greeks compared the graceful curve of such lids to the delicate and pleasing loops formed by young vines, and therefore called an eye of this variety ἑλικοβλέφαρος. Winckelmann has noted that it was the eyes of Venus, in particular, that the ancient artists were fond of adorning with this graceful curve of the lids. . . . Italian, and especially Spanish eyes, are far-famed for their classical and graceful oval form."

Almond eyes are peculiar to the Semitic and ancient Aryan races. Some of the bards of India sing the praises of an eye so elongated that it reaches to the ear; and in Assyrian statues such eyes are common. The ancient Egyptians had a similar taste; and Carus relates that some Oriental nations actually enlarge the slit of the eye with the knife; while others use cosmetics to simulate the appearance of very long eyes. According to Dr. Sömmering, the eye of male Europeans is somewhat less elongated than that of females.

Round or oval marginal curvature, however, is not the only condition of beauty in an eyelid. The surface, too, must be kept in a tense, well-rounded condition. Sunken, hollow eyes displease us not only because they suggest disease and age, but because they destroy the smooth surface and curvature of the eyelids. Thus do we find the laws of Health and Beauty coinciding in the smallest details.

The position of the eye also largely influences our æsthetic judgment. What strikes us first in looking at a Chinaman is his obliquely-set eyes, with the outer corner drawn upwards, which displeases us even more than their excessive elongation and small size. Oblique eyes are a dissonance in the harmony of our features, and almost as objectionable as a crooked mouth. True, our own eyes are rarely absolutely horizontal, but the deviation is too minute to be noticed by any but a trained observer. Sometimes, as Mantegazza remarks, the opposite form may be noticed, the outer corner of the eye being lower than the inner. "If this trait is associated with other æsthetic elements, it may produce a rare and extraordinary charm, as in the case of the Empress Eugénie."

The eyelashes and eyebrows, though strictly belonging in the chapter on the hair, must be referred to here because they bear such a large part in the impression which the form of the eye makes on us. The short, stiff hairs, which form "the fringed curtain of the eye," are attached to the cartilage which edges the eyelids. They are not straight but curved, downward in the lower, upward in the upper lid. And the Beauty-Curve is observed in still another way, the hairs in the central part of each lid being longer than they are towards the ends. In the upper lid the hairs are longer than in the lower. Their æsthetic and physiognomic value will be considered presently under the head of Expression.

In the eyebrows the Curve of Beauty is again the condition of perfection. It must be a gentle curve, however, or else it imparts to the countenance a Mephistophelian expression of irony. Eyebrows were formerly held to be peculiar to man, but

Darwin states that "in the Chimpanzee, and in certain species of Macacus, there are scattered hairs of considerable length rising from the naked skin above the eyes, and corresponding to our eyebrows; similar long hairs project from the hairy covering of the superciliary ridges in some baboons."

The existence of the eyebrows may be accounted for on utilitarian grounds. Natural Selection favoured their development because they are, like the lashes, of use in preventing perspiration and dust from getting into the eyes. Their delicately-curved form, however, they probably owe to Sexual Selection. Cupid objects to eyebrows which are too much or not sufficiently arched, and he objects to those which are too bushy or which meet in the middle. The ancient Greeks already disliked eyebrows meeting in the middle, whereas in Rome Fashion not only approved of them, but even resorted to artificial means for producing them. The Arabians go a step farther in the use of paint. They endeavour to produce the impression as if their eyebrows grew down to the middle of the nose and met there. The Egyptians, Assyrians, Persians, and Indians also used paint to make their eyebrows seem wider, but they did not unite them. On the outside border the eyebrows should extend slightly beyond the corner of the eye.

EXPRESSION

In the chapter on the nose reference was made to our disposition to seize upon any sensation experienced inside the mouth and label it as a "taste," whereas psychologic analysis shows that in most cases the sense of smell (excited during *exhalation*) has more to do with our enjoyment of food than taste; and that the nerves of temperature and touch likewise come into play in the case of peppermint, pungent condiments, alcohol, etc. We are also in the habit of including in the term "feeling" or "touch" the entirely distinct sensations of temperature, tickling, and some other sensations, to the separate study of which physiologists are only now beginning to devote special attention.

Similarly with the eyes. Being the most fascinating part of the face, on which we habitually fix our attention while talking, they are credited with various expressions that are really referable to other features, which we rapidly scan and then transfer their language to the eyes. Nor is this all. Most persons habitually attribute to the varying lustre of the eyeball diverse "soulful" expressions which, as physiologic analysis shows, are due to the *movements* of the eyeball, the eyebrows, and lashes. The poets, who have said so many beautiful things about the eyes, are rarely sufficiently definite to lay themselves open to the charge of inaccuracy. But there can be little doubt that the popular opinion concerning the all-importance of the eyeball is embodied in such expressions as these: "Love, anger, pride, and avarice all visibly move in those little orbs" (Addison). "Her eye in silence has a speech which eye best understands" (Southwell). "An eye like Mars to threaten or command." "The heavenly rhetoric of thine eye, 'gainst which the world cannot hold argument." "Behold the window of my heart, mine eye." "Sometimes from her eyes I did receive fair speechless messages." "For shame, lie not, to say mine eyes are murderers." "If mine eyes can wound, now let them kill thee." "There's an eye wounds like a leaden sword." The last three of these Shaksperian lines were evidently echoing in Emerson's mind when he wrote that "Some eyes threaten like a loaded and levelled pistol, and others are as insulting as hissing or kicking; some have no more expression than blueberries, while others are as deep as a well which you can fall into." "Glances are the first *billets-doux* of love," says Ninon de L'Enclos.

In order to make perfectly clear the mechanism by which the eye becomes an organ of speech, it is advisable to consider separately these six factors, which are included in it—(*a*) Lustre; (*b*) Colour of the Iris; (*c*) Movements of the Iris or Pupil; (*d*) Movements of the Eyeball; (*e*) Movements of the Eyelids; (*f*) Movements of the Eyebrows.

(*a*) *Lustre.*—" The physiological problem whether the surface of the eyeball, independent of the muscles that cover and surround it, can express emotion, a near study of the American girl seems to answer quite in the affirmative," Dr. G. M. Beard remarks, without, however, endeavouring to specify what emotions the surface of the eyeball expresses, or in what manner it does express them.

Dr. Magnus, on the other hand, who has made a more profound study of this question than any other writer, is emphatic in his conviction that "the eyeball takes no active part in the expression of emotions, which is entirely accomplished by the muscles and soft parts surrounding it." His view is supported by the fact that although some of the ancient sculptors endeavoured by the use of jewels or by chiselling semi-lunar or other grooves into the eyeball to simulate its lustre by means of shadows, yet as a rule sculptors and painters strangely neglect the careful elaboration of the eyeball; and in the Greek works of the best period, including those of Phidias, the eyeball was left smooth and unadorned, the artists relying especially on the careful chiselling of the lids and brows for the attainment of the particular characteristic expression desired.

Nevertheless Dr. Magnus goes too far in denying that ocular lustre can be directly expressive of mental states without the assistance of the movements of the eyebrows and lids. His own observations show that he has overstated his thesis. We can indeed, he says, infer from the appearance of the eyeball "whether the soul is agitated or calm, but we have to rely on the facial muscles to specify the emotion. This is the reason why we can never judge the sentiments of one who is masked; for the fire in his eye can only indicate to us his greater or less agitation, but not its special character. *That* we could only read in the features which the mask conceals. It is for this reason that the orthodox Mahometan makes his women cover up their face with a veil which leaves nothing exposed but the eyes, because these cannot, without the constant play of the facial muscles, indicate the emotional state. The lustre of the corneal mirror therefore indicates to us only the quantity, but never the quality of emotional excitement."

Herein Dr. Magnus follows the assertion of Lebrun, a contemporary of Louis XIV., that "the eyeball indicates by its fire and its movements in general that the soul is passionately excited, but not in what manner."

No doubt the Turk attains his object in leaving only the eyes of his women open to view, for thus the passing stranger cannot tell whether her eye flashes Love or anger. But he *can* tell whether she is agitated or indifferent: and is not that a language too? Do we not call music *the* "language of emotions," although it can only indicate the quantity of emotion, and rarely its precise quality—just like the eyes? Therefore Dr. Magnus is wrong in denying to the eyeball the power of emotional expression. Vague emotion is still emotion.

It has already been intimated in what manner emotional excitement increases the eye's lustre. It causes the blood-vessels in the sockets of the eye to swell, thus increasing the tension of the conjunctiva and the flow of the lachrymal fluid.

Besides quantitative emotion there is another thing which ocular lustre expresses, and that is Health. It is true that consumption, fever, and possibly other diseases may produce a peculiar temporary transparency of complexion and ocular lustre; but, as a rule, a bright eye indicates Health and abundant vitality.

As Health is the first condition of Love, and as the ocular lustre which indicates Health cannot be normally secured without it, women of all times and countries have been addicted to the habit of increasing the eye's sparkle artificially by applying a thin line of black paint to the edge of the lids. The ancient Egyptians, Persians, Hindoos, Greeks, and Romans followed this custom. But the natural sparkle which comes of Health and Beauty-sleep [*i.e.* before midnight, with open windows] is a thousand times preferable to such dangerous methods of tampering with the most delicate and most easily injured organ of the body.

Still another way in which the eyeball itself can express emotion is by the varying amount on it of the lachrymal fluid, to which, in my opinion, its lustre is chiefly owing. There is a supreme and thrilling sparkle of the eye which can only come of the heavenly joys of Love; but there is also "a liquid *melancholy*" of sweet eyes, to use Bulwer's words. Scott remarks that "Love is loveliest when embalmed in tears"; and Dr. Magnus attests that "especially in the eyes of lovers we often find a slight suspicion of tears." He traces to this fact a peculiar charm that is to be found in the eyes of Venus, which the Greeks called ὑγρὸν (liquid, swimming, languishing). The sculptors produced this expression by indicating the border between the lower lid and the eyeball but slightly, thus giving the impression as if this border were veiled by a liquid line of tear-fluid.

What enables the lid to keep this fluid line in place is the fact that its edge is lined with minute glands secreting an oily substance. The presence of these glands in the upper lid, where they cannot serve to retain lachrymal fluid, suggests the important inference that the lustre of the eye may be partly due to a thin film of oil spread over the cornea by the up-and-down movements of this lid. Indeed, this may possibly be the chief cause of ocular lustre.

When the lachrymal fluid habitually present in the eye becomes too abundant it ceases to express amorous tenderness, and becomes instead indicative of old age, or, worse still, of intemperance. Alcoholism has a peculiarly demoralising effect on the lower eyelid, which becomes swollen and inflamed. This probably over-stimulates the action of the oil glands in the lids, thus accounting for the watery or blear eye, eloquent of vice.

(*b*) *Colour of the Iris.*—There is nothing in which popular physiognomy takes so much delight as in pointing out what particular characteristics are indicated by the different colours of eyes. All such distinctions are the purest drivel. We have seen that differences in the colour of eyes are entirely due to the varying amount of the same pigmentary matter present in the iris. Now, what earthly connection could a greater or less quantity of this colouring matter have with our intellectual or moral traits? It is necessary thus to trace facts to their last analysis in order to expose the absurdities of current physiognomy.

Inasmuch as black-eyed southern nations are, on the whole, more impulsive than northern races, it may be said in a vague, general way that a black eye indicates a passionate disposition. But there are countless exceptions to this rule—apathetic black-eyed persons, as well as, conversely, fiery blue-eyed individuals. Nor is this at all strange; for the black colour is not stored up in some mysterious way as a result of a fiery temperament, but is simply accumulated in the iris through Natural Selection, as a protection against glaring sunlight.

Although, therefore, the brilliancy of the eye may vary with its colour, the colour itself does not express emotion, either qualitatively or quantitatively. In reading character no assistance is given us by the fact that eyes are "of unholy blue," "darkly divine," "gray as glass," or "green as leeks." Shakspere calls Jealousy a "green-eyed monster"; and the green iris has indeed such a bad reputation that blondes in search of a compliment commonly abuse their "green" eyes, to exercise your Gallantry, and give you a chance to defend their "celestial blue" or "divine violet."

Dr. Magnus suggests that the reason why we dislike decidedly green or yellow eyes is simply because they are of rare occurrence, and therefore appear anomalous; for in animals we do not hesitate to pronounce such eyes beautiful. He also explains ingeniously why it is that we are apt to attribute moral shortcomings to persons whose eyes are of a vague, dubious colour. Such eyes displease our æsthetic sense, and this displeasure we transfer to the moral sense, and thus confound and prejudice our judgment. In the same way our dislike of unusual green eyes disposes us to accuse their owners of irregularities of conduct. Moral: Keep your æsthetic and ethical judgments apart.

Conversely, in the case of snakes, our fear and horror make it difficult for us to appreciate the æsthetic charm of their colours. And all these cases show that the æsthetic sense, if properly understood and specialised, is independent of moral and utilitarian considerations : which knocks the bottom out of the theory of Alison, Jeffrey, and Co.

One more abnormality of colour in the iris must be referred to. It happens not infrequently that the colour of the two eyes is not alike, one being brown, the other blue or gray. In such cases, though each eye may be perfect in itself, we dislike the combination. What is the ground of this æsthetic dislike? Simply the fact that the dissimilarity of the eyes violates one of the fundamental laws of Beauty—the law of Symmetry, which demands that corresponding parts on the two sides of the body should harmonise.

(*c*) *Movements of the Iris.*—The jetblack pupil of the eye, as already noted, is not always of the same size. It becomes smaller if an excess of light causes the iris to relax, larger if diminution of light makes the iris contract its fibres. Another way of altering the size of the pupil is by gazing at a distant object, which causes it to enlarge, while gazing at a near object makes it smaller. According to Gratiolet and some other writers, there is still another way in which the pupil is affected, namely, through emotional excitement. Great fear, for instance, enlarges the pupil, according to Gratiolet. Dr. Magnus, however, remarks that, apart from the fact that some observers have denied that the pupil is affected by emotions, the alterations in its size are as a rule too insignificant to be noted by any but a trained observer ; so that they could not play any important physiognomic *rôle.*

Yet a large pupil is everywhere esteemed a great beauty, and is often credited with a special power of amorous expression. "Widened pupils," says Kollmann, "give the eye a tender aspect; they seem to increase its depth, and fascinate the spectator by the strangeness this imparts to the gaze. Oriental women put atropine into their eyes, which enlarges the pupil. They do this in order to give their eyes the soulful expression which they believe is imparted by large pupils, distinctly foreshadowing the joys of love."

Whether emotionally expressive or not, so much is certain that large pupils are more beautiful than small ones, for the same reason that large eyes are more beautiful than small ones, *i.e.* because we cannot have too much of a thing of Beauty.

Finally, there is this to be said regarding the lustre, colour, and size of pupil and iris, that they emphasise the language of the eye. If we play a love-song on the piano, we may admire it; but if it is sung or played on the violoncello, it makes a doubly deep impression; and why? Because the superior sensuous beauty of the voice, or the amorous tone-colour of the 'cello, paints and gilds the bare fabric of the song. A small dull-coloured eye, similarly, may speak quite as definite a language of command or entreaty, pride or humility, as any other; but the flashing large pupil and the lustrous deep-dyed iris intensify the emotional impressiveness of this language a hundredfold, by adding the incalculable power of sensuous Beauty. Thus lustre and colour are for the *visible* music of the spheres what orchestration is to audible music.

(*d*) *Movements of the Eyeball.*—The socket of the eye contains (besides the fat-cushion in which the eyeball is imbedded, the blood-vessels, and other tissues) seven muscles; one for raising the upper lid, and six for moving the eyeball itself upwards, downwards, inwards, outwards, or forwards and obliquely. To the action of these muscles the eye owes much of its expressiveness.

It has been noted that elating emotions have a tendency to raise the features, depressing emotions to depress them. The eyeball is no exception. Persons who are elated by their real or apparent superiority to others turn their eyes habitually from the humble things beneath them; hence the muscle which turns the eyeball upwards has long ago received the name of "pride-muscle"; while its antipode, the *musculus humilis*, is so called because humility and modesty are characterised by a downward gaze.

The muscle which turns the eyeball towards the inner corner, nosewards, is much used by persons who are occupied with near objects. If this convergence of the eyes is too pronounced, it gives one a stupid expression; whereas, if moderate, the expression is one of great intellectual penetration, as Dr. Magnus points out. He believes that the trick, made use of by some portrait-painters, of making the eyes appear to follow you wherever you go depends on this medium degree of convergence of the eyes.

Slight divergence of the eyeballs, on the other hand, is characteristic of children and of great thinkers—an item which Schopenhauer forgot to note when he pointed out that genius always retains certain traits of childhood. "Donders," says Dr. Magnus, "has always observed this divergent position of the eyes in persons who meditate deeply.

And the artists make use of this position of the eyes to give their figures the expression of a soul averted from terrestrial affairs, and fixed on higher spiritual objects. Thus the Sistine Madonna has this divergent position of the eyes, as well as the beautiful boy she carries on her arm." It is also found in Dürer's portrait of himself, and in a bust of Marcus Aurelius in the Vatican.

If, however, this divergence becomes too great, it loses its charm, for the eyes then appear to fix no object at all, and the gaze becomes "vacant," as in the eyes of the blind or the sick. To appreciate the force of these remarks it must be borne in mind that there is only one part of the retina, called the "yellow spot," with which we can distinctly fix an object. What we see with other parts of the retina is indistinct, blurred.

These details are here given because many will be glad to know that by daily exercising the muscles of the eyeballs before the mirror, they can greatly alter and improve their looks. Every day one hears the remark, "She has beautiful eyes, but she does not know how to use them." When we read of a great thinker, like Kant, fixing his gaze immovably on a tree for an hour, we think it quite natural; nor does any one object to "the poet's eye, in a fine frenzy rolling," for we all know that a poet is merely an inspired madman. But a young lady who wishes to charm by her Beauty must learn to fix her wandering eyes calmly on others, while avoiding a stony stare. One of the greatest charms of American girls is their frank, steady gaze, free from any tinge of unfeminine boldness. Such a charming natural gaze can only be acquired in a country where girls are taught to look upon men as gentlemen, and not as wolves, against whom they must be guarded by dragons.

Eye-gymnastics are as important to Beauty as lung-gymnastics to Health, and dancing-lessons to Grace. But of course there is a certain number of fortunate girls who can dispense with such exercises, because they gradually learn the proper use of their eyes, as well as general graceful movements, from the example of a refined mother.

Goldsmith's pretty line about "the bashful virgin's sidelong looks of love," is not a mere poetic conceit, but a scientific *aperçu*; for, as Professor Kollman remarks, "the external straight muscle of the eye was also called the lover's muscle, *musculus amatorius*, because the furtive side-glance is aimed at a beloved person."

Nor is this the only way in which the movements of the eyeball are concerned with Romantic Love. By constantly exercising certain muscles of the eyeball in preference to others, the eyes gradually assume, when at rest, a fixed and peculiar gaze which distinguishes them from all other eyes. It is comparatively easy to find two pairs of eyes of the same colour or form, but two with the same gaze, *i.e.* characteristic position of the eyeballs, never. Hence Dr. Magnus boldly generalises Herder's statement that "Every great man has a look which no one but he can give with his eyes," into the maxim that "*Every individual* has a look which no one else can make with his eyes."

Bungling photographers commonly spoil their

pictures by compelling their victims to fix their eyes in an unwonted position. The result is a picture which bears some general resemblance to the victim, but in which the characteristic *individual* expression is wanting.

Our habit of masking our eyes alone when we wish to remain unrecognised, and leaving the lower part of the face exposed, affords another proof of the assertion that the eye is the chief seat of individuality. For though the eyeball itself remains visible, the surrounding parts are covered, so that its characteristic position cannot be determined.

Now we know that Individual Preference is the first and most essential element of Romantic Love. Hence Dante was as correct in calling the eyes "the beginning of Love," as in terming the lips "the end of Love." And Shakspere agrees with Dante when he speaks of "Love first learned in a lady's eyes"; and again: "But for her eye I would not love her; yes, for her two eyes."

(*e*) *Movements of the Eyelids.*—Although the foregoing pages considerably qualify Dr. Magnus's thesis that the eyeball owes all its life and expressiveness to the movements of the eyelids and brows, yet the physiognomic and æsthetic importance of lids, lashes, and brows can hardly be too much emphasised. A very large proportion of the pleasure we derive from beautiful eyes is due to the constant changes in the apparent size of the eyeball, and the gradations in its lustre, produced by the rapid movements of the upper lid. This is strikingly proved by the fact, noted by Dr. Magnus, "that the eyes of wax figures, be they ever so artistically finished, always give the impression of death and rigidity," whereas "artificial eyes, such as are often inserted by physicians after the loss of an eye, have, thanks to the constant play of the lids, an appearance so animated and lifelike that it requires the trained eye of a specialist to detect the dead, lifeless glass-eye in this apparently so animated orb."

A complete emotional scale is symbolised in these movements of the upper eyelids. A medium position indicates rest or indifference. Joyous and other exciting emotions raise them, so that the whole of the lustrous iris becomes visible. Thus we get the eye "sparkling with joy" or the "angry flash of the eye," as well as Cupid's darts: "He is already dead; stabbed with a white wench's black eye." "Alack, there lies more peril in thine eye than twenty of their swords."

But if the lids are raised too high, so that the white above the iris becomes visible, the expression changes to one of affectation, or maniacal wildness, or extreme terror. There are persons, says Magnus, in whom the aperture between the lids is naturally so wide as to reveal the upper white of the eyes; and in consequence we are apt to accuse them of hollow pathos. I have seen not a few beautiful pairs of eyes marred by the habitual tendency to raise the lids too much—a fault that can be readily overcome by deliberate effort and practice before the mirror.

On the other hand, if the aperture between the lids is too small, that is, if the lids are naturally (or only transiently) lowered too much, we get an apathetic, drowsy expression. The Chinese eye displeases us not only by its oblique set, and the narrowness of the lid, but also because the natural smallness of the eyeball is exaggerated by the narrow palpebral aperture. The negro appears more wide awake to us, because in his eyes this aperture is wider—so wide, in fact, that he is apt to displease us by showing too much of the white sclerotic.

A very drooping eyelid being expressive of fatigue, physical or mental, *blasé* persons affect it in order to indicate their *nil admirari* attitude. But there is another secret reason why they drop their eyelids. If we lower the head and open our eyes widely, they retire within their sockets and appear hollow, suggesting dissipation or disease; whereas, if we raise the head, throwing it slightly backwards, and lowering the eyelids, we obliterate this hollow, and give the impression of languid indifference. This, rather than the "raising of the eyebrows," is what constitutes the "supercilious" expression.

It cannot be said that a supercilious appearance is specially attractive, yet the obliteration of the eyes' hollowness is an advantage; and it may be added that, since perfect health is not a superabundant phenomenon, the same reasoning explains why many faces are so much more fascinating in a reclining or semi-reclining position than when upright. Fashion, of course, being the handmaid of ugliness, does not object to hollow eyes encircled by blue rings, but even cultivates them. Yet in her heart of hearts every fashionable woman knows that nothing so surely kills masculine admiration

—not to speak of Love—as sunken eyes with blue rings.

A slight drooping of the eyelids, on the other hand, gives a pleasing expression of amorous languor. The lid, with its lashes, in this case, coyly veils the lustre of the eye, without extinguishing it. Hence, in the words of Dr. Magnus, the sculptors of antiquity made use of this slight lowering of the lid to express sensuous love; and accordingly it was customary to chisel the eyes of Venus with drooping lids and a small aperture.

In their task of moderating and varying the lustre of the eyeball, the lids are greatly assisted by the lashes. An eye with missing or too short lashes is apt to appear too fiery, glaring, or "stinging." Long dark eyelashes are of all the means of flirtation the most irresistible. Note yonder artful maiden. How modestly and coyly she droops her eyes, till suddenly the fringed curtain is raised and a glorious symphony of colour and lustre is flashed on her poor companion's dazed vision! No wonder he staggers and falls in love at first sight.

"White lashes and eyebrows are so disagreeably suggestive," we read in the *Ugly Girl Papers*, "that one cannot blame their possessor for disguising them by a harmless device. A decoction of walnut juice should be made in season, and kept in a bottle for use the year round. It is to be applied with a small hair-pencil to the brows and lashes, turning them to a rich brown, which harmonises with fair hair." Another recipe given, by a good authority, is as follows: "Take frankincense, resin, pitch, of each one half ounce; gum mastic, quarter of an ounce;

mix and drop on red-hot charcoals. Receive the fumes in a large funnel, and a black powder will adhere to its sides. Mix this with fresh juice of alderberries (or Cologne water will do), and apply with a fine camel-hair brush."

Those who wish to make their lashes longer and more regular may find the following suggestions, by Drs. Brinton and Napheys, of use: "The eyelashes should be examined one by one, and any which are split, or crooked, or feeble, should be trimmed with a pair of sharp scissors. The base of the lashes should be anointed nightly with a minute quantity of oil of cajuput on the top of a camel-hair brush, and the examination and trimming repeated every month. If this is sedulously carried out for a few months the result will be gratifying."

All such operations should be performed by another person, for the eye is a most delicate organ. Yet, not even this organ has been spared by deforming Fashion. The fact that some Africans colour their eyelids black may have a utilitarian rather than a cosmetic reason. But what shall we say to the Africans who eradicate their eyebrows, and the Paraguayans, who remove their eyelashes because they "do not wish to be like horses?"

Twin sisters ever are Fashion and Idiocy.

(*f*) *Movements of the Eyebrows.*—Herder called the arched eyebrow the rainbow of peace, because if it is straightened by a frown it portends a storm. In plain prose, the eyebrow partakes of the general upward movement from joyous excitement, and the downward movement in grief. If the eyebrows are too bushy, they overshadow the eye and produce a gloomy or even ferocious appearance. The Chinese, possibly from an instinctive perception that their eyes are not too large or bright, shave their eyebrows, leaving only a narrow fringe. Dr. Broca also notes that the eyebrow adds to the oblique appearance of the Chinese eye through a particular movement, the two internal thirds of the eyebrows being lower, and the external third higher than with us.

Though not, perhaps, directly concerned in the expression of Love, the eyebrow is not to be underrated. No detail of Beauty escapes Cupid's eyes; for do we not read of "the lover, sighing like furnace, with a woeful ballad made to his mistress's eyebrows?"

COSMETIC HINTS

As modern lovers disapprove of eyebrows meeting over the nose, superfluous hairs should be removed. Coarse irregular hairs in any part of the eyebrow should be pulled out or kept in position by a *fixateur*. "It is not well to trim the eyebrow generally, as it makes it coarse. . . . When it is desired to thicken or strengthen them, two or three drops of oil of cajuput may be gently rubbed into the skin every other night ; but here, and *always* when wiping them, the rubbing should be in the direction of the hair, from the nose outward, and *never* in the reverse direction." Among harmless dyes, pencils of dark pomatum or walnut-bark, steeped in Cologne for a week, are recommended; or, for a transient effect, a needle smoked over the flame of a candle may be used.

Regarding the general hygienic care of the eye,

the following rules should be borne in mind. Never read or work in a too weak or too glaring light, or when lying down, or with the book too near the eye. Rest the muscles occasionally by looking at a distant object. Bathe the eyes every morning in cold water, *keeping them closed.* For disorders, consult a physician immediately; a day's delay may be fatal to ocular beauty. For ordinary inflammation, an external application of witch-hazel extract, mixed with a few drops of Cologne, is very soothing. *Never* sleep with your eyes facing the window. Ninety-nine persons in a hundred do so; hence the large number of weak, lustreless eyes, early disturbances of slumber, and morning headaches. Large numbers of tourists in Switzerland constantly suffer from headaches, and lose all the benefits of their vacation, simply because they fail to have their head at night in the centre of the room, where it ought to be, because the air circulates there more freely than near the wall.

THE HAIR

CAUSE OF MAN'S NUDITY

"From the presence of the woolly hair or lanugo on the human fœtus, and of rudimentary hairs scattered over the body during maturity," Darwin inferred that "man is descended from some animal which was born hairy and remained so during life." He believed that "the loss of hair is an inconvenience and probably an injury to man, even in a hot climate, for he is thus exposed to the scorching in the sun, and to sudden chills, especially during wet weather. As Mr. Wallace remarks, the natives in all countries are glad to protect their naked backs and shoulders with some slight covering. No one supposes that the nakedness of the skin is any direct advantage to man; his body, therefore, cannot have been divested of hair through Natural Selection." Accordingly, he concludes that man lost his hairy covering through Sexual Selection, for ornamental purposes.

But if it can be shown that the nakedness of his skin *is* in some way of advantage to man, this argument falls to the ground. There are sufficient reasons, I think, for believing that Natural Selection aided Sexual Selection in divesting man of his hairy coat.

With his usual candour Darwin noticed the evidence which seemed to tell against his view. Mr. Belt, he says, "believes that within the tropics it is an advantage to man to be destitute of hair, as he is thus enabled to free himself of the multitude of ticks (acari) and other parasites with which he is often infested, and which sometimes cause ulceration." Darwin doubts, however, whether this evil is of sufficient magnitude to have led to the denudation of the body through Natural Selection, "since none of the many quadrupeds inhabiting the tropics have, as far as I know, acquired any specialised means of relief." But as primitive man's habits of cleanliness are much inferior to those of animals, this objection loses its force; and it is, moreover, weakened by the testimony of Sir W. Denison that "it is said to be a practice with the Australians, when the vermin get troublesome, to singe themselves." We also know that the ancient Egyptians shaved off their hair from motives of cleanliness.

However, it is not likely that the superior advantages of cleanliness and freedom from parasites would alone have sufficed to produce so great a change in man as the loss of his hair. It is more probable that the sun was the chief agent in accomplishing this transformation. I fail to see the force of Darwin's contention that the fact that "the other members of the order of Primates, to which man belongs, although inhabiting various hot regions, are well clothed with hair, generally thickest on the upper surface, is opposed to the supposition that man became naked through the action of the sun." For these animals commonly live in forests and on trees, where they are protected from the rays of the sun, which is not the case with man.

Furthermore, Darwin himself mentions some circumstances which point to the conclusion that the sun is the cause of man's nudity. He says, for instance, that "elephants and rhinoceroses are almost hairless; and as certain extinct species which formerly lived under an arctic climate were covered with long wool or hair, it would almost appear as if the existing species of both genera had lost their hairy covering from exposure to heat. This appears the more probable as the elephants in India which live on elevated and cool districts are more hairy than those on the lowlands."

Bearing in mind what was said in the chapter on the Complexion regarding the negro's skin, there is no difficulty in understanding why Natural Selection should eliminate the hairy covering of the skin while favouring a dark complexion. Hair not only absorbs the sun's heat, but retains that of the body; hence a hairy man not living on trees would be very uncomfortable in Africa, and likely to succumb to the enervating effects of high temperature. The negro's naked skin, on the other hand, is, as we have seen, specially devised as a *body-cooler*. The black pigment protects the underlying nerves of temperature, while the solar heat absorbed by this pigment is immediately radiated in the form of perspiration. Now we can see not only why the negro's skin is more velvety, smooth, and hairless than our own, but why its sweat-pores are larger and more numerous than in our skin.

At a later stage of evolution Sexual Selection probably came in to aid in this process of denudation. We may infer this, in the first place, from the analogous case of apes who have denuded and variously-coloured patches on the head and elsewhere, which they use for purposes of display, to attract the notice of the opposite sex; in the second place, from the fact that there are not a few tribes who pluck out their hairs. "The Fuegians threatened a young missionary, who was left for a time with them, to strip him naked, and pluck the hairs from his face and body, yet he was far from being a hairy man;" and "throughout the world the races which are almost completely destitute of a beard, dislike hairs on the face and body, and take pains to eradicate them." Darwin also notes some facts which, by analogy, seem to make it probable that "the long-continued habit of eradicating the hair may have produced an inherited effect."

In the case of the white race we cannot rely so much on the action of the sun as accounting for the absence of hair, but must place more especial emphasis on Sexual Selection. We are warranted in doing this by the consideration that Taste for Beauty is more developed in the white race, and therefore has more influence in controlling the choice of a mate. "As the body in woman is less hairy than in man, and as this character is common to all races, we may conclude" with Darwin "that it was our female semi-human ancestors who were first divested of hair," this character being then transmitted by the mothers to their children of both sexes.

The two universal traits of Beauty which chiefly guided man in the preference of a hairless skin were evidently Smoothness and Colour. One need only compare for a moment the face of a female chimpanzee, its leathery folded skin and straggling hairs, with the smooth and rosy complexion of a European damsel, to understand that, leaving touch out of consideration, sight alone would have sufficed to give the preference to the hairless skin. But since we derive less direct advantage than the tropical races from such a skin, cases of reversion to the hairy type are more common among us than with them, and our bodies in general are more hairy.

BEARDS AND MOUSTACHES

The elimination of hair from those parts of the body where it is less beautiful than a nude skin, is only one of the functions of Sexual Selection. Another equally important function is the preservation and elongation of the hair in a few places for ornamental purposes.

"We know from Eschricht," says Darwin, "that with mankind the female as well as the male fœtus is furnished with much hair on the face, especially round the mouth; and this indicates that we are descended from progenitors of whom *both sexes were bearded*. It appears, therefore, at first sight, probable that man has retained his beard from a very early period, whilst woman lost her beard at the same time that her body became almost completely divested of hair."

A long beard serves, to some extent, to protect the throat, but a moustache serves no such use, and it seems therefore more probable that beards as well as moustaches were developed in man for ornamental purposes, as in many monkeys (see, for some very curious pictures of bearded monkeys, *Descent of Man*, chap. xviii.) But why should women have lost their beards while men retained theirs? Because of the importance of emphasising the secondary sexual differences between man and woman, on which the degree of amorous infatuation depends. The tendency of evolution, as we have seen, has been to make the sexes more and more different in appearance; and as man chooses his mate chiefly on *æsthetic* grounds, he habitually gave the preference to smooth-faced women, whereas woman's choice, being largely based on *dynamic* grounds, fell on the bearded and moustached men, since a luxurious growth of hair is commonly a sign of physical vigour. Hence the humiliation of the young man who cannot raise a moustache, and the reciprocal horror of the young lady who finds the germs of one on her lip. Both are instinctively afraid of being "boycotted" by Cupid, and for ever debarred from the pleasures of mutual Romantic Love.

Women are quite right in dreading hair in the face as a blemish, for it is not only objectionable as a masculine trait, but also as a characteristic of old age, a hairy face being quite a common attribute of aged females. But with men the case is different. Though women may still be often influenced in their amorous choice by a beard, it is not, as just pointed out, on æsthetic grounds; and it is indeed very dubious if the beard can be accepted as a real personal ornament. True, the ancient Greeks respected a beard as an attribute of maturity and manhood, but their ideal of *supreme* beauty was nevertheless an unbearded youth: Apollo has neither beard nor moustache. The ancient Egyptians had a horror of the bearded and long-haired Greeks. "No Egyptian of either sex would on any account kiss the lips of a Greek," and whenever the Egyptians "intended to convey the idea of a man of low condition, or a slovenly person, the artists represented him with a beard" (Wilkinson). Similarly, in the second edition of his *Anatomy of Expression* (1824), Sir Charles Bell wrote that "When those essays were first written there was not a beard to be seen in England unless joined with squalor and neglect, and I had the conviction that this appendage *concealed the finest features*. Being in Rome, however, during the procession of the Corpus Domini, I saw that the expression was not injured by the beard, but that it added to the dignity and character of years."

These two sentences contain the whole philosophy of beards. The expression of character is not injured, but rather increased by a beard; but if it conceals the fine features of youth it is objectionable. There are men whose faces are too wide, and whose appearance is therefore improved by a chin-beard; and there are others whose faces are too narrow, and who consequently look better with side-whiskers. But in a well-shaped youthful masculine face a beard is as great a superfluity, if not a blemish, as in a woman's face.

Now, since the faces of civilised races are undoubtedly becoming more beautiful as time advances, it is comforting to know that, notwithstanding female selection, the beard is gradually disappearing. Very few men are able to raise a fine beard to-day, even with the artificial stimulus of several years' daily shaving; and the time, no doubt, is not very distant when men will go to the cosmetic electrician to have their straggling hair-bulbs in the chin killed. This may produce an inherited effect on their children; and the always smooth-faced mother, too, cannot but exert some hereditary influence on her sons as well as her daughters. The women, in turn, will inherit some of the superior æsthetic Taste of the men, and begin to see that there is more charm in a smooth than in a bearded face; while there will still be room enough for those sexual differences in facial Beauty which feed the flame of Love.

The following newspaper paragraph, though it may be a mere *jeu d'esprit*, is amusing and suggestive: "A Frenchman sent a circular to all his friends asking why they cultivated a beard. Among the answers 9 stated, 'Because I wish to avoid shaving'; 12 'Because I do not wish to catch cold'; 5 'Because I wish to conceal bad teeth'; 'Because I wish to conceal the length of my nose'; 6 'Because I am a soldier'; 21 'Because I was a soldier'; 65 'Because my wife likes it'; 28 'Because my love likes it'; 15 answered that they wore no beards."

Moustaches are much more common to-day than beards, and it is barely possible that they may escape æsthetic condemnation, and survive to the millennium. Persons with very short upper lips or flat noses, it is true, only emphasise their shortcomings by wearing a moustache; but in broad faces with prominent noses a well-shaped, not too drooping, moustache is no doubt an ornament, relieving the gravity of the masculine features and adding to their expression. As Bell remarks: "Although the hair of the upper lip does conceal the finer modulations of the mouth, as in woman, it adds to the character of the stronger and harsher emotions." "I was led to attend more particularly to the moustache as a feature of expression," he says, "in meeting a handsome young French soldier coming up a long ascent in the Côte d'Or, and breathing hard, although with a good-humoured, innocent expression. His sharp-pointed black moustache rose and fell with a catamount look that set me to think on the cause."

Young men may find in Bell's remarks a suggestion as to how they may make the moustache a permanent ornament of the human race. The movements of the moustache are dependent on the muscle called *depressor alæ nasi*. By specially cultivating this muscle men might in course of time make the movements of the moustaches subject to voluntary control. Just think what a capacity for emotional expression lies in such a simple organ as the dog's caudal appendage, aptly called the "psychographic tail" by Vischer: and moustaches are double, and therefore equal to two psychographic appendages!

Sexual Selection would not fail to seize on this "new departure" in moustaches immediately in order to emphasise the sexual differences of expression in the face, and thus increase the ardour of romantic passion. A few days ago I came across an attempt in a German paper to explain the meaning of the word Flirtation. The writer derives the word from an old expression meaning to toss or cast about. This he refers to the eyes, and thinks that the proper translation of Flirtation is *äugeln, i.e.* to "make eyes." We, of course, know that flirting is a fine art which includes a vast deal besides *äugeln*; but "making eyes" is certainly one of its tricks. Now, is it not probable that by and by, when young men will have properly trained their *depressor alæ nasi*, they will look upon the making of eyes as a feminine attribute, and, instead of winking at their sweethearts, express their admiration by some subtle and graceful movement of the moustaches? This would obliterate Darwin's assertion that Love has no special means of expression.

BALDNESS AND DEPILATORIES

Superficial students of Darwinism are constantly

making owlish predictions that ere many generations will have passed bald heads will be the normal aspect of man. But, as we have just seen in the case of beards, it is not utility or Natural Selection so much as Sexual, Æsthetico-Amorous Selection on which the evolution of Personal Beauty depends. If Natural Selection were at work alone we should, indeed, ultimately become bald; for as soon as man begins to cover his head with a cap or hat, he takes away the chief function of the hair on the top of the head, where it serves as a protection against wind and weather. But Sexual Selection now steps in and says that the hair must remain, because without it the head looks decidedly ugly, whatever its shape.

"Eschricht states that in the human fœtus the hair on the face during the fifth month is longer than that on the head; and this indicates that our semi-human progenitors were not furnished with long tresses, which must therefore have been a late acquisition. This is likewise indicated by the extraordinary difference in the length of the hair in the different races: in the negro the hair forms a mere curly mat; with us it is of great length, and with the American natives it not rarely reaches to the ground. Some species of Semnopithecus have their head covered with moderately long hair, and this probably serves as an ornament, and was acquired through sexual selection. The same view may perhaps be extended to mankind, for we know that long tresses are now and were formerly much admired, as may be observed in the works of almost every poet; St. Paul says, 'If a woman have long hair it is a glory to her'; and we have seen that in North America a chief was elected solely from the length of his hair" (Darwin).

Inasmuch as Sexual Selection or Love is impeded in its action not only by pecuniary and social considerations, but by the fact that it cannot be guided by any particular feature alone, its action is slow and sometimes uncertain. Hence the increase of bald heads. It is therefore necessary to supplement the beautifying results of Sexual Selection by means of hygienic precautions, such as avoiding airtight, warm, high hats, badly ventilated rooms, intemperate habits, and other causes of baldness. Hereditary baldness is difficult to arrest in its course; but even in such cases much may be accomplished by beginning in childhood to take proper care of the hair. Most persons—especially men—seem to imagine that combs and brushes are made solely for the purpose of arranging the hair in some approved fashion; whereas, if properly used, a brush adds as much to the *sensuous* beauty of the hair as to its *formal* appearance. To remove all the dust from the hair, and give it gloss and healthy colour, about fifty daily strokes, or more even, are recommended. Avoid irritating the scalp with fine combs or hard bristles, and wash it once or twice a week with a weak solution of ammonia or borax. Hair that is properly brushed is always glossy with its natural oil, and needs no vulgar ointment, offensive to the smell and suggestive of uncleanliness. If with these hygienic precautions the hair refuses to become beautiful, it is time to get medical advice; for the dull colour and dryness of the hair which lead to baldness are often due to constitutional disease.

Powdering the hair is fortunately no longer in vogue as it was formerly. It is a most unæsthetic habit, not only because white or gray hair is naturally suggestive of old age, grief, and decrepitude, but because the flour forms with the perspiration and with the oil of the hair a nasty compound. William Pitt "estimated, in 1795, that the amount of flour annually consumed for this purpose in the United Kingdom represented the enormous and incredible value of six million dollars."

It is estimated that the average number of hairs on the head is 120,000. This allows one to look with considerable indifference on the loss of a few hundred, all the more as in ordinary cases, even after illness, every hair lost is replaced by another. But when the papilla at the base of the hair cavity is destroyed, then baldness is inevitable. It follows from this that the only certain way of removing hair permanently from places where it is not desired is to destroy this papilla. "Plucking hair out by the root" does not destroy it. "If they are pulled out with the tweezers there is a still greater stimulus given," says Dr. Bulkley (*The Skin in Health and Disease*), "and the hairs return yet more coarse and obtrusive." The various Oriental and Occidental pastes for removing the hair have no more permanent effect than shaving. "Superfluous hairs can be removed either by the introduction of an irregularly-shaped needle into the follicle (after the extraction of the hair), which is then twisted so as to break up the papilla and produce a little inflammation, which closes the follicle ; or a needle can be inserted, and a current from a battery be turned on, when the follicle is destroyed by what is known as electrolysis. These procedures could be done only by a physician."

Concerning electrolysis Dr. S. E. Woody says in the *American Practitioner and News* that the number of hairs to return and demand a second removal will decrease with the skill of the operator and the thoroughness of the operation. He usually expects the return of about 5 per cent, but when these are in turn removed the cure is complete. " You should have the patient come only on bright days, for good light is necessary."

ÆSTHETIC VALUE OF HAIR

If not the most beautiful part of the head, hair certainly is the most beautifying. To improve the shape of mouth, nose, chin, or eyes requires time and patience, but the arrangement of the hair can be altered in a minute, not only to its own advantage, but so as to enhance the beauty of the whole face. By clever manipulation of her long tresses, a woman can alter her appearance almost as completely as a man can by shaving off his long beard or moustache.

But, alas ! If the prevalence of the bustle and wasp-waist allowed any doubt to remain as to the woful rarity of æsthetic taste among women, it would be found in the arrangement of the hair and the kind of headdresses they commonly adopt at the behest of Fashion. " Because women as a rule do not know what *beauty* means," says Mrs. Haweis (*The Art of Beauty*), " therefore they catch at whatever presents itself as a novelty. . . . They do not pause to consider whether the old fashion became them better—whether the new one reveals more clearly the slight shrinking of the jaw, or spoils the pretty colour still blooming in the cheek."

The latest head-dress foisted on the feminine world by Parisian Fashion shows most strikingly how Fashion is the Handmaid of Vulgarity as well as of Ugliness. Heaven knows, the high silk hats worn by men are bad enough, on hygienic as well as æsthetic grounds. They promote baldness and destroy all the artistic proportions of stature, making the head look by one half too high. But silk hats are a harmless trifle compared with the shapeless straw-towers, ornamented with bird-corpses, that have been worn of late by almost all women in countries which slavishly follow Parisian example. And there is this great difference between man's silk hat and woman's bird-sarcophagus—the former only results in ugliness, the second is also evidence of heartlessness, and leads to vulgarity. For what is it but vulgarity if women continue to go to the theatre for two winters with hats which make it quite impossible for those sitting behind them to see the scenery and enjoy the play—and all this in spite of innumerable sarcastic and angry protests in the journals? Is not the first rule of etiquette and good manners regard for the feelings and pleasures of others?

What would women say to a man who kept on his tall hat in a theatre until the ushers threw him out? Would they not all pronounce him either intoxicated or ineffably vulgar? Would not Schopenhauer, if he could go to an American theatre to-day, be justified in saying that women are not only the "unæsthetic sex," but also the "ill-bred sex"? And can the women who are so devoid of courtesy towards the men wonder that masculine gallantry towards women on street-cars and elsewhere seems to be on the wane?

Although there are no two heads in which the most pleasing effect is secured by precisely the same arrangement of the hair and the same style of hat, it may be laid down as a universal rule that a very high hat or arrangement of the hair is becoming to no one, for the reason above indicated. Let it be observed, says Mr. Ruskin, "that in spite of all custom, an Englishman instantly acknowledges, and at first sight, the superiority of the turban to the hat." "Guido," says Mrs. Haweis, "probably felt the peculiar charm of the turban when he placed one upon the quiet melancholy head of Beatrice Cenci." For full and bright young faces the Tam o' Shanter is the loveliest of all headdresses. But this subject is too large to be discussed in a paragraph. In Mrs. Haweis's *Art of Beauty* may be found some elegant illustrations of head-dresses placed near fashionable monstrosities; and young ladies would do well to devote an hour a day for a year or two to the study of some history of costume. Nothing awakens the sense of Beauty so rapidly as good models and comparisons.

Concerning the arrangement of the hair two more points may be noted. Is it not about time to do away with the venerable absurdity of parting the hair? If entire baldness is voted ugly, why should partial baldness be courted? The hair should be allowed to remain in its natural direction of growth. It does not part itself naturally, nor again—and this is a much more important point—does it grow backward from the forehead. The Chinese coiffure disfigures *every* woman who adopts it; and the habit of combing back the hair tightly from the forehead, moreover, often causes neuralgic headache, the cause of which is unsuspected; not to speak of the fact that such a coiffure raises the eyebrows, and thus gives a fixed expression of amazed stupefaction. The hair naturally falls over the forehead, and fringes it as beautifully as a grove does a lake.

The ancient Greek notions on this subject are worthy of attentive consideration. "Women who had a high forehead placed a band over it, with the design of making it thereby seem lower," says Winckelmann. Not only in women but in mature men the hair was so arranged as to cover up "the receding bare corners over the temples, which usually enlarge as life advances beyond that age when the forehead is naturally high." The modern fringe or "bang" is, however, an improvement even on the Greek curve of the hair over the temples. It improves the appearance of all women except those whose forehead is very low naturally; but in all cases exaggeration must be avoided.

A writer in the London *Evening Standard* thinks it is strange that the English, "who have the poorest hair in Europe, make the least attempt to show what they have," and that it has now "come to such a pass that a maiden of twenty thinks it almost indecent to wear her hair loose." He traces this to the tyranny of Fashion—the ugly majority having compelled the beautiful minority to conceal their charms. But we may be sure that ere long Beauty will revolt against Fashion. It will be another French revolution, practically,—an emphatic protest against Parisian dictation and vulgarity.

BRUNETTE AND BLONDE

> "In the old time black was not counted fair,
> Or if it were it bore not beauty's name;
> But now is black beauty's successive heir."—SHAKSPERE.

BLONDE *VERSUS* BRUNETTE

Becker tells us that among the ancient Greeks "black was probably the prevailing colour of the hair, though blond is frequently mentioned"; and he adds that both men and women used dyes, and "the blond or yellow hair was much admired." Mr. Gladstone, in his work on Homer, remarks that "dark hair is a note of the foreigner and of Southern extraction. . . . I have been assured that, in the Greece of to-day, light hair is still held as indicating the purest Hellenic blood." According to Winckelmann, "Homer does not even once mention hair of a black colour"; and again: "Flaxen, $\xi\alpha\nu\theta\acute{\eta}$ hair has always been considered the most beautiful; and hair of this colour has been attributed to the most beautiful of the gods, as Apollo and Bacchus, not less than to the heroes; even Alexander had flaxen hair."

That the Romans agreed with the Greeks in giving the preference to light hair seems probable from the extensive importations of yellow German hair for the Roman ladies, as also from the fact that "Lucretius, when speaking of the false flatteries addressed to women, quotes one in illustration, namely, that a maiden with black hair is μελίχροος (honey-coloured)—thus ascribing to her a beauty which she does not possess."

When the fair-haired Teuton overran the South a new motive for preferring blond hair arose, as a writer in the London *Standard* remarks: "Whatever the feeling of the men, we may be sure that the dark beauties of those climes felt a natural inclination to resemble the wives and daughters of the conqueror, and when we perceive their likenesses again, at the revival of art in Italy, not a black tress is to be seen. Is there a single Madonna not blond?—or ten portraits of women by the great masters? In all the gallery of Titian, we think only of a figure, naked to the waist, in the Uffizi, described as one of his mistresses. . . . But we know that the blond tint was artificial in a majority of cases—the deep black of eye and brow would show it if no evidence were forthcoming. But evidence turns up at every side . . . a hundred recipes are found in memoirs, correspondence, and treatises of the time.".

Hear another witness: "Southern Europe," says Mr. R. G. White, "is peopled with dark-skinned, dark-haired races, and the superior beauty of the blond type was recognised by the painters, who always, from the earliest days, represented angels as of that type. The Devil was painted black so much as a matter of course that his pictured appearance gave rise to a well-known proverb; ordinary mortals were represented as more or less dark; celestial people were white and golden-haired: whence the epithet 'divinely fair.'"

And the poets were quite as partial as the artists to the light type. Petrarch's sonnets are addressed to a blue-eyed Laura. Krimhild of the *Nibelungenlied* is blue-eyed, like Fricka, the Northern Juno, and Ingeborg of the *Frithjof's Saga*, and the Danish princess Iolanthe, as Dr. Magnus points out; and in the French folk-songs "the girls are almost as invariably blond as in the songs of Heine," as a writer in the *Saturday Review* (1878) remarks, adding that "there is even such an expression as *aller en blonde*, 'to go a-wooing,' which proves the universality of the belief in fair beauties."

Concerning England, a writer in the *Quarterly Review* declares that Shakspere mentions black hair only twice throughout his plays; and that in the National Gallery of that date (1853) there was not a single female head with black hair.

BRUNETTE *VERSUS* BLONDE

Thus we have evidence showing that during the epoch preceding the general prevalence of Romantic Love, the blonde type was considered the ideal of beauty throughout Europe—in Greece and Italy as well as in Germany, Scandinavia, France, and England. And where the hair was not naturally blond, artificial means were used to make it so.

But as soon as Love appears on the scene and sharpens the æsthetic sense, we find a reaction in favour of brunettes. There can be no doubt of this, for it is attested not only by personal opinions and observations, but by accurate statistics. The *Quar-*

terly Review just referred to believed that blondes were gradually decreasing in England, and the *Saturday Review* asserts that "some years ago Mr. Gladstone, whom nothing escapes, declared that light-haired people were far less numerous than in his youth. Many middle-aged persons will probably agree with him." "The time was," the writer adds, "when the black-haired, black-eyed girl of fiction was as dark of soul as of tresses, while the blue-eyed maiden's character was of 'heaven's own colour.' Thackeray damaged this tradition by invariably making his dark heroines nice, his fair heroines treacherous sirens." Byron, we may add, also showed a passionate preference for brunettes ; and does not another great love-poet, Moore, speak of "eyes of unholy blue"?

Speaking of the Germans, the anthropologist Waitz remarks that "the blond and red hair, the blue eyes and light complexion, which most of them had at the period of the Roman wars, have not disappeared, it is true, but certainly diminished greatly in frequency. In Jarrold we find the analogous statement that as late as the time of Henry VIII. red hair predominated in England, and that at the beginning of the fifteenth century gray eyes were more common, dark eyes and dark hair less common, than now." As this change is correlated in both these countries with a gradual refinement of the features, does it not indicate that modern æstheticoamorous selection favours the brunette type?

Waitz's assertion regarding the gradual decrease in the number of blondes in Germany is strikingly confirmed by the results of a series of statistical investigations undertaken under the supervision of Professor Virchow. Almost eleven million school children were examined in Germany, Austria, Switzerland and Belgium, and the results showed that Switzerland has only 11·10, Austria 19·79, and Germany 31·80 per cent of pure blondes. Thus the very country which, since the days of ancient Rome has been proverbially known as the home of yellow hair and blue eyes, has to-day only 32 pure blondes in a hundred; while the average of pure brunettes is already 14·05 per cent (and in some regions as high as 25 per cent). The 53·15 per cent of the mixed type are evidently being slowly transformed into pure brunettes, thanks to intermarriages with the neighbours who are of the dark variety east and west, as well as south of Germany.

In England Dr. Beddoe has collected a number of statistics which also bear out the theory that brunettes are gaining on blondes. Among 726 women examined he found 369 brunettes and 357 blondes. Of the brunettes he found that 78·5 per cent were married, while of the blondes only 68 per cent were married. Thus it would seem that a brunette has ten chances of getting married in England to a blonde's nine. Hence Dr. Beddoe reasons that the English are becoming darker because the men persist in selecting the darker-haired women as wives.

In France a similar view has been put forth by M. Adolphe de Candolle in the *Archives des Sciences*. He found that when both parents have eyes of the same colour 88·4 per cent inherit this colour. "But the curious fact comes out that more females than males have black or brown eyes, in the proportion, say, of 49 to 45 or of 41 to 39. Next, it appears that with different coloured eyes in the two parents, 53·09 per cent of the progeny followed the fathers in being dark-eyed, and 55·09 per cent followed their mothers in being dark-eyed. An increase of 5 per cent of dark-eyed in each generation of discolorous unions must tell heavily in the course of time. It would seem," adds *Science,* to which I owe this summary of De Candolle's views, "that, unless specially bred by concolorous marriages, blue-eyed belles will be scarce in the millennium."

WHY CUPID FAVOURS BRUNETTES

How are we to account for this undeniable change in favour of brunettes? Is it merely a matter of Taste and Fashion? Are we simply going through a period of brunette-worship which in turn will be followed by a century or two of blonde-worship, and so on *ad infinitum?* or are there reasons for believing that Cupid will abide by his present decision, and continue to eliminate blondes? There are several such reasons, which may best be discussed separately, under the heads of Complexion, Hair, and Eyes.

(1) *Complexion.*—The dark skin is more soft and velvety than the light skin, and therefore more agreeable to the touch; hence, as Winckelmann remarks, " he who prefers dark to fair beauty is not on that account to be censured; indeed, one might approve his choice, if he is attracted less by sight than by the touch." But the eye, too, is likely to be more pleased by a brunette than a pure blond complexion. In the dark skin the pigmentary matter tones down the

too vivid red of the translucent blood, wherefore the brunette complexion appears more mellow and delicate in its tints than the Scandinavian blonde, in which a blush suggests a hectic flush, and its normal whiteness the pallor of ill-health or a lack óf invigorating and beautifying sunshine.

The brunette complexion, in a word, suggests to the mind the idea of *stored-up sunshine*, i.e. *Health;* and as Health is what primarily attracts Cupid, this, combined with his taste for delicate tints and veiled blushes, partly accounts for his preference of the dark type. Youthful freshness is another bait which tempts Cupid; and it is well known that the dark complexion does not, as a rule, fade so soon as the blond.

That the brownish skin is commonly healthier than the white is also shown by its being less subject to the irregularity in the secretion of pigmentary matter which causes freckles. These blemishes, like smallpox marks, are much rarer among the dark than among blond races and individuals.

The skin of blondes who are exposed to a hot sun and raw weather becomes red, inflamed, and decidedly unbeautiful, while a brunette's complexion only becomes a shade darker, and possibly all the more attractive. This suggests another reason why the brunettes have an advantage over blondes in the country, where love-making is chiefly carried on in summer. Yet it will not do for the blondes to avoid the sunshine on this account, for that will make them anæmic and prematurely old.

There is a class of extreme blondes to whom sunlight is not only irritating, but positively painful.

They are called albinos, because there is no brown pigment whatever in any part of their body—skin, hair, or iris. The Dutch call them Kakerlaken or cockroaches, because, like these animals, they avoid the light. Such anomalous individuals occur also among animals; and Darwin has noted regarding birds that albinos do not pair, apparently because they are rejected by their normally-coloured comrades. This fact has a remote bearing on our argument, for blondes are intermediate between albinos and brunettes.

It would appear, indeed, as if not only the complexion but the general constitution of the dark type were superior to that of the blond type. In the chapter on the Complexion it was stated that a dark hue is regarded in Australia and elsewhere as evidence of superior strength. The ancient Greeks, Winckelmann tells us, although they called the young with fair complexions "children of the gods," looked upon a brown complexion in boys as an indication of courage. Professor Topinard states that "the fair races are especially adapted to temperate and cool regions, and the South is looked upon as almost forbidden ground. The brown races, on the contrary, have a remarkable power of becoming acclimatised." Several writers have even endeavoured to account for the gradual increase in the proportion of brunettes by connecting it with the modern tendency towards centralisation of the population in large cities, where the blondes, being unable to resist their unsanitary surroundings, are eliminated, while the more vigorous and fertile brunettes survive and multiply.

One reason why tourists are more impressed by

the prevalence of beauty in southern than in northern regions, is because the working classes are more beautiful in the South than in the North; and the working classes, of course, constitute the vast majority of the population everywhere. "In northern countries," says Mr. Lecky, "the prevailing cast of beauty depends rather on colour than on form. It consists chiefly of a freshness and delicacy of complexion which severe labour and constant exposure necessarily destroy, and which is therefore rarely found in the highest perfection among the very poor. But the southern type is essentially democratic. The fierce rays of the sun only mellow and mature its charms. Its most perfect examples may be found in the hovel as in the palace, and the effects of this diffusion of beauty may be traced both in the manners and the morals of the people."

Another advantage to the study and development of Personal Beauty lies in the fact, noted by Ruskin, "that in climates where the body can be more openly and frequently visited by sun and weather, the nude both comes to be regarded in a way more grand and pure, as not of necessity awakening ideas of base kind (as pre-eminently with the Greeks), and also from that exposure receives a firmness and sunny elasticity very different from the silky softness of the clothed nations of the North."

(2) *Hair.*—"That noble beauty," says Winckelmann, "which consists not merely in a soft skin, a brilliant complexion, wanton or languishing eyes, but in the shape or form, is found more frequently in countries which enjoy a uniform mildness of

climate." "This difference shows itself even in the hair of the head and of the beard, and both in warm climates have a more beautiful growth even from childhood, so that the greater number of children in Italy are born with fine curling hair, which loses none of its beauty with increasing years. All the beards, also, are curly, ample, and finely shaped; whereas those of the pilgrims who come to Rome from the other side of the Alps are generally, like the hair of their heads, stiff, bristly, straight, and pointed."

Nevertheless, the hair is the blonde's one feature in which, so far as the head itself is concerned, she may dispute the supremacy with the brunette. Light hair is finer than dark hair, and there is more of it to the square inch; and as for the colour, who will say that a girl with "golden locks which make such wanton gambols" is inferior in beauty to one who is "robed in the long night of her deep hair"?

But if the positive tests of Beauty—Colour, Lustre, Smoothness, Delicacy, etc.—do not permit us to give the preference to dark hair, it is otherwise when we come to the negative tests. A fine head of blond hair *may* be as beautiful as a head of brown hair, but it is not so apt to be beautiful; it has a tendency to become "stiff, bristly, straight, and pointed." There are various reasons for believing that light hair as a rule is not so healthy, not so well-nourished, as dark hair. Every reader must have noticed among his friends that the blondes are much more likely than the brunettes to complain of dry and refractory hairs, and difficulty in keeping them in shape.

"The end of long hair is usually lighter in colour than its beginning," as Professor Kollmann remarks: "at a distance from the skin the hairs lose their natural oil as well as the nourishing sap which comes from their roots." This implies that the colour of the hair becomes darker with increasing vigour and vitality. We have seen that the same is true of the colour of animals in general, the healthiest being the most vividly coloured, and the males commonly darker than the less vigorous females; and as for plants, who has not noticed how easy it is to trace the course of an invisible brooklet in a meadow, not only by the greater luxuriance, but the much darker colour of the grass which lines its banks?

Once more, we know that old age, great sorrow, terror, headaches, or insanity, diminish the pigmentary matter in the hair and make it lighter—gray or white; and that by frequently brushing blond hair we not only make it more glossy and shapely, but at the same time darker.

Red hair is probably an abnormal variety of blond hair, since it does not occur among the darker races. It is disliked not only because it is so often associated with freckles, but because it is commonly dry, coarse, and bristly. The Brahmins were forbidden to marry a red-haired woman; and the populace of most countries, confounding moral with æsthetic impressions, accuses red-haired people of various shortcomings. "Sandy hair, when well brushed and kept glossy with the natural oil of the scalp, changes to a warm golden tinge. I have seen," says the author of the *Ugly Girl Papers*, "a most obnoxious head of colour so changed by a few years' care that it became the admiration of the owner's friends, and could hardly be recognised as the withered, fiery locks once worn."

An American newspaper paragraph, for the truthfulness of which I cannot vouch, recently stated that twenty-one men in Cincinnati, who had married red-haired women, were found to be colour-blind. A person who is colour-blind mistakes red for black.

(3) *Eyes.*—But it is when we leave the scalp that the superiority of dark over light hair becomes most manifest. That black eyelashes and eyebrows are infinitely more beautiful than light-coloured ones, is admitted without a dissentient voice; and it is needless to add that brunettes, whether gray or black-eyed, are almost certain to have dark eyelashes, while blondes are almost certain not to have them. Hence the painting of light eyelashes has been a common artifice among all nations and at all times; and Mrs. Haweis goes so far as to sanction the use of nasty gray hair powder because it "makes the eyebrows and eyelashes appear much darker than they really are." I have, however, seen black eyelashes on several young ladies who could hardly be classed as brunettes, and who assured me on their conscience that they had not dyed them. Can it be possible that Sexual Selection (*i.e.* the æsthetic overtone in Romantic Love) is endeavouring to evolve a type of Beauty in which golden locks will be allowed to remain, while the eyelashes will be changed to black? The only objection to this surmise is that the hair in other parts of the face (chin and upper lip), though rarely of the same

colour as that on the scalp, is almost always lighter in hue. But, whether or not Love can accomplish the miracle of making black lashes universal, the fact remains that they are in all cases a thousand times more charming than yellow or red lashes, and also more apt to be long and delicately curved, coyly veiling the mysterious lustre and fire of the iris.

Concerning the iris, in turn, it cannot be denied that it is most beautiful when black (dark brown), or so deeply blue or violet as to be easily taken for black. This superiority of the dark hue is due partly to the fact that a brown eye is commonly more lustrous than a light eye, and partly to the law of contrast; for a light-coloured iris obviously does not present such a vivid contrast to the white of the eye as a brown iris, and is therefore apt to seem vague, watery, and superficial in expression. The light blue or gray eye appears shallow. All its beauty seems to be on the surface, whereas the "soul-deep eyes of darkest night" appear unfathomable through their bewitching glamour.

What is the etymology of the word bella donna? Was it given to the plant on account of the beauty of its cherry-like berries? or was it not rather chosen by some poet who noted the wondrous effect of these poisonous berries in changing all eyes into black eyes by enlarging the pupils, thus making every donna a bella donna, or "beautiful lady"? Great, indeed, must be the fascination of a large pupil, since so many women have braved the danger to health, and the certainty of impairment of vision, which follow the use of this poison as a cosmetic.

It was noted in an earlier part of this volume that young men are led to propose chiefly in the evening, because the twilight enlarges the pupil, thus not only beautifying *her* eyes, but enabling him to see *his own* divine image reflected in them, proving his Monopoly of her soul. A brunette's dark eyes on such an occasion appear to be *all* pupil: how, then, can you wonder that brunettes are gaining on blondes?

However, let not the blondes despair. As they become scarcer they will for that very reason be valued the more as curiosities, and the last of them, should she fail to find a husband, will be able to command a handsome salary in a museum or as a comic opera singer.

Moreover, there is no reason why physiologists should not ere long discover the secret of changing the tint of the skin, hair, and iris to suit one's taste. All children are born with light eyes, but a great many exchange them for dark eyes as soon as they realise their mistake. We also know that ill-health temporarily changes the colour of the hair. According to the *Popular Science Monthly*, " Prentiss records a case of a patient to whom muriate of pilocarpine was administered hypodermically, and whose hair was changed from light blond to nearly jet black, and his eyes from light blue to dark blue." The eating of sorghum is also said to favour the evolution of a brunette colour. But it is to the electricians that we must look for a harmless and efficient method of stimulating the secretion of pigmentary matter in the iris, skin, and hair. The man who first discovers how to change blondes to brunettes will acquire a fame as great as Newton's or Shakspere's, and when he dies Cupid will appoint him his private secretary.

"John," we can hear a woman say to her husband twenty years hence—"John, Laura is now five years old. Don't you think it is time to send her over to Dr. Electrode? I don't object to her yellow hair, but I do think her complexion, iris, and eyelashes should be made several shades darker. She will then stand a better chance in the marriage-market when she gets older."

NATIONALITY AND BEAUTY

Beauty, like Love, has its national peculiarities, based on climate, customs, traditions, mental and physical. As the description of all these differences between the various peoples in the world would require several volumes the size of this, it cannot, of course, be attempted here even roughly. Nor is this necessary, for most of these national peculiarities are variations which have more ethnologic than æsthetic interest. Many of them have been considered in the preceding pages to illustrate the Evolution of Personal Beauty; and something has been said episodically regarding Greek, Hebrew, Georgian, and Mediæval Beauty. Polish women are famous for their beauty, but as I have never been in Poland nor in Russia, I do not feel competent to pronounce judgment on the common verdict, and will therefore limit my observations to the six nations whose Love-customs I have endeavoured to describe. And even in these cases I cannot claim that the following remarks have any greater value than such as attaches to mere casual jottings. In most European countries the nations are as wildly mixed as in the United States, though less recently; and it is therefore extremely difficult to draw any general conclusions, as is shown by the conflicting opinions of tourists. Moreover, each nation is variously subdivided, so that some things are, *e.g.* true of North Germany which are not true of South Germany, and so in other countries. Yet there are a few points on which travellers commonly agree, and these will be briefly considered here. The highest beauty is pretty much the same the world over—in Japan as in France; and even among the savages of Africa young girls are to be found who, but for their colour, would be pronounced beauties in Europe. Most nations are on their way towards this highest type of Beauty, and they occupy different stages of evolution according to their attitude and advantages regarding the four principal sources of Personal Beauty—Hygienic Habits, Mixture of Nationalities, Romantic Love, and Mental Refinement.

FRENCH BEAUTY

Widely as tourists commonly differ in their opinions as to the prevalence of Beauty in various countries, on one point there seems to be a universal agreement—viz. that nowhere in Europe is it so rare as in France. Thackeray notes that nature has "rather stinted the bodies and limbs of the French nation." Walker, in his work on Beauty, remarks that "the women of France are among the ugliest in the world"; and Sir Lepel Griffin puts the truth pointedly in these words: "National vanity, where inordinately developed, may take the form of asserting that black is white, as in France, where the average of good looks, among both men and women, is perhaps lower than elsewhere in Europe. If a pretty woman be seen in the streets of Paris, she is almost certainly English or American; yet if a foreigner were to form an estimate of French beauty from the rapturous descriptions of contemporary French novels, or from the sketches of *La Vie Parisienne*, he must conclude that the Frenchwoman was the purest and loveliest type in the world in face and figure. The fiction in this case disguises itself in no semblance of the truth."

Yet there have been French writers who felt the shortcomings of their nation in regard to Personal Beauty. One of them says that you find in the Frenchman "the love of the graceful rather than the beautiful"; and in the following characterisation of his countrywomen, by M. Figuier, it is easy to see that he lays much more emphasis on their grace and the expressiveness of their features than on their Beauty proper: "There is in her face much that is most pleasing, although we can assign her physiognomy to no determinate type. Her features, *frequently irregular*, seem to be borrowed from different races; they do not possess that unity which springs from calm and majesty, but are in the highest degree expressive, and marvellously contrived for conveying every shade of feeling. In them we see a smile though it be shaded by tears; a caress though they threaten us; and an appeal when yet they command.

Amid *the irregularity of this physiognomy* the soul displays its workings. As a rule the Frenchwoman is short of stature, but in every proportion of her form combines grace and delicacy. Her extremities and joints are fine and elegant, of perfect model and distinct form, without a suspicion of coarseness. With her, moreover, art is brought wonderfully to assist nature" (*The Races of Man*).

It appears, indeed, as if Frenchwomen, who are naturally bright and quickwitted, endeavoured to make up in grace what they lack in beauty. Hence nothing is more common than Frenchwomen who are so fascinating with their graceful little ways and movements that one almost or quite forgets their homeliness. No French girl ever needs to be taught how to use her eyes to best advantage ; and, as a clever newspaper writer has remarked, French girls " can say more with their shoulders than most girls can with their eyes ; and when they talk with eyes, hands, shoulders, and tongue at once, it takes a man of talent to keep up."

Of course it would be absurd to say that no specimens of supreme Beauty are to be found in France ; but they are scarce as strawberries in December. The general tendency of women to become either too stout or too lean after they have got out of their teens, is apparently more pronounced in France than elsewhere in Europe. And as for the men, they can be recognised anywhere, either by their almost simian hairiness or their puny appearance. What a difference in stature and general manly aspect between a regiment of French and one of English or German soldiers ! And the superiority of the English soldiers to the French in vigour and beauty is more than "skin-deep"; it appears to extend to the very chemical composition of their tissues: for Professor Topinard remarks in his *Anthropologie* that he enunciated more than twenty years ago "a fact which was more or less confirmed by others, namely, that the mortality after capital operations in English hospitals was less by one-half than in the French. We attributed it to a better diet, to their better sanitary arrangements, and to their superior management. There was but one serious objection offered to our statement. M. Velapeau, with his wonderful acumen, made reply, at the Academy of Medicine, that the flesh of the English and of the French differed; in other words, that the reaction after operations was not the same in both races. It is, in effect, an anthropological character."

Thus the "wonderful acumen" of two French scientists has established the fact that French deterioration is shown not only in a surprisingly low birth-rate, but in the general inferiority of the French constitution: for the ability to resist the effects of wounds or illness is evidence of a sound constitution.

That the chief cause of French ugliness, degeneration, and infertility lies in their contemptuous treatment of Romantic Love, must be apparent to any one after reading the preceding chapter on French Love. French parents may point triumphantly to cases of genuine Conjugal attachment in their sons and daughters, whose marriages were based on social or pecuniary considerations. But they forget the *grandchildren*. It is they who suffer from these ill-assorted, fortuitous unions. Only the children of Love are beautiful and destined to multiply.

French indifference to the claims of Love also explains why another leading source of Beauty—the mixture of races—is inoperative in their country. The French are a very mixed nation. In the North, says Dr. Topinard, "we find the descendants of the Belgae, the Walloons, and other Kymri; in the East, those of Germans and Burgundians; in the West, Normans; in the centre, Celts, who at the same epoch at which their name took its origin consisted of foreigners of various origins and of the aborigines; in the South, ancient Aquitanians and Basques; without mentioning a host of settlers like the Saracens, who are found here and there, Tectosages, who have left at Toulouse the custom of cranial deformities, and the traders who passed through the Phocæan town of Marseilles." But the advantages which might result to Personal Beauty from such a mixture of peoples are neutralised through the universality of money-marriages, notwithstanding that these must in some cases bring together the descendants of different races. For a mixture of races is not necessarily and always an advantage, but only when it enables a lover to profit by the greater physiognomic variety in finding a mate whose qualities will blend harmoniously with his own.

In the case of a third primal source of Beauty—Mental Culture—we find again that its action is impeded through the anomalous position of Love in France. Inasmuch as adulterous love-making is the only kind of Love-making sanctioned by French custom and described in French literature, it is necessary to withhold most books and periodicals from the young of both sexes, who are thus compelled to grow up in ignorance. "The burden of ignorance presses sorely upon her," says M. Figuier of the Frenchwoman: "It is a rare thing for a woman of the people to read, as only those of the higher classes have leisure, during their girlhood, to cultivate their minds. And yet even they must not give themselves up too much to study, nor aspire to honour or distinction. The epithet *bas bleu* ('blue-stocking') would soon bring them back to the common crowd — *an ignorant and frivolous feminine mass.*"

Note that this is the confession of a patriotic Frenchman. The fact that there have been a few brilliant Frenchwomen, famous for their *salons*, has created the impression that most Frenchwomen are brilliant, whereas the majority appear to be utterly without intellectual interests or ambition. Nor could this possibly be otherwise, considering the extremely superficial education which even the most favoured receive in the nuns' schools. And not a few of them bring home from these schools something worse than ignorance, viz. the constitution and habits of an invalid. Not only the girls, even the boys in French schools are never allowed to play without supervision. Healthy romping is considered undignified in young girls, and when they get a little older the high-heeled, pointed shoes prescribed by Fashion take away any desire they may feel to indulge in beautifying exercise. Uncomfortable shoes and clothing, combined with the necessity of having a chaperon, even to simply cross the street, prevent French girls from indulging in those long walks to which English girls owe their fine physique. Nor do the French show such a devotion to the bath-tub and other details of Personal Hygiene as their neighbours across the channel.

Thus we see that the French, thanks to their conservative, Oriental customs, are placed at a disadvantage as regards every one of the four main sources of Beauty — Romantic Love, Mixture of Races, Mental Culture, and Hygiene. And it is not only Personal Beauty that suffers. A writer in *La Réforme Sociale* complains that "family feeling is dying out, the moral sense is growing weaker . . . the country is falling into a state of anæmia." And another writer in the same periodical, after noting the alarming fact that although France has gained eight million inhabitants since 1805, the number of births is no larger than it was then, calls upon those interested in these symptoms of national decay to investigate the local causes of it.

But it is needless to look for "local causes." The disease is a national one, and calls for constitutional treatment. Let the French, in the first place, instead of locking up their girls till they are ready to be sold to a rich *roué*, initiate them into the arts of Anglo-American Courtship, and then allow Romantic Love to take the place of money as a matchmaker. That the effect of such a change would be miraculous may be inferred from the fact that the products of a few generations of American love-making—French girls in Canada and the United

States—are vastly superior in Beauty and Health to their transatlantic cousins.

In the second place, the French must give up the notion that disease is aristocratic. "In almost all countries," says M. About, "there exists a class distinguished from the masses as the aristocracy. In this social miscellany the women have small white hands, because they wear gloves and do not work; a pale complexion, because they are never exposed to the sun; a sickly appearance and thin features, because they spend the four months of the winter at balls. Hence it follows that 'distinction' consists in a faded complexion, sickly appearance, a pair of white hands, and thin features. The Madonnas of Raphael are not '*distingué*,' and the Venus of Milo also is very deficient in that quality."

After they have ceased to ridicule Love and to worship Disease, it will be in order for the French to cultivate their æsthetic Taste. That of all European men Frenchmen show the worst taste in dressing is commonly admitted; but the preposterous superstition that French*women* have a special instinct for dressing tastefully is so firmly rooted in the mind of women elsewhere, that nothing short of a miracle would be able to eradicate it. The reason why the roots of this superstition are so deep is this: Frenchwomen rarely have any great beauty of figure or features. Hence they devote all their time to devising means for hiding their formal defects and distracting the attention of men by some novelty or eccentricity of apparel. In America and Germany, where the majority of the women are also ugly, these tricks are eagerly copied; and the pretty girls are compelled to yield to the tyranny of the majority, as has been fully explained in the chapter on the Fashion Fetish.

Englishwomen have, to a large extent, emancipated themselves from Parisian Fashion Tyranny, aided by the protests of the men against self-inflicted ugliness. And it is one of the healthiest signs of the times that in America, too, the men are beginning to break the ice of gallant timidity, and telling the women plainly what they think of their hideous Parisian fashions. Not long ago an intelligent woman wrote to the Boston *Transcript*, asking : "Why will not the press, instead of growling and snarling at *the poor women who cannot help themselves*," ask the theatre managers to compel the women to take off their high hats, which, she admits, ninety-nine in a hundred women consider a nuisance? Yet they "cannot help themselves!" The poor women! What a terrible slavery! the pretty women of America *compelled* to adopt the fashions originated by the ugliest women of Europe in order to hide their defects!

If American women must have models, let them go to Spain or Italy for them, especially in the matter of headdresses. Of the Spanish mantilla, which can be adapted to the style of every face, Prosper Mérimée says that "it makes ugly women pretty, and pretty ones enchanting." And a German lady on her way to Spain bought on her way, as a matter of course, the latest Parisian hat. "But when I arrived in Madrid," she writes, "my genuine Parisian hat seemed of such apelike ugliness that I felt actually ashamed to wear it. For my taste had been corrected and improved at sight of the first mantilla I saw; and I am convinced that a large majority of German women and girls possess quite as much sense of beauty as I, and will therefore prefer the Spanish mantilla to any hat made by the most noted *modiste* in Europe."

ITALIAN BEAUTY

Although differences in form, complexion, and physiognomy are to be noted in different parts of France, they are less pronounced than in Italy, concerning which it is therefore more difficult to make general statements. "The barbarian invasions in the north, and the contact with Greeks and Africans in the south," says M. Figuier, "have wrought much alteration in the primitive type of the inhabitants of Italy. Except in Rome and the Roman Campagna, the true type of the primitive Latin population is hardly to be found. The Grecian type exists in the South, and upon the eastern slope of the Apennines, while in the North the great majority of faces are Gallic. In Tuscany and the neighbouring regions are found the descendants of the ancient Etruscans. . . . The mixture of African blood has changed the organic type of the Southern Italian to such an extent as to render him entirely distinct from his Northern compatriots, the exciting influence which the climate has over the senses imparting to his whole conduct a peculiar exuberance."

In their estimate of Italian Beauty tourists differ widely. The raptures and ecstasies of some writers are explained by others as due to the æsthetic intoxication produced by sudden contact with a new type; and they claim that a few years' residence suffices to dispel these illusions. On the judgment of the Italians themselves it is not safe to rely, for that is tinged too much by local patriotism, the Milanese claiming the pre-eminence in Beauty for themselves, while the Venetians, Florentines, Romans, and Neapolitans blow their own horns respectively. Professor Mantegazza thinks that the men are handsomer in Italy than the women, of whom he allows only about ten per cent to have any claims to real Beauty. Sir Charles Bell notes that "Raphael, in painting the head of Galatea, found no beauty deserving to be his model; he is reported to have said that there is nothing so rare as perfect beauty in woman; and that he substituted for nature a certain idea inspired by his fancy." Montaigne, who travelled in Italy in the latter part of the sixteenth century, expressed his surprise at the rarity of beauty in women and girls, who at that time were kept in more than French seclusion. A German author, D. J. Volkmann, wrote in 1770 that "there are few beautiful women in Rome, especially among the higher classes; in Venice and Naples more are to be seen. The Italian himself has a proverb which says that Roman women are not beautiful" (quoted by Ploss).

Byron, in one of his letters, gives a glowing description of an Italian beauty of the Oriental type whom he met, and then adds: "Whether being in love with her has steeled me or not, I do not know; but I have not seen many other women who seem pretty. The nobility, in particular, are a sad-looking race—the gentry rather better." In another place he writes that "the general race of women appear to be handsome; but in Italy, as on almost all the Continent, the highest orders are by no means a well-looking generation."

Yet was it not Byron who wrote of Italy that it is "the garden of the world," and that its "very weeds are beautiful?" And does not this apply to the race as well as the soil? It is because they constantly live in a garden, in the balmy air and mellowing sunshine, that Italians can to a certain extent defy the laws of personal Hygiene, and flourish under conditions which would torture us to death. Miss Margaret Collier remarks, in *Our Home by the Adriatic*, that in the rural communities, even among the well-to-do, to ask for a bath is to create alarm as to the state of your health. And Berlioz speaks somewhere of Italian peasant-girls "carrying heavy copper vessels and faggots on their heads; but all so wretched, so miserable, so tattered, so filthily dirty, that, *in spite of the beauty of the race* and the picturesqueness of their costume, all other feelings are swallowed up in one of utter compassion."

Could the cosmetic value of fresh air and sunshine be more strikingly attested than by the fact that Berlioz could speak of "the beauty of the race," notwithstanding the national indifference to the laws of cleanliness?

In regard to Romantic Love as a source of Beauty, the Italians also occupy a somewhat anomalous position. In the rural districts French matrimonial methods seem to be largely followed. Miss Collier mentions a young lady who visited her to receive her congratulations on her approaching marriage, and who, on being asked the name of her future husband, replied naïvely, "Oh, I don't know; papa has not yet told me that." The peasantry, however, are free to choose their own mates, and it is among them that Italian Beauty is accordingly most prevalent. In the cities the method of love-making is "operatic," as we saw in the chapter on Italian Love; but the main point is that Individual Choice is not made impossible as in France, and that the Italians worship Love as a law instead of looking on it with contemptuous cynicism and ridicule.

The way in which the Mixture of Races affects Italian Beauty affords a fresh illustration of the superiority of the Brunette type. In Germany, by general consent, Beauty is much more frequent in the South, where brunettes abound, than in the North, where they are scarce. Hence we may conclude that the Blonde type is improved by the intermixture of the Brunette type. But is the Brunette type of Northern Italy improved to the same degree by the admixture of Northern Blondes? Not in my judgment. Venice and Milan and Bologna, it is true, boast many beautiful women; but has any tourist in writing about these cities ever expressed much admiration for Italian Blondes? And are not Naples and Capri, the paradise of Brunettes, commonly regarded as the region where Italian Beauty is seen at its best? Here it is chiefly dark races that have intermingled, hence the eyes are sure to be of a deep brown colour; whereas in Northern Italy the introduction of blonde blood produces the lighter, less decided tints of the iris which we do not admire. This disadvantage, it is true, is also encountered in South Germany, but it is neutralised by the gain of dark eyebrows, and long black lashes, and the more supple and rounded limbs of the South.

That mental culture adds much to Italian beauty cannot be said, for Italian women of all classes are noted for their intellectual indolence. But atonement is largely made for this by their extreme emotional susceptibility. Blue skies, rank vegetation, pretty scenery, and a natural love of music have softened and trained their feelings ; and though the Italian climate does not favour profound artistic culture, it warms the blood and incites the features to give expression to every passing mood. It is this habit of emotional expression that has given a unique charm and the power of graceful modulation to Italian features. As a German artist, Herr Otto Knille, remarks of the Italians, "They pose unintentionally. Their features, especially among the lower classes, have been moulded through mimic expression practised for thousands of years. Gesture-language has shaped the hands of many into models of anatomic clearness. They have a complete language of signs and gestures, which each one understands, as, for instance, in the ballet. Add to this the innate grace of this race . . . and we see that the Italian artist has an abundance of material for copying, as compared with which the German artist must admit his extreme poverty. Whoever has lived in Italy is in a position to appreciate these advantages. . . . Think of the neck, the nape, and the bust of Italian woman, the fine joints and the elastic gait of both men and women. Nor are we much better endowed as regards the physiognomy. The German potato-face is not a mere fancy —the mirror which A. de Neuville has held up to us, though clouded with prejudice, shows us an image not entirely untrue to life. We artists know how rarely a head, especially one which lacks the enchanting charm of youth, can be used as a model for anything but flat realism. Most German faces, instead of becoming more clearly chiselled and elaborated with age, appear more spongy, vague, and unmeaning."

Winckelmann's remarks on Italian Beauty are in the same vein: "We seldom find in the fairest portions of Italy the features of the face unfinished, vague, and inexpressive, as is frequently the case on the other side of the Alps; but they have partly an air of nobleness, partly of acuteness and intelligence; and the form of the face is generally large and full, and the parts of it in harmony with each other. The superiority of conformation is so manifest that the head of the humblest man among the people might be introduced in the most dignified historical painting, especially one in which aged men are to be represented. And among the women of this class, even in places of the least importance, it would not be difficult to find a Juno. The lower portion of Italy, which enjoys a softer climate than any other part of it, brings forth men of superb and vigorously-designed forms, which appear to have been made, as it were, for the purposes of sculpture."

In confirmation of my statement that in Northern as in Southern Italy it is the Brunette type that chiefly excites the admiration of the tourist, I may finally cite Heine's remarks on the women of Trent. For, although Trent is a town of the Austrian Tyrol, it yet is practically an Italian community. Had not business called him southwards, Heine relates in his *Journey from Munich to Genoa*, he would have felt tempted to remain in this town where "beautiful girls were moving about in bevies. I do not know," he adds, "whether other tourists will approve of the adjective 'beautiful' in this case; but I liked the women of Trent exceptionally well. They were just of the kind I admire —and I do love these pale, elegiac faces with the large black eyes that gaze at you so love-sick; I love also the dusky tint of those proud necks which Phœbus already has loved and browned with his kisses; . . . but above all things do I love that graceful gait, that dumb music of the body, those limbs with their exquisitely rhythmic movements, luxurious, supple, divinely careless, mortally languid, anon æthereal, majestic, and always highly poetic. I love such things as I love poetry itself; and these figures with their melodious movements, this wondrous concert of femininity which delighted my senses, found an echo in my heart, and awoke in it sympathetic strains."

SPANISH BEAUTY

In Spain, as in Italy, Germany, France, and the United States, we find more Personal Beauty in the Southern than in the Northern regions. This coincidence cannot be accidental, but attests the great cosmetic value of sunshine and plenty of fresh air. Perhaps no other portion of the globe has such a paradisiacal climate as Andalusia, where the inhabitants practically pass all their time in the open air,—on verandahs and in their cosy little galleries, and fragrant orange groves, in whose shade they can spend the hot part of the day, while the nights are cooled by balmy mountain or sea breezes. To these natural hygienic advantages add the unusually happy mixture of nationalities, and the fact that Romantic Love is much less impeded in its sway than in France or Italy, and we see at a glance to what the young Andalusian owes the undulating lines and luscious plumpness of her figure, her ravishing facial beauty, and her graceful gait, or "melodious movements," as Heine would say.

Surely the goddess of Beauty herself mixed the national colours that make up the Spanish type. When Spain was added to the Roman dominion she was, as Mr. E. A. Freeman remarks, "the only one of the great countries of Europe where the mass of the people were not of the Aryan stock. The greater part of the land was still held by the *Iberians*, as a small part is even now by their descendants the Basques. But in the central part of the peninsula *Celtic* tribes had pressed in, and . . . there were some *Phœnician* colonies in the south, and some *Greek* colonies on the east coast. In the time between the first and second Punic Wars, Hamilcar, Hasdrubal, and Hannibal had won all Spain as far as the Ebro for *Carthage*." Among the other nations which successively overran the country were the Goths, Vandals, Suevi, and Moors; to whom must be added large numbers of Jews and Gypsies, of which latter race Spain still possesses about 50,000.

Most of these nations had some favourable physical traits which Sexual Selection had the opportunity to fix upon and perpetuate ; while sundry incongruities must have been neutralised and obliterated by the intermingling of races. And another important consideration is, that this intermingling of nations was effected so many centuries ago that it is now no longer a heterogeneous physical mixture, but a true "chemical," or physiological, fusion, in which dissonances and incongruities are less likely to occur than in countries where the mixture is more recent.

That the addition of Greek and Roman blood, redolent of ancient civilisation, to the original Spanish stock was an advantage is obvious. The Goth brought his manly vigour ; the Gypsy his concentrated essence of Brunetteism ; the Arab his oval face, dusky complexion, the straight line connecting nose and forehead, the small mouth and white teeth, the dark and glossy hair, the delicate extremities and gracefully-arched foot, and above all, the black eyes and long black eyelashes. If Shakspere is right in saying that there is no author in the world "teaches such beauty as a woman's eye," then Andalusia easily leads the world in Personal Beauty. The prosiest tourist becomes poetic in describing the Andalusian's "black eye that mocks her coal-black veil." Large and round are these eyes, like those of Oriental Houris ; long and dense their black lashes, which yet cannot smother the mysterious fire and sparkle which their iris appears to have borrowed of the Gypsies. In many cases there is a vague, piquant indication of the almond-shaped palpebral aperture—one of the Semitic traits derived from the Phœnicians, Jews, and Saracens. And then, what woman can make such irresistibly fascinating use of her eyes as the Spanish brunette?

M. Figuier thus sums up the physical characteristics of the Spanish woman: " She is generally brunette, although the blonde type occurs much more frequently than is usually supposed. The Spanish woman is almost always small of stature. Who has not observed the large eyes, veiled by thick lashes, her delicate nose, and well-formed nostrils? Her form is always undulating and graceful; her limbs are round and beautifully moulded, and her extremities of incomparable delicacy. She is a charming mixture of vigour, languor, and grace."

"The appearance of a Spanish woman," says Bogumil Goltz, " is the expression of her character. Her fine figure, her majestic gait, her sonorous voice, her black, flashing eye, the liveliness of her gesticulations, in a word, her whole external personality indicates her character."

It is to be noted that whereas French Beauty appears to be visible to French eyes only, and regarding Italian Beauty opinions differ, all nations unite in singing the praises of " Spain's dark-glancing daughters." To the French and German testimony just cited may now be added a few Italian, English, and American witnesses.

Signor E. de Amicis, in his interesting work on Spain, says of the women of Madrid that " they are still the same little women so besung for their great eyes, small hands, and tiny feet, with their very black hair, but skin rather white than dark, so well-formed, erect, lithe, and vivacious." But, like all other tourists, he reserves most of his remarks on Spanish women for his chapters on Andalusia, although this is the part of Spain which also offers the richest material for description in its architecture and scenery. Concerning the women and girls of Seville, as seen in the large tobacco factory which employs 5000 females, he says: "There are some very beautiful faces, and even those that are not absolutely beautiful, have something about them which attracts the eye and remains impressed upon the memory—the colouring, eyes, brows, and smile, for instance. Many, especially the so-called *gitane*, are dark brown, like mulattoes, and have protruding lips; others have such large eyes that a faithful likeness of them would seem an exaggeration. The majority are small, well-made, and all wear a rose, pink, or a bunch of field-flowers among their braids. . . . On coming out of the factory, you seem to see on every side for a time, black pupils which look at you with a thousand different expressions of curiosity, ennui, sympathy, sadness, and drowsiness."

The same writer found that "The feminine type of Cadiz was not less attractive than that celebrated one at Seville. The women are a little taller, a trifle stouter, and rather darker. Some fine observer has asserted that they are of the Greek type; but I cannot see where. I saw nothing, with the exception of their stature, but the Andalusian type; and this sufficed to make me heave sighs deep enough to have blown along a boat and obliged me to return as soon as possible to my ship, as a place of peace and refuge."

Mr. G. P. Lathrop's description (in *Spanish Vistas*) of the girls in the Seville factory is pitched in a somewhat lower key than Signor de Amicis's: "Some of them," he writes, "had a spendthrift, common sort of beauty, which, owing to their southern vivacity and fine physique, had the air of being more than it really was. . . . There were some appalling old crones. . . . Others, on the contrary, looked blooming and coquettish. Many were in startling deshabille, resorted to on account of the intense (July) heat, and hastened to draw pretty pañuelos of variegated dye over their bare shoulders when they saw us coming. . . . The beauty of these Carmens has certainly been exaggerated. It may be remarked here that, as an offset to occasional disappointment arising from such exaggerations, all Spanish women walk with astonishing gracefulness, and natural and elastic step ; and that is their chief advantage over women of other nations."

A writer in *Macmillan's Magazine* (1874), after referring to "the stately upright walk of the Spanish ladies, and the graceful carriage of the head," notes that a mother will not allow her daughter to carry a basket, so as not to destroy her "queenly walk"; and "her dull eye too will grow moist with a tear, and her worn face will kindle with absolute softness and sweetness, if an English señor expresses his admiration of her child's magnificent hair or flashing black eyes."

The description given by the same writer of a scene he witnessed along the Guadalquiver, suggests one reason of the healthy physique and vitality of Spanish women : " An old mill-house, with its clumsy wheel and a couple of pomegranates, shaded one corner of this part of the river; and under their shade, sitting up to their shoulders in the water, on the huge round boulders of which the bottom of the river is composed, were groups of Spanish ladies. Truly it was a pretty sight! They sat as though on chairs, clothed to the neck in bathing-gowns of the gaudiest colours—red, gray, yellow, and blue; and, holding in one hand their umbrellas, and with the other fanning themselves, they formed a most picturesque group."

Washington Irving, in a private letter, paints this picture of a Spanish beauty whom he saw on a coast steamer: "A young married lady, of about four or five and twenty, middle-sized, finely-modelled, a Grecian outline of face, a complexion sallow yet healthful, raven black hair, eyes dark, large, and beaming, softened by long eyelashes, lips full and rosy red, yet finely chiselled, and teeth of dazzling whiteness. Her hand . . . is small, exquisitely formed, with taper fingers, and blue veins. I never saw a female hand more exquisite." The husband of this young lady, noticing that Mr. Irving was apparently sketching her, questioned him on the matter. Mr. Irving read his sketch to the man, who was greatly pleased with it; and this led to a delightful though brief acquaintance.

In another letter, Washington Irving writes to a friend: "There are beautiful women in Seville as . . . there are in all other great cities; but do not, my worthy and inquiring friend, expect a perfect beauty to be staring you in the face at every turn, or you will be awfully disappointed. Andalusia, generally speaking, derives its renown for the beauty of its women and the beauty of its landscape, from the rare and captivating charms of individuals. The generality of its female faces are as sunburnt and void of bloom and freshness as its plains. I am convinced, the great fascination of Spanish women arises from their natural talent, their fire and soul, which beam through their dark and flashing eyes, and kindle up their whole countenance in the course of an interesting conversation. As I have had but few opportunities of judging them in this way, I can only criticise them with the eye of a sauntering observer. It is like judging of a fountain when it is not in play, or a fire when it lies dormant and neither flames nor sparkles."

Byron, in *Childe Harold*, waxes enthusiastic over the Spanish woman's "fairy form, with more than female grace"—

" Her glance how wildly beautiful ! how much
Hath Phœbus wooed in vain to spoil her cheek,
Which glows yet smoother from his amorous clutch !
Who round the North for paler dames would seek ?
How poor their forms appear ! how languid, wan, and weak !"

But in a letter from Cadiz Byron notes the weak as well as the strong points of Spanish women. "With all national prejudice, I must confess, the women of Cadiz are as far superior to the English women in beauty, as the Spaniards are inferior to the English in every quality that dignifies the name of man. . . . The Spanish women are all alike, their education the same. . . . Certainly they are fascinating ; but their minds have only one idea, and the business of their lives is intrigue. . . . Long black hair, dark languishing eyes, clear olive complexions, and forms more graceful in motion than can be conceived by an Englishman used to the drowsy, listless air of his countrywomen, added to the most becoming dress, and, at the same time, the most decent in the world, render a Spanish beauty irresistible."

"Their minds have only one idea," is an exaggeration, for the Andalusian women are famed for a considerable amount of innate wit, rivalling the brightness of their eyes. Yet of deeper intellectual interests there are none. Of the total population of Spain only a quarter can read and write; for although schools exist in abundance, they are very generally neglected; and the estimation in which teachers are held is seen from the fact that out of 15,000 one half receive an annual salary of less than twenty pounds sterling.

Mental Culture avenges itself bitterly on the women of Spain, as of other Southern countries, for this neglect of its claims. While the freshness of youthful Beauty remains, all is well, for then the sensuous charms are so great that intellectual claims can be ignored. But when this freshness fades, then it is that the features begin to show a lack of mental training. Intellectual apathy masks the face, and gives it an expression of vacuity; exercise is neglected, and indolence, combined with excessive indulgence in fattening food, soon destroy the lovely contours of the figure and the fairy-like gait. "A Spanish woman of forty appears twice as old," says Goltz.

Thus we see that for perfect and permanent Beauty *all* its sources must be kept open and utilised.

Attention must finally be called to one feature of Andalusian Beauty which all tourists emphasise, namely, the small stature of the women, to which they largely owe their exceptional grace of gait. And there are reasons for believing that the perfected woman of the millennium will resemble the Andalusian Brunette, not only in complexion, hair, eyes, gait, and tapering plumpness of figure, but also in stature. In other words, it seems that Sexual Selection is evolving the *petite* Brunette as the ideal of womanhood.

Among the ancient Greeks who were not swayed by Romantic Love, Amazons were greatly admired, as previously noted; and Mr. Gladstone remarks that "stature was a great element of beauty in the view of the ancients, for women as well as for men; and their admiration of tallness, even in women, is hardly restrained by a limit."

From this Greek predilection modern æstheticoamorous Taste differs, for several weighty reasons. The first is that a very tall and bulky woman, though she may be stately and majestic, cannot be very graceful; and Grace, as we know, is as potent a source of Love as formal Beauty. Again, there is something incongruous and almost comic in the thought of a very large woman submitting to Love's caresses; and *le ridicule tue*. Thirdly, great stature is rarely associated with delicate joints and extremities. But the principal reason why the modern lover disapproves of Amazonian women, mental and physical, is because they are quasi-masculine. Romantic Love tends to differentiate the sexes in stature as in everything else. True, Mr. Galton, after making observations on 205 married couples, came to the conclusion that "marriage selection takes little or no account of shortness and tallness. There are undoubtedly sexual preferences for moderate contrasts in height; but the marriage choice appears to be guided by so many and more important considerations that questions of stature exert no perceptible influence upon it. . . . Men and women of contrasted heights, short and tall or tall and short, married just about as frequently as men and women of similar heights, both tall or both short; there were 32 cases of one to 27 of the other."

But Mr. Galton's argument is rather weak. He admits that "there are undoubtedly sexual preferences for moderate contrast in height"; and his own figures show 32 to 27 in favour of mixed-stature marriages, in most of which the women must have been shorter, owing to the prevalent feminine inferiority in size. And in course of time the elimination of non-amorous motives of marriage will assist the law of sexual differentiation in suppressing Amazons.

The modern masculine preference for *petite* female stature is, furthermore, attested by an irrefutable philological argument which will be found in the following citation from Crabb's *English Synonymes*: "*Prettiness* is always coupled with simplicity; it is incompatible with that which is large; a tall woman with masculine features cannot be *pretty*. Beauty is peculiarly a female perfection; in the male sex it is rather a defect; a man can scarcely be *beautiful* without losing his manly characteristics, boldness and energy of mind, strength and robustness of limb;

but though a man may not be *beautiful* or *pretty*, he may be *fine* or *handsome.*" " A woman is *fine* who with a striking figure unites shape and symmetry; a woman is *handsome* who has good features, and *pretty* if with symmetry of feature be united delicacy."

Burke believed that it is possible to fall in love with a very small person, but not with a giant. There is, indeed, a natural prejudice in the modern mind against very tall stature even in men. Thus, we read in Fuller's *Andronicus:* "Often the cockloft is empty in those whom Nature hath built many stories high"; and Bacon is reported to have said "that Nature did never put her precious jewels into a garret four stories high, and therefore that exceeding tall men had ever very empty heads." An apparent scientific confirmation of this belief is found in Professor Hermann's *Nervensystem* (ii. 195), where we read that "when the body becomes abnormally large, the brain begins to decrease again, relatively, as Langer found in measuring giant skeletons." And another sign of regression is found in the fact that tall men are apt to have relatively too heavy jaws.

GERMAN AND AUSTRIAN BEAUTY

Although the Germans of to-day are by no means a pure and distinct race, they are less thoroughly and variously mixed than most other European nations; and this is one of the main reasons why Personal Beauty is comparatively rare in the Fatherland. It is rarest in the northern and central regions, where the original Blonde type is best preserved, and becomes more frequent the nearer we approach the Brunette neighbours of Germany—Italy, Austria-Hungary, and Poland—whose women have been aptly called "the Spaniards of the north." France forms an exception. There, thanks to the imprisonment of Cupid, ugliness is so rampant that intermarriage only intensifies the natural homeliness, —a fact of which any one may convince himself by spending a few days in the borderland between France and Germany.

Partly owing to this lack of variety in the national composition of the Germans, partly to the custom of chaperonage, Romantic Love has not as wide a scope of selective action as elsewhere; and as if these impediments to the increase of Beauty were not sufficient, they are augmented in a wholesale fashion by the parental illusion that the Love-instinct is a less trustworthy guide to a happy marriage than "Reason," *i.e.* the consideration that the bride has a few thousand marks and belongs to the same social clique as the bridegroom. Like their French neighbours, the Germans in these cases forget the claims of the *grandchildren* to Health and Beauty—*i.e.* the harmonious fusion of the complementary parental qualities by which Love is inspired.

But in regard to the third source of Beauty—Mental Culture—the Germans surely are pre-eminent among nations, it will be claimed. In one sense, no doubt, they are. Almost all Germans can read and write, and no race equals them in special erudition. But erudition is not culture. The German system of education is exceedingly defective, because it cultivates too largely the lowest of the mental faculties

—the Memory. The number of scientific, historic, and philological facts a German schoolboy knows by heart is simply astounding; but he has not digested them, and cannot apply them practically. No attempt is made to cultivate his higher faculties —his imagination, originality, or the gift of expressing a thought in elegant language. Were a candidate to show the wit and brilliancy of a Heine or a Shakspere, it would not add one grain to the weight his pedantic professors attach to his work. They will not favour the growth of qualities in which they themselves are so conspicuously deficient. Note, for example, the vast contempt with which the pedants of the University of Berlin look down on "the German Darwin," Professor Haeckel, because he dares not only to be original, but to write his books in a language clear as crystal, and adorned with wit, satire, and literary polish.

Other nations are proud of their great men *even before they are dead;* not so the Germans. Nor are the Germans really a literary nation, as a whole. Many books are written there, but they rarely come under the head of *literature;* and their circulation, on the average, is not one-tenth that of English, French, and American books. Beer is more popular than books.

No, the pedantic erudition, which alone is officially honoured in Germany, is not synonymous with Mental Culture. It does not vivify the features sufficiently to mould them into plastic shape. Hence the prevalence of the "spongy features" and Teutonic "potato-faces" referred to by a German artist quoted in the chapter on Italian Beauty. "The true national character of the Germans is clumsiness," says

Schopenhauer; and again: "The Germans are distinguished from all other nations by the slovenliness of their style, as of their dress." And the Swiss Professor, H. F. Amiel, remarks in his *Journal Intime* that "the notion of 'bad taste' seems to have no place in German æsthetics. Their elegance has no grace in it; they cannot understand the enormous difference there is between distinction (which is *gentlemanly, ladylike*) and their stiff *Vornehmheit*. Their imagination lacks style, training, education, and knowledge of the world; it has an ill-bred air even in its Sunday dress. The race is poetical and intelligent, but common and ill-mannered."

It must be admitted, however, that the Germans have made great progress in external refinement and manners since their late war with France, one of the greatest advantages of which to them was that it destroyed the mystic halo which had for many generations surrounded the imported Parisian Fashion Fetish. What the Germans need now is a period of Anglomania. They have already ceased to laugh at the Englishman for travelling with his bath-tub, and have found it worth while to provide him with that commodity in the hotels. In course of time bath-tubs in private German houses may be expected to become more common than they are now; and after a generation or two shall have given proper attention to skin-hygiene, freckles and other cutaneous blemishes will be less prevalent than at present. In their houses the Germans are really as tidy as any nation; but their indifference to the appearance of their collars and cuffs often leads one to suspect the contrary.

The next thing the Germans ought to learn of the

English is greater gallantry toward the women, who are too apt to be looked upon as household drudges, whom it is not necessary to educate or amuse. Especially ruinous to female Beauty is the hard field labour required of the women who have the misfortune to belong to a nation which has not yet outgrown its condition of mediæval militarism. A German physician, quoted by Dr. Ploss, notes the fact that the beauty and bloom of youth last but a short time with the working classes of North Germany: "The hard labour performed before the body is fully developed too easily destroys the plumpness, which is an essential element of beauty, draws furrows in the face, and makes the figure stiff and angular. Often have I taken a mother who showed me her child for its grandmother."

The author of *German Home Life* remarks in a similar vein: "German girls are often charmingly pretty, with dazzling complexions, abundant beautiful hair, and clear lovely eyes; but the splendid matron, the sound, healthy, well-developed woman, who has lost no grain of beauty, and yet gained a certain magnificent maturity such as we in England see daily with daughters who might well be her youngest sisters—of such women the Fatherland has few specimens to show. The 'pale unripened beauties of the North' do not ripen, they fade." And no wonder, for either the girls belong to the poorer classes and lose their beauty prematurely from overwork; or, if they are of the well-to-do classes, they get no Beauty-preserving exercise at all. "German girls," the Countess Von Bothmer continues, "have no outdoor amusements, if we except skating when the winter proves favourable. Boating, riding, archery, swimming, croquet—all the active, healthy outdoor life which English maidens are allowed to share and to enjoy with their brothers is unknown to them. . . . Such diversions are looked upon by the girls themselves as bold, coarse, and unfeminine. . . . It is in vain that you tell them such exercises, far from unsexing them, fit them all the better for the duties of their sex ; it is difficult for them to hear you out and not show the scorn they entertain for you."

German men, as a rule, are much handsomer than their sisters, and they owe this superiority partly to the fact that their minds are not so vacant, and partly to the prolonged physical training which is the one redeeming feature of their military system. Nevertheless, especially in South Germany, the men too often lose their fine manly proportions in an enormous *embonpoint*, the penalty of drinking too much beer. Nor is the acquisition of a turnip shape the only bad result of the German habit of spending every evening in a tavern. The air in these beer-houses is so filthy, so soaked with vile tobacco smoke and nicotine, that after sitting in it for an hour the odour haunts one's clothes for a week, and poisons the lungs for a month. It is this foul atmosphere, combined with the stupefying effect of the beer, that accounts for German heaviness and clumsiness in appearance, attitude, gait, and literary style.

These disadvantages might be to some extent neutralised if, on returning to his bedroom, the German would spend the rest of the night, at least, in fresh air. But no ! He dreads the balmy night air as he would a dragon's breath, although Professor

Reclam and other great authorities on Hygiene have told him a million and sixty times that night air is more salubrious than day air, except in swampy regions.

Tourists in Switzerland often wonder why it is that the natives, notwithstanding their glorious Alpine air, are, with rare exceptions, so utterly devoid of Beauty. Partly this is due to the hard labour and scanty food to which most of them are condemned; but the main reason is that they enjoy their health-laden air only in the daytime and in summer. At night and in winter they close their windows hermetically, and in the morning the atmosphere in such a room is something which no one who has ever breathed it will ever forget.

When the Germans visit Switzerland they carefully imitate the example of these ignorant peasants, thus depriving themselves of all the benefits of an Alpine tour. An eye-witness last summer told me of the following encounter in a Swiss hotel between an English lady and a German. The dining-room being hot to suffocation, the English lady opened a window, whereupon the German immediately got up and closed it. The English lady opened it again, and again it was closed; whereupon she pushed her elbow through the glass, and thenceforth enjoyed the fresh, fragrant air, to the horror and indignation of the assembled Teutons.

All these remarks of course apply to the Germans only in a very general way. Among all classes in Germany specimens of Beauty may be found that could hardly be surpassed anywhere else. Pretty faces are more frequent than elegant figures, which commonly are too robust and masculine. German girls are the most domestic and amiable in the world, and it is their amiability and depth of feeling that gives their mouth such a sweet expression and refined outlines. When German girls are educated, as often they are in America, their faces beam in irresistible beauty. The most beautiful non-Spanish eyes I have ever seen belonged to a girl in Baden; and the most roguish blue eyes I have ever seen, to a Würtemberg girl. Regular Italian features are not uncommon in Bavaria, although snub-noses are most frequent there. The Bavarian complexion, though somewhat too pale, is beautifully clear; and I have almost come to the conclusion that this is in some way connected with the national habit of drinking beer three times a day. It might be worth while to inquire whether there is a beautifying ingredient in beer which might be obtained without its stupefying effects.

The Germans commonly consider the maidens along the Rhine their most favourable and abundant specimens of Beauty; but Robert Schumann, who had a fine eye for feminine Beauty, emphasised the amiability rather than the beauty of these maidens in the following passage from one of his private letters: "What characteristic faces among the lowest classes! On the west shore of the Rhine the girls have very delicate features, indicating amiability rather than intelligence; the noses are mostly Greek, the face very oval and artistically symmetrical, the hair brown. I did not see a single blonde. The complexion is soft, delicate, with more white than red; melancholy rather than sanguine. The Frankfort girls, on the other hand, have in common a sisterly trait—the character of German, manly, sad earnestness which we often find in our quondam free cities, and which toward the east gradually merges into a gentle softness. Characteristic are the faces of all the Frankfort girls: intellectual or beautiful few of them; the noses mostly Greek, often snub-noses; the dialect I did not like."

Concerning the peasant women of Saxony, Mr. Julian Hawthorne remarks in his *Saxon Studies:* " Massive are their legs as the banyan root; their hips are as the bows of a three-decker. Backs have they like derricks; rough hands like pile-drivers." And again : " Handsome and pretty women are certainly no rarity in Saxony, although few of them can lay claim to an unadulterated Saxon pedigree." " We see lovely Austrians, and fascinating Poles and Russians, who delicately smoke cigars in the concert gardens. But it is hard for the peasant type to rise higher than comeliness; and it is distressingly apt to be coarse of feature as well as of hand, clumsy of ankle, and more or less wedded to grease and dirt. Good blood shows in the profile; and these young girls, whose faces are often pleasant and even attractive, have seldom an eloquent contour of nose and mouth. There is sometimes great softness and sweetness of eye, a clear complexion, a pretty roundness of chin and throat. Indeed, I have found scattered through half a dozen different villages all the features of the true Gretchen; and once, in an obscure hamlet whose name I have forgotten, I came unexpectedly upon what seemed a near approach to the mythic being."

One thing must be admitted. The Germans are the most systematic and persevering nation in the world. They took music, for instance, from her Italian cradle, and reared her till she developed into the most fascinating of the modern muses. They lead the world in scientific research; and within a few years they have terrified the English monopolists by a sudden outburst of thorough-going Teutonic industrial activity and world-competition. Let but the Germans once make up their mind that they want Personal Beauty, and lo! they will have it in superabundance. The Professorships of Hygiene, which are now being established at the Universities,* will doubtless bear rich fruit. If Bismarck discovered the full significance of Anglo-American Courtship, he would forthwith order an hour of it to be added to the daily academic curriculum; and if he realised the importance of racial mixture, he would order shiploads of South American and Andalusian brunettes to be distributed among his officers as wives. Nor would female education be any longer neglected, were it fully understood how essential it is to Personal Beauty and true Romantic Love, the basis of happy conjugal life.

What *can* be done with German stock if it is duly mixed with Brunette ingredients, is shown at Vienna, which, by the apparently unanimous consent of tourists, boasts more beautiful women than any other city in the world. Austria has about ten per cent more of the pure Brunette and fourteen per cent more of the mixed types than Germany. The dark blood of Italians, Hungarians, Czechs, flows in Viennese veins, and there is also a piquant suspicion of Oriental beauty. The Viennese woman combines Andalusian plumpness of figure and grace of movement, with American delicacy of features and purity of complexion. The bust is almost always finely developed and rarely too luxuriant; and the joints are the admiration of all tourists and natives. Speaking of England, Mr. Richard Grant White says that " Plump arms are not uncommon, but really fine arms are rare; and fine wrists are still rarer. Such wrists as the Viennese women have . . . are almost unknown among women of English race in either country." And the Countess von Bothmer thus describes the neighbours of Germany :—

"Polish, Hungarian, and Austrian women, whom we, in a general, inconclusive way, are apt to class as Germans, are 'beautiful exceedingly'; but here we come upon another race, or rather such a fusion of other races as may help to contribute to the charming result. Polish ladies have a special, vivid, delicate, spirited, haunting loveliness, with grace, distinction, and elegance in their limbs and features that is all their own; you cannot call them fragile, but they are of so fine a fibre and so delicate a colouring that they only just escape that apprehension. Of Polish and Hungarian *pur sang* there is little to be found; women of the latter race are of a more robust and substantial build, with dark hair and complexion, fine flashing eyes, and pronounced type; and who that remembers the women of Linz and Vienna will refuse them a first prize? They possess a special beauty of their own, a beauty which is rare in even the loveliest Englishwomen; rare, indeed, and exceptional everywhere else; a beauty that the artist eye appreciates with a feeling of delight. They have the most delicately articulated joints of any women in the world. The juncture of the hand and wrist, of foot and ankle, of the *nuque* with the back and shoulders, is what our neighbours would call 'adorable.'

"But alas that it should be so! The full gracious figures—types at once of strength and elegance—the supple, slender waists, the dainty little wrists and hands, become all too soon hopelessly fat, from the persistent idleness and luxury of the nerveless, unoccupied lives of these graceful ladies."

ENGLISH BEAUTY

Like the Viennese, the English afford an illustration of what can be done with Teutonic stock by a judicious admixture of dark blood. Although the mysteries of English ethnology have not been completely unravelled, the original inhabitants of the British Islands appear to have been "composed of the long-headed dark races of the Mediterranean stock, possibly mingled with fragments of still more ancient races, Mongoliform or Allophylian" (Dr. Beddoe). In the later history of the race Romans, Germans, Danes, and Normans added their blood to this mixture. The Celtic-speaking people who in the time of the Roman Conquest inhabited South Britain, partook, according to Dr. Beddoe, "more of the tall blond stock of Northern Europe than of the thickset, broad-headed, dark stock which Broca has called Celts." But the true Blonde invasion of Britain did not occur till towards the beginning of the fifth century, when the Low-Dutch tribes, the Angles and Saxons, came over from the river Elbe and the coast region, and drove the Britons to the west of the island, where they were called the Welsh, which is an old German appellation for foreigners.

The inference naturally suggests itself that the predilection for Blondes shown in English literature up to a recent date (as noted in the chapter on Blondes and Brunettes) may be traced to this fact that the conquering race was fair, and that consequently dark hair and eyes stigmatised their possessor as belonging to the conquered race. This condemnation of the Brunette type (on *non-æsthetic* grounds, be it noted) is forcibly illustrated by the following lines of the shepherdess Phebe in *As You Like It*—

> " I have more cause to hate him than to love him ;
> For what had he to do to chide at me ?
> He said mine eyes were black and my hair black,
> And, now I am remember'd, scorned at me."

But when this temporary aristocratic ground of preferring the Blonde type was neutralised through the lapse of time, and Romantic Love, that potent awakener of the æsthetic sense, appeared on the scene and opened men's eyes to the inferior beauty of that type, then began the reaction in favour of Brunettes, which has been going on ever since. This view is strikingly confirmed by the following remarks of Mr. Charles Roberts in *Nature*, January 7, 1885 :—

"American statistics show that the blond type is more subject to all the diseases, except one (chronic rheumatism), which disqualify men for military service, and this must obviously place blondes at a great disadvantage in the battle of life, while the popular saying, 'A pair of black eyes is the delight of a pair of blue ones,' shows that sexual selection does not allow them to escape from it. It is more than probable, therefore, from all these considerations, that the darker portion of our population is gaining on the blond, and this surmise is borne out by Dr. Beddoe's remark that the proportion of English and Scotch blood in Ireland is probably not less than a third, and that the Gaelic and Iberian races of the West, mostly dark-haired, are *tending to swamp the blond Teutonic of England by a reflex migration.*"

Obviously, the ideal Englishwoman of the future will be a Brunette. Thackeray had a prophetic vision of her when he described Beatrix Esmond: " She was a brown beauty: that is, her eyes, hair, and eyebrows and eyelashes were dark; her hair curling with rich undulations, and waving over her shoulders " [note that] ; " but her complexion was as dazzling white as snow in sunshine; except her cheeks, which were a bright red, and her lips, which were of a still deeper crimson . . . a woman whose eyes were fire, whose look was love, whose voice was the sweetest love-song, whose shape was perfect symmetry, health, decision, activity, whose foot as it planted itself on the ground was firm but flexible, and whose motion, whether rapid or slow, was always perfect grace,—agile as a nymph, lofty as a queen—now melting, now imperious, now sarcastic—there was no single movement of hers but was beautiful. As he thinks of her, he who writes feels young again and remembers a paragon."

Sexual Selection, however, has not limited its

efforts to the improvement of the colour of the hair, eyes, and complexion; the form of the features and figure has also been gradually altered and refined. An examination of the portraits in the National Gallery showed to Mr. Galton "what appear to be indisputable signs of one predominant type of face supplanting another. For instance, the features of the men painted by and about the time of Holbein have unusually high cheek-bones, long upper lips, thin eyebrows, and lank dark [?] hair. It would be impossible, I think, for the majority of modern Englishmen so to dress themselves, and clip and arrange their hair, as to look like the majority of these portraits." And again: "If we may believe caricaturists, the fleshiness and obesity of many English men and women in the earlier years of this century must have been prodigious. It testifies to the grosser conditions of life in those days, and makes it improbable that the types best adapted to prevail then would be the best adapted to prevail now."

Yet this improvement in the British figure and physiognomy is far from universal. The English are beyond all dispute the finest race in the world, physically and mentally; but the favourable action of the four Sources of Beauty, to which they owe this supremacy, does not extend to all classes. The lowest-class Englishman or Irishman is the most hideous and brutal ruffian in the world. Of Mental or Moral Culture not a trace; and whereas "the Spaniard, however ignorant, has naturally the manners and the refined feelings of a gentleman" (*Macmillan's Magazine*, 1874), as well as a love of the beautiful forms and colours of nature : the Englishman of the corresponding class has nerves and senses so coarse that he is absolutely impervious to any impressions which do not come under the head of mere brutal excitement. In this class there is no Mixture of Races, but a worse than barbarian promiscuity; Romantic Love is of course miles beyond the conception of imaginations so filthy and sluggish; and Hygienic neglect here finds its most hideous examples in the Western World.

In his *English Note-Books* Hawthorne speaks as follows of "a countless multitude of little girls" taken from the workhouses and educated at a charity school at Liverpool: "I should not have conceived it possible that so many children could have been collected together, without a single trace of beauty or scarcely of intelligence in so much as one individual; such mean, coarse, vulgar features and figures betraying unmistakably a low origin, and ignorant and brutal parents. They did not appear wicked, but only stupid, animal, and soulless. It must require many generations of better life to wake the soul in them. All America could not show the like."

"Climate," he says in another place, "no doubt has most to do with diffusing a slender elegance over American young womanhood; but something, perhaps, is also due to the circumstance of classes not being kept apart there as they are here: they interfuse amid the continual ups and downs of our social life; and so, in the lowest stations of life, you may see the refining influence of gentle blood."

Taine, in his *Notes on England*, thus sketches

the lowest of the Englishmen: "Apoplectical and swollen faces, whereof the scarlet hue turns almost to black, worn-out, bloodshot eyes like raw lobsters; the brute brutalised. Lessen the quantity of blood and fat, while retaining the same bone and structure, and increasing the countrified look; large and wild beard and moustache, tangled hair, rolling eyes, truculent muzzle, big, knotted hands; this is the primitive Teuton issuing from his woods; after the portly animal, after the overfed animal, comes the fierce animal, the English bull." "The lower-class women of London," says another French writer, Mr. Max O'Rell, "are thin-faced or bloated-looking. They are horribly pale; there is no colour to be seen except on the tips of their noses."

Personal Beauty in England diminishes in quality and frequency, not only as we go from the upper to the lower classes, but also if we leave London and go to other cities. How far sanitary and educational differences account for this state of affairs, and how much is due to a habitual and natural immigration of Beauty to a place where it is most sure of appreciation, it is not easy to say. Hawthorne thus records the impression made on his artistic eyes by an excursion party of Liverpool manufacturing people: "They were paler, smaller, less wholesome-looking, and less intelligent, and, I think, less noisy than so many Yankees would have been. . . . As to their persons," the women "generally looked better developed and healthier than the men; but there was a woeful lack of beauty and grace,—not a pretty girl among them, all coarse and vulgar. Their bodies, it seems to me, are apt to be very long in proportion to their limbs—in truth, this kind of make is rather characteristic of both sexes in England."

A French writer, quoted by Figuier, Dr. Clavel, makes a similar statement: "The level plains, which are as a rule met with in England, are not favourable to the development of the lower extremities, and it is a fact that the power of the English lies, not so much in their legs, as in the arms, shoulders, and loins. . . . The barely-marked nape of his neck and the oval form of his cranium indicate that Finn blood flows in his veins; his maxillary power and the size of his teeth evidence a preference for an animal diet. He has the high forehead of the thinker, but not the long eyes of the artist. . . . In dealing craftily with his antagonist, he is well able to guard himself against the weaknesses of feeling. His face rarely betrays his convictions, and his features are devoid of the mobility which would prove disadvantageous."

The Englishwoman, according to the same writer, "is tall, fair, and strongly built. Her skin is of dazzling freshness; her features are small and elegantly formed; the oval of her face is marked, but it is *somewhat heavy toward the lower* portion; her hair is fine, silky, and charming; and her *long and graceful neck* imparts to the movements of her head a character of grace and pride. So far all about her is essentially feminine; but upon analysing her bust and limbs, we find that the large bones, peculiar to her race, interfere with the delicacy of her form, enlarge her extremities, and lessen the elegance of her postures and the harmony of her movements. . . . She lacks a thousand feminine instincts, and this lack is revealed in her toilette, the posture she assumes, and in her actions and movements."

M. Taine also was convinced of the frequent lack of taste in dress and bearing in Englishwomen. Yet it is noticeable, and cannot be too much emphasised, that he *goes to Spain and not to France* for a comparison: " Compared with the supple, easy, silent, serpentine undulation of the Spanish dress and bearing, the movement here (in England), is energetic, discordant, jerking, like a piece of mechanism." Nor does Taine in other respects venture to hold up his own countrywomen as models. He repeatedly refers to the superior beauty of the English complexion: "Many ladies have their hair decked with diamonds, and their shoulders, much exposed, have the incomparable whiteness of which I have just spoken, the petals of a lily, the gloss of satin do not come near to it." And though he thinks that ugliness is more ugly in England than in France, he confesses that "generally an Englishwoman is more thoroughly beautiful and healthy than a Frenchwoman." "Out of every ten young girls one is admirable, and upon five or six a naturalist painter would look with pleasure." "Lady Mary Wortley Montague, who came to see the Court of the Regent in France, severely rallied our slim, painted, affected beauties, and proudly held up as a contrast 'the natural charms and the lively colours of the unsullied complexions' of Englishwomen." "The physiognomy remains youthful here much later than amongst us, especially than at Paris, where it withers so quickly; sometimes it remains open even in old age; I recall at this moment two old ladies with white hair whose cheeks were smooth and softly rosy; after an hour's conversation I discovered that their minds were as fresh as their complexions. Even when the physiognomy and the form are commonplace, the whole satisfies the mind; a solid bony structure, and upon it healthy flesh, constitute what is essential in a living creature."

That is it precisely. The Englishman is the finest *animal* in the world; and it is because other nations so often forget that one must be a fine animal before one can be a fine man, that the English have outstripped them in colonising the world, and imposing on it their special form of culture and manners. As Emerson remarks, in his Essay on *Beauty*, " It is the soundness of the bones that ultimates itself in the peach-bloom complexion; health of constitution that makes the sparkle and the power of the eye." "We are all entitled to beauty, should have been beautiful, if our ancestors had kept the laws,—as every lily and every rose is well."

The London *Times* characteristically speaks of " that worst of sins in English eyes—uncleanliness"; and it is in England alone of all European countries that cleanliness is esteemed next to godliness. The Frenchman's paradoxical exclamation, "What a dirty nation the English must be that they have to bathe so often!" is not so funny as it seems. The English, as can be seen in the uneducated classes, *would be* the dirtiest people in the world, thanks to their fogs and smoke, if they were not the most cleanly. It is the magic of tub and towel that has compelled M. Figuier to admit that although the

Englishwomen "do not offer the noble appearance and luxurious figure of the Greek and Roman women," yet "their skins surpass in transparency and brilliancy those of the female inhabitants of all other European countries."

It is needless to dilate on the other hygienic habits to which the English owe their Health, notwithstanding their often depressing climate,—the passion for walking and riding, for tennis, boating, and other sports, which, moreover, have the advantage of bringing the sexes together, and enabling every Romeo to find his Juliet. One cannot help admiring the independence and common sense of the respectable London girls who go home on the top of the 'bus, enjoying the fresh air and varied sights, instead of being locked up in the foul-aired interior. They know very well, these clever girls, that their cheeks will be all the rosier, their smiles more bewitching, their eyes more sparkling after such a ride. In countries where there are fewer *gentlemen* such a thing would be considered as improper for a girl as it is for a man to give a girl a chance to choose her own husband. Do the French agree with the Turks that women have no souls, since, in Taine's words, a Frenchman "would consider it indelicate to utter a single clear or vague phrase to the young girl before having spoken to her parents?" Taine imparts to his countrymen the curious information that in England men and women marry for Love, but he does not appear to realise how much of their superior Beauty—which he acknowledges—they owe to the habitual privilege of choosing their own wives for their personal charms, instead of having them selected by their parents for their money value. He does, however, realise the effect this system of courtship has on conjugal life; for in his *History of English Literature* he refers to the Englishwoman's extreme "sweetness, devotion, patience, inextinguishable affection,— a thing unknown in distant lands, and in France especially; a woman here gives herself without drawing back, and places her glory and duty in obedience, forgiveness, adoration, wishing and pretending only to be melted and absorbed daily deeper and deeper in him whom she has *freely and for ever chosen.*"

And there is another English custom the value of which Taine realises and acknowledges: "In France we believe too readily," he says, "that if a woman ceases to be a doll she ceases to be a woman." True, it is only a decade or two since the superstition that a higher education would "destroy all the feminine graces" has been successfully combated even in England; but there has always been a vast amount of home education, and the girls have profited immensely by the unimpeded opportunity of meeting the young men and talking with them, and by the fact that the purity of tone which pervades English literature has made all of it accessible to them. Hence the charming intellectual lines which may be traced in an English woman's face.

What the English still need is gastronomic and æsthetic training. After a few generations of sense-refinement the lower part of the English face will become as perfect as the upper part is now. Cultivation of the fine arts and freer facial expression of the emotions are the two great cosmetics which will put the finishing touch on English Beauty.

AMERICAN BEAUTY

England and America — which of these two countries has the most beautiful women, and which the largest number of them? Few questions of international diplomacy have been more frequently discussed than these problems in comparative æsthetics. But as in most cases patriotism has taken the place of æsthetic judgment in forming a verdict, few tangible results have been reached. There is too much exaggeration. Many English tourists have denied that there is any remarkable Beauty at all in the United States, and Americans have said the same of England.

If these sceptical Englishmen had only spent an hour on either side of the New York and Brooklyn Bridge at 6 P.M., they would have seen Beauty enough to bewilder all their senses; and if the American sceptics, next time they go to London, will spend a shilling in buying penny stamps at a dozen of those small post-offices so profusely scattered all over the city, they will see enough feminine Beauty in an hour to make them wish to stay in London the rest of their life,—especially if they remember that an advertisement for eleven girls to fill these postal clerkships has been answered by as many as 2000,—the majority of whom, presumably, were as good-looking as those who got the places, since postal clerks are not selected for their Beauty, but for their intelligence and efficiency.

A few specimens of the sweeping generalisations of tourists may here be cited. According to Richard Grant White, "The belief, formerly prevalent, that 'American' women had in their youth pretty doll faces, but at no period of life womanly beauty of figure, is passing away before a knowledge of the truth, and I have heard it scouted here by Englishmen, who, pointing to the charming evidence to the contrary before their eyes, have expressed surprise that the travelling bookwriters . . . could have so misrepresented the truth." Yet the same author indulges in the following absurdly extravagant statement: "Beauty is very much commoner among women of the English race than among those of any other with which I am acquainted; and among that race it is commoner in America than in England. I saw more beauty of face and figure at the first two receptions which I attended after my return than I had found among the hundreds of thousands of women whom I had seen in England."

The late Dr. G. M. Beard, though an acute observer, allowed his patriotism a still more ludicrous sway over his imagination: "It is not possible," he says, "to go to an opera in any of our large cities without seeing more of the representatives of the highest type of female beauty than can be found in months of travel in any part of Europe!"

Possibly Sir Lepel Griffin had read these lines when he was moved to pen the following counter-extravagances: "More pretty faces are to be seen in a day in London than in a month in the States. The average of beauty is far higher in Canada, and the American town in which most pretty women are noticeable is Detroit, on the Canadian border, and containing many Canadian residents. In the Western States beauty is conspicuous by its absence, and in the Eastern towns, Baltimore, Philadelphia, New York, and Boston, it is to be chiefly found. In New York, in August, I hardly saw a face which could be called pretty. . . . In November New York presented a different appearance, and many pretty women were to be seen, although the number was comparatively small; and at the Metropolitan Opera House even American friends were unable to point out any lady whom they could call beautiful. A distinguished artist told me that when he first visited America he scarcely saw in the streets of New York a single face which he could select as a model, though he could find twenty such in the London street in which his studio was situated."

Volumes might be filled with similar unscientific generalisations, but it would be a waste of space. My own general impression is that there are more pretty girls in America, and more beautiful women in England; that the average Englishwoman has a finer, healthier figure and colour, the American greater mobility and finer chiselling of the features. If English hands and feet are often somewhat large, American hands are just as often too small,—the greater blemish of the two, because it usually goes with too thin limbs. Irish girls of the best classes appear to be intermediate. Some of the finest figures and faces in the world belong to them; an Andalusian could hardly be more plump and graceful than many Irish and Irish-American girls. The Scotch, in the opinion of Hawthorne, "are a better-looking people than the English (and this is true of all classes), more intelligent of aspect, with more regular features. I looked for the high cheek-bones, which have been attributed, as a characteristic feature, to the Scotch, but could not find them. What most distinguishes them from the English is the regularity of the nose, which is straight, and sometimes a little curved inward; whereas the English nose has no law whatever, but disports itself in all manner of irregularity. I very soon learned to recognise the Scotch face, and when not too Scotch, it is a handsome one."

Comparative Æsthetics is still in its infancy, and many years will doubtless elapse before it will become an exact science, in place of a collection of individual opinions based on vague impressions. The statistics which have lately been collected regarding the proportion of Blondes and Brunettes in various countries, may be regarded as the beginning of such a science. The next step should be the collection of a series of national composite portraits after the manner in which Mr. Galton has formed typical faces of criminals, etc. If in each country a number of individuals of pronounced national aspect were photographed on the same plate, the result would be a picture which would emphasise the typical national traits, and enable one to judge how far they deviate in each case from regular Beauty.

In most European countries it would be comparatively easy to obtain characteristic composite portraits of this kind. But in America the difficulties would perhaps be insurmountable. For there the mixture of nationalities is too great and too recent to have produced any national type. The women of Baltimore, New York, Boston, and San Francisco—what have they in common with one another any more than with their cousins in London? Almost one-third of the inhabitants of New York are foreign-born, including about half a million Irish and Germans. A fusion of these has been going on for generations, while others have retained their national traits; and to look, therefore, for a special type of New York Beauty would be absurd. Thanks to this large number of foreigners—not always of the most desirable classes—there is less Beauty in New York in proportion to the number of inhabitants than in most other cities of the United States. When people imagine they can tell from what American city a given woman comes, they are hardly ever influenced in their judgment by physiognomy or figure, but by peculiarities of dress, speech, or manner.

Dr. Weir Mitchell says that in America you may see "many very charming faces, the like of which the world cannot match—figures somewhat too spare of flesh, and, especially south of Rhode Island, a marvellous littleness of hand and foot. But look farther, and especially among New England young girls; you will be struck with a certain hardness of line in form and feature, which should not be seen between thirteen and eighteen at least. And if you have an eye which rejoices in the tints of health, you will miss them on a multitude of the cheeks which we are now so daringly criticising." The notion that there is too much angularity of outline in New England faces and forms is a widespread one, and to some extent founded on truth; yet many of the plumpest, rosiest, and most charming American women come from Boston—as if to make amends for their antipodes, whom Mr. R. G. White describes as "certain women, too common in America, who seem to be composed in equal parts of mind and leather, the elements of body and soul being left out, so far as is compatible with existence in human form."

Concerning the multitudinous mixture of nationalities in the United States one thing may be asserted confidently: that the finest ingredient in it is the English. Yet it has long been held that the English blood deteriorates in the United States; that the descendants of the English, like those of the Germans and other nations and their mixtures, gradually lose the sound constitution of their ancestors. Hawthorne, in his *Scarlet Letter*, was probably one of the first to give expression to this belief. Speaking of the New England women who two centuries ago waited for the appearance of Hester, he says: "Morally, as well as materially, there was a coarser fibre in those wives and maidens of old English birth and breeding than in their fair descendants, separated from them by a series of six or seven generations; for throughout that chain of ancestry every successive mother has transmitted to her child a fainter bloom, a more delicate and briefer beauty, and a slighter physical frame, if not a character of less force and solidity, than her own. . . . The bright morning sun, therefore, shone on broad shoulders and well-developed busts, and on round and ruddy cheeks, that had ripened in the far-off island, and had hardly yet grown paler or thinner in the atmosphere of New England.

Yet in his *English Note-Books*, written after the *Scarlet Letter*, he relates that he had a conversation with Jenny Lind: "She talked about America, and of our unwholesome modes of life, as to eating and exercise, and of the ill-health especially of our women; but I opposed this view as far as I could with any truth, insinuating my opinion that we were about as healthy as other people, and affirming for a certainty that we live longer. . . . This charge of ill-health is almost universally brought forward against us nowadays,—and, taking the whole country together, I do not believe the statistics will bear it out." But why does he in another place speak of English rural people as "wholesome and well-to-do,—not specimens of hard, dry, sunburnt muscle, like our yeoman?" and on still another page: "In America, what squeamishness, what delicacy, what stomachic apprehension, would there not be among three stomachs of sixty or seventy years' experience! I think this failure of American stomachs is partly owing to our ill-usage of our digestive powers, partly to our want of faith in them."

Mrs. Harriet Beecher Stowe exclaims that "the race of strong, hardy, cheerful girls . . . is daily lessening; and, in their stead, come the fragile, easy-fatigued, languid girls of a modern age, drilled in book-learning, ignorant of common things." Dr. E. H. Clarke writes in his *Sex and Education*, which should be read by all parents: "'I never saw before so many pretty girls together,' said Lady Amberley to the writer, after a visit to the public schools of

Boston; and then added, 'They all looked sick.' Circumstances have repeatedly carried me to Europe, where I am always surprised by the red blood that fills and colours the faces of ladies and peasant girls, reminding one of the canvas of Rubens and Murillo; and I am always equally surprised on my return by crowds of pale, bloodless female faces, that suggest consumption, scrofula, anæmia, and neuralgia."

Dr. S. Weir Mitchell remarks that "To-day the American woman is, to speak plainly, physically unfit for her duties as woman." Dr. Allen, quoted by Sir Lepel Griffin, remarks that a majority of American women "have a predominance of nerve tissue, with *weak muscles* and digestive organs"; and Mr. William Blaikie says that "scarcely one girl in three ventures to wear a jersey, mainly because she knows too well that this tell-tale jacket only becomes a good figure."

Dr. Clarke relates that when travelling in the East he was summoned as a physician into a harem where he had the privilege of seeing nearly a dozen Syrian girls: "As I looked upon their well-developed forms, their brown skins, rich with the blood and sun of the East, and their unintelligent, sensuous faces, I thought that if it were possible to marry the Oriental care of woman's organisation to the Western liberty and culture of her brain, there would be a new birth and loftier type of womanly grace and form."

There is, doubtless, much truth in these assertions. It is distressing to see the thin limbs of so many American children, and the anæmic complexions and frail, willowy forms of so many maidens. What the American girl chiefly needs is more muscle, more exercise, more fresh air. A large proportion of girls, it is true, become invalids because their employers in the shops never allow them to sit down and rest; and standing, as physiologists tell us, and as has been proved in the case of armies, is twice as fatiguing as walking. As if to restore the balance, therefore, the average well-to-do American girl never walks a hundred yards if a street car or 'bus is convenient; and the men, too, are not much better as a rule. One of the most disgusting sights to be seen in New York on a fine day is a procession of street cars going up Broadway, crowded to suffocation by young men who have plenty of time to walk home. In the case of the women, the cramping French fashions, which impede exercise, are largely to blame.

Fresh-air starvation, again, is almost as epidemic in America as in Germany. Although night air is less dreaded, draughts are quite as much; and people imagine that they owe their constant "colds" to the *cold* air with which they come into contact, whereas it is the excessively *hot* air in their rooms that makes them morbidly sensitive to a salubrious atmosphere. If young ladies knew that the hothouse air of their parlours has the same effect on them as on a bunch of flowers, making them wither prematurely, they would shun it as they would the sulphurous fumes of a volcano. Why should they deliberately hasten the conversion of the plump, smooth grape into a dull, wrinkled raisin?

It is through their morbid fondness for hothouse air and their indolence that American women so often neutralise their natural advantages: thanks to the fusion of nationalities and the unimpeded sway of Romantic Love, they are born more beautiful than the women of any other nation; but the beauty does not last.

It must be admitted, however, that a vast improvement has been effected within the last two generations. Beyond all doubt the young girls of fifteen are to-day healthier and better-looking than were their mothers at the same age. It is no longer fashionable to be pale and frail. Anglomania has done some good in introducing a love of walking, tennis, etc., as well as the habit of spending a large part of the year in the country.

Mr. Higginson, Mr. R. G. White, and many others, have insisted on this gradual improvement in the health and physique of Americans; and Dr. Beard remarks in his work on *American Nervousness:* "During the last two decades the well-to-do classes of America have been visibly growing stronger, fuller, healthier. We weigh more than our fathers; the women in all our great centres of population are yearly becoming more plump and more beautiful. . . . On all sides there is a visible reversion to the better physical appearance of our English and German ancestors. . . . The one need for the perfection of the beauty of the American women—increase of fat—is now supplied." Yet the one cosmetic which 20 per cent of American women still need above all others is the ability to eat food which they scorn as "greasy," but which is only greasy when badly prepared. It is to such food that Italian and Spanish women owe their luscious fulness of figure.

Dr. Clarke's work on *Sex and Education* made a great sensation because he pointed out that the ill-health of American women is largely due to the brain-work imposed on them at school. Now the superior beauty of American women is admittedly largely due to the intelligent animation of their features, to the early training of their mental faculties. Is this advantage to be sacrificed? Dr. Clarke's argument does not point to any such conclusion. He simply contended that the methods of female education were injurious. "The law has, or had, a maxim that a man and his wife are one, and that the one is the man. Modern American education has a maxim, that boys' schools and girls' schools are one, and that the one is the boys' school." Girls need different studies from boys to fit them for *their* sphere in life; and above all they need careful hygienic supervision and periods of rest.—Dr. Clarke's book affords many irrefutable arguments in favour of one of the main theses of the present treatise: that the tendency of civilisation is to differentiate the sexes, mentally and physically. It is on this differentiation that the ardour and the cosmetic power of Romantic Love depend. Hence the hopelessness of the Virago Woman's Rights Cause, especially in America, where the women are more thoroughly feminine than elsewhere. It is said that when the first female presidential candidate announced a lecture in a western town, *not a single auditor* appeared on the scene. American women, evidently, are in no immediate danger of becoming masculine and ceasing to inspire Love.

Women, however, must be educated and thoroughly, for it has been abundantly shown in the preceding pages that only an educated mind can feel true Romantic Love. But their education should be feminine. They need no algebra, Greek, and chemistry. What they need is first of all a thorough knowledge of Physiology and Hygiene, so that they may be able to take care of the Health and Beauty of their children. Then they should be well versed in literature, so as to be able to shine in conversation. Their artistic eye should be trained, to enable them to teach their children to go through the world with their eyes open. Most of us are half blind; we cannot describe accurately a single person or thing we see. Music should be taught to all women, as an aid in making home pleasant and refined, and as an antidote to care. Natural history is another useful feminine study which enlarges the sympathies by showing, for example, that birds love and marry almost as we do, wherefore it is barbarous to wear their stuffed bodies on one's hat.

Education, Intermarriage, Hygiene, and Romantic Love will ultimately remove the last traces of the ape and the savage from the human countenance and figure. Climate will perhaps always continue to modify different races sufficiently to afford the advantages of cross-fertilisation or intermarriage. The remarkable fineness of the American complexion, for instance, has been ascribed to climatic influences, and with justice it seems, for, according to Schoolcraft, the skin of the native Indians is not only smoother, but more delicate and regularly furrowed than that of Europeans. The notion, however, that the climate is tending to make the American like the Indian in feature and form is nonsensical. The typical " Yankee" owes his high cheek-bones and lankness to his indigestible food ; his thin colourless lips to his Puritan ancestry and lack of æsthetic culture.

Even if climate did possess the power to modify the forms of our features, it would not be allowed to have its own way where these modifications conflicted with the laws of Beauty. Science is daily making us more and more independent of crude and cruel Natural Selection, and of the advantages of physical conformity to our surroundings. Hence Sexual Selection has freer scope to modify the human race into harmony with æsthetic demands. Perhaps the time will come when the average man will have as refined a taste and as deep feelings as a few favoured individuals have at present ; that epoch will be known as the age of Romantic Love and Personal Beauty.

INDEX

ABOUT, E.: fashionable disease, ii. 397
Absence: effect on Love, i. 409
Addison: familiarity, i. 295, 413
Æsthetic sense: developed from utilitarian associations, ii. 116; training the, 121; highest product of civilisation, 233, 346
Æsthetic suicide, ii. 200, 203
Affection: impersonal, i. 17-26; for dismal scenery, 20
Affections, personal: love for animals, i. 26; maternal love, 30; paternal, 33; filial, 36; brotherly and sisterly, 37; friendship, 39; romantic love, 42; differentiation of, 289
Age: which preferred by Cupid, ii. 62; beauty of old, 112; and decrepitude, 112; ears in old, 268; eyebrows, 339; hair, 364, 370
Air: fresh, ii. 84; necessary to Beauty, i. 298; ii. 87, 214, 260, 294, 295, 369, 405
Albinos, ii. 329, 382
Alcock, Dr.: colour of tropical man, ii. 309
Alfieri: first love, i. 328, 344
Alison: on taste, ii. 302
Allen, Grant: origin of æsthetic sense, ii. 116
Amazons, i. 305
Ambidexterity, ii. 231, 290
American beauty, i. 284; ii. 58; South American, 87; quadroons, 91; rapid development of, 98; feet, 157; frank gaze, 350, 426, 431, 438-450; complexion, 449

American Love: courtship, i. 189; flirtation, 196, 203; Gallantry, 254; and Beauty, 284; at eighteen, 309; replaces German and French courtship, ii. 38, 47-59
Amicis, E. de: Spanish beauty, ii. 408
Amiel, H. F.: on Germans, ii. 419
Animals: love for, i. 26; ignored in Christian ethics, 28; love among, 53; jealousy, 63, 205; kissing, 365, 367; as tests of Beauty, ii. 106; arctic, why white, 310
Apes: caressing, i. 361; kissing, 362, 365; ugliness of, ii. 110; feet, 145, 152; gait, 150; legs, 171; abdomen, 194; arms, 222; hands, 227; jaws, 233; nude patches, 361; hair, 368
Apollo, ii. 364
Arabian beauty, ii. 407
Aryan Love, ancient, ii. 115
Asceticism and ugliness, ii. 80
Augustine, St.: love and jealousy, i. 205
Austrian beauty, ii. 88, 407

BACH, A. B.: chest-exercise, ii. 217
Bachelors, i. 311
Bacon: friendship, i. 19, 42; amorous hyperbole, 260; celibacy and genius, 316; love and genius, 332; employment *versus* love, 411; stature and intellect, 415
Bain, Prof., i. 361; ii. 124, 132
Baldness, ii. 367
Ballet-dancing, ii. 171

Ballrooms: unhealthy, ii. 161, 221; for birds, 162
Balzac: prolonging Love, i. 349; how his love was won, 404; hand of great men, ii. 226
"Bangs," ii. 199, 373
Banting, ii. 192
Bathing, ii. 317, 410, 419, 435
Beard, G. M.: eyeball, ii. 341; American beauty, 439, 447; jaws, 233
Beard, the, ii. 361, 386
Beauty, in flowers, origin of, i. 12, 13; dependent on Health and Cross-fertilisation, 16
Beauty, Personal: the æsthetic overtone of Love, i. 51; admiration of, by animals, 70; by savages, 96; among Hebrews, 115; Hindoos, 119; Greeks, 133; Romans, 142; mediæval, 173; feminine *versus* masculine strength, 185; arouses jealousy, 213; when only skin-deep, 249; and intellect, 249; refines Love, 283-288; feminine, in masculine eyes, 283; masculine, in feminine eyes, 284; neglected after marriage, 296; lost prematurely, 298; "skin-deep," 304; elimination of ugly and masculine women, 305; fatal to bachelors, 311; physical, a source of Love, ii. 62; facial, 63; dependent on Health, 74; independent of utility, 75; Greek, 77; increased through Hygiene, 82, 113; effect of crossing on, 85; Jews, 89; quadroons, 91; increased through Love, 92, 95; as a fine art, 103, 246; tests of, negative, 107; positive, 118; human less frequent than animal, 108; lost in degradation, 111; and age, 112; expression *versus* form, 136; proportion, 144; feet, 146, 155; value of exercise, 157, 224; lower limbs, 171; Hygiene and civilisation, 173, 209; lacing fatal to, 188, 190; corpulence, 191; rare, 198; chest, 208, 213; increased by deep-breathing, 217; neglect of, a sin, 219; neck and shoulder, 219; finger-nails, 228; jaw, 233; characteristic, 236; dimples, 239; lips, 240; cheeks, 255; colour and blushes, 259; ears, 266; noses, 285; Greek, 285; arm and hand, 291; cosmetic value of gastronomy, 293; of fragrant air, 295; of sunlight, 315, 320; skin, 304, 313, 362; eyes, 323, 337 *seq.*, 407; beards, 362; moustaches, 365; sexual selection preserves hair, 368; sensuous, of eyes, 348; of hair, 369, 370; *versus* Fashion, 198, 375; Brunette *versus* Blonde, 375; national traits, 389; race-mixture and Love, 394; and mental culture, 95, 413; stature, 414; beautiful and pretty, 415
Beauty-sleep, ii. 84, 85
Beauty-spots, ii. 303
Beddoe, Dr.: brunettes and blondes, ii. 379; races of Britain, 427
Beer, ii. 193, 421, 423
Beethoven: Love-affairs, i. 336, 340, 348
Bell, Sir Charles: the lips, i. 364; Greek beauty, ii. 136; woman's gait, 176; facial expression, 242; beards, 364
Belladonna, ii. 387
Berlioz: love-affairs, i. 318, 330
Birds: affections of, i. 56; intermarriages, nuptial mass meetings, 59; courtship, 60; love-dances, 62, 83; jealousy, 63; coyness, 65; choice of a mate, 68; source of colours, 70; love-calls, 82; female seeks male, 82; display of ornaments, motives of, 84; æsthetic taste of, 86; murdered for vulgar women, 241; billing, 368
Blackie, Prof.: Goethe's love-affairs, i. 340
Blaikie, W.: American physique, ii. 445
Blind, why love is, i. 264, 325
Blonde *versus* Brunette, ii. 375, 428
Blushes, ii. 259; eyes of Albinos, 329

Index

Bodenstedt: Oriental women, i. 297; Georgian women, ii. 97
Bones, ii. 234
Bothmer, Countess von: French Love, ii. 6, 9; German women, 30; English flirtation, 46
Brain, the, ii. 298, 416
Brandes, Georg: feminine Love at thirty, i. 309, 316
Breath, offensive, ii. 255
Breathing, healthy, ii. 187; deep, magic effects of, 214, 295
Brinton and Napheys, ii. 185, 253, 271, 290, 356
Brotherly and sisterly love, i. 37
Browne, Lennox: corset ruins grace, ii. 189; consumption, 217
Brunette *versus* Blonde, ii. 65, 377-389, 402, 414, 416, 423, 428
Bryant, i. 406
Büchner, L., i. 7, 55
Bulkley, Dr.: care of skin, ii. 317; removing hairs, 370
Bunyan: kissing, i. 375
Burke: delicacy, ii. 127; smoothness, 129; neck and breasts, 208; love and stature, 416
Burns: Love and cosmic attraction, i. 9; amorous hyperbole, 261; first love, 328; ardour of his love, 334; fickleness, 339; undercurrents, 342; a lover's dream, 354; kissing, 371
Burton, i. 6, 415
Bustle, the, ii. 178, 371
Byron, Lord: affection for mountains, i. 20; epitaph on dog, 27; woman's Love, 195; waltzing, 208; the coquette, 229; Romantic Love, 261; love-affairs, 324; first love, 328; a poet's love, 337; Swift, 337; kissing, 379; refusals, 386; how to win love, 388, 403; sarcasm on marriage, 414; money and "love," 421; Italian Love, ii. 15; Love inspired by inferior beauty, 65; black eyes, 378; Italian beauty, 400

CALDERWOOD: on affection, i. 18

Calisthenics, ii. 214
Campbell, Sir G.: Aryan cheekbones, ii. 257
Camper's angle, ii. 297
Canada: Love-matches and Beauty, i. 284; ii. 175, 396
Capture of women, i. 91
Caresses, i. 361
Carew, i. 409
Celibacy: mediæval notions of, i. 148; bachelors, 311; and genius, 316
Cervantes, i. 323; ii. 24
Chamfort, i. 360
Chaperonage: in Greece, i. 124, 282; Rome, 139; mediæval, 166; modern, 191, 203, 278, 290, 299, 307; in France, 310; ii. 2 *seq.*; England, 5, 46; Italy, 14; Spain, 20; Germany, 33; America, 48, 50; evils of, 351
Characteristic, the, ii. 235
Cheeks, ii. 255; colour and blushes, 259, 364
Chemical affinities, i. 4-10
Chest, the, ii. 63, 208, 214
Chesterfield: birth of "flirtation," i. 200; flattery, 392
Children: head, ii. 298; eyes, 349
Childs, Mrs.: Love and marriage, i. 195
Chin, ii. 238
China: Love in, i. 189; jealousy, 207, 213; aristocracy of intellect, 336; standard of Beauty, ii. 102; mutilation of the feet, 142; dancing, 163; cheeks, 255; eyes, 337, 353, 356
Chiromancy, ii. 228
Chivalry: militant and comic, i. 157; poetic, 162
Choice, sexual. *See* Individual Preference
Chopin: musician for lovers, i. 272
Christianity and Love, i. 155; sympathy, 239; and Beauty, ii. 94
Circassian women, ii. 88, 263
City air, ii. 295; city life, injurious to health, 174
Civilisation: and Beauty, ii. 258; and noise, 273

Clarke, E. H.: American Health and Beauty, ii. 444; sex and education, 448
Clavel, Dr.: English Beauty, ii. 433
Cleanliness, i. 154; ii. 160, 435
Climate, ii. 449
Clough and Beauty, i. 382, 403, 404, 448
"Colds," ii. 446
Coleridge: fruitless Love, i. 194; best marriages, 304; virtue and passion, 349; compliments, 393; love and absence, 409
Collier, Miss M.: Italian Love and Hygiene, ii. 401
Collier, R. L.: English and American courtship, ii. 45
Colour: a normal product, proportionate to vitality, i. 70; Typical and Sexual, 71; Protective and Warning, 77; means of recognition of species, 79; complementary, 276; ii. 130; in cheeks, 259; ears, 270; skin, 304, 362; of man's skin, original, 310; eyes, 324, 345
Complementary qualities: colours, i. 275; guide Love, ii. 11, 64
Complexion: white *versus* black, ii. 304; Scandinavian and Spanish, 315; cosmetic hints, 315; freckles, 319; brunette *versus* blonde, 380, 423; English, 434, 436; injured by hot air, 446
Compliments, i. 391
Confidence, value of, to lovers, i. 382, 387
Conjugal love: among animals, i. 55; savages, 291; Hebrews, 110; Greeks, 121; Romans, 139; troubadours, 165; self-sacrifice, 258; in France, 260; differs from Romantic, 288-304; modern, 292; essence of, 294; feminine deeper than masculine, 298; and friendship, 412
Constable, i. 267
Consumption, nurseries of, ii. 217, 218
Coquetry: in birds, 65; and flirtation, i. 196; historic excuse for, 199; essence of, 228; masculine, 229; and high collars, 387
Corpulence, ii. 63, 190; how to reduce, 193; in old England, 430
Corset: fatal to Beauty, ii. 184-193; causes corpulence, 190, 195; ruins chest, 219
Cosmetic hints (*see* also Hygiene and Exercise): how to refine the lips, ii. 252; ears, 270; odours, 292; complexion, 315, 322; electricity, 322; eyelashes, 355; eyes, 357; hair, 367; scalp, 369; colour of eyes, 389; fresh air, 401
Cosmic attraction, i. 4-10
Costume, study of, ii. 373
Court-plaster, ii. 303
Courts of Love, i. 166
Courtship: among animals, i. 59; facilitated by love-calls, 81; display of ornaments, 84; among savages, 90; Hebrews, 112; Greeks, 124; Plato on, 125; advice to mediæval girls, 171; definition and value of, 189; playing at, 197; modern, 201, 203, 278; mediæval, 383; French, ii. 5; Italian, 16; Spanish, 22, 23; German, 27; American and English, 38, 44, 47, 56; the object of dancing, 161; needed in France, 396; Germany, 425
Cousins: Love and kissing, i. 377; as chaperons, ii. 52
Coyness: an overtone of Love, i. 49; among animals, i. 64; among primitive maidens, 103; Hindoos, 120; Greeks, 124; mediæval, 161; modern, 183-204; a feminine weapon, 185; disadvantages of, 190; lessens woman's Love, 192; displaced by flirtation, 197; of fate, 273; after marriage, 296; varies, 405; how to overcome, 407; needed in Germany, ii. 33
Crimes, against Health and Beauty, ii. 219, 249
Criminal types, ii. 96
Crinoline craze, the, ii. 179

Index

Cross-fertilisation: advantages to Health and Beauty, i. 13; ii. 85
Crossing, ii. 66; a source of Beauty, 85-92
Crowe and Cavalcaselle, ii. 15
"Cunning to be strange," i. 185
Cupid's arrows, i. 135
Curing Love, art of: i. 247, 314, 408-424; absence, 409; travel, 410; employment, 411; contemplation of married misery, 411; of feminine inferiority, 415; focussing her faults, 419; reason *versus* passion, 421; Love *versus* Love, 422
Curvature, ii. 123, 146, 172, 183, 188, 208, 213, 219, 239, 337, 338

DANCING: love-dances of birds, i. 62, 83; and grace, ii. 160; and courtship, 161; birds, 162; Greeks and Romans, 163; why men no longer care for, 165; evolution of dance-music, 166; dance of Love, 169; ballet, 170
Dante, i. 3, 175-178, 268, 317, 323, 345; ii. 252, 353
Darwin: on flowers and insects, i. 11; benefactor of animals, 30; animal jealousy, 63; coyness, 64; sexual selection, 70-81; love charms and calls, 81; birds displaying their ornaments, 85; English Beauty, 233; female tenderness, 241; masculine females, 305; expression of Love, 359; amorous desire for contact, 361; origin of kissing, 367; feminine inferiority, 416; taste, ii. 102; symmetry in nature, 119; bird dances and courtship, 162; Hottentot bustle, or steatopyg, 179; jaws and hands, 232; lip mutilations, 244; expression of emotions, 247; Siamese notions of Beauty, 256; blushing, 261; Albinos, 382; movements of ears, 267, 273; point of, 269; mutilations, 271; the nose, 278; sense of smell, 293; Indian heads, 300; movements of the scalp, 303; complexion, 307; eyebrows, 339; loss of man's hair, 358
Darwinism, new proof for, ii. 200
Decrepitude, ii. 112
Deformity: fatal to Love, ii. 63; elimination of, 94
Degradation: a cause of ugliness ii. 111
Delicacy, ii. 127, 234, 239
Depilatories, ii. 367
De Quincy: inferiority of feminine imagination, i. 417
Diagnosis of Love, i. 407
Diderot: effects of Love, i. 388
Dimples, ii. 226, 238
Disease: kills Love, ii. 62; a cause of ugliness, 112, 124; resulting from tight shoes, 144; from lacing, 186, 189; hollow eyes, 337; and Fashion, 397, 447
Display of ornaments, by animals, i. 83
Don Juans, among birds, i. 57
Draughts, stupid fear of, ii. 84
Drayton, i. 267
Dress, improprieties of, ii. 186; woman's, for woman, 199; in France, 397
Dryden: on Love, i. 142, 267; Love *versus* Love, 423
Dühring, Dr.: German money-marriages, ii. 28
Dürer, ii. 350

EARS: a useless ornament, ii. 266; physiognomic theories, 272
Eckstein: antiquity of Love, i. 15
Education of Girls, i. 251; the right kind, 313, 418; effect of, on Beauty, ii. 96, 448, 449
Egypt: Love in, i. 108; horror of beards, 363
Electricity, as a cosmetic, ii. 322, 370, 389
Eliot, George: on first Love, i. 222
Elopements, i. 98, 301
Elson, L. C.: Troubadours and Minnesingers, i. 167
Emerson: poetry and science, i. 14; lovers' sympathy, 50; on

lovers, 216; amorous hyperbole, 262, 264, 386; balm for rejected lovers, 408; ocular expression, ii. 341; Health and Beauty, 435
Emotional differentiation, i. 288
Empedokles, i. 5, 288, 330
Engagements, ii. 45, 46; broken, 57
English Beauty, i. 233; feet, ii. 153, 157; open-air games, 175; mouths and chins, 249; nose, 287; beards, 364; Brunettes gaining on Blondes, 379; physique, 393, 396, 427-443
English Love: courtship, i. 189; flirtation, 196, 203, 309, 314; kissing, 374, 380; ii. 37-47; Goldsmith on, 55
Epicures: why handsome, ii. 294
Erasmus: kissing in England, i. 374
Erotomania, i. 356
Evolution of Love, i. 1, 179, 277, 288, 290; of Beauty, ii. 100; of taste, 101; great toe, 152
Exaggeration: characteristic of bad taste, i. 98
Exclusiveness, amorous. *See* Monopoly
Exercise: effects on Beauty, i. 298; ii. 78, 174; reduces fatness but increases muscle, 193, 224; in France, 395, 413, 421, 427
Exogamy, i. 91
Expression: improves form of features, i. 250; facial, of Love, 359; of lips, 364; of Beauty, ii. 101, 134-140; mouth, 234; facial, 242, 313; of vice, 848; of lust, 248; ears, 273; eyes, 332, 339-356; dog's tail, 367; Italian, 403
Eyes, i. 264, 420; smiling, ii. 243; the most beautiful feature, 323; colour of, 324; lustre, 331, 341; form, 335; lashes and brows, 338, 386, 353-356; expression of, 339; movements of iris, 346; of eyeball, 348; of lids, 352; of brows, 356; "making eyes," 367; dark *versus* light, 386; Spanish, 407, 409

FACE, the, ii. 236, 296, 365

Factories: unhealthy, ii. 218; whistles, 274
Fashion: the Handmaid of Ugliness, ii. 103; a disease, 141; mutilates the feet, 141, 154; frustrates advantages of dancing, 161; prescribes absurd hours, 165; its essence vulgar exaggeration, 178; crinoline craze, 179; wasp-waist mania, 184; lacing, 186; Fashion Fetish analysed, 195; and Darwinism, 200; repeats itself, 201; ludicrous features, 203; masculine, 204, 207; disgusting pictures, 208; deforms the breasts, 211; finger-nails, 229; gloves, 231; right-handedness, 231; teeth, 243; powders and paints, 260, 313, 314; ears, 271; noses, 278, 288; *versus* Taste, 279; forehead, 296, 299, 301; court-plaster, 303; eyebrows, 339; hollow eyes, 354; mutilates eyes, 356; head-dresses, 371; tyranny of ugliness, 374; in France, 395; and bad manners, 398
Fat, cosmetic value of, i. 193, 212
Feet, the: size, ii. 140; fashionable ugliness, 141; tests of Beauty, 145; not enlarged by *graceful* walking, 158
Feminine Beauty: in masculine eyes, i. 283; prematurely lost, 298; ii. 76; rarer than masculine, 77; greater than masculine, 125; bosom, 126, 208, 219, 223; face, 237; nose, 286; forehead, 199, 296, 374; wrinkles, 301; skin, 362; beard, 363, 415
Feminine Inferiority, i. 415-419; ii. 15
Feminine Love: less deep than masculine, i. 193; ii. 13; desire to please, i. 255; dynamic, not æsthetic, 285, 404; ii. 62; at thirty, i. 309; expression of, 360; lessens delicacy, 407; Fichte on, ii. 31, 220
Feminine virtues, i. 157; mediæval culture, 169; cruelty, 241; devotion, 257

Index

Femininity, standard of, ii. 41
Fichte: feminine Love, ii. 31
Fickleness of genius, i. 337
Figuier, ii. 313, 391, 395, 399, 408
Figure: a good, inspires Love, i. 247; Oriental, ii. 445; plump, 447
Filial Love, i. 36
Finger-nails, ii. 228
Fletcher, i. 267
Flirtation: and coquetry, i. 196; definition of, 198; *versus* coyness, 198; in France, ii. 14; in Spain, 22; Germany, 33; England, 46; with the eyes, 355, 367
Flower love and beauty, i. 10-17
Flower, Prof.: walking, ii. 151; toes, 153; nose-rings, 288
Forehead, the, ii. 199, 236; Beauty and brain, 296; fashionable deformity, 299, 374
Fragrance, a tonic, ii. 295
France: the source of vulgar Fashions, ii. 141
Franklin, B.: early marriages, i. 303; advantages of large families, 303
Freckles, not caused by sunshine, ii. 319, 381, 419
French Beauty: rare as Love-marriages, ii. 11; feet, 157; ugly fashions, 200; brunettes and blondes, 379; general, 391-399; in America, 396; compared with English, 434
French Love: Chivalry, i. 159; Troubadours, 164; no flirtation, 198, 203; grandchildren sacrificed, 260; lower classes, 282; feminine, at thirty, 309, 314; killed by ridicule, 389; ii. 1-14, 123, 394
French, T. R.: nose-breathing, ii. 292
Freytag, G.: mediæval German marriages, ii. 26
Friendship, i. 39-42; among animals, 54; female, in Greece, 130, 288; advantages over conjugal love, 412
Fringe, ii. 199, 373

GAIT, graceful, ii. 149, 159; defects in woman's, 176, 178, 180; in Spain, 410, 414, 434
Gallantry: an overtone of Love, i. 49; among animals, 62; among savages, 106; birth of, in Rome, 147; crazy mediæval, 161, 253; modern, 252; conjugal, 296; extravagant forms of, 355; feminine, 390; flattery in actions, 393; Italian, ii. 15; Spanish, 22; German, 29; American, 53; true, 200; why on the wane, 373
Galton: on Coyness, i. 200; callous feelings, 239; morals and large families, 303; heredity of genius, 322; woman's senses less delicate than man's, 417; ancestral influences, ii. 67; criminal types, 96; stature and marriage, 415; change in English physiognomy, 430
Gastronomy: cosmetic value of, ii. 294; England, 437; America, 444
Gautier, Th.: woman has no sense of beauty, ii. 199
Genius: emotional, i. 3, 144, 177; and Health, 286; and marriage, 316; and Love, 323, 349; modern, abundant, 326; in Love, 327; amorous precocity, 327; ardour, 332; *versus* rank and money, 336; fickleness, 337; multiplicity, 341; and Monopoly, 343; fictitiousness, 344
Georgian women, ii. 97
German Beauty: i. 232; Bavarian corpulence, ii. 194; Brunettes gaining on Blondes, 379; physiognomy, 404; general, 416-426
German Love: chivalry, i. 159; Minnesingers, 166-168; in Folksongs, 169; word for courtship, 189, 203; in novels, 230, 314; gallantry, 384; compared with French, ii. 3, 25-37
Girls: of the Period, i. 191; plain, chances of getting married, 247; pretty, apt to be spoiled, 249,

321; wrong education, 251, 418; cages *versus* nets, 296; hints on men, 300; American and English, 301; best education for, 313; easily duped, 359; in France, ii. 3; Germany, 30; know when they are ugly, 68; should skate, 176; how to acquire a fine figure, 194, 225

Gladstone: Greek hair, ii. 375, 378; stature, 414

Godkin, E. L.: true character of milliners, ii. 198

Goethe: *Elective Affinities*, i. 7; affection for nature, 24; ancient love, 186; first Love, 219; intellect and Love, 252; love-affairs, 324, 331, 340, 342; unhappy marriages, 413; transitoriness of Love, ii. 35; aversion to noise, 276

Goldsmith: on Love, i. 187, 265; his first love, 339; English Love, ii. 55

Grace: where found, ii. 69, 127; of gait, 149; acquired by dancing, 160; destroyed by corsets, 189; movements of the head, 220; French, 393; Italian, 403; Spanish, 410, 414

Gradation: ii. 120, 147, 172, 208, 219, 226, 314, 336

Grandchildren: sacrificed to money-marriages, i. 257, 260, 392, 416

Gratiolet, ii. 347

Greek Beauty: i. 133; sources of, ii. 77; animals as ideals, 109; no expression, 136, 137; feet, 148; gymnastics, 193; hands, 229; chin, 240; lips, 242; ears, 268, 272; beards, 364; arrangement of hair, 374; colour of hair, 375; stature, 414

Greek Love, i. 120, 186, 253, 288, 306

Griffin, Sir L.: French women, ii. 391; American women, 439

Grose: noses, ii. 279

Grote, G.: Platonic love, i. 128; Greek Beauty, 133; Amazons, 306

Gymnastics: among Greeks, ii. 193

Gypsy, Spanish, ii. 407

HAECKEL, Prof., ii. 268, 418

Hair: how to wear, ii. 199, 429; on the arm, 223; cause of man's nudity, 358; how to remove, 367; preserved by Sexual Selection, 368; æsthetic value of, 371; blonde and brunette, 375, 383; red, 385

Hamerton, P. G.: Love and age, i. 222; feminine sympathy, 251; embers of passion, 422; French Love, ii. 4, 9, 10, 12

Hammond, Dr. W.: Delirium of Persecution, i. 353; erotomania, 356

Hand, ii. 221, 226, 232

Handel, i. 319

Harrison, J. P.: length of first and second toes, ii. 153

Hartmann, E. von: pleasure and pain, i. 269; masculine and feminine Love, ii. 31

Hats, tall, ii. 207; hideous French, 200, 372, 398

Haweis, Mrs.: Fashion *versus* Beauty, ii. 371; turban, 373; hair-powder, 386

Hawthorne, N.: a love-letter, i. 400; English Beauty, 430, 431; American physique, 442

Hawthorne, Julian: German Beauty, ii. 424

Haydn, i. 318, 331

Hazlitt, i. 413

Head, the, deformities of, ii. 103; and hair, 368

Health: correlated with Beauty in flowers, i. 12, 16; in animals, 74; men and women, 285; source of Love, ii. 62; source of Beauty, 74-85, 106, 436; and delicacy, 129; exercise, 174; lacing, 186; sins against, 249; and colour, 134, 304, 312; and lustre, 331, 343; eyelids, 337; and sunshine, 381; in Italy, 401; England, 436; America, 443

Hebra, Prof.: freckles, ii. 319

Hebrews: Love among ancient, i. 110; sense of beauty, 115; absence of jealousy, 207; beauty and ugliness of, ii. 89; noses, 281, 283
Hegel: colour of the skin, ii. 304
Heine: flower and butterfly love, i. 16; the word love, 17; joy and torture, 51; persiflage of coyness, 190, 192; jealousy, 208, 212; on first Love, 219; his marriage, 252; poet for lovers, 272, 324; his first love, 329; his true love, 334; æsthetic love, 338; multiplicity, 341; wedding music, 415; woman's character, 415; curing Love with Love, 423; French Love, ii. 3; an emotional educator, 34; Italian Beauty, 405
Helmholtz: overtones, i. 47
Herder: Love, i. 113; eyes of great men, ii. 351
Heredity: of genius, i. 322
Hetairai, i. 127
Higginson, T. W.: sexual likeness, i. 279; American physique, 441
Hindoo Love maxims, i. 117
History of Love, i. 108
Holland, F. W.: morals and large families, i. 303
Holmes, O. W.: feminine barbarity, i. 243; refined lips, ii. 249
Homer: Helen's Beauty, ii. 80, 394
Honeymoon, i. 263, 302
Horwicz, i. 26, 33, 384
Hottentots: notions of Beauty, ii. 179
Howells, W. D.: monogamy, i. 214; feminine self-abnegation, 413; Italian courtship, ii. 16-18; broken engagements, 57; playful flattery, 58
Hueffer, F.: Troubadours, i. 164
Hume: uncertainty augments passion, i. 199; mixed emotions, 275
Humphrey, Dr.: walking, ii. 151
Hungarian Beauty, ii. 88
Huxley: female education, i. 418; ape's foot, ii. 150
Hygiene, modern: a source of Beauty, ii. 82; of the feet, 157; legs, 175; chest, 214, 216; fatal consequences of neglect, 217; eyes, 357, 425; hair, 369; in England, 436
Hyperbole: emotional, an overtone of Love, i. 51; in ancient Aryan Love, 119; modern, 260-266; after marriage, 295; pathologic analogies, 352, 355; contact, 362; and genius, 389; in America, ii. 58

INDIANS, American: wooing, i. 277; standard of Beauty, ii. 101; muscular power, 172; deformed skulls, 300
Indifference, feigned: value to lovers, i. 386
Individual Preference: an overtone of Love, i. 48; among animals, 67; savages, 91, 95; Hebrews, 112, 126; Greeks, 125; Romans, 140; mediæval times, 152, 180; modern, 277-283, 301; in France, ii. 6; Italy, 17; Spain, 22; Germany, 27; England, 38, 437; America, 57; Schopenhauer on, 73
Individualism *versus* Fashion, ii. 201
Individuality, i. 278; and nationality, ii. 57, 138, 352, 394
Individuals: sacrificed to species, ii. 60, 70
Insanity and Love: analogies, i. 350; erotomania, 356
Intellect and Beauty, i. 99, 249, 250, 348; ii. 95, 97, 99, 437
Intellect and Love, i. 99, 119, 127, 133, 196, 144, 246, 252, 309, 325, 336, 347; ii. 32, 56, 63
Intoxication, amorous, i. 262, 316
Iris, ii. 326, 345, 347
Irving, Washington: transient Love, i. 339; intellect and Beauty, ii. 95; Spanish Beauty, 411
Italian Beauty: ii. 15, 19; feet, 153, 156; nose, 279; hair, 376, 384; complexion, 383; general, 399-405

Italian Love : chivalry, i. 163 ; no word for courtship, 189, 314 ; ii. 14-19, 401

JÄGER, G.: personal perfumery, ii. 293
James, Henry : American women, i. 254 ; Daisy Miller, ii. 49
Japan : jealousy, i. 207, 213
Jaws, the, ii. 232
Jealousy : an overtone of Love, i. 49 ; among animals, 63 ; moral mission of, 99 ; occasional absence among savages, 100 ; Greek, 124 ; mediæval, 165 ; modern, 205-214 ; retrospective and prospective, 211 ; aroused by Beauty, 213, 276 ; conjugal, 295 ; Oriental, 297 ; morbid, 355
Jeffrey : on Taste, ii. 102 ; theory of Beauty, 114
Jews. *See* Hebrews
Johnson, Dr.: second Love, i. 217 ; marriage and Love, 413
Jowett, Prof.: Sokrates, love and friendship, i. 412

KANT : women ensnared by counterfeit lovers, i. 389 ; value of smiles, ii. 252
Karr, A.: Woman's Love, i. 414
Keats : amorous hyperbole, i. 262 ; paradox, 268 ; Beauty and Love, 283 ; love-letters, 394-397
Kissing, i. 228, 364 ; among animals, 365 ; savages, 366 ; origin of, 367 ; ancient, 372 ; mediæval, 374 ; modern, 376 ; love-kisses, 377 ; art of, 380 ; varieties of, ii. 241 ; on the ears, 270 ; cheeks, 259
Knight : Beauty and utility, ii. 115, 122
Knille : Italian Beauty, ii. 403
Kollmann, Prof.: feminine Beauty, i. 126 ; walking, 171 ; muscular development, 175 ; gait, 176 ; breasts, 209 ; face, 235 ; nose, 276 ; hair, 384 ; results of crossing, ii. 89
Koran, the : on woman's soul, i. 150

Krafft-Ebing : Insanity and Love, i. 276, 357

LA BRUYÈRE : how to win love, i. 390 ; on use of paint, ii. 314
Lacing : fatal to Beauty, ii. 185
Lamartine : genius and Love, i. 337 ; love-affairs, 404
Lamb, Chas.: amorous paradoxes, i. 266 ; love-affairs, 339
Language of Love : words, i. 358 ; facial expression, 359 ; caresses, 361 ; kissing, 364
La Rochefoucauld : Love and friendship, i. 42 ; and absence, 409
Lathrop, G. P.: Love - making in Spain, ii. 21 ; Spanish Beauty, 410
Laughter, ii. 253
Lavater : chin, ii. 238 ; ocular lustre, 331
Lawson, F. P.: effect of education on Beauty, ii. 96
Leanness, ii. 63, 190 ; how to cure, 193
Lecky : on kindness to animals, i. 29 ; family affections among Greeks, 121 ; asceticism and chastity, 149 ; feminine devotion, 257 ; southern type of Beauty, ii. 383
Lenau : love-letters, i. 397 ; music and Love, 411
Leo, Judah : on Love, i. 5, 6
Lessing : every woman a shrew, i. 415
Life : prolonged through hygienic care, ii. 82
Lips, i. 364, 371 ; expression of scorn, 234 ; refined, 239 ; lip language, 240 ; effect on, of æsthetic culture, 249
Liszt, i. 318
London, ii. 275
Longfellow, i. 422
Love-charms (and calls) : among animals, i. 81 ; for women, 401 ; ii. 260
Love-dramas, among flowers, i. 14
Love-maxims : Hindoo, i. 17
Love, Romantic : a modern sentiment, i. 2, 288 ; superior to friendship, 42 ; to maternal love,

43; secures to man the benefits of cross-fertilisation, 45; overtones of, 46-51; a great moral, æsthetic and hygienic force, 46, 156; among animals, 53; savages, 87; Egyptians, 108; Hebrews, 111; ancient Aryans, 115; more traces of modern in Indian poetry than in Greek and Roman, 118; among Greeks, 120; origin of, 137; among Romans, 139; Mediæval, 148; wooing and waiting, 162; dependent on refinement, 163; maid *versus* married woman, 169; birth of modern, 175; order of development proved, 179; at the altar, 181; in novels, 182; pleasure of pursuit, 185; value of procrastination, 186, 189; coyness lessens woman's, 192; masculine deeper than feminine, 193, 414; ii. 12; modern jealousy, i. 205; passion or admiration, 209; is transient, 217, 289; is first best? 218; Heine on first, 219; first is not best, 221; individual *versus* the species, 223; coquetry, 228; opposed by rank, 230; intensifies emotions, 235; stimulates social sympathy, 240; selfish aspect of, 241; at first sight, 61, 245; inspired by a fine figure, 247; by sympathy, 251; responsible for general growth of Gallantry, 254; refines men, 256; impels toward self-sacrifice, 256, 259; in France, 260; emotional hyperbole, 260, 280; intoxication of, 262; honeymoon, 263; mixed moods and paradoxes, 266; course of true, 273; lunatic lover and poet, 275; and conjugal, 277; individual choice, 278; and culture, 282; idealised by Beauty, 283-288; responsible for Beauty, 284; differs from conjugal, 288; elements of, in conjugal affection, 295; makes men embarrassed, 300; free choice does not always imply Love, 301; eliminates ugly and masculine women, 305; inspired by Beauty, 311; a duty, 314; must be mutual, 315; genius is amorous, 322; *a creative impulse*, 324; imagined is real, 325; arouses genius, 327; precocious, 327; most intense in men of genius, 333; fickle, 337, 347; loving two at once, 341; "sublimed" by Beauty, 349; pathologic analogies, 350; erotomania, 356; language of, 358; facial expression of, 359; caresses, 361; kissing, 364; how to win, 380-408; feminine, and genius, 387; effects of, 387; compliments, 391; love-letters not necessarily slovenly, 396; extracts from, 396-400; charms for women, 401; masculine, and vanity, 403; opposed to viragoes, 404; proposing, 405; signs and tests of, 407; how to cure, 408; effect of absence on, 409; effects of marriage on, 412; poisoned by humiliation, 421; *versus* Love, 422; chances of recovery, 424; national peculiarities, ii. 1; massacred in France, 2; Italian, 15, 19; Spanish, 19; German, 25; English, 37, 55; American, 47; a cause of Beauty, 25, 58, 72; points out woman's sphere, 44; obedience to, a moral duty, 34; Schopenhauer's theory of, 59-73; sources of, 62; complementary, explanation of, 68; leads to happy marriages, 71; a source of Beauty, 92-95; displaces cruel Natural Selection, 94, 258; is inspired by grace, 129, 149, 158; more concerned with form than with colour, 133; guided by subtle signs, 136; individualisation and "beauty-spots," 138; neglects no detail of Beauty, 139; the object of dancing, 162; killed by fashionable deformity, 186; feminine and masculine, 220; maintains æsthetic proportion, 238; related to Health and Beauty, 243; beautifies the face, 95, 247; special expression of, 248; beautifies the lips, 251; the cheeks, 258; and fresh air, 260; and blushes, 266; inspired by a musical voice, 276; beautifies the nose, 283; eliminates high feminine foreheads, 296, 299; method of amorous selection, 312; awakens the sense of beauty, 313; banishes rouge, 314; inspired by eyes, 323, 352; beautifies the eyes, 330; eyebrows, 339, 357; large pupils, 347; *musculus amatorius*, 351; killed by sunken eyes, 354; preserves the hair, 368; favours brunettes, 65, 377, 428; eyelashes, 386; and Beauty, 394; favours small women, 414; *versus* reason, 417; and Beauty in England, 436; sexual differentiation, 448; in America, 448; age of, 450

Lovers: selfish bores, i. 216, 236; quarrels, 271; musician and poet for, 272; falsetto, 360; ii. 277

Love-sickness: real, i. 356

Love-stories: none in Greek literature, i. 122

Lubbock, Sir J.: on flowers and insects, i. 13; absence of certain emotions in savages, 88; kissing, 366

Lungs: hygiene of, ii. 215

Lustre, ii. 130; in eyes, 331, 341

Luther: and marriage, i. 156

Lynn-Linton, Mrs.: Girl of the Period, i. 299

MACAULAY: Petrarch's love, i. 346

Madonna, Sistine, ii. 350; blond, 376

Magnus, Dr. Hugo: colour of the eye, ii. 330; lustre, 332; expression, 341; portraits, 349; individuality, 351

Manicure secrets, ii. 230

Manners: essence of good, ii. 372; Spanish 430

Mantegazza: on courtship, i. 189; ι2 caresses, 363; Esquimaux nose, ii. 278; Italian noses, 278, 290; wrinkles, 302; Italian Beauty, 400

Manu, laws of: on woman, i. 116

Mariolatry: influence on woman's position, i. 156

Marlowe: amorous hyperbole, i. 266; half-kisses, 380

Marriage: among animals, i. 57, 59; Egyptian trial, 109, 280; modern ideal of, 110; in Greece, 125; in Rome, 149; and chivalry, 160, 165; Love *versus* expediency, 181; maiden *versus* wife, 184; through accident, 223; men becoming cautious, 251; Love not a motive in France, 260; of men of genius, 264, 316, 320; money *versus* Beauty, 284; "the sunset of Love," 289; conditions of happy, 292-294; nets and cages, 296; of love, *versus* "reason," 299; ii. 417; hints, i. 302; chances for ugly women, 307; age for, advancing, 308; misery of, 411-415; in France, ii. 6; Germany, 26; America, 58; based on Love, 60; and dancing, 165; and noses, 276; and complexion, 315; Albinos, 382; and stature, 415

Masculine Beauty: in feminine eyes, i. 284; more common than feminine, ii. 77, 135, 213, 219, 223; face, 237; nose, 286; forehead, 296; wrinkles, 301; beard, 363, 365, 415; in Germany, 421

Masculine Love: deeper than feminine, i. 193, 414; ii. 13; coquetry, i. 229; Gallantry, 254; beautifying impulse, 287; insincerity, 300; comic expression of, 360; won *via* Vanity, 403; increases delicacy, 407; *versus* feminine, ii. 31

Masculine vanity, i. 403

Masculine women: eliminated as old maids, i. 305, 404

Massage, ii. 224

Maternal Love, i. 30; among animals, 54, 293

Mediæval Love, i. 148; celibacy, *versus* marriage, 148; woman's lowest degradation, 150; negation of feminine choice, 152; Christianity and love, 155; chivalry, militant and comic, 157; poetic, 162; female culture, 169; Personal Beauty, 173; Spenser on Love, 174; Dante and Shakspere, 175

Mediæval Ugliness: causes of, ii. 81

Meditation beautifies the face, ii. 349

Mental Culture: a source of Beauty, ii. 95; France, 395; Italy, 403; Spain, 412, 413; Germany, 417; England, 437; America, 448

Middleton, i. 267

Mill, J. S.: female self-denial, i. 259; companionship in marriage, 294; woman's sphere, 312

Milliners' cunning, ii. 197

Milton, i. 172, 318

Minnesingers, i. 166

Mitchell, Dr. W.: American physique, ii. 442

Mitchell, P. C.: monkeys' kisses, i. 365

Mixed Moods and Paradoxes of Love, i. 51, 266-277, 295

Mixture of races (*see* also Crossing): and Love, ii. 394; in France, 394; Italy, 399; Spain, 406; Germany, 416; England, 407, 427, 442

Modesty: a source of Coyness, i. 184; and blushes, 263

Monogamy: favours the development of Love, i. 103; in Egypt, 109

Monopoly: an overtone of Love, i. 48; among savages, 101; in ancient Aryan Love, 119; modern, 214-226; and genius, 342; three are a crowd, 354; in Lenau's love-letters, 399; masculine and feminine Love, ii. 31, 388

Montagu, Lady: on woman, i. 414

Montaigne: on marriage, i. 414; Italian Beauty, ii. 15

Moore, T.: genius and marriage, i. 317, 321; first love, 328

Moral impressions: confounded with æsthetic, ii. 346

Mormons, i. 101

Mountains: feelings inspired by, i. 19

Mouth: muscles of, ii. 240; self-made, 252

Muscles: development of, ii. 62; use and disuse, 100; the plastic material of Beauty, 193; of an athlete, 224; facial, 246; mouth, 247

Music: of male birds, does it charm the females? i. 81; dance-music, 166; Chopin's funeral march, 271; fans love, 411; ii. 105, 121, 231, 250, 348

NATIONALITY: and Beauty, i. 411; ii. 389; and Love, 1

Natural Selection: a cause of Beauty, i. 70 *seq.;* replaced by Love, ii. 94, 258; blushes, 261; complexion, 308; eyebrows, 339; loss of hair, 359, 368

Neck, ii. 219

Negroes: African, strangers to Love, i. 89; American, can they love? 106; ugliness of, ii. 87; standard of Beauty, 102, 107; feet, 147; legs, 172, 227; teeth, 243; lips, 245; cause of blackness, 309; complexion, inferiority of, 313; eyes, 324, 327, 329, 354; hair, 368

New York: a silly fashion in, ii. 203; noise in, 275, 295; effeminate men, 447

Nordau, Max: love in Germany, i. 282

Norton, C. E.: on Dante, i. 175

Nose, the: shape and size, ii. 277; evolution of, 279; Greek and Hebrew, 283; fashion and cosmetic surgery, 287; important functions of, 291

Nose-breathing: importance of, ii. 215, 291

Novels: Love in, i. 17

Novelty: and first Love, i. 225

Nudity: cause of man's, ii. 358

ODOURS: cosmetic value of, ii. 292
Old Maids, i. 305
O'Rell, Max: French chaperonage, ii. 7; English degraded women, 432
Origin of Love, i. 137
Ornamentation: non-æsthetic, ii. 103
Ovid: on tricks of Gallantry, i. 1; rarity of Beauty in Rome, 142; art of making love, 144; Gallantry, 148; conception of Love, 189; enduring a rival, 208; estimate of, 323; loving two at once, 341; how to cure love, 409, 411, 419

PARADOXES of Love, i. 266-277, 337
Parasols, ii. 321
Pascal: self-conscious lovers, i. 353
Paternal love, i. 33; animals, 54, 293, 172
Pepys: Spanish wooing, ii. 21
Perfume: personal, ii. 292; cosmetic value of, 297
Pessimism, erotic, ii. 60, 72
Petrarch: as a love-poet, i. 345
Photographs: why inferior to portraits, ii. 135; why so often bad, 351
Physiognomy: comparative, ii. 107; ears, 272; colour of the eyes, 345; variety in, and Love, 394; language of passion, i. 246
Pity and Love, i. 241
Planché: wasp-waists, ii. 185
Plato: on Courtship, i. 125; ii. 49; "Platonic" Love, i. 128; origin of Love, 137; pre-matrimonial acquaintance, 204; mixed mood of love, 268; irrational love, 350; feminine inferiority, 416; Love and Beauty, ii. 93
Pleasure and pain, i. 269
Ploss: love-charms, i. 402; Germanic marriages, ii. 26
Plumpness: inspires Love, ii. 63
Polish Beauty, ii. 426
Polygamy: among animals, i. 58; conducive to Jealousy, 101; among Hebrews, 111; in India, 116; neutralises conjugal love, 291
Portraits, ii. 135, 349; typical, 441
Pretty: definition of, ii. 415
Pride: in paternal love, i. 35; in Romantic Love, 50; and vanity, 226-233; in conjugal love, 295; masculine vanity, 344; wounded, cures Love, 421
Proportion, ii. 119; facial, 296; stature, 298
Proposing, i. 113, 228, 244, 387, 405, 406
Prudery, i. 201; ii. 199
Purchase of wives, i. 93
Puritans: sins of, against Health, ii. 249

QUADROONS: beauty of American, ii. 91; graceful gait, 155

RAILWAY whistles, ii. 274
Raleigh: deep love, i. 359, 413
Rank: an enemy of Love, i. 230; ii. 6
Raphael: on Beauty, ii. 400
Realism: emotional, desirable in novels, i. 110
Reclam, Prof.: dust in lungs, ii. 291; night air, 84, 422
Richardson, W. B.: the ideal city, ii. 83
Right-handedness, ii. 231
Roberts, Charles: brunettes and blondes, ii. 427
Roberts, J. B.: nasal deformities, ii. 290
Rochefoucauld, La: women, love, and friendship, i. 42; pleasure of love, 315
Roman Beauty, i. 142; hair, ii. 376
Roman Love, i. 139-148
Rousseau: on woman's Love, i. 193; his last love, 331, 403
Rückert: kissing, i. 378
Ruskin: poetry and science, i. 14; love of dismal scenery, 21; amorous paradoxes, 268; woman's work, ii. 42, 43; health and beauty, 74; and utility, 75; hap-

Index

piness essential to beauty, 82; intellect beautifies the features, 96; taste of savages, 105; beauty and utility, 108; degradation and ugliness, 111; wild scenery, 117; symmetry, 118; curvature, 123; colour, 130, 133; moderation, 184; expression in the mouth, 234; virtue and Beauty, 253; Greek features, 284; turban, beauty of, 373; southern Beauty, 383

Russian old maids, i. 310

SAPPHO: as a Love-poet, i. 130

Savages: development of maternal love, i. 32; parental love, irregular, 33; filial love weak, 36; strangers to Romantic Love, 87; ii. 69; inferior to birds, i. 87; courtship, 90; regard for beauty, 96; Jealousy and Polygamy, 99, 206; Gallantry, 252; masculine women, 279; notions of Beauty, 286; ii. 102; conjugal attachment, i. 292; kissing, 367; sense delicacy, 371; inferior to us in Health, ii. 76; taste, 101, 233; tests of Beauty, 107, 356; ugliness of, 110; dancing, 162; muscular development, 172; noses, 279; paint, 313

Scalp: movements of, ii. 302

Scandinavian complexion, ii. 315, 381

Scherer: on mediæval German Love, i. 169

Scherr, J.: on witchcraft trials, i. 151; Wieland in love, 342; Petrarch, 346; mediæval courtship, 383; mediæval Spanish women, ii. 20

Schiller: Minnesingers, i. 167

Schopenhauer: on the Will, i. 5; æsthetic enjoyment, 29; final cause of colour in animals, 80; love at first sight, 245; self-sacrifice, 259; torments, 271; celibacy and genius, 316; genius and woman's love, 387; unhappy marriages, 414; theory of Love,
ii. 59-73; animal Beauty, 108; masculine and feminine beauty, 126; small feet, 145; the unæsthetic sex, 196; noise and culture, 276; noses and marriage, 277, 288; Germans, 418

Schumann, R., i. 261; love-affairs, 343; on German Beauty, ii. 423

Schweiger - Lerchenfeld: Italian women, ii. 16; Spanish love-making, ii. 22

Schwenninger cure for corpulence, ii. 191

Scotch Beauty, ii. 440

Scott, Sir W.: on Dryden and Love, i. 144; and marriage, 318, 348; masculine vanity, 403

Seeley, Prof.: Goethe on Love, ii. 35

Selden: marriage, i. 415

Self-sacrifice: an overtone of Love, i. 49, 211, 252; conjugal, 258, 302; in feminine Love, ii. 31; Schopenhauer on, 59, 71, 72

Sellar, Prof.: Ovid, i. 323

Seneca: Beauty, i. 413

Sensuality and Romantic Love, i. 123

Service for a wife, i. 94

Sex: the unæsthetic, ii. 196; and education, ii. 448

Sexual differentiation, i. 278; ii. 363, 414, 448

Sexual Selection (*see* also Love and Individual Preference): among animals, i. 70; primitive men, 96; effect on chest, ii. 208; loss of hair, 223, 359; blushes, 261; ears, 267; noses, 283; complexion, 307; eyes, 323, 325; masculine and feminine, 363; preserves hair on head, 368; action uncertain, 369; *versus* Natural Selection, 450

Shakspere: treatment of Love, i. 3, 178; invests inanimate objects with human feelings, 4; on Beauty, 52; coyness and modesty, 185; woman's Love, 193; amorous hyperbole, 261; course of true love, 273; what inspires love in women, 285; marriage of, 318; amorous character of, 323; blind love, 325; lunatic and lover, 350; kissing, 378; winning love, 381; refusals, 386; flattery, 391; unsought love, 406; tests of Love, 408; love never fatal, 408; reason as Love's physician, 421; hereditary Beauty, ii. 93; feet, 139; the beautiful and the characteristic, 235; poet of Love, 252; blushes, 261; expression in the eyes, 340, 353; love inspired by eyes, 352; Blondes and Brunettes, 375, 377

Shelley: paradox of Love, i. 268; loving and being loved, 315; amorous disposition of, 324, 348

Shoes: tight, objections to, ii. 143; improvements in, 159

Shoulders, the, ii. 219

Simcox, G. A.: on Gallantry, i. 147; mediæval ugliness, ii. 81; noses, 287

Skating: effects on Beauty, ii. 175

Skin. *See* Complexion

Sleep: and noise, ii. 84, 274; refreshing, 215

Smoothness, ii. 129, 208, 223, 270, 361, 365

Soap: should be used on the face, ii. 302, 319; good and bad, 317

Solomon's Song, i. 113

Sources of Love, ii. 62

Southey: woman's faith, i. 414

Southwell, i. 267

Spanish Beauty: feet, ii. 157; grace, 177, 410, 434; chest deformed by Fashion, 211; lips, 250; mantillas, 200, 398; complexion, 383; general, 405-416; refinement, 420

Spanish Love: chivalry, i. 159; falling in love, 245, 314; extravagant Gallantry, 355; ardour, ii. 16, 19-25

Spencer, Herbert: on primitive paternal love, i. 33; filial love, 36; analysis of Love, 50, 52; money-marriages, 181; woman's sphere, 313; origin of kissing, 367; irregular mixture of ancestral qualities in children, ii. 66; individuals *versus* the species, 70; female savages uglier than male, 77; intellectual and physical beauty, 90; evolution of Beauty, 101; muscular power of savages, 172; laziness of savages, 174; masculine Fashion, 205

Spenser: Love and friendship, i. 174

Staël, Mme. de: on Beauty and intellect, i. 52; Love *versus* parental dictation, ii. 14

Stature and Beauty, ii. 414

Stays: for deformed women, ii. 195

Steatopyga, ii. 179

Steele: kissing, i. 364; love-letters, 396

Stenches and noises, ii. 275

Stendhal: Love and age, i. 221; Love in France, 282; humiliation poisons Love, 421; ii. 2

St. Jerome: on the education of girls, i. 154

Stockings: best kind, ii. 160

Suckling: lovers' pallor, i. 360

Suicide: from Love, i. 195

Sunshine: good for the complexion, ii. 306; does not cause freckles, 320; and Health, 381, 401, 405

Surgery, cosmetic, ii. 271, 288

Swift: marriage, i. 296; love-affairs, 337

Swiss, the, ii. 422

Symmetry, natural tendency to, in flowers, i. 16, 118, 289, 346

Symonds: on Italian Love, i. 163; formal code of Love, 171; Petrach, 346; Shelley, 348

Sympathy: and affection, i. 18; an overtone of Love, 50, 233-252; development of, 237; in conjugal love, 294

TAINE, H.: English Beauty and Love, ii. 432 *seq.*

Taste: æsthetic theories of, ii. 101; disputing about, 120, 233, 246, 256; *versus* Fashion, 279; sense of, 293; non-æsthetic standard, 428

Teeth: ii. 232, 237, 243; care of, 255
Tennyson: kissing, i. 377
Tests of Beauty: negative, ii. 106; positive, 118
Thackeray: advice to lovers, i. 203; Love, 268; to women, 403; simpering Madonnas, ii. 81; dark heroines, 377; French physique, 390
Thaxter, Mrs.: women and birds, i. 243
Thomson, i. 350
Toe, great, evolution of, ii. 152
Topinard: early decrepitude of savages, ii. 76; life prolonged in France, 83; crossing, 87, 90; nose, 278; deformed skulls, 300; dark races, 382; French nation, 394
Tourgenieff: on a dog's love, i. 27; first love, 327.
Trollope, A.: American Gallantry, ii. 53
Troubadours, i. 164, 355, 357
Trousers, ii. 205
Turks, ii. 88
Tylor, E. B.: the ape's gait, ii. 150; arms, 222; negro's finger-nails, 228; blushing, 262; ears, 272; nose, 278; skulls, 300
Tyranny of ugly women, ii. 198, 374

UGLINESS: follows ill-health in animals, i. 74; in women, 298; no bar to marriage, 307; mediæval, ii. 80; due to simian resemblance, 108; savage features, 110; degradation, 111; decrepitude and disease, 112; tyranny of, 198; due to indolence, 214; a sin, 219; "beauty-spots," 303
Use and disuse, effect of, on organs, ii. 100
Utility and Beauty, ii. 108, 116

VEILS, ii. 321
Vice: destroys Beauty, ii. 248, 345
Viragoes, i. 280, 305
Virchow, Prof.: Brunettes and Blondes, ii. 379

Virgil: Love-episode, i. 142
Vogt, Carl: sexual divergence, i. 279; negro's feet, ii. 147; females and animals, 154; thighs, 171
Voice, a musical, ii. 276
Voltaire: on ancient and modern friendship, i. 42; standard of taste, ii. 101

WAGNER, R.: leading motives, literary application of, i. 183; analogies between Love and music, 226; feminine devotion, 256; marriage, 318; a musical kiss, 379; ii. 105, 241
Waist, ii. 183
Waitz: Magyars, ii. 88; Chinese complexion, 306, 311; decrease in number of blondes, 378
Walker, A., i. 413; woman's gait, ii. 178; French Beauty, 391
Walking, ii. 149, 160
Wallace, A. R.: on choice exerted by animals, i. 69; Natural *versus* Sexual Selection, 70-81; beauty correlated with health in animals, 74; sources of colour in animals, 77; chest of Amazon Indians, ii. 213; hair on arm, 223
Waltz: the dance of Love, ii. 169
Warner, Chas. D.: women and birds, i. 243
Wasp-waist mania, the, ii. 184, 371
Wealth, vulgar display of, ii. 197
White, R. G.: blonde type, ii. 376; Viennese Beauty, 426
Wieland: love-affair, i. 342
Wife: capture, i. 91; purchase, 93; service for, 94; capture and coyness, 183; selling, ii. 39
Wilde, Oscar, ii. 206
Winckelmann: Greek Beauty, ii. 79, 109; curvature, 125; breasts, 210; Greek chest, 213; hand, 226; chin, 239; dimples, 240; lips, 242; ears, 268; nose, 277; eyes, 336; hair, 374, 375, 384; dark complexion, 380, 382; Italian Beauty, 405
Winning Love, art of: i. 1, 66, 120, 185, 203, 208, 380-408;

brass buttons, 380; confidence and boldness, 382; pleasant associations, 383; perseverance, 385; feigned indifference, 386; compliments, 391; Love-letters, 394; for women, 401; proposing, 405; how to meet coyness, 407; spicing flattery with burlesque, ii. 58

Witchcraft, trials for, i. 151

Woe, ecstasy of, i. 269

Woman: weak in impersonal emotions, i. 25; strong in conjugal and maternal love, 30; inferior to man in Romantic Love, 30, 193; prefers manly to handsome men, 97; position in Egypt, 108; among Hebrews, 111; in India, 116; ancient Greece, 123; Rome, 139; mediæval degradation, 150; proverbs about, 155; oasis of culture, 169; position in France, 172; cruelty to birds, 241; intelligent, 250; in public life, 258, 281; loses Beauty prematurely, 298; employment problem, 312; ii. 40; uniform worship, i. 380; discourages deep Love, 387, 388; inferior to man, 415; Huxley's ideal, 418; in mediæval Spain, ii. 20; indifferent to loss of Health, and the consequences, 76; superior in Beauty to man, 126; deplorable conservatism, 165; penalty of indolence, 194; has no sense of beauty, 195, 199, 212, 220, 371; needs no stays, 195; deficient in taste, 196; duped by sly milliners, 197; object of dress, 199; needs æsthetic instruction, 201; riding hat, 206; fashion preferred to good manners, 373

Wooing. *See* courtship

Woody, S. E.: electrolysis for removing hairs, ii. 371

Wrinkles, ii. 228, 301

YANKEE, ii. 450

Young, i. 318

ZIMMERMANN, O.: Ecstasy of woe, i. 269

Zola, ii. 252

THE END

www.ingramcontent.com/pod-product-compliance
Lightning Source LLC
Chambersburg PA
CBHW022056300426
44117CB00007B/482